THE OCTOPUS

Europe in the
Grip of Organised Crime

Brian Freemantle

THE OCTOPUS

Europe in the
Grip of Organised Crime

ORION

The right of Brian Freemantle to be identified as
the author of this work has been
asserted by him in accordance with
the Copyright, Designs and Patents Act 1988.

First published in Great Britain in 1995 by
Orion
An imprint of Orion Books Ltd
Orion House
5 Upper St Martin's Lane
London WC2H 9EA

A CIP catalogue record for this book is available
from the British Library

ISBN 1 85797 609 6

Typeset by Deltatype Ltd, Ellesmere Port, Cheshire
Printed in Great Britain by Clays Ltd, St Ives plc.

International crime gangs have
expanded from traditional spheres
of activity such as prostitution,
the arms trade and trafficking in
drugs to money laundering, the
trade in nuclear technology and
human organs and the transport
of illegal immigrants.

Boutros Boutros Ghali,
UN Secretary General,
opening a conference on
worldwide organised crime.
Naples. 21.11.94

*Again for Maureen
who is owed much more*

Contents

Author's Note

The original concept of this book was to examine the forecast explosion of indigenous crime *within* the European Union when its internal border restrictions were removed, on January 1, 1993.

Almost from the outset it became obvious that this wouldn't work. And not because three of the twelve countries at that time forming the Union – the United Kingdom, Ireland and Denmark – didn't remove the restrictions anyway, arguing with politicians' logic that such internal barriers were their external boundaries as well, so they had to be retained to keep crime out. Which, of course, they didn't. Or because France, too, kept its restrictions at its border with Belgium until March 1995, worried at the possible flood of illegal immigrants and drugs that might pass through, via Belgium, from Holland.

The unsettling reality is that 'Fortress Europe' (cliché Number One), from inside which 340,000,000 Europeans would look safely out at everyone else in the world over a rigidly law-enforced 'Ring of Steel' (cliché Number Two), was an idea which could never have worked.

Ahead of any other multinational industry, organised crime calculated the enormous potential of the European Union through all its formative stages: the mobs of the world – not just European – were the first to go into business, the very first, in fact, to become true Europeans, even if a lot don't qualify from either birth or nationality.

The drug mafias of Colombia and Bolivia and Peru formed joint venture links with the mafias of France and Italy. Which in turn forged associations with the mafias of Russia and Poland. Which made independent connections back in Latin America, thus completing the circle. The incredibly violent Jamaican 'Yardies' who set up shop in England enforce their rule with Russian Kalashnikovs exported by the container load by Russian mobs. Those same mobs – and those from Poland and Hungary – smuggle children and young girls through that rusted 'Ring of Steel' to stock Europe's sex market. There is competition in the live skin trade from Serbian gangs from the dismembered Yugoslavia, which feed Europe's sexual appetite, giving ethnic cleansing an even more obscene definition by supplying Croatian and Muslim girls to Holland and Germany. And then they double their profit by arming their Balkan war with Eastern bloc weaponry bought with their skin trade earnings.

Organised crime groups in America are the chief exporters of video and blue movie pornography and paedophilia to the European Union. European pornographers – particularly German – have business arrangements with Chinese Triads to make paedophilia films in Thailand and Sri Lanka. Each Triad is long established in every European capital and works with fellow gang members in Communist China, easing illegal Chinese immigration into the member states on expertly forged documentation. The Triads provide drugs to Europe's Asian population and extort protection money from European-based Asian businesses. There are sometimes bloody battles for control with Vietnamese clans disputing their market position in Europe. Both import the heroin for Europe's addicts. So do gangs from Turkey and Africa.

And amid all this the institutions of the Union let it be defrauded of an estimated yearly £6 billion – some estimates put that figure at £10 billion – by its own citizens as well as by external organised mafias because its member governments invariably put their individual national interest before all else. Better the easy fudge, placating the all-powerful farmers' lobbies of the Union than any serious attempt at reform. Nothing will change by the entry of Sweden, Finland and Austria into the market. The yearly size of the fraud will simply expand.

While I have found it necessary therefore to discuss external involvements in the internal European crime scene – for clarity and objectivity – I have kept as far as possible within my original remit.

A further aspect of that remit needs to be examined, however: an encroachment upon civil liberties and human rights every bit as dangerous as the threat from organised crime.

No police force or law enforcement agency anywhere in the Union attempts to minimise the scale of the organised criminality with which it is confronted. None feels the need to exaggerate, either: it would in fact be difficult to. But their awareness of this has encouraged demands from them for legislation and restrictions that they openly concede could infringe personal liberties. Their justification is that honest citizens have to sacrifice some personal freedoms for law and order protection. That justification is invariably coupled with the question – 'What has an honest man got to fear?'

The answer to that question came from a Strasbourg jurist who refused to be quoted by name: 'A country without crime is a country without freedom.'

Therefore, as important as I believe it is to examine in depth the major crime organisations threatening Europe, I believe it essential also to look at all potential erosions of human rights. This book is not, however, a doom-laden prediction of the death of civil liberty. It is merely a warning.

It is not written, either, as yet another treatise upon the Mafia, either the traditional Sicilian founding fathers or the organised crime offspring that are customarily referred to under that generic title. The unarguable fact is that the mafia – with the Sicilian and Italian at the forefront – are experts at their chosen profession, making it impossible to write about the European underworld *without* frequent references to them and their influence.

Neither, finally, is this book intended in any way to be anti-European. One does not have to be anti-European to find much – too much – to criticise in the arrogant empire-building of non-elected Commission bureaucrats. Or in the way national governments are cynically prepared to let their taxpayers be robbed blind rather than show sufficient political will (a phrase that will recur often in this book) to correct absurd and out-of-date grant, aid and price-support mechanisms.

One has just fervently to hope the worst predictions of too many professional criminologists don't come true. Having studied for two years the growth and strength throughout Europe of organised crime, I fear that hope is a forlorn one.

Winchester, 1995.

Acknowledgements

Considering the subject matter of this book, I was surprised that, out of almost a hundred people and organisations I approached, only five refused outright to meet me. All were politicians.

Not unnaturally, although many of my informants were prepared to be publicly identified, there were many others who talked only on condition of their total anonymity: more than half of those feared violent physical retribution if their identities were known. Others, particularly men and women involved in investigation and intelligence analysis, felt their operational functions would be jeopardised. I agreed to this because I believed that I would gain enormously in content, even though it obviously meant I would be unable to attach an identifying source to any of their information that I used which I professionally regret in a non-fiction work.

During the eighteen months research for this book I travelled nearly ten thousand miles throughout the European Union, visiting and re-visiting many cities and capitals and countries.

The first, logically, was Brussels, centre of the European universe for thousands of European Union bureaucrats. There I was given every conceivable help by Christopher White, a correspondent with unmatched knowledge of the Union and of the workings of the European Parliament, to which he was once attached. In Brussels, too, I gained valuable insight into the fight against fraud from Budgetary Committee member and Labour MEP for Birmingham West, John Tomlinson, and from Terry Wynn, Labour MEP for Merseyside East. Their guidance prepared me for an encounter with Per Knudsen, then newly-appointed head of the Community's fraud hunters, the *Unite de Co-ordination pour la Lutte Anti-Fraude*, and with Knudsen's assistant, Philip Kermode. The Union's Common Agricultural Policy (CAP) is the main source of that fraud and I benefited from meeting agricultural expert Brian Gardner and ebullient Irish spokesman Gerard Kiely. Fellow Irishman Daniel Mulhall was also extremely helpful. And later, in Luxembourg, Gabriel Cipriani, spokesman for the Court of Auditors, patiently provided me with the first of many official reports that revealed the extent of CAP deception.

Strasbourg was another city I had repeatedly to visit. One of those trips was to attend a conference of the European Council of Police Unions, where I discussed with Roger Bouiller, the council's administrative secretary, both the harmonisation of European police forces and the infringements of human rights likely to be caused by foreseen legislation. I was also fortunate to meet on that occasion Dr Jiri Vandas, from the Interior Ministry of the Czech Republic and Dr Janos Bertok, from the Hungarian Ministry of the Interior. At that stage the fledgling European FBI, Project Europol, occupied temporary accommodation in Strasbourg, prior to its permanent move at the end of 1993 to The Hague. I learned much about Europol from German Chief Superintendent Peter Vowe.

On a previous visit to the city I met officials at the Council of Europe who have been an on-going source of help throughout the preparation of this book. Those willing publicly to be thanked are Mrs Christine Dennemeyer and Ms Sabine Zimmer. There were others who chose to remain unnamed. The Pompidou Group's Christopher Luckett was the first of over a dozen interviewees on Europe's illegal drug problems, and lawyer Hans Nilsson was enlightening on the subject of computer fraud. It was on yet another visit to Strasbourg that I heard from Netherlands Socialist MEP and criminal expert Pieter Stoffelen how close, in his opinion, organised crime is to overwhelming Europe's dis-organised legal systems.

In Lyon I was given every facility by Interpol's Secretary General, Raymond Kendall, by Mr Kendall's *Chef de Cabinet*, Miguel Chammoro, and by his criminal intelligence chief, Lucas Christopanos.

I travelled to the Sicilian capital of Palermo to meet Leoluca Orlando, who, as head of the anti-Mafia party, La Rete, is at the top of the Cosa Nostra's target list and because of this is one of Italy's most protected politicians. I thank Mr Orlando for his time and one of his aides, Andreas Scrosati, for his patience in arranging our meeting. I further thank Mr Scrosati for making possible the meeting in Rome with another then La Rete MP, Nando Dalla Chiesa, whose father, General Carlo Alberto Dalla Chiesa, was assassinated by the Mafia. It was in Rome, too, that I met Judge Liliana Ferraro, who leads Italy's anti-Mafia campaign as head of the Justice Ministry's penal affairs department and who keeps in her office mementos of her predecessor, Judge Giovanni Falcone – blown to pieces in Palermo by a Mafia bomb – as a reminder that she could suffer the same fate herself. Also in Rome I was greatly assisted by the wise guidance of an old friend, Gianluigi ('Gigi') Melega. And I renewed my acquaintance with correspondent Ronald Singleton who throughout the writing of this book has been an invaluable source of information and help.

Most of my meetings during several visits to Paris had to be on the basis of anonymity, and I gained much from them, particularly at encounters near the Champs-Elysées and others off the Faubourg Saint Honoré. People I can thank there are William Langley and Ann-Elizabeth Moutet, and professor of criminology Dr Xavier Raufer. It was through the courtesy of Professor Raufer that in June 1994, I was given a unique opportunity to meet virtually every world expert on the global Mafia at the XXth annual conference of the Institut de Criminologie, where they were discussing the organised crime threat to world economies. Professionals to whom I remain indebted include Evgenie Liakhov, organised crime specialist at the Russian military academy in Moscow; Crescencio Arcos, principal US deputy Secretary of State for Narcotic Matters; Judge Bruno Siclari, chief of the National AntiMafia Directorate (DIA) at the Italian Ministry of Justice and the investigator into Italy's illegal P2 Masonic Lodge: Judge Giancarlo Caselli, successor to murdered anti-Mafia judge Paolo Borsellino; Kwok Cho-Kuen Albert, Chief Superintendent of the Organised Crime and Triad division of the Hong Kong Police; Baltazar Garzon, minister in charge of organised crime, narcotics and money laundering in Spain; Latin American cartel expert Peter Lupscha, professor of political sciences at the University of New Mexico; Jean-Francois Sampieri, Marseille investigating judge and the foremost authority on French organised crime; investigative judge Thierry Jean Pierre, money laundering expert at the French Ministry of Justice before his 1994 election to the European Parliament in Strasbourg; and the deputy head of Scotland Yard's organised crime unit, Detective Chief Superintendent Roy Clark.

I travelled extensively in Germany, to Bonn, Cologne, Wiesbaden and Berlin. Again many meetings had to be on a non-attributable basis. For his help in Bonn I am grateful to John England and also Interior Ministry official Dr Michael Griesbeck. I greatly appreciated the views of the underworld problems confronting reunified Germany that were given to me by Eduard Lintner, MP and Parliamentary State Secretary to the Minister to the Interior, by Chief Superintendent Jurgen Maurer, head of the Bundeskriminalamt's organised crime division, and by Chief Superintendent Peter Kroemer, who leads the unit investigating nuclear smuggling through his country from the bordering states of the former Soviet Union. Back in England Sam Cummings, the world's biggest dealer in small arms, told intriguing stories of sinister approaches from the former communist empire.

It was in The Hague, in the Netherlands, that Dutch criminologist and Justice Ministry advisor Dr Jan van Dijk again suggested to me that crime was so well organised and internationally financed that the European Union has limited time to defeat it. This was by no means an opinion restricted to himself or Euro-MP Pieter Stoffelen. Others in the Netherlands whom I can thank for their help are correspondent Mark Fuller, and Henk Klein Beekman, who leads perhaps the most unusual trade union in Europe, the Association of Dutch Sex Club owners.

I was given an example of Irish hospitality and friendship in Dublin by Garda trade union official John Greene, whom I first met in Strasbourg with fellow official Tony Fagan, and through John met Garda Representatives' General Secretary John Ferry. Chief Superintendent Anthony Hickey, at that time head of the drugs branch, and Stephen Rea, assistant editor of the Garda Review, also provided essential guidance on terrorist activities both north and south of the Irish border.

In England I received extensive cooperation from a large number of people.

I was welcomed to the XVth international conference of Data Protection and Privacy Commissioners in Manchester by the then registrar, Eric Howe. I thank him and his assistant, Mrs Pat Mellor. The gathering enabled me to meet practically every official responsible for safeguarding individual computer-held data and personal material in every country in the European Union. Those who gave unsparingly of their time were Anita Bondestam, Director-General and head of the Swedish Data Inspection Board; Essex Chief Constable John Burrow, CBE, chairman of the Association of Chief Police Officers' working group on data protection; Christian Schricke, head of the legal directorate and chairman of the OECD Commission on Computer Information and Privacy; and Dr Professor Spiros Simitis, of Frankfurt University and former Data Protection Commissioner for the German state of Hesse. I also met Stewart Dresner, Director of Privacy Law and Business, the leading international data protection information service. Through him – later – I was introduced to the service's researcher, Brazilian-born Deborah Fisch Nigri, LLB, who gained her Doctorate of Philosophy in law specialising in computer crime and who has proved an invaluable source of guidance into a multi-million-pound, if arcane, activity. It was in Manchester, too, that I renewed my acquaintance with Andrew Puddephatt, who gave me the benefit of his long experience as General Secretary of Liberty of official authority abuse of human rights. I was given further information about such abuse by Halya Gowan, of Amnesty International. I also thank that organisation for guiding me to Dr Jean Claude Alt, of the *Clinique des Franciscaines*, at Versailles, and Dr Ron Guttman, a surgeon at the McGill Transplant Centre at the Royal Victoria Hospital in Montreal, who talked at length about the theft – sometimes involving murder – of organs from children and young adults for transplant operations.

Two Euro-MPs I had been unable to meet in Strasbourg made time to spend with me in England. For their consideration I am grateful to Sir Jack Stewart-Clark, Conservative member for East Sussex and a drug trafficking specialist, and Peter Price, until his 1994 election defeat the Conservative member for London South East, who brought an accountant's scrutiny to the sometimes curious financial affairs of the Union.

Anthony Hooper, QC, talked to me on behalf of the General Council of the British Bar, on the many worrying changes being proposed for the British criminal justice system and Anthony Scrivener, QC, provided further invaluable expertise.

I was flattered to find a previous non-fiction work of mine on drug trafficking and addiction (*The Fix*) listed as one of the books of reference in the Organised Crime Unit of the National Criminal Intelligence Service. And thank most sincerely the then head of that unit, Detective Inspector Graham Saltmarsh, MA, for his guidance and continuous assistance in the preparation of this book, during which he was given the responsibility of heading the Service's financial section. Thanks are also necessary to the Triad expert at the unit, Detective Sergeant Michael Ball, Michael Ross, deputy head of the Drugs and Money Laundering branch, Detective Sergeant Ian Langrish, attached to the Interpol section and Louise Ellis, the then Executive Officer in charge of the Paedophile Unit.

Many police officers and investigators whom I met asked not to be identified. Superintendent Michael Hames, at the time of my research the outspoken and deeply committed head of Scotland Yard's Obscene Publications Squad, was fortunately not one of them. I am also glad that Richard Coyles, the chairman of the Police Federation of England and Wales and Dave F. Hayward, from the Sergeants' Central Committee of that Federation, were also not among those so reticent. Glad, too, that after some initial reluctance John Alderton, the former Chief Constable of Devon and Cornwall – and one time Research Fellow with the Centre for Police Studies at Exeter University – agreed to share with me his views and concerns about British law and order.

Expert and valued guidance upon that subject also came from a number of permanent officials – all of whom insisted upon remaining nameless – at Britain's Home Office. And from the nearby British Treasury I was helped to understand the workings of British financial institutions through which, daily, cosmic sums of money pass, vast amounts of it the proceeds of crime.

Perhaps not surprisingly I had the greatest difficulty persuading people to talk to me – either on or off the record – about the protective association between the Mafia, European Freemasonry and the Brussels-based Commission, the unelected executive arm of the Union. Leoluca Orlando had no such hesitation. Neither did Euro-MP John Tomlinson and former Strasbourg colleague Peter Price. Nor John Hamill, curator, spokesman and historian of the United Grand Lodge of England.

I express gratitude, too, to the multi-lingual former intelligence officer and multi-assassination attempt survivor who initially guided my enquiries into influence-manipulating Freemasonry.

He will recognise his considerable contributions from various passages in this book.

Septuagenarian Melville Mark, a wealthy property developer, was the only person, other than some policemen and politicians, prepared openly to discuss his refusal – in France – to become a victim of the Mafia. In view of the level of Côte d'Azure assassinations – one particularly close to someone with whom Mr. Mark was negotiating – I consider that refusal a brave one, despite his reluctance to call it such.

James Emson, CBE, managing director of the Art Loss Register, and former policeman Colin Reeve, chief security officer for the London auctioneers Christie's, have helped me enormously in my researches into fine art crime, as has another former detective, art insurance loss adjuster John Suter.

I owe additional thanks to Jame Emson for the long distance introduction to Madame Banka Sulc in war-racked Zagreb, who disclosed the pillaging of Croatian works of art.

I am equally grateful to those inhabitants of the European fine art, antique and restoration environment who trusted me sufficiently to talk at length and with openness. I remember with particular pleasure a farmhouse luncheon. And a dinner party that went on far too late into the night in a house where the antiques really *were* genuine and the host a friend.

The refusal of this particular group of people to be identified was not because they were personally involved (they stressed they had to know the tricks to avoid being tricked themselves) but because they would suffer – materially, not physically – for breaking ranks by admitting there was any cheating or illegality at all. One was either in – or out – of the ring. To be out of the ring was virtually to be out of business.

For her more than competent professional translations of a number of French documents I thank Philada Rogers, to whom some of the facts about violence, larceny, corruption and murder must have seemed incongruous in the leafy tranquillity of Dorset.

A number of people I met were self-admitted professionals of the trade which is the subject of this book. Crime. Any identity they provided would probably have been false anyway and so often we only bothered with first names. Whenever possible – which was often – I checked their anecdotal stories with independent, sometimes official sources. Those I could not check and which appeared too fanciful I have omitted.

To them all – the named and the unnamed – I remain extremely grateful.

CHAPTER ONE

The Wages of Sin

Crime pays. It always has done. Not, of course, for the street people or the amateurs. They are swept up, like the disposable dross they are, as much victims as those upon whom they prey. The people for whom crime pays are the professionals, the men and women who operate it as a business, conducted through structures closely resembling legitimate multi-national corporations and conglomerates, their boardroom-like heirarchies serviced by accountants and financial advisors.

The crime that pays is organised crime, which I examine in this book under the eight general headings: the illegal arms trade, the illegal drugs trade, money-laundering, computer crime, prostitution and pornography, illegal imigration, terrorism and fine art.

But each of these crimes overlap, one on to another, because the professionals who organise them as businesses rarely confine themselves to one but trade in several.

The crime most worrying world governments, the smuggling of nuclear material and technology – as well as of conventional arms – from the former Soviet bloc is inextricably linked to illegal drug trafficking. The cosmic profits from both activities require highly sophisticated money-laundering techniques, that convert dirty money into clean. Most of those techniques depend upon the border-crossing ease of computers, which additionally fosters other entire areas of crime. One is computer sex, which links with the more traditional prostitution and pornography industry. To feed that industry men and women are taken, often by force, from the enormous trade in illegal immigrants. It is also fed by the kidnap or purchase of children and young adults from Latin America or Eastern Europe, which source in turn services a further, most horrifying crime, identified by the United Nations' Dr Boutros Ghali, the trafficking in human organs. Drugs finance the terrorism with which some religiously-dominated Middle East states – eager purchasers of nuclear and conventional weapons – actively seek to destabilise Europe. Those states have raised additional terrorist finance by selling their country's fine art through European auction houses. Through those same auction houses is also traded the huge amounts of fine art stolen throughout the fifteen countries of the European Union, as well as those looted wholesale from the former Soviet empire.

These, then, are the crimes and their general headings which the UN's Secretary General itemised – coincidentally to their being the ones I chose to discuss in this book – as those threatening not just Europe but world democracy. He did so at a conference attended by delegates from 139 countries in Naples in November 1994. That conference concluded that such crimes – and their organised perpetrators – *did* pose the danger Boutros Ghali had warned of.

Regrettably, law enforcement agencies in the EU singly and universally refuse to acknowledge the danger. Just as they refuse to take the necessary action to confront it.

Which is not the only advantage enjoyed by the mafias of Europe and their business partners outside. A further and essential aid to organised crime is the concealment and protection offered by a particular European variety of Freemasonry, each country's being recognised by the word 'Orient' in its title.

Because of its acknowledged criminal connections and because it flouts the accepted principles of the Brotherhood, 'Orient' Free-masonry is proscribed by the world-governing British organisation. Despite which secret, closed-door Orient Freemasonry, and the equally secret mafia groups it nurtures, have flourished in Europe. And since the end of the Cold War have spread their tentacles throughout the former communist empire.

I do not lightly nor without evidence make this accusation. It is based upon conversations with concerned officials of the British lodge, with Euro-MPs and with assassination-threatened men and women brave enough publicly to denounce the connections.

Because of their inconceivably vast profits, the crimes discussed in this book are those judged by Europe's disorganised law enforcement and intelligence agencies to be the European Union's most significant illegalities. And because they are illegal, and so provide no audited, publicly available accounts, it is only possible to estimate very approximately the tax-free profits such crimes generate. But from the indicators by which experienced international investigators make their calculations – insurance adjustments, provable gains admitted during arrest confessions, and drug street prices – the proceeds of organised crime are measured in multi-billions.

The illegal, nuclear-led arms trade and the illegal drugs industry are so closely intertwined that it is virtually impossible to separate either as the top earner.

Certainly the world is awash with mind-bending, mind-altering substances. And the European Union is geographically and culturally at the centre of this narcotics whirlpool, being sucked ever downwards. One overall figure suggested to me was that the annual worldwide income from drug trafficking was £328 billion.[1] An acknowledged British authority[2] put it even higher, at £500 billion. Even taking the lower figure, however, £131 billion of that comes each year from within the European Union.[3] The income from illegal arms dealing – in both weaponry and in expertise – brings in comparable sums: some analysts put the profits even higher than those derived from illegal drugs.

Such staggering, totally tax-free yearly incomes make it possible for organised crime literally to buy governments. And through them, in effect, countries. That fact, particularly as it applies to the unstable new republics of the former Soviet Union, formed the basis of the apocalyptic warning given by Dr Boutros Ghali at that November 1994 conference in Italy, the very country where such a scenario had already become reality.

It is because Italy provides the case history example of that 'crime wins' apocalypse that I examine in detail the criminality, violence and corruption that led to the replacement of the Italian First Republic with a Second, the corruption-battered first administration of which crumbled within eight months of coming to office. And that led to the position there of the traditional and original Mafia. I talked with Palermo mayor and European MP Leoluca Orlando, founder of the anti-Mafia party La Rete and the first man to identify the masonic crime-arms-and-drug connection, as a result of which he must now live surrounded by more than a dozen armed bodyguards. He insisted[4]:'The new frontier, the new horizon of the world, is no longer the fight between communist and capitalist. It is the fight between legality and illegality. The problem is to know if in the future the governments of the world will be legal or illegal.'

Similarly, the former deputy Commissioner at Britain's New Scotland Yard and a two-term secretary general of the 179-nation Interpol organisation conceded to me that enforcement efforts made against one arm of the largest of crime businesses is already lost. He acknowledged: 'Drugs are unstoppable.'

As well as armaments and drugs, the Midas wealth at the disposal of organised crime – and the nation-destabilising potential it possesses – has spawned a third sophisticated, highly technical area of crime activity. Each feeds the profits from the other: the first is entirely dependent upon the second, which couldn't operate without the income from the first.

It's called money-laundering.

The money derived from crime – most certainly the huge amounts generated from the range of illegalities described in this book – is 'dirty', just as an identifiable stolen object is 'hot', provably linking its thief to his larceny. And just as a stolen article has to be fenced as quickly as possible – both in order to separate the robber from the evidence of his crime and to gain a rapid profit on the transaction – so dirty money has to be washed. The never-ending avalanche of cash must be purged of its guilt-proving connection, through recognised legal channels operated by legitimate financial institutions. These make it squeaky-clean by making it totally explainable. It is then moved sideways several times, buying convenient cash-transacting facilities such as banks or casinos or property developments, the normal activities of which further scrub and rinse and sanitise it.

Money-laundering is the responsibility of organised crime's accountants and financiers: the Japanese mafia, the Yakuza, are believed by one specialised British law enforcement unit to have located a specifically-named financial division of their organisation in England, in order to move their money through London's world-leading City establishments. Usually, however, the initial staging posts for such manoeuvres are the tax haven bank secrecy countries of the world, which I will identify here, along with the various mechanisms they employ. The computer is the principal tool by which these money magicians make billions disappear – at the touch of a keyboard, not the wave of a magic wand: unless its source is questioned at the moment of its very first handling by a legal institution, dirty money vanishes forever, transferred thousands of miles from one country to another in a fraction of a second.

Seizing its vast profits is one of the very few ways in which organised crime can be effectively confronted. Cash flow is the life blood of any business; cut it off and the business will wither and die. Remarkably, in view of the lack of any genuinely real political will or crime enforcement cooperation in the EU, its fifteen member states have agreed that organised crime's illegal fortunes are its Achilles' heel. With rare foresight and commitment, they have further agreed to adopt legislation targeting this wealth. Regrettably, here again as in the different ways in which the fifteen nations all attempt to unify any EU legal suggestion, the ways in which they have individually adopted the European money laundering Conventions and Directives are, to say the least, uneven. So the crime-beating effort is flawed and stands little chance of success.

As well as providing an indispensible money laundering service, computers offer golden possibilities for fraud, with estimated profits close behind those from arms dealing and illegal drugs. For such crime exact figures are even more impossible to estimate, because few, if any, financial institutions – including *every* leading world bank – admit that their systems can be broken into. To make such an admission would acknowledge the unacceptable truth: that *no* computer programme or database is totally protected from unauthorised plundering by a determined hi-tech intruder. And this truth would shatter public and customer confidence, already damaged when an unknown hacker[5] plucked from British Telecom's supposedly impenetrable records the secret telephone numbers of virtually every UK intelligence organisation, as well as those of the Royal Family, of the country's defence installations and of senior government leaders, including the prime minister. And again, in January 1995, when it was learned that a 16-year-old British boy – nicknamed 'Datastream' – hacked into the US government's most sensitive computers to watch supposedly highly secret communications between Washington and American agents in North Korea during the 1994 crisis over nuclear inspection. Not only did he read the transmissions – and enter top secret systems detailing US government payroll and procurement records – he also made his discoveries available, as did the unknown British Telecom intruder, on a bulletin board on Internet, the global communications network that can be accessed by thirty-five million users!

Rather than concede their systems are vulnerable, financial institutions prefer secretly to bear the entire cost of whatever hackers steal. After all, even if they were to trace the computer thief, the laws that exist are so poorly framed and difficult to enforce that any high profile prosecution would almost certainly fail, further eroding public confidence.

It might be limited in screen size but a computer's VDU is the world's biggest and most comprehensive pornographic cinema, totally uncensored and totally unpreventable. Again, because the porn available in Europe is illegally supplied, its amount is totally impossible to calculate; its source is not restricted, even, to Europe. It is as easy for computer-literate European operators – the majority of whom statistically are children – to call up sexually or violently deviant material from Miami as it is to call it up from Madrid. Certainly that availability runs into the hundreds of thousands of images, both stills and movie-simulated, the latter possible by the further technological miracle of image enhancement. The United Kingdom has attempted to legislate against such pornography in a much-flawed Act[6] but the reality, as with so many other efforts to stem organised crime, is that the legislation is virtually impossible to enforce, as I later make clear.

The European porn movie business has outlets other than computer screens. The trade in films and videos is enormous, extending far beyond the Community's boundaries and catering for every taste. Young children are kidnapped or purchased to become victims of the worst of paedophile depravities, some even involving babies as young as fourteen months. Although British police claim never to have seized or even seen such a film, 'snuff' movies – in which children as well as adults are actually murdered on screen – exist.

The live sex market flourishes too. Youngsters of both sexes, preferably in their middle teens, are tricked or beaten into prostitution: in Amsterdam I was told of salesmen offering sex club owners a selection of bewildered East European girls at £2,000 a head, packed into minivans awaiting inspection.

Of all the crimes examined in this book, equal in horror to that of snuff movies, the most appalling is that identified in his Naples speech by Boutros Ghali: the kidnap or purchase of waifs or young adults from whom are stolen – often fatally or disfiguringly – organs to save the life of a terminally ill person prepared to pay whatever price to go on living. Although the extent of the body-snatching industry is disputed within the medical profession, the UN Secretary General has no doubt that it exists. Neither has the European Parliament, which has passed resolutions demanding EU legislation against the crime. Astonishingly, none has so far been enacted.

Bringing illegal immigrants into the European Community is a highly organised criminal activity too, from which emanate – in addition to vast profits – several other felonies, often resulting in serious social unrest. Since they enter on forged papers, persons or families smuggled into Europe are at the blackmailing mercy of the organisation which supplies their false documentation and which can threaten exposure whenever it chooses, making the immigrants as much slaves as are the sex-fodder girls brought in by minivan from Eastern Europe; indeed, a large proportion of those girls are ferried illegally across EU borders simply in order to give additional powers of enforcement to their already physically intimidating ponces. Few illegal immigrants have sufficient money to pay in advance for themselves and their families to be smuggled into the EU. They agree promissory notes on which the daily multiplying interest is impossible to pay. Some go into crime unprompted, but others are forced into it, simply so that they can pay their debts. Their daughters and sons go into prostitution. Many illegal immigrants are from the Far East and Africa, where illegal drugs are indigenous: drug trafficking and transportation is the predominant crime in which they become involved.

Predictably, this makes *all* immigrants – legal or illegal – alienated, the objects of violent, often murderous hate attacks from EU citizens who perceive drugs as the biggest single threat to the fabric of their society. Additionally, the post-war prosperity of Europe – particularly of Germany and France – was assisted by legal foreign workers. Now that the prosperity is faltering, bringing inexorable, long-term unemployment, foreign workers are seen as job-stealers, which creates another – even more widespread – reason for physical attack. Today, in every country in the EU, racially-motivated gangs are not just prepared to but are anxious to kill, encouraged by fascist groups increasingly being accepted and voted into the mainstream of European politics by people for whom xenophobic 'foreigners-out' insularity – the very antithesis of the European Union – is a popular credo.

European law enforcement officers collectively label these murderous gangs 'football hooligans', or 'skinheads'. This is totally misleading, suggesting groups of stumbling lager louts draped in football scarves, or rebellious, shaven-headed but basically harmless adolescents. The gangs are none of these things. The are the highly organised foot-soldiers of internationally-linked far right fascist movements, dedicated to fomenting civil unrest throughout the European Community.

This ambition is one they share with the organisers of another crime I examine in detail in this book, the terrorism based in the Middle East. These ME states have been responsible for in-calculable violence and murder, sometimes even of massacre, in practically every country in the European Union. One such state – Iran – currently supports with money and arms *every* national terrorist organisation in Europe, and knowingly sustains their murderous, crime-supported, crime-generating activities. Several such states are eager purchasers of nuclear material and expertise currently haemorrhaging from the former Soviet Union.

The prime source of funding for Iran's destabilising efforts in the name of its religion is illegal drugs, particularly heroin. Another, in the past, was the sale, at a fraction of their true value, of the incredible heritage of art and national treasures collected by the former Shah.

The ayatollahs were not the first to combine crime with art. Art theft, fakery and forgery were among the foremost businesses of organised crime long before Tehran realised their potential. Although the suggestion was derided by at least one official of a leading London auction house, I have been persuaded during my researches for this book that the global profit from stolen and faked works of art ranks closely behind that of arms and drug dealing in the mafias' money-making league table. There *are* covetous 'Mr Bigs' for whose solitary, darkened-room pleasure priceless works are stolen to order, particularly Japanese Yakuza leaders who have curious preference for French Impressionists. Old Master thefts are those that make world headlines, but for every masterpiece snatched from a country house or gallery wall there are thousands of the highest value second or middle category works that attract less publicity but enormous sums of money.

The collapse of communism throughout the former Soviet Union has had a phenomenal effect upon fine art crime. Officials of some of the former satellite countries have used the word 'rape' to describe to me the looting from their countries of heritage treasures: the British director of an international organisation formed to trace stolen artefacts showed no surprise at the suggestion of a Polish official that, every ten minutes of every day, a priceless piece of his country's patrimony vanishes into Western Europe.

For every genuine antique or fine art piece moving along the robbers' route across Europe there are a dozen fakes, some crafted so superbly that they defy identification by respected international experts. Sometimes – as in the later examined case involving a particular British aristocratic family – the scam is so well thought-out that the fake is supported by the original authenticating documents.

In his Naples speech the UN's Secretary General identified the choice confronting not just the European Union but the entire world as 'the rule of law over the rule of the jungle'.

Organised crime made its choice a long time ago. Europe hasn't. And is showing no signs of doing so.

Very occasionally a big fish – the equivalent of a director or a senior executive – gets landed, prompting politicians chasing the voting appeal of law and order to call press conferences about battles being fought and wars being won.

Genuine law enforcement experts rarely claim such victories. Experienced criminologists never do. They know there's always a new crime king ready to ascend the briefly empty throne. Just as, at the lowest level, there is always another layer of disposable dross to rise to the surface to replace imprisoned street dealers, pimps, muggers and drug mules.

Genuine crime experts know also – but will admit only in private and then unattributably – that crime not only pays, it's winning. Organised crime is already so wealthy and so deeply entrenched in the fabric of legitimate society that it will very soon be beyond the control of any legal system.

Which is frightening. What is even more frightening is that no effective legal opposition is being created in the European Union to confront this threat.

The EU needs a cohesive, truly federated FBI, a combined police and investigatory agency composed of officers and experts from each of its current fifteen member states. And it needs a properly and fully federated system of laws as applicable and as legally binding upon Greek citizens in the south as upon Swedish citizens in the north.

It has neither. Nor will it have, for too many years in a far too distant future. By which time it will be too late.

A pretence is being made, a ragbag of empty undertakings and unenforced agreements, none of which has genuine substance or is backed by genuine commitment. Member governments lack any real will to make the Union succeed. Their justice and interior ministers issue pious communiques pledging the harmonisation and integration of their national forces, all of which bitterly argue and fight among themselves, each to protect their own internal empires. None is willing to surrender even the smallest degree of authority or power to an external, supra-national body.

The embryo of such a body already exists. Its name, appropriately, is Europol and from the enthusiasm of its strongest advocate, Germany, it might at face value appear that my pessimistic forecasts are unfounded. Sadly, though, the Europol that Germany champions is a pan-Europe police force in which Germany sees itself as the dominant influence, if not its head. Which situation, throughout the other nations of the Union with still too recent memories of two world wars, ranges from the unpalatable to the totally unacceptable. And their opposition is fuelled by Interpol, which as an international police liaison facility lacks the operational function absolutely essential for an FBI-type organisation, but which still considers itself the only international anti-crime agency that Europe needs. Europol, in the opinion of Interpol's Secretary General Raymond Kendall, is qualified only to become one of his divisions.

Jan van Dijk, a professor of criminology and Directorate head of Crime Prevention at the Dutch Ministry of Interior, held back during our meeting at The Hague from specifying any cataclysmic deadline for law and order unity in the EU. He did believe, however, that time was fast running out for EU governments to show the currently abjectly lacking political will and for national enforcement agencies to put aside pride and territorial jealousies and harmonise into a united front against organised crime. A Netherlands Euro-MP, Pieter Stoffelen, against whom there have been four death threats but who still insists on travelling without a bodyguard, had no such hesitation in specifying a time limit. With

over a decade's experience of European criminality, gained on the
legal committee of the Parliamentary Assembly, he told me he
thought two years was the maximum period after which the
various mafias would become unbeatable.[7] John Ferry, who brings
immense practical experience to his job as General Secretary of the
Irish police trade union, shared these views[8] and French criminologist Dr Xavier Raufer was similarly pessimistic.

At a June 1994 conference organised in Paris by Professor Raufer
and attended by the world's top anti-mafia specialists I did not
encounter one professional who believed they were winning any
battles, let alone wars, against organised crime. Which made
hardly surprising at the United Nations gathering of 139 countries
in Naples five months later that Secretary General Boutros Ghali
should suggest such crime presented the single most serious threat
to world democracy.

Although I identify the gangs and conglomerates by their
individual names and titles throughout the course of this book, I
have chosen frequently to use the word mafia – with a small 'm' – as
a generic term for organised crime. The founding societies to
which the expression properly refers are those of Italy, with the
Cosa Nostra of Sicily the original title holders. It was the Cosa
Nostra that defined every mafia's most important requirement to
be its sworn-in-blood vow of *omerta*, the pledge never to disclose
any detail of its activities. The secrecy rituals of the Orient
freemasons are more symbolic than the literal death-for-dishonour
oaths of the Cosa Nostra but the secrecy is nevertheless meticu-
lously maintained by European masons, in both east and west.
This makes each the perfect blood brother for the other, and
provides secure shell-within-a-shell concealment for both.

Among themselves masons understand the Mafia concept of
'influence' and cultivate it assiduously. In this way freemasonry
creates – as my coming Italian examples will show – a usefully
discreet forum where men of Mafia influence can meet men of
respectable commercial or political influence.

I have been convinced by the Euro-MPs to whom I have earlier
referred that masonic shields are frequently thrown up to defend
Brotherhood bureaucrats who occupy convenient positions of
power in the EU's permanent institutions: this particular European
freemasonry is politically deeply committed and wields a great deal
of influence. There are European lodges linking the very highest
levels of certain national governments manipulating policy

decisions to the advantage of those governments, and cynically – even criminally – flouting the democratic principles by which the European Union is treaty-bound to operate.

CHAPTER TWO

By Way of the Orient

The proscribed freemasonry lodges that cloak organised crime and manipulate political influence to the particular benefit of certain European Union countries share a common element: their titles include the word 'Orient'. Of them all, the *Grande Orient Lodge de France* is considered the most active and the most powerful: members of the families of two former French leaders have held high office in it and still retain active connections with it.[1] It has a highly influential membership within the European Commission in Brussels and in the European Parliament in Strasbourg. The successful opponents of demands from British Labour MEPs for a publicly open register of freemasons, particularly among officials at the European Commission, were later closely involved in defending a parliamentary employee who deposited a large sum of money he was responsible for administering into an interest-bearing personal account in a London bank. It earned £50,000, about which parliament knew nothing. The £50,000 interest, technically due to the parliament, was never recovered.

Belgium has active Grand Orient lodges, with members in the upper echelons of the Commission who are in a position to affect decisions and thinking of the non-elected executive of the European Union. A particularly prominent and politically active Belgian family has strong links with the country's Grand Orient. I am unable, legally, to name these people.

And in Italy the insidiousness of unofficial freemasonry partially emerged in 1981 with the revelation that an Orient lodge offshoot called *Propaganda Due* (P2) was actively planning a coup d'etat against the government. P2 was a secret lodge, unconnected with the official and legal Grand Lodge d'Italia, which has 18,000 members. The disclosure that leading politicians, police, the secret service and the judiciary were all members of P2 brought down the government. P2 was declared illegal and was supposedly disbanded. It was not. And has not been.[2] In 1994 it was declared legal again. An appeal against that 1994 decision technically keeps it unlawful.

Only 950 of P2's 2,600 members were ever identified. Those that remained undiscovered continued to meet secretly throughout its alleged banning and provided concealment for organised crime and influence peddling. Other secret Orient lodges were formed and are still operating. They hide terrorists, some of whom were responsible for the bombing of the Uffizi Gallery in Florence in May 1993. There were other terrorist bombings, prior to that, in one of which P2's suave and avuncular Grand Master Licio Gelli was implicated. In the spring of 1993 Giuliano di Bernardo even abandoned his attempts to clean up the Italian lodge (regarded as legal, although not by the controlling English body) of which he was then Grand Master. After examining lodge records di Bernardo quit with the declaration 'I have seen a monster.'[3] He moved from Rome to Milan and formed the Grand Regular Lodge of Italy. He also undertook to cooperate fully with magistrates investigating links between organised crime and masonry. And issued the edict that anyone wishing to join his breakaway lodge had to produce an examining magistrate's certificate that they were not involved in any criminal activity, Mafia association or political corruption.

Forty-six-year-old Palermo mayor Leoluca Orlando, whose unruly black hair is showing grey-flecked signs of the death threat strain under which he constantly lives, insists[4] organised crime – in the case of Italy, the traditional Mafia groups – gets it strength from binding ties with masonry. Only Germany, he believes, has a proper awareness of how serious the problem is. He goes as far as to say the old Mafia tradition of one Family's allegiance to one Godfather has changed. Now, under the protective secrecy of masonry, organised crime is being run in Europe and beyond by committees of professional criminals. Orlando likens the new *cupola* or controlling commission to 'a constellation of stars'.

It is an ever-expanding constellation.

Within one year of the collapse of communism in the Soviet Union, the unofficial Orient Lodge of Italy had masterminded the formation of two lodges in the Czech and Slovak republics, two in Poland, two in Hungary and one in Russia. Unofficial French masons – the official movement's word for such dispossessed members is 'irregular' – encouraged the opening of lodges in the former Czechoslovakia, Romania, the split up Yugoslavia, Hungary and Russia. All were formed, initially, as lodges-in-exile and met in Paris. Beneath their cover the mafias of the former communist empire have flourished and consolidated: the Orients provide the hidden conduit for links between the organised crime of East and West.

The burly Leoluca Orlando, who believes he prevented – although perhaps only delayed – his assassination by naming the masons who protect the Mafia chieftains planning to kill him, warned: 'Through masonry the Mafia is going all over Europe. It means the fight is not a Sicilian or an Italian fight. The problem is an international one. The problem is to know who will be able to build a future with legality or with illegality.'

The modern history of Freemasonry, to which today 6,000,000 belong worldwide, began in 1717. By being the first the English Grand Lodge became the movement's governing body, overseeing the development of masonry throughout Europe. In just over fifty years, Brotherhoods were formed in every country in Europe. The Nazis banned the movement during the Second World War – as did Mussolini in Italy – and it was outlawed during the communist era in the Soviet Union. Catholics were prohibited from being members by the Vatican, which considered masonic ritual blasphemous. That church ruling, since relaxed, brought anti-clericalism into the Orient lodges.

Such anti-clericalism emerged publicly in 1878 when the Grand Orient Lodge of France removed all references to a Supreme Being from its ritual and constitution, as a result of which London withdrew recognition. According to masonic scholar and historian John Hamill, it was then that French masons broke a further rule by involving themselves in politics. Today they have cultivated political manoeuvring into an art form. Some Euro-MPs complain that masonic political commitment permeates every level of the European Union.

It was not until 1972 that the English governing body officially accepted the Grand Orient of Italy: before then, says Hamill, the history of Italian masonry was 'fairly checkered'. It subsequently survived the P2 scandal – upon the dishonest assurance that the Italian parent organisation had definitely closed down the machiavellian Gelli's private fiefdom – but finally had recognition withdrawn again because of the large number of members involved in the political scandals and Mafia atrocities at the beginning of the 1990s.

Visits by British masons to Germany's Grand Lodge were banned in 1990, ostracising the Germans for allowing the proscribed Italian and French Brotherhoods to attend meetings. The Grand Orient of Belgium is denied recognition from London, too. During our meeting at the palatial London headquarters of World Freemasonry Hamill assured me that to forbid inter-county visits was a serious censure within the movement. He also talked openly of the strong influence unrecognised lodges exert within Brussels and the European Parliament. 'The Grand Orients have always been very politically minded, very minded on social policies as a group rather than as individuals who are freemasons.'

It was as long ago as 1985 that the British Socialist MEP Group floated their masonic registration idea for the institutions of the united Europe. It came at a Madrid conference of Socialist parties in the then European Community, and promptly led to a walk-out by Henri Saby, leader of the French Socialists, and Mario Dido, his Italian counterpart.

That was four years after the emerging scandal of P2 had given the first indication of the very tiniest tip of a huge law breaking masonic iceberg. By that time the government of Arnaldo Forlani had collapsed under the weight of the scandal. The Justice Minister himself, Adolpho Sarti, had been one of the first to go, accused through his links with the lodge of political espionage and endangering the security of the very state he was sworn to safeguard. Colonel Antonio Viezzer, a former Secret Service chief, had gone, too, alleged to have passed state secrets to Gelli in his suite at Rome's Excelsior Hotel, on the via Veneto. Pietro Longo, Social Democrat leader and budget minister in the succeeding government of Bettino Craxi, denied being a member of the banned lodge, even though he was listed on seized membership documents. Those documents gave the names of fifteen generals and admirals. One was the head of the armed forces. Two others commanded the country's intelligence services. The final score of men of influence driven from office – in addition to serving members of the government – was 38 MPs and magistrates and 185 military and security service officers.

Bewildered Italians – and European parliamentarians – thought there could never be a bigger political embarrassment.[5] They were wrong.

There was the affair of Roberto Calvi, a member of P2 and a money launderer for the Mafia, who was found hanged beneath Blackfriars Bridge in London in June 1982. Shortly before the financial institution he headed, Banco Ambrosiano, had collapsed with fraudulent debts of $1.3 billion. It was to be another eleven years before an independent enquiry, using scientific techniques unavailable when Calvi's body was found, proved he had been murdered: the first inquest finding had been suicide, the second an open verdict. London police reject criticism that their investigation was flawed. An Italian supergrass named as the killer Mafia narcotics trafficker Franco di Carlo, subsequently jailed for twenty-five years for drug offences committed after Calvi's death. In Rome a frail Czech bishop, Mgr Pavel Hnlica, admitted paying £5 million for the contents of the briefcase Calvi had with him in London. One of the two Italians selling them, Flavio Carboni, had been with Calvi in London. Mgr Hnlica's cheques were drawn against the Vatican's private bank, the Institute of Religious Works (IOR). Before his death, Calvi was deeply involved in money transfers – a lot of it Mafia cash[6] – throughout the world with the IOR's President, Chicago-born Archbishop Paul Marchincus, a giant of a man who looks more like the college boxer he once was than a man of the cloth. His Vatican links earned Calvi the nickname 'God's Banker', although the slight, balding, heavily moustached Calvi resembled more a junior clerk than a banker. Calvi's briefcase reputedly contained highly embarrassing details of the Vatican's part in the money laundering. The papers were never recovered. Marchincus remains beyond the law, in the protection of Vatican sovereign sanctuary.

It did not take eleven years to reach the verdict of murder against another of Gelli's banking associates. Michele Sindona was a member of P2 and a long time friend of Calvi. In 1980, convicted of fraud and perjury by a Manhattan court, he was returned to Italy for trial for commissioning murder, for which he was jailed for life. He – like Calvi – knew a great deal that might have discomforted the church – he personally knew Pope Paul VI – the masonic lodges and the Mafia. He agreed to talk to investigators. Before he could, in September 1986, cyanide was slipped into his coffee in his video-monitored cell in Voghera prison. He died instantly. His killer was never found.

Throughout it all, Licio Gelli, the serious faced *éminence grise* of the whole intricate affair, remained relatively untouched and untroubled. Although he was tried for a number of right wing terrorist atrocities, the admitted fascist who lists his profession as a mattress manufacturer and who once tried to bribe Pope Paul VI with a gold plated bed, has rarely been jailed. Ten years imprisonment was imposed *in absentia* after he had been found guilty of being the paymaster for the 1980 bombing of Bologna railway station that killed 86 people: at the time of the trial Gelli fled to Argentina, whose president, General Galtieri, he greatly admired. Gelli had spent time in Argentina immediately after the war, not returning to Italy until the early sixties.

Arrested on a secret visit to Switzerland to check his numbered Swiss account, Gelli was extradited back to Italy early in 1988, but, under the conditions of his extradition, he could not be charged with, or made to serve a sentence for, anything other than a bankruptcy offence involving the dead Roberto Calvi's Banco Ambrosiano. Because he was supposed to be suffering from a severe heart condition needing surgery – which has never been performed – the robust, fit-looking Gelli was freed from a maximum security jail to the comfort of his own home, Villa Wanda, in the Tuscany township of Arezzo. On his frequent trips to Florence in a bullet-proofed Fiat the bespectacled Gelli was accompanied by guards whose salary was paid by the Italian state: nominally – very nominally indeed – Gelli was under technical house arrest. He remains so today, after a 1994 confused term of imprisonment in connection with P2, which is anyway being appealed against.

The first indication that Gelli had remained as active as ever in his covert freemasonry – from which several other hidden, Mafia-linked lodges had spawned – came in 1993. With it came the confirmation that masonry and Mafia involvement had spread deep within the Commission of the European Union in Brussels.[7]

The discovery was made by Dr Agostino Cordova, one of Italy's foremost anti-Mafia investigating magistrates and the public prosecutor for the Calabrian town of Palmi. His probe into the possible defrauding of the Commission by Calabrian pig breeders uncovered correspondence between Gelli and the Calabrian lodge at Roccella Ionica. Almost at once Dr Cordova found his enquiries hampered to the point of total obstruction. His investigatory staff was cut by half. His offices frequently underwent unannounced inspections from the Italian Justice Ministry. His deserved nomination as chief prosecutor of the country's anti-Mafia commission was blocked by former Socialist Justice Minister Claudio Martelli. Another deserved promotion, that of public prosecutor of Naples, was also prevented. So frustrated did Dr Cordova become he protested openly to the Anti-Mafia Commission and claimed corrupt police members of crime-dominated lodges were impeding him. He supported that accusation by supplying the Council of Judiciary, the governing body of Italian jurists, with a list of magistrates who were using their masonic affiliations to protect organised crime. He also told the Anti-Mafia Commission that one of its members was an until then undiscovered member of P2.

Such claims brought no surprise for Leoluca Orlando. He talks of 'hundreds and hundreds' of unsolved murders throughout Italy, dating the cover-up to as far back as the end of the war. He makes a heavy joke about Agatha Christie writing of perfect crime. 'When all the crimes are perfect the problem is the State is not perfect.'[8]

Despite blatant official obstruction, Dr Cordova was finally, in late 1922, able to link Gelli publicly to the Calabrian Mafia, the 'Ndrangheta. A further 128 people were named as being involved with Gelli in a massive arms and drugs conspiracy. Sources close to Dr Cordova[9] talk of his Calabrian investigation uncovering a network of crime-oriented lodges far more extensive than anything suspected in the original P2 debacle. Illegal cells are believed to exist in Rome, Milan and Florence: Gelli is a frequent visitor to Florence. The masonic-mafia partnership has been confirmed to examining magistrates by Pietro Maria Muscolo, a high official of an illegal Grand Orient. Even so, like so many other Italian criminal investigations into people in high places, the Calabrian enquiry is likely to run into legal cul-de-sacs and remain unresolved. This has already happened to many of the criminal accusations levelled at Licio Gelli.

Dr Cordova's 1992 allegations did more than name the man who officiated at the marriage between crime and Freemasonry. They connected the two activities that give organised crime the means to overwhelm Europe's fragmented, back-biting law enforcement agencies: drug trafficking coupled with arms dealing.

And just as the criminal groups have a limitless supply of narcotics from the Far East and Latin America – and of psycho-tropics from within the Union itself – so there are equally bottomless sources of weaponry.

Guns – even artillery – are available from Russia and Latvia and Lithuania and the Ukraine and Poland and Hungary and the former Czech and Slovak Republics and what used to be designated on maps as East Germany. It is in Germany – with money funnelling through a wide spread of European banks – that most of the arms deals are arranged by the closely allied organised crime groups.

A huge amount is conventional ordnance. But there is also nuclear material for atom bombs. And men and women ready and willing to be hired to make them.

CHAPTER THREE

Weapons of War

So alarmed is Germany, being at the hub of this trade in nuclear terrorism, that two intelligence units – K14, at Kiel, and another in the Organised Crime Bureau in the federal police HQ at Wiesbaden – have been established to investigate what world governments recognise to be potentially the most devastating business ever operated by organised crime. Chancellor Helmut Kohl personally protested at Russia's involvement in this trade to President Boris Yeltsin at a G7 financial meeting in Italy in July 1994. Which was hypocrisy upon hypocrisy. It was only concerted Western pressure upon Bonn which forced Germany to cancel at the end of 1994 a construction contract for two nuclear reactor plants at the Iranian port of Bushire. By January 1995, Moscow had signed a deal with Tehran to complete the £525 million project. And after four separate shipments of weapons-graded plutonium were seized entering Germany in August 1994, Kohl despatched Bernd Schmidbauer, Germany's Intelligence Minister, to Moscow for urgent talks to stem the flow. One stunning discovery coming from those talks was that virtually throughout the former Soviet Union there is no police system sufficiently motivated or efficient to prevent the nuclear trade.

German-based Russian mafia are involved. So are the traditional Italian Mafia, also from German cells. A Serbian mafia group acts as the fulcrum. South African entrepreneurs take part in continent-spanning trafficking. And despite international conferences and supposedly binding control agreements, some intelligence sources[1] talk of official government connivance in Russia and in former Soviet republics eager for the hard foreign currency available.

Those same sources identify the customer countries as Libya, Iraq, Iran and Algeria. Pakistan somewhat surprisingly was revealed as a client after the August seizure. America's CIA and three European counter-espionage services are positive that Iran possesses four complete nuclear devices.[2] Emissaries from Libya and a Lichtenstein head-hunting agency have been identified offering lucrative Libyan work contracts to scientists and technicians in Moscow and some formerly-closed nuclear facility cities.[3] A number of one-time Soviet experts have already moved to the Middle East. Some have been named.[4] One was Vladimir Kubov, a senior researcher at Moscow's Kurchatov Institute for Atomic Energy Research. Another was Philip Gurkhanian, a nuclear physicist from a facility in Nagorno-Karabakh. A third was Arsen Hamidiadeh, who worked at the Atomic Research Institute in Kazakhstan, the Muslim republic with traditional ties with Iran, from where, in March 1992, an authoritative American publication quoted intelligence sources reporting that three nuclear warheads had vanished.[5] A fourth scientist identitied was Alexandr Ahmediadeh, a physicist from Turkmenistan.

Defence ministers from Britain, Italy, France and Germany secretly discussed at the end of 1994 and into 1995 the creation of a £20 billion 'Star Wars' shield to protect Europe from surprise nuclear attack from the Middle East.

By 1992 the exodus of Russian scientists to the Middle East was well under way. Conservative intelligence assessments were of up to 12 resident in Algeria, 4 in Libya, 50 in Iraq – including a team from the Arzamas-16 nuclear weapons institute – and as many as 14 nuclear scientists, 50 engineers and 200 technicians in Iran.[6]

In a radio interview in January, 1992, Germany's then Foreign Minister, Hans-Dietrich Genscher, called the former Soviet nuclear scientists 'wandering technological mercenaries' being recruited by 'irresponsible potentates who have the dangerous ambition of building weapons of mass destruction'. A month later the then Dutch Foreign Minister Hans van den Broek estimated at an EC Foreign Minister's meeting in Lisbon that there were 4,000 Russian scientists qualified to supervise the building of a nuclear weapon.

And in May of that year the EC and America each agreed to contribute £14.5 million towards building an International Science and Technology Centre in Moscow to employ displaced Russian nuclear scientists. Japan also contributed.

There are four main Russian mafia groups involved in trafficking nuclear weaponry and material. They are the Dolgopruadnanskaya, the Chechens, the Ukrainians and the Georgians. In each are soldiers – some with experience of serving at atomic weapon sites during the Cold War – from the greatly disbanded Red Army and the much reduced former KGB. All the Russian mafiosi are headquartered in Moscow – with operating links in all major Russian cities and former republics – but they organise nuclear smuggling from their permanent German bases: they work from areas in Hamburg and Munich, but their biggest concentration is in what used to be East Berlin. They cooperate with minimal friction – in the manner of any huge interdependent, multi-national conglomerate – with gangs of the Sicilian Cosa Nostra, the Neapolitan Camorra and the Calabrian 'Ndrangheta and the newly formed Sacre Corona (which can be translated appropriately as 'Holy Wreath') from Puglia, in the heel of Italy. They have established themselves over a wide area in Germany, with recognised turf in Rhine Main, the Ruhr, Rhine-Neckar, Munich, Saarland and Franconia.[7] A third, very important group is the Serbian Ravna Gora. There are historically close ties between Russia and Serbia. The Ravna Gora are particularly active in Belgium and the Netherlands, but their centre in what used to be East Berlin handles the arms and nuclear weapons deals.

Each of the groups prefers working out of the eastern part of the country, where they are helped by indigenous gangs made up from ex-officers of the Stasi, the former East German Secret Service. In July 1994, Manfred Kittlaus, the director of a special Berlin police unit investigating the Stasi, warned Bonn in an official report that before German unification in 1990, the East German intelligence organisation stole almost £11 billion, which former officers are now using to finance organised crime. One reason for criminal organisations preferring to operate from what was once East Berlin became clear during my meeting in Bonn with Eduard Lintner, the State Secretary to the German Interior Minister.[8] At the time of our encounter, even though police divisions in the west were being decimated to staff the east, there was an overall 15,000 shortfall in police strength. Leipzig, also in the east, is a favoured city for joint planning meetings by the international Mafia.

'We can do anything we like there,' confirmed a man I met in Germany who claimed to be a member of the Dolgopruadnanskaya.[9] 'The Stasi ran the place when the communists were in power. Nothing much has changed since. It's safe.'

He called himself Oleg. And made jokes that the woman with him, who was blonde and half his age and who giggled a lot, was named Olga. 'I'm screwing my twin: everything I do is against the law.' The girl giggled. He spoke with a thick Slavic accent and was rudely arrogant to waiters, snapping his fingers for attention when he wanted to use the hotel's mobile telephone, which was often. The Zippo-type lighter for the heavy cigars was gold, like the Rolex with a diamond encircled face, the diamond topped ring and the identity bracelet. He appeared to wear more jewellery than the girl, although she had her share, mostly diamonds again. He said he knew I couldn't be 'bad people' – meaning the law – because I was English. When I said I was a writer interested in crime, he became boastfully expansive. It was he who mentioned the Dolgopruadnanskaya first, not I. 'We're the best: we go back as far as Brezhnev.' He identified, unprompted, other Moscow mafia: the Chechens, who operated in Germany ('They think they're the leaders but they're shit, really') and the Lubertsy and the Ostankino clans. He'd been personally involved in obtaining nuclear materials – 'hot stuff – you know what I mean by hot? Hot so you're a stupid bastard if you get too close and touch it. Others do that. They don't know what they're doing.' He could tell me a lot, if he wanted to: maybe he'd think about it. We arranged to meet that evening, when he had thought about it. I have no way of knowing if he was genuinely involved in the crimes he seemed to know so much about or whether he was merely showing off to the giggling girl, who spoke sufficient English to understand our exchanges: certainly he told me things about nuclear smuggling I had not at that time learned but was to hear later. I might have discovered even more had I told him what my next, already-scheduled appointment was, and so taken away his suspicions in advance, but the possibility of my being followed never occurred to me. It obviously should have done. When I returned to my hotel the anonymous waiting message read, simply, 'Appelallee 45,

Biebrich.' That is the address in the Wiesbaden suburb of the Organised Crime Bureau of the Bundeskriminalamt, Germany's federal police to which the cautious Russian had trailed me. The man who called himself Oleg and his giggling companion never kept our appointment.

At that Wiesbaden meeting at the Bundeskriminalamt, Chief Superintendent Peter Kroemer, head of the unit investigating atomic smuggling, was meticulous in trying to separate the facts from the more exaggerated fiction surrounding the crime. He was sceptical, for instance, of the much-vaunted Doomsday material, Red Mercury.

Evidence about this substance is conflicting: Russian government officials appear to have confirmed its existence, and after his election successes in 1993 the Russian nationalist leader Vladimir Zhirinovsky talked of a weapon beyond the comprehension of the rest of the world. Certainly intelligence sources confirm[10] the existence of a substance called Red Mercury, which is a compound of mercury and antimony oxides. In powder form it is stable, but it supposedly becomes explosive when converted into a liquid under pressure and by radiation. In theory Red Mercury can be employed in a nuclear device as a substitute for the traditional explosives used to implode upon the plutonium under the intense energy of a neutron cannon. The theory continues that the mercury compound makes possible atomic weapons as small as a hand grenade. Libya and Iraq are known to have paid in excess of £1 million for samples: in 1992 while carrying out a UN sanctions investigation imposed upon Iraq after the Gulf War, a United Nations nuclear inspection team discovered dossiers naming Red Mercury in a Baghdad government office.[11] Containers of the alleged material have been seized by police in Poland, Bulgaria, Italy and Germany.

Superintendent Kroemer insisted none of the samples tested by European scientists was capable of creating an atomic device. 'If there is such a component, we haven't come across it yet.'

The current importance of Red Mercury, he thought, was as a scam to cheat gullible buyers out of millions of pounds, a confidence trick that was working with some success.

The deeply-felt concern of the United States that an unstable Middle East country or well-financed terrorist group might be able to hold Europe to nuclear ransom is such that Washington has made Scientific Officers at all its appropriate overseas embassies responsible for monitoring the illegal trade in atomic weaponry. I was guided in the mystery of Red Mercury by one such officer, in conditions of anonymity so strict I will not even indicate which European capital we were in, except to make it clear it was *not* London. My informant, a qualified physicist, had heard of Red Mercury and studied some discussion papers on it but still did not know what it was supposed to be or do. His view – like that of Superintendent Kroemer – was that it was one of the most successful confidence tricks ever perpetrated. 'And because of what they want it for and who they are, I'm damned glad these guys are being suckered by the sting: bad guys cheating bad guys. Great!'

However, other American intelligence analysts,[12] while not arguing against the assessment that Red Mercury lacks explosive properties, advance a different but very practical use for the substance. They suggest that, after claiming to have reduced its military cooperation with Middle East terrorist states under Western aid pressure following the collapse of communism, Moscow set up private venture enterprises to continue that cooperation through its old and new intelligence agencies. These in turn forged links with Russian organised crime, and under the disguise of 'private venture' were able, in fact, to provide nuclear materials, forbidden by international proliferation treaties. And the Red Mercury? A clever hoax to divert Western counter-intelligence from the smuggling of the genuine article.

The pool – lake is more accurate – of available skilled manpower and nuclear material is enormous. American intelligence estimates that at the time of the dissolution of the Soviet empire there were more than 10,000 scientists employed specifically on direct-energy research, in addition to almost 1,000,000 with a high degree of atomic experience and expertise: at the height of the Cold War there were eighty Russian cities closed from any outside contact, where research and development was conducted.[13] The number of former $50-a-month scientists lured to the Middle East by salaries in excess of $3,000 a month can be measured in terms of hundreds.[14] My scientific monitoring informant stressed, however, that although the extent of recruitment was dangerously high, what he referred to as 'a considerable infrastructure' was still necessary for a bomb or device to be completely manufactured in any of the four intelligence-identified Middle East countries. He considered a far more worrying threat to be the outright purchase from the operating Mafia clans of ready made war-headed rockets in the 155mm range. And the greatest threat of all was that the smugglers would get their hands on the sort of Russian-manufactured biological or chemical weapons that Iraq's Saddam Hussein possessed during the Gulf War – but did not use for fear of matching retaliation. It is America's fear of Russian-organised crime obtaining Doomsday weapons that led the Federal Bureau of Investigation to obtain permission from President Boris Yeltsin in May 1994 for the Bureau officially to open a permanent office in Moscow. FBI Director Louis Freeh spelled out the apprehension of both America and Russia when he said: 'We must take action before a major nuclear incident occurs.'

Only one source[15] upon which I have drawn has suggested that Red Mercury is being offered for sale to the middlemen Continental mafia. I have found no independent corroboration, but there is overwhelming proof that from its trading in other nuclear material and weaponry organised crime is making profits equalling – some assessments are that it even exceeds – the cosmic income from drugs. A single warhead is priced at £14 million. Echoing widely held 'can't win' fears concerning the overall fight against organised crime, referred to in the opening to this book, the judgement of an American enquiry[16] is chilling:–

'So extensive have these networks become that it is unlikely, so long as there remains a market for the weapons and materials being sold, that any amount of law enforcement methods short of police state tactics will be able to seriously disrupt them.'

I have the names of fifteen registered companies in Germany and Austria allegedly involved in the illegal shipment to Europe and the Middle East of weaponry from Russia and its former satellite countries. I know the names of banks in Germany and Austria through which the vast profits are alleged to have been channelled: Swiss banks are also involved. For legal reasons, I cannot disclose them. Vienna, capital of one of the new entrants into the European Union, is also an active entrepreneurial city: during the Cold War it was one of the busiest crossroads between East and West. Now it's even busier.

The American enquiry[17] describes specific examples of nuclear smuggling; these have been independently disclosed to me in practically identical detail.[18] In practically every instance, the former virtually unpoliced Yugoslavia is the highway. It is the most-used trafficking route between the East and the client states of Iran, Iraq, Libya and Algeria. It is, additionally, a substantial recipient of all types of conventional arms, for its indigenous war. Croatia even perfected a barter system to finance the trade: in return for a guaranteed supply of conventional weapons it has stored, safe from any official international interruption or interference, nuclear material on its way to the Middle East.

The most frightening evidence of nuclear material moving through Europe became known late in 1992. At the end of a German investigation the material was believed to have passed through five countries: it could, according to police with whom I spoke, have crossed even more.

The story began in Switzerland when a Pole, Krysztof Adamski, sought medical help at a Zurich clinic which diagnosed severe radiation sickness. It transpired that he had contracted the fatal illness from carrying 200 grams of Caesium 137 and Strontium 90 – the radioactive components of nuclear fission – in his breast pocket. They were samples, for a potential customer, of the goods on offer.

Bundeskriminalamt investigations suggested that the radio-active, bomb-making equipment had originated in Lithuania. From information provided by the dying Adamski, it emerged that the shipment was being routed from the former Soviet republic through Romania and Poland before reaching Germany. In the first of two separate interceptions, the Germans seized, near Munich, just over 2 kilos of what was described as 'highly enriched' uranium, of weapons-graded strength. It was being transported, insufficiently encased in anti-radiation protection, in a BMW driven by a Czech courier. According to scientific assessment, the amount was almost 10% of that necessary to make a basic atomic bomb. In another swoop near Frankfurt 200 grams of Strontium-90 similar to that which was killing Adamski, were recovered from a Polish-registered BMW. Again it was inadequately sealed. The driver had a left luggage key to a locker in which was found a further consignment of Caesium-137 and Strontium-90. In the car also were documents showing that the Polish and Russian nuclear mafia had a further 20 kilos of weapons, graded uranium as well as other radio-active material for prospective purchasers. There were insufficient clues to where it was being hidden: some of it was throught to be in Poland. The Germans decided more than 9 kilos had already entered their country.

They tried to set up a sting operation, pretending to be Middle East buyers with money for at least 9 kilos of enriched uranium, capable of bomb building. A Polish crook, Zbiginiew Fuitowski, acted as intermediary. The German mistake was to insist that delivery be made in Frankfurt – and so within their legal jurisdiction – instead of the established marketplace of Croatia. Suspecting the sting, the organised crime group did not turn up at the appointed time and place to conclude the deal. Which meant there was still a large amount of improperly protected radio-active uranium on the loose. That it was unprotected seemed to be confirmed when both of the BMW drivers – the sort of disposable dross I referred to at the beginning of this book – were found to be suffering from fatal doses of radiation. They and Adamski insisted under questioning that *all* the 20 kilos was somewhere on German soil, although all three denied knowing where.

Alerted at government level by Bonn, Polish detectives raided the home in Terespol, Eastern Poland, of one of the dying courier drivers. Almost 2 kilos of uranium – leaking like all the rest – was discovered in a bathroom. Under separate pressure from Bonn, officers from the Russian Interior Security Ministry raided a house close to a military defence installation at Udmertskaya and recovered 100 kilos of radio-active substances.

The sheer amount of deadly material moving unchecked – but more importantly unprotected – through cities and towns in which thousands of people live has led some analysts to speculate on the possible emergence of an entirely different sort of terrorism. It would have needed less than the 200 grams seized in Frankfurt to have poisoned the entire water supply of the city. It would be difficult for any city authority to resist a ransom demand based on a threat to introduce such material into reservoirs.

The complete security from any official interference for the various mafia groups trading in war-ravaged Croatia was discovered by another investigation – this time into one of the biggest mafia clan leaders operating in Germany. He is a Russian named Aleksandr Viktorovich Kutzin. He is said to be linked to the Dolgopruadnanskaya. Unlike their counterparts in Italy and America, those who head clans are not referred to as Godfathers. A Russian mafia family is called a brigade. Therefore, in the correct Russian nomenclature, Kutzin is a brigadier. He operates – and completely hides the trail of his transactions – through a maze of more than forty companies carefully established in Vienna, Munich, Warsaw and Moscow. His deals are so well concealed that unless he – or an accomplice prepared to identify him – is arrested during an actual smuggling operation, Kutzin is virtually beyond prosecution. He has homes in Germany and Russia, but travels constantly. His deputy is a Pole, Wojciech Grabowski. In February 1991, Kutzin received an order for conventional weapons – SA7bs, AK-47 rifles with accompanying ammunition – destined for Croatia. It was placed by Anton Kikas, a Croatian with freedom of movement throughout the world on a Canadian passport: the deal was financed through a bank in Klagenfurt, Austria, with $1,000,000 contributed to Croatia by sympathisers outside the former Yugoslavia. That initial deal was to lead to an intricate, continent-wide relationship between Kikas and Kutzin.

It developed almost immediately. Zagreb found difficulty in financing its arms requirements from the former Eastern bloc. From Germany came the solution: Kutzin would barter conventional weaponry in return for Zagreb guaranteeing safe and incurious storage for the nuclear material transitting through the country. Via Kikas, Croatia agreed. And even improved upon the deal. In addition to safe storage, Croatia would provide false documentation to conceal the fissile shipments once they had crossed the border on their way south.

The Russian quickly discovered another benefit from knowing Anton Kikas. The Croatian had already established a fleet of charter aircraft to ferry guns from South Africa to arm his countrymen. They were leased from an American company, but were registered as being operated by a Ugandan-registered corporation. Its headquarters were in the Kenyan capital of Nairobi. During 1991 the planes brought weapons from South Africa to Zagreb, staging in the Ethiopian capital of Addis Ababa. Once the link had been established between Kutzin and Kikas, additional flight plans were introduced. At night the planes flew 'special cargo' from the former Soviet bloc countries into Zagreb, under the agreed discreet storage deal.

The European-African axis came to light in 1991 when two Yugoslav MIG-21s forced one of the charter Boeing 707s (registration 5X-UCM) to land at Belgrade. Its cargo was South African-manufactured ordnance.

This interruption did not stop the nuclear trade. Kutzin continued to smuggle nuclear material for any buyer with sufficient cash, using Croatia as the staging post. When South Africa expressed an interest in nuclear know-how, Pretoria became such a customer. In Zagreb a personal assistant to President Tudjman was given an intermediary function. A scientific institute in Zagreb supervised all nuclear transfers.

There was another seizure – again of only conventional weaponry – at Regensburg, Germany, in December 1991. But it was the subsequent arrest of an underling which gave investigators the most detailed information about the activities of Kutzin and Kikas. One of the gang was an Arab, with Yugoslavian citizenship, who had links with the PLO.

There is no indication of any members of the Kutzin mafia becoming contaminated by radioactivity. But during my researches I was assured at least sixteen couriers, apart from Adamski and the other two members of his gang, had died from contact with what they were handling. The majority were said to be Polish. At the time of writing, Kutzin and Kikas are still operating.

Another barter user of the Croatian 'safe haven' arrangement is one of the few known women arms dealers. Her name is Rita Draxler. For several months in the early part of the 1990s she operated from a fourth floor suite of a Vienna hotel. I know of no known photograph of her: she is described as 'attractive, although hard featured'. She works with a Yugoslav man whose name on police records, Marijan Sokolovic, is suspected by some intelligence analysts to be an alias: they have no other identity.

Those records – and details of the Draxler mafia – resulted from an interrogation of Sokolovic when he was arrested in Vienna in November 1991, after a European-wide investigation ranging through Switzerland, Italy and Austria. Sokolovic revealed he was the constantly travelling link man between Rita Draxler's European-based operation and her nuclear suppliers, who lived in Russia, Vitali Fedorchuk and Oleg Petrovski. Both had been members of the former Soviet intelligence apparatus, Fedorchuk of the defunct KGB, Petrovka of the military GRU. Under that same interrogation, Sokolovic disclosed that the Russians could acquire tactical nuclear warheads with a range of thirty to sixty kilometres. The asking price was £14 million. They were stolen from army depots around Irkutsk. Iraq and Libya were named as the client countries for the components after they were smuggled from Russia to the former Yugoslavia, where they were stored in the Croatian city of Sibenik. The Draxler mafia does not take sides in the Balkan conflict: it does business with both Croats and Serbs.

Blanketed by false Croatian documentation, the nuclear parts were trucked to Bulgaria – the port of Varna is a major transit city –

and then to Turkey before entering Iraq. It was suggested to me that the Draxler family worked to a shopping list supplied by Saddam Hussein's top atom scientists and technologists. Some are, of course, Russians lured to Baghdad by hugely attractive salaries.

The investigation that lifted the very corner of the curtain on the Draxler mob began in Italy. In late 1991 there was reliable underworld information of radioactive hardware being offered for sale in the lakeside town of Como, close to the Swiss border. The geographical importance of this location became clear with the arrest in Switzerland of the honorary consul to Honduras, Friedrich Refner, who was seized while actually carrying uranium in the boot of a car the smugglers had hoped would be protected by diplomatic immunity. Swiss investigations quickly discovered that the uranium had been supplied by a Draxler clan banker, Karl Friedrich Federer, who was keeping a supply – 30 kilos of uranium and 10 kilos of plutonium – in a Zurich bank vault.

Sokolovic's name first came up during the Italian investigation in Como, after that city's assistant public prosecutor Romano Dolce –who specialised in nuclear smuggling investigations – had himself been arrested in May 1994, but not convicted on charges of complicity with organised crime in arms and nuclear material dealing. When Sokolovic was detained in Vienna in November 1991, he was carrying a small amount of plutonium.

Rita Draxler remains the Godmother to her family, although Italian police hold an arrest warrant for her following the seizure in December 1991, of a shipment of 32 kilos of plutonium bars stolen from storage silos in the Ukraine. At that time the Ukraine, which in January 1994, agreed to surrender its nuclear arsenal, was the world's third largest atomic power, with 1,600 Soviet-era warheads under its somewhat frail control. The bars seized by the Italians were destined for Iraq, after storage in Sibenik while the financial aspects of the deal were finalised. The Italian authorities learned of the Ukraine consignment from their original investigation in Como and its connection with the Swiss arrest of Karl Federer.

Considering the appalling terrorist potential of nuclear trafficking – and the apparent deep concern world authorities feel about it – the decisions of courts to which governments look for deterrent sentencing is astonishing. Sokolovic, for example, was released by the Austrian authorities after only four months in jail, and has resumed his position in the still operating Draxler mafia.

And a Briton convicted by a court at Flensburg, northern Germany, of trying to smuggle £50 million worth of plutonium received an 18 months suspended sentence in December 1993. The man, Norman Derbyshire, tried to negotiate the sale of 60 kilograms to a former British intelligence officer turned arms dealer named Rupert Turp. Turp alerted police in Germany and Bulgaria: Sofia is another established trading post and it was there the deal with Derbyshire was struck. His defence, after his arrest in Germany, was that he was only the middleman for the Swedish mastermind, identified in court as Bo Hartman.

At least three people who guided me on nuclear terrorism – one the scientific expert – were bitterly critical of court leniency. The American said: 'It's inconceivable that courts, hearing the evidence and knowing the cataclysmic consequence of just a few grams of uranium and plutonium, seem to treat the crime as something hardly more serious than a traffic offence.'

Detective Chief Superintendent Kroemer disclosed that Interpol had convened top secret discussions in Moscow to try to persuade the Russian authorities to impose tighter control over both conventional and nuclear weaponry. A reply to that request is still awaited from the government of President Yeltsin. In view of the gross inefficiency – as well as widespread corruption and even connivance within Russian law enforcement and militia – it could be a long wait. And the reply might be meaningless if it ever arrived.

There is deep concern by every European government at just how much hardware of all sorts, not only nuclear, is being traded. In fact intelligence suggests that some items were being offered in 1994 at half the price demanded two years earlier, although still on a multi-millions per warhead scale – which further suggests that there was actually a glut in the market place.

At a time when there are approximately 40 conflicts throughout the world that can be classified as wars – with the intractible Balkan bloodletting the one most occupying the European Union – the market is understandably thronged with eager customers.

Multi-millionaire Philadelphian Sam Cummings, the world's biggest small arms dealer, lives in Monte Carlo but conducts his business from Manchester, England, and offers the rifle-advocate's justification – 'it's not guns that kill, it's the people who use them'. When we met,[19] the courtly American had just returned from a buying expedition in the former Soviet Union. 'I've been in the business for more than forty years. I've never seen so much stuff available. There's enough weaponry throughout the bloc to keep wars going for decades. It's scarcely worth the trouble to reload: you might as well just pick up another gun.'

Sam Cummings trades legitimately, under proper licensing procedures. The Moscow, Italian, Serbian and German mafias do not. They've lifted the sluice-gate to flood Europe with every sort of killing device. 'The surprise is not that it's happened,' says Cummings, philosophically, 'It's that more people aren't being slaughtered. But they will be. It's just a matter of time.'

Cummings is talking of wars.

But the guns that are pouring westwards from the former Soviet Union are not just supplying armies. They're equipping drug dealers and gangsters on the streets of every European city. And people are being slaughtered there, too.

CHAPTER FOUR

Guns Will Make Us Powerful[1]

There were triple-decker headlines in Britain in February 1994, when police in Liverpool raided an empty ground floor apartment in Breckfield Road North and uncovered an arsenal of sub-machine guns and assault rifles. There were seven Czech Model 25 9mm submachine guns and two Russian Kalashnikov AKM assault rifles. There were bullets for both among the assorted 250 rounds of ammunition seizure. That arsenal also included an Israeli-made Uzi 9mm submachine gun, an Italian Armi-Jager AP80 rifle and an American-manufactured Armelite AR-15 rifle. The Armelite is so powerful that victims struck in a non-lethal part of the body sometimes die from the impact shock.

Commentators claimed astonishment. The police didn't. Although it was the largest ever haul in that particular city there had been others, elsewhere, as well as intelligence warnings months before that mafia groups well established in England were importing consignment loads of weaponry from the former Soviet territories and Europe. There had already been in Manchester what had once seemed to be an insanity confined to the streets of America: 'drive-by' shootings by gunmen amusing themselves casually blasting with live, flesh-shattering ammunition through the open windows of cruising cars. On the day of that February seizure, ambulance paramedics in Manchester announced they were donning bullet-proofed vests before going out on emergencies: they sometimes got caught in crossfire between warring gangs responding to calls.

The Eastern bloc weapons trade into England is masterminded by the Russian mafia, from luxury enclaves in London. I have been told[2] of Russians buying, from suitcases crammed with cash, houses for £3 to £4 million in exclusive areas like St John's Wood and Hampstead. 'They don't have a banking culture, although they are learning how to wash their money through our financial systems. At the moment they still only trust cash. And they have plenty of it.' Four clans have been positively identified to me.[3] The Dolgopruadnanskaya, already a dominant force in Germany, are well entrenched. So is a Chechen family whose main, controlling base is in Moscow, not the breakaway Chechen republic that Boris Yeltsin moved with such bloody brutality to crush at the end of 1994 and the beginning of 1995. There are Ukrainian mobs. And groups made up from the former Red Army.

Illegal drugs, that bedrock upon which all organised crime is founded, provide the income and a linked demand for the weapons. A gun – several if possible and certainly one that is automatic – is an essential accoutrement for every Jamaican in the notoriously violent Yardie gangs in the established trafficking centres of London and Manchester and Liverpool. They trade cannabis from their Caribbean homeland, from which they derive their patois-based title of Yardies. But the most lucrative – and constantly growing – business is cocaine from Latin America, to purify into crack. That comes predominantly from Colombia: even if it is produced in Bolivia or Peru, the Colombians – the major trafficking family is based in the town of Cali[4] – are the international traders. London has resident organised crime groups from Colombia, too and the Colombians are as violent as the Jamaicans: they are eager arms-buyers. So, also, are the biker clans, the Hell's Angels and the Outlaws. Some police authorities regard the bikers as the biggest 'Murder Incorporated' in the world, responsible for more murders than any other organised crime group.[5]

The Hell's Angels and the Outlaws are indigenous English gangs, called Chapters. Known members of those Chapters are individually registered among the 3,000 profiles of professional criminals on a database maintained and constantly updated at the London headquarters of the National Criminal Intelligence Service. From that 3,000, 330 are specially designated 'core nominals'. That marks them as either complete gang groups or gang leaders.

The Russian mafia families and the Yardies and the Hell's Angels and the Outlaws are not the only organised crime mobs in London: just those most prone to gun violence. The four known Triad groups, who have divided the Chinatowns of every European city between them, kill and maim with the same ferocity – I have seen photographs of victims in gang wars with limbs practically sliced from bodies – but they usually fight with the machete-type swords which feature in all their rituals. And the Italian Cosa Nostra and Camorra and 'Ndrangheta, although gun users, avoid authority-attracting violence whenever possible: it's bad for business. It is a philosophy newly imported from American organised crime – which also has emissaries in London – through the changing Italian parent families in Palermo and Calabria and Naples.

The only way, in fact, in which organised crime in the United Kingdom differs from the rest of Europe is that it does not have the additional protective shell of Freemasonry beneath which to bury its activities. Or has not – as happened in the case of Italy – insinuated itself at a sufficient level within government, the law or the judiciary to operate with virtual impunity.

Early in 1994, alarmed by the upsurge of violence and related murders, Scotland Yard coordinated Britain's eight area drug squads in a countrywide strategy aimed at armed narcotic gangs. The National Criminal Intelligence Service began a programme of pin-pointing the sources and true extent of illegal weaponry entering the country: that programme supplements the database already containing 3,000 organised criminal identities. A year earlier, in another move against violent crime, officers of South Yorkshire's armed response units, which constantly patrol the county in vehicles carrying pistols, Heckler and Koch rifles and body armour, were given permission to unlock their weapons upon the radioed authority of a duty inspector instead of having to go through the time-consuming procedure of getting approval from an assistant chief constable. By 1994, nearly all Britain's other forty-two police authorities had armed and body-armoured rapid response units trained and ready to go first into any shooting situation.

The February 1994, arms seizure in Liverpool made its headlines because the haul was a significant escalation from the handgun and shotgun type of weaponry that until that time had customarily been intercepted.

The fear among many anti-crime professionals is that with so much conventional military hardware so freely available there could be a further, and bloodier, move into rocketry and other battleground equipment. All that is needed is money, which will never be a problem for drug-financed mafiosi. None has so far made a purchase because there is no practical use or benefit from such a weapon. *At the moment.*

For the criminal – and for countries wanting to remain within the bounds of conventional warfare – anything in the normal armaments catalogue is awaiting immediate delivery. And is just as easily obtained in London as anywhere else in the European Union.

It was not the ease of British procurement which primarily bought balding, thick-set Ruslan Outsiev to London, with his slimmer and swarthier brother Nazerbeck, in 1992. But Britain's relaxed attitudes were the cause of both men being murdered in their £1 million penthouse in Bickenhall Street, Marylebone. At the time the killings were described as Russian mafia executions and there were unsubstantiated theories of gang wars about to erupt on the streets of London. From subsequent police analysis to which I have had access,[6] however, it is clear that organised crime was only very peripherally involved. The brothers were Chechen, but by nationality, not through membership of any ethnic mob. Although styling himself Chechenia's deputy prime minister, Ruslan was, in fact, the deputy chairman of the President's Council of Chechenia, an oil-rich state in the northern Caucasus whose self-proclaimed independence from Russia – not recognised by London – Boris Yeltsin crushed by the beginning of 1995. The Outsiev brothers were living in the English capital because of Russia's recognition refusal. At night they indulged in sensuous extravagance: at the subsequent trial of one of the two men accused of their killing there were stories of £2,000 tips at restaurants and six-at-a-time call-girl orgies. By day, meanwhile, the Outsievs tried to create the essentials for establishing an infrastructure in their breakaway country: negotiable currency, stamps, identity cards and passports.

Chechenia – the entire population of which was deported from their homeland by Stalin – is an Islamic state, although not fanatically fundamentalist. A more fervent Muslim republic in the former Soviet Union, Azerbaijan, is at war with its Christian neighbour, Armenia, over the possession of the enclave of Nagorno-Karabakh. And Armenian intelligence, composed of

former KGB personnel well aware from organised crime connections of how easy it was to get battleground weapons from
London-based mafia, became convinced late in 1992 that Ruslan
and Nazerbeck Outsiev were negotiating to buy 2,000 Stinger
surface-to-air missiles that could have tilted the balance of the
conflict in Azerbaijan's favour. It was to prevent that purchase that
Ruslan Outsiev was killed, by three bullets in the back of the head.
His brother – in hospital at the time of the assassination – was killed
in identically the same way on the day of his discharge, to prevent
his talking or seeking revenge. The killer, a London-based
Armenian intelligence agent named Mkritch Martirossian, hanged
himself in the police cell in which he was awaiting trial. His
conspirator in the plot, fellow Armenian Gagic Ter-Ogrannsyan,
was given two life sentences at an Old Bailey trial in October 1993.

There are indications, from the after-trial analysis, that Ruslan
Outsiev was indeed trying to make contacts with British-based
arms dealers, both legitimate and gang-dominated: in a statement
to the police before his death Martirossian claimed to have pleaded
with Ruslan to abandon the purchase.

It was not the only approach the Azeri government made
through London dealers – despite the fact that there was an official
British government embargo against British arms exports to the
former Soviet republic. But then, British government departments
have been known to interpret arms embargoes with the logic –
quite apart from the honesty – of the Mad Hatter whom Alice met
in Wonderland.

In early 1992 – before the Outsiev brothers settled in London – an
Azeri government delegation made a private visit to Sam
Cummings at his Manchester complex, seeking Russian-made
weapons. They complained that since their independence, they
could not officially obtain guns they wanted from Moscow and
therefore needed a supplier with Cummings' capacity. They
offered to pay in gold.

'I said we could supply them: we have enough in Manchester for
one division, no problem,' recalls Cummings, who knew socially
Mikhail Kalashnikov, inventor of the terrorists' favourite tool.
Being an American domiciled in France – supplying non-British
weapons – Cummings would not have been bound by the British
embargo.

Cummings still made licensing enquiries. After being assured by
an executive of his American office that no US weapons would be

involved, a US State Department official, according to Cummings, said: 'OK. We don't say yes, we don't say no, but we say maybe, after we make a few more enquiries.' When Cummings relayed that response to the British Foreign Office – who until his approach were totalling unaware of an Azeri arms delegation even being in the country – an official said: 'What kind of answer is that?'

Cummings didn't know, either. Unable to get a sensible, yes or no decision from Washington, Cummings, who has supplied other newly independent former Soviet states, did not accept the Azeri contract. He believes it was completed instead by entrepreneurial arms dealers – he refuses, just, to use the word mafia – within the former bloc, from a massive sale of conventional weaponry in the Ukraine.

I understand[7] that Iran, anxious to spread its fundamentalism to another Moslem country, was also a willing provider, approaching the Azeris unasked. The Iran involvement completed both an elaborate and ironic circle.

The Azeris wanted only Soviet-manufactured ordnance, compatible with what they already possessed from their past as a client state of Moscow. As emerged from the German seizure in Regensburg, at the end of 1991, the Kutzin mafia were trafficking vast quantities of Russian equipment through Germany: the Regensburg interception alone included 1,500,000 rounds of Russian ammunition, as well as 3,000 AK-47 rifles. More got through than was stopped. Some moved along the familiar Dolgopruadnanskaya route, from southern Germany into Croatia. From there it continued its wide curve into Iran, where it crossed the country at its eastern borders to re-enter the Azeri republic – to which Russia wouldn't export direct – finally to reach the Azeri capital of Baku.

The other identified German-controlled mafia, run by Rita Draxler, has also cooperated with the Berlin-based Dolgopruadnanskaya to supply arms to Iran. Which, in turn, carried on its arms dealing to neighbouring Islamic states in an effort to extend its fundamentalist influence. In 1991, for instance, Draxler coordinated a £39 million order of precisely the sort of Stinger missiles that would cost the Outsiev brothers their lives just over a year later. The Draxler operation – as usual following the Croatian safe haven route – also included Milan missiles.

I have discovered no evidence that during their apparently disappointing English expedition in 1992 the Azeri delegation had more success shopping with the London-based Dolgopruadnan-skaya mafia. I would be surprised, however, if they didn't.

Some routings of Eastern bloc military equipment to terrorist customers have been more direct. In November 1993, a container load of armaments was intercepted at Teesport by British Customs officers and agents from MI5, the country's counter-intelligence agency responsible for anti-terrorist investigations. Hidden beneath a concealing cargo of ceramics were more than 300 AKM assault rifles, all equipped with bayonets, pistols, thousands of rounds of ammunition, hundreds of hand grenades, more than two tons of military explosive and detonators to activate it. The AKM rifle, manufactured in both Romania and Hungary, is an updated, much improved version of the AK47 from which a bullet can kill from shock alone, like the American Armelite. The AKM can fire at the rate of 600 rounds a minute. Value of the haul was put at £350,000.

The seizure was not a chance discovery. It resulted from liaison between MI5 and Polish intelligence, which had earlier warned London of an Irish group looking for arms in Warsaw. At London's request the group were put under surveillance. Britain's external intelligence service, MI6, were brought into the monitor-ing operation. The munitions container was watched being loaded aboard the Polish merchantman *Inowrock* at Gdynia on 19 November. It arrived at Teesport – after crossing the Baltic and the North Sea under intense scrutiny which at times included aerial surveillance – five days later. Had it not been seized, the container would have crossed England to be ferried over the Irish Sea to Belfast.

There the extremist Ulster Volunteer Force, an illegal Loyalist organisation, were waiting to receive it.

The haul came at a time when the prospect of dialogue between the British government and Sinn Fein, the political wing of the Republican IRA, was being secretly negotiated. Protestant Loyalists in the province believed they had been excluded from a peace process in which they felt they were entitled to participate on equal terms. According to Northern Ireland observers, if the Teesport cargo had reached the resentful Protestant paramilitary force, there could have been a bloodbath. One police official to whom I talked[8] used the word carnage.

The shipment confirmed a warning a few months earlier from RUC Chief Constable Sir Hugh Annesley that extreme Loyalists – who in the preceding three years had killed more victims than their rival Republicans – were seeking to improve their bomb-making capacity, which still lagged behind that of the IRA.

Admitting that the cargo was for them, a UVF official in Belfast called it a 'logistical setback', but added that they were 'unbowed and unbroken'. The UVF statement pledged to 'scour the world for arms'.

They'd found some by June 1994. And used them to slaughter six Catholics – one an old man of 87 – as they sat in the village pub in Loughlinisland, twenty miles from Belfast, watching a World Cup soccer match between Ireland and Italy. The UDV killers laughed as they ran away.

The IRA had always had better logistical supply, because it was regarded as a freedom-fighting revolutionary organisation by revolutionary states, of which Libya has always considered itself the leader. Libya was a chief arms supplier to the Republicans when the Eastern bloc was communist-controlled and it could obtain weapons and explosives with Moscow's permission. It has remained so afterwards, simply switching its suppliers from official sources to Russian and European mafias.

Virtually all the Czech-manufactured Semtex explosive used in dozens of outrages on the British mainland – including the Warrington shopping precinct slaughter of a twelve-year-old and a three-year-old toddler in 1993, the £500 million City of London bombing the same year, the attack upon the Grand Hotel, Brighton, in October 1984, which came close to killing Margaret Thatcher during the Conservative Party conference, and the massacre of 11 Royal Marine bandsmen at their music school in Kent in 1989 – was stockpiled from Libyan supplies.

And there are enormous stockpiles still in Ireland.

One expert in Irish policing[9] estimates that the IRA possesses enough Libyan-supplied material for a campaign lasting twenty years. It is buried in underground concrete bunkers, covered with six feet of topsoil. The concrete is one foot thick, with no manhole entry. 'It's just complete concrete and they have no intention of touching those arms for years and years: they see it as a long term war, a war of attrition.' As well as Semtex, the sealed concrete vaults hold Kalashnikov rifles, rockets, rocket launchers, hand grenades and hand guns. In 1992 Ireland's Garda mounted a search-and-find campaign codenamed Operation Silo. The 150 tons of ordnance recovered were estimated to be only twenty per cent of what is stored on both sides of the Irish border.

The British peace initiatives with the IRA, from which the justifiably suspicious Loyalists feared in November 1993 they were being excluded, were confirmed a month later in a joint declaration of a willingness to talk – once the IRA renounced violence – by the British and Irish governments. These initiatives were almost immediately manipulated by the Northern Ireland Republican movement into a propaganda extravaganza which left the British government looking deservedly ridiculous. In one of his most telling caveats to any peace process, Sinn Fein President Gerry Adams – whose denial of IRA membership extends to issuing libel writs against those who claim otherwise – said in January 1994, that the IRA could fight on for another twenty-five years. The less publicity-adept Loyalist movement, which later endorsed the peace effort, has a similar armanents capacity, coupled with a willingness to revert to it if those peace efforts fail. Because the mainland attacks of the IRA were always headline grabbing the misleading belief was largely held in Britain that the IRA were more violent than the Loyalists. They weren't. Within Northern Ireland itself they frequently carried out more killings and bombings than the IRA. But in any case, the destructive capacity possessed by both movements will certainly fuel organised crime in the region, should the current ceasefire prove lasting.

Anti-terrorist experts regard Semtex as the most dangerous of all explosives held by terrorist organisations like the IRA or the Ulster Volunteer Force, or by terrorist countries like Libya. It was just over 2lbs of Semtex that in 1989 blew up the PanAm Boeing 747 over Lockerbie, in Scotland, and killed 270 people. British forensic scientists are working to perfect an odour-activated device to detect the Czech-made explosive, which has virtually no smell, nor any use other than military. So far they have not succeeded, and it remains possible still for Semtex to get aboard aircraft. In January 1994, Britain's Department of Transport authorised an exercise to test the efficiency of baggage checks at London's Heathrow Airport. Semtex under a variety of concealment – once in a doll popular on British television – successfully evaded the security of American, United, KLM Royal Dutch and Virgin Atlantic airlines.

British police intelligence analysts do not limit their concern to Eastern Europe as the sole arms suppliers of organised crime gangs. In an assessment I have studied[10] they warn that the removal of Customs barriers in the European Union made it much easier to bring guns into England from the Continent. There was 'little risk' of detection by British Customs officers. In France and Belgium – a world leader in firearm ownership – it is possible for a UK citizen to buy a pump action shotgun simply by producing a passport.

Governments themselves are, of course, arms dealers also. With the collapse of the Soviet Union the government of Hungary offered its entire small arms industries to the portly, affable Sam Cummings, literally lock, stock and barrel. So did the Czechs, which incidentally would in theory have given Cummings some insight into the country's Semtex programme. 'I didn't want to do it for a number of reasons. The main one was I was too old. I don't have the twenty years more that it would take to get them properly turned around. And I have enough headaches with our own plants that we work with in different parts of the world. So I didn't want to do it, but if I had been the Agency (CIA), or Six (MI6), I would have.' Cummings, once a weapons expert for the CIA, didn't want the Russian small arms concession either, when it was offered to him – 'from Vladivostok to St Petersburg. Millions and millions of rifles and pistols and so forth. But the market is flooded with Kalashnikovs: who wants them any more?'

The Russian mafia and European organised crime, that's who.

And as for the official manufacturing industries, Western governments want them.

Cummings understands that the weapons production facilities of both Hungary and the Czech republic have been largely acquired by the arms-exporting firms of France. Paris has also acquired a large interest in a Belgian firm which in turn owned the Winchester rifle company of America. The French, says Cummings admiringly, are very astute people.

There is little to admire about the British government and its hypocritical, if not dishonest, arms dealing. For several months in 1993 and even longer into 1994 there was an ignominious parade of present and past government ministers – including Margaret Thatcher – fidgeting under examination at a public enquiry prime minister John Major had been forced into convening to explain why the government had been prepared to sit back and let innocent men be jailed rather than admit it broke its own arms embargo against trading with Baghdad.

Throughout the late 1980s the British firm Matrix Churchill sold advanced machine tools to Saddam Hussein during the build-up to the Gulf War, when Iraq was, in fact, at war with Iran – and even while the Gulf War was being fought, Matrix Churchill equipment was used to modify Scud missiles. The British government – and Britain's MI6 – knew what the company was doing. Matrix Churchill told them, and in any case the managing director, Paul Henderson, was acting as an agent for the intelligence service. Yet when unwitting British Customs arrested Henderson and two fellow directors, Whitehall attempted to conceal the truth. Which was that London was content to go on supplying both sides – Iran as well as Iraq – in a conflict in which it is estimated one million people died.

Had it not been for the honesty of just one man – Alan Clark, successively Minister of Trade and Minister for Defence Procurement – who confirmed in the court in which the three were being tried that the British government had been breaking its own guidelines, Henderson and the two other directors would have probably been jailed, becoming further victims. Instead, the charges against them were dropped. I have no doubt, having studied both the case and the subsequent enquiry conducted by Lord Justice Scott, that the details of the Matrix Churchill debacle were discussed as high as Cabinet level, although this, of course, is denied just as so much else is denied in this miserable affair.

'Where's it say governments obey or follow their own rules?' wonders Cummings, cynically.

In the case of Britain, the answer seems nowhere. While the Matrix Churchill enquiry was still in progress there came to light another blatant breach by the government of its own restrictions. It took until 1994 to come out, but in 1988 Margaret Thatcher signed a committing agreement with Malaysian Premier Dr Mahathir Mohammed to sell £1.8 billion of British arms to Malaysia. At the same time, another parallel agreement was reached for Britain to contribute £234 million in aid towards the construction of a dam, the Pergau project later described by senior British civil servants as 'an abuse of the aid programme'. According to government rules, to avoid the accusation that such programmes are used as 'sweeteners', their allocations are supposed to be kept quite independent of arms negotiations or sales. When details of the linked arrangement became public, Dr Mahathir declared Malaysia would revert to the 'Buy British Last' campaign that the Margaret Thatcher deal was negotiated specifically to overcome: the House of Commons was told in April 1994, that Dr. Mahathir's seven month ban had cost £2 billion and 40,000 jobs in England. Baroness Thatcher refused to give evidence to a House of Commons select committee enquiry, which found that Lord Younger was guilty of 'reprehensible' conduct. In November 1994, the High Court ruled that the Foreign Secretary had broken the law allocating the aid in connection with the Pergau dam project.

And on and on go the examples, with weary cynicism.

The world's arms trade – official as well as unofficial – is monitored in Sweden by the Stockholm International Peace Research Institute. The investigations showed that between 1987 and 1991, Indonesia was the sixth largest recipient of British weapons systems. In June 1993, British Aerospace gained a £500 million contract for twenty-four Hawk fighter-trainers: there are plans to purchase sixteen more. In April 1993, Indonesia's Air Marshal Sibun was quoted by the country's news agency, Antara, as saying: 'The planes will be used not only to train pilots, but also for air-to-ground attack in cases of emergency. In fact the Hawks were made especially for air-to-ground assault.'

A year later, a television programme[11] alleged that British aircraft were being used in 'the genocide' of East Timor.

In a book about organised crime, do such matters belong? I believe so.

In June 1994, the Vatican published a report[12] eight years in preparation, urging world governments to limit the manufacture and supply of weapons. 'Never before has our earth known so much armed conflict, fed by a proliferation of arms.'

CHAPTER FIVE

There's No Business Like Snow Business

This chapter heading is not a misprint. Rather, it's a word-play from *Annie Get Your Gun* that perfectly sums up the illegal drugs trade that underpins all other European – and worldwide – crime. To quote – as I might again and again – the opinion of Interpol's Secretary General, Raymond Kendall, illegal drugs are 'un-stoppable'. No addict with the money – and if he or she hasn't got the money they can always steal or sell their bodies to get it – need go without. Few do. Few will. None have to.

There's cocaine – snow – from South America. Heroin from the Golden Triangle of Thailand, Burma and Laos or the Golden Crescent of Afghanistan and Pakistan, greatly supplemented by Turkey. Cannabis from virtually everywhere. All three, in lesser quantities, from at least five countries in Africa. Psychotropics from backstreet laboratories mostly operating in the Netherlands. Truly unstoppable.

In Italy a synonym for their all-embracing Mafia is *la piovra*. It means 'octopus', the out-stretched tentacles of which are the routes along which the bulk of narcotics come into Europe. The only flaw in the metaphor is that the octopus has more than one head, and more than eight law-crushing arms.

And as with every other aspect of well organised crime engulfing the EU virtually unopposed, the Eastern bloc, led by the mafias of Russia, is offering ever wider trafficking conduits.

Although cocaine and its purified derivative – crack – occupy the headlines of the moment, heroin is still regarded as the predominant drug of abuse, Europe-wide.[1] In the Golden Triangle it comes from the multi-million, once CIA-supported empire established close to the Thai township of Chiang Mai by a Buddha-fat warlord named Khun Sa. In the Golden Crescent the poppies which produce the morphine gum from which heroin is extracted come from the sprawling organisation headed by former Pakistan MP Ayub Khan Afridi. Like Khun Sa during the Vietnam war, the saturnine Afridi was befriended during the Afghan conflict by America's CIA because of his cross border contacts in Kabul. Now he is on the run from his bunker-designed anti-aircraft gun emplaced home near the Khyber Pass after being named in a US court indictment as the biggest drug baron in Pakistan. His business continues in his absence.

When the Soviet Union was intact, both Khun Sa and Ayub Afridi had to move their heroin westwards either through Afghanistan and Iran into Turkey and then along what used to be known as the Balkan Route, through the former Yugoslavia, or more indirectly – but still westwards – via the Italian Mafia or Chinese Triad middlemen.

The Yugoslavian war has interrupted the Balkan Route. It's still used – four tons were seized in transit at the height of the fighting in 1993 – but far safer entry points into Europe are now available further east. Heroin now detours – assisted by murderously competitive Serbian and Croatian gangs, in turn poached upon by the mafias of Hungary, Russia and the Czech Republic – by way of once communist-restricted trails through Bulgaria and Romania.

In the future – even after the end of the Balkans War – the Asian heroin traders will have an even greater and wider choice of access routes into Europe. There is an intention to build twenty more international airports throughout the massive landmass of Russia.[2] Those new airports will be in addition to – not replacements for – those already existing, through which illegal drugs are already being moved, and will further supplement the drug-gateway airports of the Czech and Slovak Republics, Hungary, Poland, Romania, Bulgaria and the fifteen newly independent countries that once formed the Soviet Union. According to the Pompidou Group's Christoper Luckett 'the possibilities (for traffickers) are quite staggering'. Or as Raymond Kendall says, 'unstoppable'.

Not all the heroin and locally-grown cannabis will travel

onwards to Europe. Like the Americans in Vietnam, Russians developed a drug culture from their involvement in Afghanistan. Russia now has an estimated 2,000,000 addicts[3] whom their mafias fight to the death to supply. Poland has more than 300,000 addicts[4] who, uniquely in the drugs world, inject the juice of unripened poppy heads and a liquid created from 'poppy straw', poppies from which the opiate sap has not been extracted.[5] The republics of both Czech and Slovakia have addict populations running into thousands: Britain has sent customs teams to the Czech Republics and Hungary to train border authorities on methods of drug interception. This is a rare and pitifully small-scale example of enforcement authorities working together in relative harmony.

Despite this internal consumption, there's still a lot of heroin, measured in terms of tons, moving from the east to feed the addicted of the European Union. Of whom, in total, there are an estimated one million.[6] I believe that to be an under-estimate. The greatest problem in any study of drug trafficking or addiction is that *all* figures have to be guessed at. Indeed, some academic researchers[7] complain that, in the absence of empirical statistics, drug policies are often driven by emotive exaggeration. With the benefit of his Europe-wide overview with the Pompidou Group, however, Christopher Luckett suggests there are in each of four major European countries – the United Kingdom, France, Germany and Italy – 150,000 opiate addicts, with Spain slightly lower, at 100,000. In his foreword to the most current examination of Germany's drug control programme,[8] Chancellor Helmut Kohl uses the figure of 70,000 for his country, which does not include any input from the former East Germany. Paris-based criminologist Xavier Raufer comes close to Luckett, with a figure of 120,000 for France. An Italian drug intelligence officer who refused to be identified thought 150,000 was 'about right, but who really knows?' Whether as the result of a refusal to indulge in alarmist exaggeration or a desire to minimise the failure of ill-considered policies is debatable, but Britain's Home Office points out that only 28,000 British addicts are officially registered, although privately accepting 90,000 as a more realistic overall figure.

The masonically-protected Italian mafias of Cosa Nostra, Camorra and 'Ndrangheta – as always quantum leaps ahead of the divisive, squabbling enforcement authorities – realised the illegal drugs potential of Eastern Europe both as customer states and shipment routes as early as 1990.

It was drugs – all illegal drugs, not just heroin – that headed the agenda of the first known summit of Eastern and Western mafias.[9] And in a secret society in which deferential hand-kissing is expected and accorded, it is significant that it was the German-domiciled Italians – representing not just their own organisations but as emissaries of the Latin American and Asian groupings – who went to the organised crime families of the east, not the other way round. Luciano Violante, at the time chairman of Italy's Anti-Mafia Commission, describes Russia as 'a kind of strategic capital of organised crime from where all the major operations are launched'.

The first gathering was in Warsaw, in March 1991. The second was in Prague in October 1992.[10] The agenda for both was the same – illegal drugs, money laundering and nuclear arms smuggling. Present at those Warsaw and Prague gatherings are understood to have been leaders of the ubiquitous Dolgopruadnan-skaya, Chechen, Ramenki and Stankino. There were also delegates from the Ukraine. There is no police or security intelligence confirmation of subsequent yearly conferences but some analysts[11] believe similar summits of the global mafia have occurred annually. One is suspected to have taken place in Moscow in 1993.

There are at least 2,600 organised crime gangs in Russia, of which forty match in size and structure the Mafias of Italy or New York.[12] Certainly the Russian conduit is being used – and will be used even more when the twenty additional airports are built – to ferry cocaine in tandem with heroin into Europe to contribute to the industry's £131 billion a year drugs income. At the time of writing, however, the predominant trafficking is still along more traditional circuits. And circuitous they are, to evade the customs' classic 'profile identification' which results in rigorous Target One checks of any cargo originating, no matter how apparently legitimate, from Colombia – the primary source country – or from Peru or Bolivia. Shipments are shuttled sideways, to appear to originate in, for example, Venezuela: I learned that it was at the Venezualan port of La Guaira that cocaine worth £400 million was loaded in January 1994, bound initially for Poland and from there back into Western Europe: one and a half tons were intercepted by British Customs at Birkenhead. Ecuador or Brazil or Paraguay or Argentina are also used as false origination points. Jamaica – whose shoot-for-fun Posse or Yardie gangs are the major distributors in Britain – is the main, though not the only, shipping island in the Caribbean. Mexico is a transit country to the north. Even further north, Colombians deeply entrenched in New York move cocaine and cannabis via that city, across the Atlantic towards Europe.

And the movement continues to be circuitous, even after the original country of consignment has been one step removed. A stop-over in Africa – Nigeria is the favoured staging post – is frequently used. The final link in the chain is often Rome or Palermo or Catania and the waiting Italian Mafia. In fact, motherships laden with cannabis and cocaine ply regularly between Colombia and the Iberian peninsula, always heaving-to safely outside territorial waters to rendezvous with smuggling boats from Portugal or the fishing fleets from Spain's virtually unpoliced and inlet-riven Galicia coast: in February 1994, Francisco Jose Torres, a sea captain from Galicia, was jailed for 30 years by an Edinburgh court for smuggling £100 million worth of cocaine into Britain in 1991. Two years later – in 1993 – a total of five tons of cocaine was seized in Spain: analysts estimate that haul to represent less than five per cent of what enters Europe every year through Spain alone.[13] Without advanced intelligence it is possible to check only a very small proportion of the million-plus containers that arrive every year at Antwerp in Belgium, or Rotterdam or Amsterdam in Holland. Britain is one of the European Union members whose better-than-average customs interception rate is begrudgingly acknowledged by South American traffickers. To circumvent its high success rate, cocaine destined for the UK is frequently addressed for transit through a British port or airport to another European country – where it will be regarded less suspiciously, having come from England – only to be shipped *back*, from its new point of origin lessening suspicion still further.

The controlling Colombian mafia families, referred to as cartels, who have established gangs in virtually every country in the European Union, originate from Cali, a town eighty miles inland from the Pacific. They replaced the even more infamous cartels of the country's chief trading city, Medellin, in the late 1980s. They did so by pragmatically deciding the violence perpetrated by the Medellin 'boss of bosses', Pablo Escobar – who actually declared war upon the country's government, at times appeared to be winning it and ended up with a £4 million dead-or-alive price on his head – was counter-productive, incompatible with a world-wide business worth £161 billion a year.[14] It was not an entirely pragmatic business decision, of course. The Cali mobsters also wanted revenge upon Escobar for having blown up an Avianco jet on a shuttle flight between Bogota and Cali in 1989: among 107 people killed were two leading Cali gangsters. That killing gave the Cali cartels reason to finance a vigilante movement known as Los Pepes (People Persecuted by Pablo Escobar) that was able to gain control of Escobar's business when he was killed, as was inevitable, in December 1993.

The Cali 'boss of bosses' is, in fact, a double act, the brothers Gilberto and Miguel Rodriguez Orejuela. Both are named in trafficking indictments issued in America. I have been told they have installed gang members in London.[15] Other Cali cartel leaders with cells liaising with indigenous mafiosi are Ovido Londono, Hernando Restrepo Ochoa, Francisco Herrera and Jose Santa Cruz. As well as cornering the cocaine market, the Cali mobsters are now cultivating heroin: they are not yet in a marketing position to challenge the Asian mafias' supplies to Europe but drug observers believe it will only take three or four years.

The quantity of cocaine they are shipping to the European Union is enormous. The US Drug Enforcement Administration calculates that 200 tons enter undetected every year. John Lee, a senior DEA official, told an international police conference in London in 1993: 'Massive quantities of drugs are flowing into Europe as the cartels expand their drug market.' Echoing the familiar warning ignored by European governments and disregarded by insular police forces, he added: 'The threat to democracy posed by drug traffickers is not limited to the Third World.'

It's not limited to heroin or cocaine, either. One of the commonest and oldest slang expressions for marijuana is weed. It *is* a weed and grows like one, practically everywhere – even as far north as Scandinavia.

There are huge plantations producing cannabis in the three Latin American countries. It's grown on every West Indian island: it's the most important agricultural crop in Yardie-dominated Jamaica, with a yearly income put by an EU monitoring body[16] close to £900 million. In Africa, Nigerian gangs have begun to grow it – as they are cultivating the coca plant for cocaine and the opium poppy for heroin – to ship northwards into Europe. The cannabis industry thrives in every North African country, both for local consumption and for their customers across the Mediterranean. It is landed nightly in France and Gibraltar and Italy and

Sicily and Malta and Greece by boat, for delivery to the waiting Italian and French mafias. A favoured route is the shortest, across the narrow mouth of the Mediterranean from the North African Spanish protectorate of Ceuta, or a little further west, from Tangier. Marijuana is treated as an equally important crop as the opium poppy in Turkey. Its growth is expanding, because of the realised market of the European Union, in the former Soviet republics of Kazakhstan and Tajikistan. The protracted civil war in the Lebanon did nothing to interrupt the marijuana production in the Bekaa Valley, between the central mountain range and Syria: from its main city, Baalbek, the Palestinian Liberation Organisation traded millions of pounds worth to purchase arms. The Iraq-Iran war did not halt the cannabis flow from Iran, either. Marijuana cultivation in Afghanistan is as extensive as that of the poppy fields. In the Netherlands, a special cannabis grown in a special way makes it the country's second most important agricultural crop, second only to tulip production.

Ireland is one member state that has used that word of Interpol's Secretary General – unstoppable – to warn the European Union[17] that it fears itself to be a highway along which an enormous amount of all those drugs gets through the so called Ring of Steel. And without the allocation of resources from Brussels sufficient to buy a fleet of patrol boats, the route cannot be blocked.

The Republic's eloquent police trade union General Secretary John Ferry describes his country – strategically placed on the drug shipping routes from America, Latin America and from North African suppliers skirting the obvious Spanish landfall – as 'the open backdoor to Europe for the major drug barons'.[18] Ferry continues: 'I am afraid that we will bury our heads in the sand so long that it may be too late when the initiative is finally taken. I believe we probably will lose this war.' For Europe to allocate the huge amount of money necessary to equip Ireland's police and Customs and navy with sufficient vessels and manpower properly to close the door would be politically unacceptable. Ferry regards that reluctance as short sighted. 'The reality is that we not only try to protect the UK but we are now trying to protect Europe from the world drug epidemic. That's why I think we can legitimately look to Europe and expect it will say "OK. So you are our back door and we are happy to close it".'

Dublin has first hand experience of the epidemic Ferry believes to be engulfing Europe. The Irish capital alone, with a population of approximately one million, has at least 7,000 heroin addicts: possibly more. When I was there I stayed at the excellent Shelbourne Hotel. A few months earlier an Italian doctor and his wife had been awoken by a burglar in their room. When the thief was challenged, he brandished a hypodermic partially filled with blood and said he was HIV positive and would stab the woman, infecting her with AIDS, if they didn't hand over their valuables. Which of course they did. The threat of stabbing with an infected hypodermic is a frequent defence of drug-addicted shoplifters or muggers when challenged in other parts of Europe, particularly France. I did not personally see any such warnings but Ferry assured me that in Dublin there are street signs advising tourists not to carry cameras or obvious valuables that addicts can target or snatch.

Illegal drug seizure figures in England for 1994 show trafficking and consumption rising relentlessly, with every indication of that increase climbing progressively higher: the amount of intercepted cocaine was a 224 per cent increase on the previous year. Based on their findings from the biggest detailed research in Britain's schools, Exeter University predicted that by 1995 almost half of all sixteen year old boys and a third of sixteen year old girls in British education would have experimented with illegal drugs.

The total value of the 51 tons of drugs seized in 1994, at street prices level, was put by British Customs and Excise analysts at £550 million. Customs authorities claim an overall drug seizure rate of ten per cent. A truer Europe-wide figure, unattributably agreed,[19] is five per cent. But even calculated by the official estimate the value of drugs to organised crime is over £5 billion a year in Britian, just *one* of the Union's member states.

In January 1994, the then British Customs Chief Investigator Douglas Tweddle admitted: 'The drug problem is Britain is worse than it has been in the past. The violence which is linked with drug trafficking undoubtedly has been increasing. There has been a growing number of murders in inner city areas linked with drug smuggling.'

In London alone, the Metropolitan police and the National Criminal Intelligence Unit identified twelve murders and twenty-eight attempted murders as crack related. There is no analytical intelligence from other cities to show how many of England's other four hundred murders in 1993 were drug-linked.

The 620 kilos of heroin intercepted during 1994 was a record, sufficient for 280 million injections. Those mathematics, like all mathematics involving drugs, are open to interpretation, because they are entirely dependent upon the degree of adulteration practised by dealers. Heroin is normally a white powder – the processing in Mexico creates a browner product, known as 'Mexican Mud' – which is refined from the original morphine base, the sap which seeps from a lanced opium poppy bulb. The powder is dissolved, usually in water – although sometimes in lemon juice or vinegar for the added acidity kick – by heating over a low flame. On the street it is never sold pure. To make it go further and increase its profitability, it is normally mixed – 'cut' – with other white powders, ranging from whitewash scraped from walls to talcum powder, flour, sugar or even, fortunately very rarely, the killer poison strychnine. Every time a user injects, he's gambling with the strength of his fix, guessing – and hoping – it will be around the normal 35 to 40 per cent, to which most junkies are accustomed. Occasionally, either because the dealer is inexperienced or has sufficient not to need to stretch his supply, the percentage is much higher. Every year in England and Europe there are recorded deaths of addicts shooting up heroin of 60 or 70 per cent purity.

Drugs intelligence[20] puts the price of heroin throughout Britain and Europe generally at between £70 and £80 a gram. A gram is normally broken up and sold in wraps – 'dime bags' – at £10 each. Heroin is a soporific, like the opium from which it is derived. A user goes 'on the nod', drowsily freed from all worries.

By comparison cocaine is an exhilarating stimulant, infusing a sensation of energetic, 'I can do anything' euphoria. In Peru, where the power of the drug was learned centuries ago, coca is considered a sacred plant, a religious belief now shared by most of the world's dedicated users.

To produce cocaine, a paste is distilled from the leaves of the coca plant by steeping them in kerosene, sulphuric acid and an alkali. Hydrochloric acid is added to provide what is scientifically a salt – cocaine hydrochloride. In 1980 the Colombian Cartels – then headed by the indulgently fat, moustached Pablo Escobar – were squeezing every last cent out of their manufacturing by selling on the streets of Medellin and Cali the impurity-packed, acid-tainted detritus from the bottom of their processing vats. They aptly called it bazooka. It was smoked – with tobacco or marijuana – and within weeks addled the minds of its users. Bazooka – which was only ever sold in Colombia, never tried on the more sophisticated America and Europe market – produced extreme, often homicidal violence.

It was a frightening harbinger of what was to follow, just five years later in America and three years after that in Europe.

Predictably it was the business-minded Orejuela brothers from Cali who devised the new market leader.[21] Powdered cocaine has always been the rich man's drug, snorted through tubes often made from rolled up $100 or £50 notes from four or five separated lines laid out on a hard – usually glass – surface. What the Cali mafia demanded was a new drug for the masses that was easier to use and hooked its users forever: something like bazooka, only cleaner.

According to US Drug Enforcement records, they got it first in 1983. Two years later it was being described as an epidemic in America. It arrived in Britain in 1990.

It's called Crack.

The simplicity of its manufacture is on the level of school boy chemistry. Cocaine is mixed with baking powder. Water is added and the 'cake' cooked until the mixture hardens. When it does so sufficiently, the baking powder splits, to disclose – with the cracking sound that gives it its name – crystals of pure cocaine hydrochloride. Sold in quantities about the size of a peanut, in street parlance it's a 'rock'.

Cocaine powder is sometimes dissolved and injected, but the traditional way of taking it is to inhale through a tube, into the nostrils. Although studies show crack is being dissolved and injected, it is usually smoked. Nasally inhaled cocaine, absorbed through the mucous membranes, gives a high that can last as long as half an hour. The hit from smoking crack – rushing straight to the brain via the blood stream or through fume-filled lungs – can dissipate after as little as thirty seconds: three or four minutes is considered a long high. But the intensity of the euphoria is staggering: so much so that, like the instant after-effect of bazooka, a user's sole preoccupation is to score again. I have been assured by treatment specialists[22] that addiction can become pronounced after just two sessions. Total dependency is measured in terms of just a week. One intelligence assessment[23] says: 'The compulsion to use crack is so strong that it is widely considered to be an addiction that cannot be cured.'

In 1989, an American DEA official, Robert Stutman, warned a

conference of British police chiefs that the United Kingdom would be facing the epidemic America was experiencing within three years. Crack did arrive but not immediately in the dire proportions predicted. The crack unit formed by the Metropolitan police as a precautionary measure was disbanded. By 1993, after seizures had risen by almost four hundred per cent over a three year period, the police still denied it had been a mistake disbanding its anti-crack force. In 1994 2.2 tons of cocaine was intercepted entering Britain.

Britain's drug intelligence analysts predict[24] that crack will continue to increase as an abuse problem, although no-one is yet using the word 'epidemic'. The ease with which it might become one is reflected in street prices. A gram of powdered cocaine costs £50. Much more crack can be produced from powdered cocaine: a rock comes for as little as £10, peaking at £25.

Cannabis retains its market lead popularity in Britain, although in 1994 the amount seized, 47 tons, showed a slight drop on the previous year's total of 51 tons. Only just over 10 tons of that was the leafy, herbal part of the marijuana plant, which is shredded like tobacco to be smoked. Over 42 tons was hashish, the resin scraped from the dried leaves of the plant and compressed into blocks. The resin is also smoked, although it can also be added to food or made into a drink. The Jamaican Yardies enjoy it as a tea. At prices ranging between £25 to £40 a quarter ounce, the value of the overall 51 tons was put at £176 million. The cannabis grown in a special way in the Netherlands is identified by British intelligence[25] as 'skunk' or 'skunkweed' (*Niederweit* in Holland) because of its pungent smell during growth. That growth is hydroponic: under strong artificial light, without soil – in sand or vermiculite – and flooded in water. The normal level of hallucinogenic tetra-hydrocannabinol (THC) in the strongest, sinsemilla strain of ordinary cannabis can be six per cent. 'Skunkweed' can go as high as thirty per cent: ten to twenty per cent is average.

By far the greatest statistical increase in the course of one year was in the seizures of synthetic drugs, the psychotropics. The Netherlands is identified[26] as the major European producing country.

All drug use is cyclical, rising and falling on the whim of popularity: Ecstasy is currently a strong favourite. The danger with Ecstasy sold to teenagers at rave parties is that there is no way of knowing which chemicals or process have been employed in its manufacture.

The drug methylenedioxyamphetamine (MDMA) is the genuine Ecstasy, but it is the least seized in police and Customs raids. There are more than 1,000 different chemicals in the MDA range, all of which give, either more or less, a feeling of euphoria which settles into a sensation of well being, accompanied by hallucination. Although MDA is not addictive, there is a danger of dancers at rave parties – the scene at which it is usually taken – collapsing from heatstroke or dehydration.

The impurity of the manufacture of some tablets – which sell for between £10 to £20 a pill – sometimes kills. There is also the danger that what is bought as Ecstasy doesn't qualify chemically at all under the MDA rating but is, in fact, ketamine, an animal anaesthetic used in veterinary treatment. In 1993 the British authorities seized 554 kilograms of what was being marketed as Ecstasy, valued from those street prices at £58 million. The following year there was an 88 per cent increase, sufficient to have made 2,300,000 tablets.

Amphetamines – which normally come as a white powder, in a wrap, and fuel the rave culture more than Ecstasy – are the second most popular drug in Britain, after cannabis. Unlike Ecstasy, however, amphetamine – most popularly known as Speed or Whizz – can lead to psychological dependence. Its effect is great energy and alertness. It costs around £10 a gram, the usual amount in a wrap: that dosage is sufficient for two sessions. The effect of a hit lasts up to three hours. In 1993, 543 kilos with a street value of £75 million were kept out of the hands of teenagers.

LSD, the favourite of the 1960s, underwent one of the recognised cyclical drops at the beginning of the 1990s. But by the middle of the decade was on the increase again, the supply dominated by Dutch traffickers.

The 275,000 shots picked up in 1993 represented a five per cent decrease over the previous year. LSD – lysergic acid diethylamide – is customarily infused into paper, which is then ingested or dissolved. The paper infusions are fashioned in customised designs: thirty new motifs appeared in 1993. It can also be produced as a pill. Violently hallucinogenic, it creates distorted sight and sound perceptions and also distorts the user's sense of time and reality. It is known to have given people the impression they can fly: Frank Olson, a scientist upon whom the CIA tested it, flung himself through the 13th floor window of New York's

Statler hotel in a flying pose. It, too, is popular at rave parties and sells for as little as £2.50 to £4 a dose.

Tranquillisers – known generically as benzodiazepines – are also drugs of addiction traded on the streets of Europe.

Best known are chlordiazepoxide, diazepam, and temazepam. Average price is £1 a capsule. Although usually swallowed, tranquillisers are sometimes heated three or four at a time to be dissolved and then injected, to give a feeling of drowsiness.

At school playground level – more in Britain than in any other European Union country – there is also the abuse of solvents: lighter fuel, aerosols, glue, paint and cleaning fluids. Children usually inhale the fumes with their faces enclosed in plastic bags to retain the potency. Solvent abuse – usually referred to as glue sniffing – can and does kill.

Solvents are bought over the shop counter.

The three main drugs of abuse – heroin, cocaine and cannabis – are sold on street corners or in 'shooting galleries' or 'crack houses'.

Two organised crime gangs specialise in the trade. One is virtually unique to the United Kingdom. Both know a lot about killing. Of all the organised crime groups I describe in this book, these two are the acknowledged experts.

CHAPTER SIX

A Yard of Their Own to Call Home

Ninety per cent of the crack and cocaine trade in the United Kingdom is conducted by Jamaican gangs known as Yardies. Such gangs do not exist or operate in any other part of the European Union. Every Yardie owns at least one gun: rapid firing automatics or rifle or machine gun calibre are preferred. Britain's Metropolitan Police Commissioner Sir Paul Condon did not cite them specifically by name but it was the level of gun violence and brutality of the Yardies that led to his predicting[1] it was sadly inevitable that British police would be armed, as a matter of course, by the turn of the century.

British police intelligence[2] believe the headquarters of the Yardies is in the Moss Side district of Manchester – the first city in the country to experience drive-by shootings – and that the Yardies were to have been the customers of an arsenal of assault rifles and machine guns discovered in Liverpool in February 1994. For obvious reasons I will not identify the serving officer who suggested that the danger of Yardie violence in the city had been officially minimised during the 1993 negotiations with the International Olympics Committee for Manchester to host the 2000 Olympic Games. Three taxi drivers refused even to consider taking me to Moss Side: two said I was mad and the third wouldn't even direct me to walk there on foot. An Asian accepted the fare only when I explained I wanted simply to drive through, not to stop at an address. What I saw was a decayed, graffiti-daubed area of very few white faces, a ghetto of high rises and two storey terraces close together, nothing planned, just dumped. There were some boarded up buildings like the crack house I had seen in New York's drug-supplying Little Italy, but no obvious activity around them. One black group of teenagers yelled and threw a bottle, which broke on the road behind. My Asian driver suggested they maybe hadn't liked his colour: there was a lot of racism. Or maybe they didn't want to be looked at by a sightseer. There was very little *movement* of people: although it was mid-morning, with everyone behind closed doors it could have been late at night. The driver refused to drop me off: I'd said I didn't want to stop. He might be liable if anything happened to me – which was very probable. Certainly I'd never get another taxi, to take me out of the area. If I wanted to take the risk, I could walk back in when he'd dropped me outside the area. He didn't want the responsibility. What was the point of walking around a place like this? Back at the hotel I realised from a map that he had only taken me to the very outskirts: it might even have been safe enough for me to have walked.

There are Yardie gangs in Liverpool too, where the arms cache was uncovered. They exist also in Birmingham, Bristol and London. In London their turf – undisputed other than by rival Yardies gangs who kill and rob each other for additional drug supplies – are areas of Peckham, Hackney, Stoke Newington, Clapham and Brixton. Street patrol policemen in Brixton were issued with bullet-and-knife proof body armour in March 1994, after two constables were shot, fortunately neither fatally. Police Commissioner Sir Paul Condon promised again more guns would be issued to police.

As well as controlling the crack and cocaine business, the Yardies also handle all distribution of whatever percentage of the £900 million Jamaican cannabis industry is directed to England. It is not possible to estimate the extent or value of that percentage.

It was the Cali Cartel – as always led by the Rodriguez Orejuela brothers – that formed the bond with the Yardies, soon after crack was refined in Colombia in 1983. The Jamaicans then literally blasted their way into the American crime scene to control the US crack dealing, and they were to do the same in England seven years later. By 1991, the US Justice Department estimated there were close to 40,000 Jamaican mobsters in the country. And that, in a five year period, they had been responsible for more than 5,000 murders. In America the organised gangs are referred to as Posses, not Yardies. The most infamous American group is the Shower Posse – believed to be under the direction of a Colombian who worked in New York[3] – so called because they assassinate by showering theirs victims with automatic weapon fire.

When the Rodriquez Orejuela brothers were ready to bring the Colombian cocaine business to Europe it made logical business sense to leave the distribution in the United Kingdom to the Jamaicans: until 1962 Jamaica had been part of the British Commonwealth, and so England had a high proportion of second and third generation Jamaicans permanently resident in the country. Although their common language is English, which reinforced the business logic, Yardies communicate among themselves in an almost impenetrable patois, and it is that patois and the close connection with their native Jamaica from which the British-based gangs derive their title. In Jamaica 'the Yard' is the street term for home – not for backyard as is sometimes suggested – and the gangs like the association with their roots.

One leading Yardie mobster who transferred from the American Shower Posse to Britain was Christopher (Tuffy) Bourne, who usually wore a thin moustache and his hair and chin beard close-cropped. Facial hair is a useful Yardie fashion accessory, easily shaved or regrown to alter appearances. Bourne was deported three times from Britain as the chief Yardie leader, always re-entering on a forged, new-name passport (black book in Yardie patois) before being shot to death in a London gang fight in May 1993. In March 1994, Raymond (Emma) Grant, a contender for Yardie leadership, was jailed for life for Bourne's murder.

Other Yardie thugs sought in Britain are brothers Ron and Oliver Francis, thought to be hiding from American FBI questioning in connection with nine murders. Robert (Rambo) Peart, whom Canadian police want to question in connection with drug dealing, armed robbery and kidnapping, is also believed to have been seen in London and Manchester. His whereabouts are uncertain. Michael Morrison, who delights in the nickname Pumpie because he kills with a pump-action shotgun, fled to England from a crack dealing indictment in America's Kansas. His current whereabouts are unknown also. So are those of Neville (Scorcher) Grant, a known Yardie leader who is suspected to be trading in drugs after illegally re-entering a Britain from which he has already been deported four times, on a fifth 'black book'. Grant's nickname denotes the speed at which he travels between drug deals on a high powered motorcycle.

British immigration authorities each month deport a number of Jamaicans regarded as undesirable, or as definite Yardies. They also subject Jamaican arrivals – particularly those coming for holidays or to visit relatives – to tight scrutiny. In December 1993, there was a civil liberty uproar when a total of 190 on a Christmas holiday charter flight were detained at Gatwick airport. Amid claims of racism by civil libertarians, twenty-seven were refused entry.

Irrespective of the Schengen Agreement – the computer-based 'Fortress Europe' entry control system which came into being with the Maastricht Treaty and which governs the admission of non-citizens from outside the European Union, of which the United Kingdom is not a signatory – all European member states will have external entry visa controls by 1996. This is one of the measures demanded by the Maastricht Treaty, which activated a previously agreed clause also – Article 100c – of the European Community Treaty. The British government will then be able to comply with its civil liberty assurances that no visa regulations will be imposed by London upon the 350,000 Jamaicans who visit the country each year, but bring the shutters down anyway by invoking a binding European Union stipulation from Brussels. This will be a convenient way of digging itself out of the hole it has dug for itself in a typically inept effort to avoid the racist tag.

After persistent campaigns by black civil rights groups, the Home Office changed its policy towards suspected Jamaican arrivals. Instead of holding them in detention while their entry rights were established, immigration officers were instructed officially to list them as 'refused entry' – but to grant them temporary admission. The conditions were that they should remain at designated addresses and keep in telephone contact with the police. The outcome was as predictable as night following day: while genuine visitors followed the rules, 'black book' Yardies and first-time drug trafficking recruits disappeared into Britain's Jamaican underworld, ridiculing the system (which deserved ridicule anyway). Five months before the Christmas charter flight swoop, Charles Wardle, Britain's then Immigration Minister, told the House of Commons that in the previous year over 750 Jamaicans allowed in under the current system had vanished. In February 1995, Wardle resigned his succeeding portfolio as Trade

Minister so that he could publicly pressure premier John Major to put immigration control on the agenda for the 1996 inter-governmental conference redefining the Maastricht Treaty. Article 7a of the existing Maastricht accord restricting immigration was not, according to Wardle, 'worth the paper it was written on'.

Home Secretary Michael Howard in June 1993, ordered Scotland Yard – which had earlier disbanded a Yardie squad as it had also disbanded its crack unit – to re-establish a taskforce targeting Yardie organised crime. In July Detective Chief Super-intendent Roy Clark, Scotland Yard's deputy head of criminal intelligence, went to Kingston, Jamaica to set up a criminal liaison system with the Jamaican police. Other British police officials negotiated with American enforcement authorities for an exchange of criminal profiles between the United Kingdom and the United States. Part of that arrangement was that the Federal Bureau of Alcohol, Tobacco and Firearm's database listing all the Posse groups and their leaders would be made available to Britain.

Two months after the American cooperation was agreed, unarmed community policeman Patrick Dunne was gunned down in Clapham, south London, when he stumbled upon an argument between crack-peddling Yardie mobs. The murder weapon was a 9mm automatic, one of the guns most favoured by Yardie gangs.

Ironically, the officer appointed to investigate PC Dunne's killing was Detective Superintendent John Jones, the former head of the Yardie unit Scotland Yard had earlier decided to be unnecessary.

The Yardies' propensity for – or rather pleasure in – violence is matched by the biker gangs, the other organised crime group whose chief activity is drug trading and transportation. And unlike the Yardies, the biker gangs do not confine themselves to England but operate throughout the European Union. There are chapters (biker groups) in every country in the Union. Their mobility and tight clan structure makes the bikers the most cohesive and all-embracing criminal organisation blanketing Europe. Some police assessments[4] claim bikers are more violent and are responsible for more murders and intimidation in the United Kingdom[5] than even the Yardies. Interpol has created special monitoring units, tracking the bikers – 'the fastest growing criminal organisation in the world'[6] – throughout every country in which they are established.

In Britain, the National Criminal Intelligence Service has set up a similar specialised section. Canada – which considers itself particularly afflicted with biker criminality – is providing both European agencies with an exclusive bikers' database holding over 30,000 entries.

That database has endorsed evidence, independently gathered by both Interpol and NCIS, of cooperating links between the bikers and both traditional Italian mafia and Colombian cartels. It is the Colombian connection upon which enforcement authorities are concentrating, having determined that one of the chief European entry points – if not the main entry point – for Cali cocaine and crack is via the Iberian peninsula. With the additional advantage of a language similarity – the attraction of England for the Yardies – drug officers believe the strongest European Union base for the Colombian mafia is in Portugal and Spain.

Just as the French interpret most European legislation to Gallic benefit their police and customs are using legislation enacted before the Second World War to modify this interpretation of the Shengen cross-border agreement. The old law, passed in the 1930s, quite simply allows them to have an expandable frontier. Technically the French border can be moved inwards from the positively marked frontier with any of its neighbours for a distance of sixty kilometres. Normally they operate in a thirty kilometre range, and anyone entering that deep *cordon sanitaire* can be challenged. The French invoke the 1930s law not just across the Spanish frontier but also across their separated-by-Belgium border with the Netherlands.

Bikers, astride Harley Davidson motorcyles wearing Nazi helmets, individually decorated with recognised leathers (colours) and boastful, often Nazi, insignia, used to be the easiest criminal groups for police to profile. Not any longer. The regalia – and the motorcycles – are retained, but more and more only for publicity effect: apeing the efforts towards respectability of virtually every organised crime group I have encountered, the bikers try to hide their criminality beneath a Robin Hood cloak of charity-organising and fund-raising. According to English targeting intelligence[7] when they wish to move about Europe undetected they discard their identifiable uniform and, instead of motorcycles, they drive Mercedes and BMWs. I have even heard of bikers at the wheels of Rolls Royces.[8] Even more astonishing, those dedicated to breaking the law cynically use it. The most commonly known bikers – and most infamous – are the Hell's Angels: they have in England copyrighted the recognisable items of their regalia and are prepared to issue legal injunctions to prevent that copyright being infringed.[9] They have developed their own intelligence services, obtaining the restricted telephone numbers and biographies of detectives profiling them, and complain to the National Criminal Intelligence Service in London if the unit describes the Hell's Angels in what they regard as a derogatory fashion.

The Hell's Angels originated in 1947 in San Bernardino, California. It did not develop into an international organisation until Ralph (Sonny) Barger founded the Oakland Chapter, in the suburbs of San Francisco. Barger, much tattooed, now comfortably middle aged, is still the revered messiah of the cult.

Criminal intelligence got their first indication of what sort of organisation the Hell's Angels were in 1983, when a defecting member testified before a US Congressional committee that an American initiate had to commit murder – 'roll bones' – before acceptance, this effectively precluding any undercover police infiltration. The hooded witness – whose name was in fact Clarence (Addie) Crouch, a former vice president of the Cleveland Chapter – testified that an initiate, before chapter witnesses, also had to engage in sex with a child under age, and with a woman over 65, and finally had to commit necrophilia.[10]

The English offshoot of the genuine Hell's Angels is the largest outside America, although its accredited strength is surprisingly small. There are only twelve chapters, the total membership of which is put at 200, but there are additional fetch-and-carry gofers, known variously as 'prospects' and 'hangarounds'. They have 'honour' members also, drawn from the professional classes of barristers, doctors and accountants who have refined the leadership's now respectable commercial persona, while shrewdly encouraging the easily-mocked Nazi-helmet-and-bike image to remain the public impression.

The English Chapter celebrated the border-free integration of the EU in 1993 by registering a company called Hell's Angel's Europe Inc. to bring even more closely together the Continental chapters and coordinate their operations in all the European member countries. As with other organised crime groups, police intelligence predicts a massive expansion into Eastern Europe and Russia. Chapters there are already known to have been formed.

A secondary bikers' group in the United Kingdom is the

Outlaws. Although they are numerically larger than the Hell's Angels, they are not regarded by police as being so well organised or as well-connected with other mafias. There are about seven hundred fully initiated Outlaws making up sixty gangs, and they have a large number of 'prospects' 'hangarounds' and 'honorary' affiliates. Like the Hell's Angels, they now work in business suits. As well as cocaine and cannabis, they bring huge quantities of psychotropics into England from Holland, Europe's leading producing country. They are are also the couriers of the Dutch-grown 'skunkweed'.

There are further suggestions[11] that they – and their Hell's Angels rivals – are substantial carriers to England of psychotropics from Poland and Hungary, whose indigenous gangs are increasing producers of this specific range of drugs. In border-tightening training visits to these two countries British police and Customs officers have identified both biker groups as a particular trafficking problem.

Criminal intelligence estimates the yearly income of both groups in the hundreds of millions,[12] which is why City-suited accountants are so important to them. That much illegal money is then laundered until it becomes as respectable as the Hell's Angels and the Outlaws like to appear themselves.

CHAPTER SEVEN

Money Makes the World Go Around

The immediate cash profits from organised crime are so vast that they have to be transported in suitcases or even in bulk-carrying containers: at just the London end of one international seizure there was so much in so many boxes that it took accountants twenty-three days just to count it![1] There's the Pompidou Group's estimate of £131 billion for Europe alone. Or the lesser figure, of £56 billion worldwide, agreed upon by both the Paris-based Organisation for Economic Co-operation and Development and the Financial Action Task Force set up by G7, the world's seven richest countries. Which don't, incidentally, include any of the drug-producing states.

As I stressed earlier, both figures are informed guesses. What isn't a guess is that, once obtained illegally, the huge cash amounts have to be converted into something legal. The Watergate scandal that drove the late US President Nixon from office gave the world the title for the process[2]: money laundering. Organised crime has perfected the art. World – and all European – governments are trying to become equally expert at pursuing, finding and then seizing the drug fortunes. At the moment this is one of the few – practically the *only* – effective way of attacking the millionaire drug traffickers and their billionaire suppliers.

The EU has three pieces of 'hunt the money' legislation. One is a 1991 EC Directive legally binding every member state to introduce into its own individual legal system a money laundering law. Second is a money laundering Convention passed by the Council of Europe, which the British government was the first to ratify in September 1992. Every other country in the Union now has done the same, some more determinedly than others. It was France's Professor Raufer who described his country's relevant statutes as 'absolutely useless'.[3] The third money laundering enforcement regulation is the 1988 UN Convention against Illicit Traffic in Narcotic Drugs and Psychotropic Substances, more conveniently referred to as the Vienna Convention.

Essential to tracing any drugs fortune or asset is early identification of the first stage in the washing cycle: in bankspeak it's called 'placement'. If the placement is missed, the chances of finding the money, or whatever asset that money has been used to purchase, is virtually impossible. For that reason every EU country is, under a European-agreed system, putting upon financial institutions the onus – enforced by penalty – for spotting the initial suspicious placement. Those institutions – banks, investment companies, brokers, building societies, credit card companies and bureaux des changes – are required by the 1988 Basle Statement of Principles on Money Laundering to report cash or asset movements they consider questionable. In the case of the United Kingdom, that report must be to the financial section of the National Criminal Intelligence Service.

The United Kingdom already had money laundering legislation in place before the three international conventions. There was the 1986 Drug Trafficking Offences Act and the Criminal Justice (International Co-operation) Act. A new Criminal Justice Bill which became law in 1994 enshrined most of the provisions of the 1986 Drugs Act, in particular making it an offence, punishable by imprisonment, for any legitimate money manager or handler to fail to report suspicious transactions. The edict to every such manager is 'know your customer'. In 1993, NCIS was notified of 12,000 transactions deemed suspicious. After investigation only £10 million was seized which prompted some police intelligence officers seriously to doubt the money market's commitment to obeying the law. One officer described as laughable the ratio between successful seizures and reported suspicions.

Of particular concern at the time of writing is the potential use by organised crime of futures dealing on the London commodity exchanges. A requirement of European law now is that detailed records be kept and maintained of all such transactions. The officer who was cynically unimpressed at the seizure ratio told me the records on some future dealing weren't much more reliable than figures written down on the backs of envelopes. An analysis[4] by the National Criminal Intelligence Service observes caustically that it is interesting to note how, despite the legal penalties in Britain against money laundering, an open invitation to a conference[5] at which international money laundering was a major topic was accepted by not one single official from any financial regulatory body in the United Kingdom – including the supervisory Bank of England which proclaims a determination to protect the integrity of the world's banking system.

Placement crosses the first hurdle of the laundering process. The money has been rinsed to lose its initial grubbiness. It is still too provably close to its illegal source, however. So the washing process clicks into its next cycle: in further bankspeak, this is 'layering'. This describes the moving of the money or assets through a series of transactions that distance them so far from their placement source that they are totally untraceable. Once that's achieved, the crime revenue is 'integrated' – legitimised beyond any investigation or enforcement, certainly beyond that of any tax-probing authority. Organised crime has won. As it usually does.

The most obvious of the myriad ways for the mafias and the cartels to separate their identifying money from its identifying source is physically to carry it – the placement stage – from one country to another, in boxes or suitcases. The removal of internal border controls in the European Union has made this easier than ever before.

Furthermore, the EU's external Ring of Steel is not for one moment preventing the money bag carrier moving to and from the East. Russia and its former satellite countries have, in fact, become the biggest laundries in Europe. And are likely to remain so, for years to come.

In 1992, ten bank officials were assassinated by the European-established Moscow mafias for refusing to legitimise through their banks the criminal profits from phoney shell companies: forty of the Russian capital's 260 banks are controlled by organised crime.[6] Leoluca Orlando told me: 'In Eastern Europe the Mafia is buying banks, because there the banks are weak'.[7]

Germany's Bundeskriminalamt believe that the Chechen mafia,

in particular, are ahead of other Russian groups using the financial centres of Frankfurt to clean their money. An anonymous British businessman – whose integrity I trust – recalled[8] a train journey from Moscow through the Baltic states on which two men were locked into their carriage – with a key to unlock it from the inside in the event of emergencies – with 'several suitcases full of cash' which had earlier been smuggled unimpeded eastwards from Berlin. Their eventual destination was Sweden, where he believes they successfully opened money-washing bank accounts. Russian mobsters are known by Britain's National Criminal Intelligence Service to have opened accounts in the Channel Island of Jersey, one of the world's bank secrecy and tax haven states.

Over 200,000 joint venture companies have been set up in Moscow[9] to engage in phoney trading to legitimise criminal income and expenditures between Russia and the rest of the world. A Russian Interior Ministry official[10] has told British police that more than £16 billion has been moved *out* of Russia back into Western banks along this route. To make the laundering system work, all those companies need is linking arrangements with companies in the European Union: in England such companies are believed to be spread around many major cities, although the majority are thought to be in London. In one of London's leading socialite clubs, I was told by an Indian entrepreneur that I could name my own price for an introduction to friends in Moscow that would lead him to a joint venture tie-up. 'There's more money in Russia,' he said, 'than it's possible to count, just waiting to be scooped up.'

An NCIS[11] briefing warns: 'Senior Russian financiers have themselves concluded that it is now impossible to conduct legal business in their own country. They cite the all-pervasive hold by criminal groups on banks, industries and joint venture . . . the money that doesn't find its way to London, Frankfurt or Zurich is used to buy up legitimate businesses and property. The criminal organisations thus become a kind of venture capital fund, bank-rolling car dealerships and rental franchises, restaurants, night-clubs, hotels and, of course, casinos. An agreed estimate among both crime groups and police sources is that about half of Russia's commercial banks are under criminal control. Last year (1992) alone Chechen gangs siphoned off $500 million (£328.9 million) in a massive bank fraud the equivalent of one third of the sum provided by the IMF (International Monetary Fund) to stabilise the rouble.

The normally stable international banking business has become a dangerous place . . . The economy's criminalisation is so pervasive that there is often a fine line between gangsters, corrupt bureaucrats and the new entrepreneurs who find it virtually impossible to operate in Russia without breaking the law or having some contact with Russia's Mafia. There is a crude view of business: disputes are settled with guns and the legal system is in a state of collapse.'

Always, too, criminals and masons work together. Leoluca Orlando insisted during our meeting[12]: 'In Eastern Europe there is a very strong masonry and there is a very strong mafia and they are very big together.' So much money was being laundered in the former communist countries, in Orlando's opinion, that organised crime was going beyond buying up banks actually to buying up *parts* of the various states. 'The investment in East Europe will be the biggest money-cleansing operation in the history of humanity.'

To complete the final integration stage in concealing their fortunes, launderers frequently move into tax haven and bank secrecy states. The attractions are obvious. There are few or no taxes, and there are few or no questions asked about the source of newly-arriving wealth: none of the tax haven bolt-holes is a signatory to any international convention or directive, although a British Treasury official assured me that all havens with British connections were gradually introducing their own anti-laundering regulations.

No tax at all is exacted on no-questions-asked deposits in the Bahamas, the Cayman Islands, or the Turks and Caicos islands of the Caribbean. Or the islands of Vanuatu and Nauru, in the Pacific. Low tax countries include Bermuda, the Netherland Antilles, the British Virgin Islands, Monserrat, Panama, Liechtenstein, Monaco, Bahrain and Hong Kong.

As well as imposing little or no tax, these countries offer bank and commercial secrecy, enforce no currency controls, and have businesses – even banks or insurance companies – which are easily purchased by launderers and then operated as legitimate enterprises. Such available-for-sale companies are often openly advertised in international publications, such as the *International Herald Tribune*.[13] Once acquired, such shell companies – which normally have one local resident as the person named on the deed of incorporation – permit as much money as the trafficker wishes to manipulate to be moved through their accounts. Very often there are several such shells, between which the crime income can be juggled and moved further to hide it. All the haven countries have the additional advantage of state-of-the-art communications, enabling money to be moved in seconds by wire transfer.

It's not essential to bother with shell companies. Having placed and layered their money in an offshore bank, mafia organisations frequently finish the integration by transferring as much as they want to draw upon into a further bank, although not one in the country in which they reside and operate. In their country of residency, they then borrow from their own bank, one in which they are established and recognised, thus avoiding the know-your-customer trap created by the European Union legislation – happy at last to disclose the amount on deposit in the foreign bank as collateral for the loan.

Switzerland is a bank secrecy country but bitterly resents any suggestion it is a haven for laundering the proceeds of crime. It has, in fact, had a code of practice for many years to identify narcotics money and had evolved, in advance of the EU directive, a system for prosecuting financiers who knowingly handled such proceeds. Under Swiss law, a money manager has to report any transaction from an unknown customer over 25,000 Swiss francs. Some other European countries operate a suspicion ceiling, but Britain has intentionally avoided creating a trigger figure, leaving the suspicion-arousing amount to the discretion of individual finance houses.

The British legislative decision not to impose an arbitary sum was taken to defeat a known laundering method that avoids leaving a paper trail. It's called 'smurfing'. It's labour intensive, time consuming but effective. The only requirement is to know the figure at which any transaction attracts attention: and then operate the laundering just below it. Teams of smurfs deposit dirty money just below the limit in dozens of small bank accounts.

Alternatively, still below that limit, they buy – for cash – negotiable instruments, cashiers' cheques, bank drafts or money orders, which can then be realised whenever the money is needed.

A unique variation on smurfing emerged in 1993 in Paris, coincidentally confirming for the first time the presence in Europe of the Japanese mafia, the Yakuza. Dozens of Asians – mostly students – descended upon luxury leather boutiques: later, after the smurfing operation had finished, mystified police were able to identify 300 specific buyers. Delighted leather boutiques admitted ten-at-a-time purchasing groups. The students bought recklessly, always using brand new 500 franc notes which police later learned were being drawn from Luxembourg banks by five of the Yakuza gang, commuting daily. The leather goods were shipped to twenty fake companies in Tokyo, where they were sold at a lower price than they had been bought for in Paris. The loss didn't matter: it was an acceptable write-off in the business of turning dirty money into clean.

Detective Inspector Graham Saltmarsh, head of the laundering crime unit at Britain's NCIS and a money laundering expert, believes a specialised branch of the Japanese mafia, the *Sokaiya*, is operating undetected in the City of London. The Bundes-kriminalamt and Interpol think the Yakuza are active in every other leading financial centres of Europe. The Yamaguchi-gumi, based in Kobe, are the biggest group. The Matsuda-gumi are almost as powerful. The Sumiyoshi-Rengo and Inagawar-kai are based in Tokyo. All operate a rigidly controlled heirarchical system, impenetrable to any undercover infiltration. All organised crime groups have their initiation ceremonies and rituals but the Yakuza rituals are more bizarre than most. Traditionally they completely tattoo their bodies in patterns so tightly intricate that naked it is impossible to detect that they are unclothed. If a soldier – a *kobun* – transgresses he pleads forgiveness from his Godfather – an *oyabun* – by ceremonially severing a finger at the first joint with a short samurai sword.

The *Sokaiya* active throughout Europe operate on behalf of all the foremost Yakuza gangs. They prey particularly upon busi-nesses and financial institutions with Japanese connections, by which they are known and feared. Blackmail of senior executives – sexual entrapment is frequently used – is a favoured way of gaining compliance. NCIS believe the *Sokaiya* lead every other world mafia in their exploitation of London's financial outlets for money laundering.

Japanese police officers are permanently seconded to enbassies in EU capitals. In London the Japanese detectives have a good working relationship with NCIS. But Inspector Saltmarsh acknow-ledges the difficulty of fighting such a unique organisation as the Yakuza, whose code of silence is such that 'it makes the Sicilian observance of *omerta* sound like a licence to gossip'. And it is compounded by the refusal of terrorised Japanese businessmen and bankers in London to admit they are under any gangster pressure.

Yet it is only through the financial sector that any sort of police lead can be established into the Yakuza. Their *Sokaiya* deal with registered financial institutions throughout the money centres of the European Union.

The other main Asian organised crime group – Triad societies – frequently use what is known as underground banking to move their drugs and extortion money in and out of the EU and to and from Asia. Four Triad societies have been positively identified in the European Union: 14K, Wo Shing Wo, Wo on Lok and San Yee On. All have members domiciled in London and England's principal provincial cities. NCIS has a special Triad division under Hong-Kong trained Detective Sergeant Michael Ball, and all British police forces have been warned that a large number of Triad gangsters will flood into the country before Hong Kong reverts to communist Chinese control in 1997. An NCIS intelligence analysis[14] estimates that a total of 500,000 Chinese will quit the colony before 1997 for various part of the world, and since, under the 1990 British Nationality (Hong Kong) Act, 50,000 heads of household can apply for UK citizenship for themselves and their families, averaging four members to each family, this creates a possible legal influx of 200,000.

The inevitability of Triads being washed up on Europe's shores, intentionally, on such a tide doesn't end there. Portugal has offered citizenship to most of Macau's 500,000 population when the enclave reverts to China in December 1999: some will choose to stay but in excess of 400,000 are expected to leave. NCIS warns: 'There is no doubt that in addition, a large number of Chinese criminals will try to use Macau (where a brisk trade in forged or illegally obtained documents is used to gain Portuese and EC passports) for illicit access to Europe and possibly the UK.' The underground banking system used by these groups is heavily dependent upon trust or family ties. It is therefore ideally suited to such close-knit societies of blood-brother oaths and automatic death for betrayal: 'I will be killed by myriads of swords' is the Triad initiation acceptance of the penalty for disclosing *any* society secret.

The mechanics of underground banking are not complicated. In the country where the crime proceeds are generated, a Triad launderer deposits the dirty money with a man who operates as an unregistered and therefore unofficial banker. This banker acknowledges the deposit by providing a receipt which is often as bizarre as a currency note torn in half or a special marker, known as a 'chop', the other half of which is already held by an overseas accomplice. He then notifies that accomplice – another unofficial banker in the foreign country where the clean money is required to be drawn – of the relevant amount. When the launderer or his society presents his own half of the chop the money is paid out in local currency, less substantial commission and fees, which is how the underground bankers make their profit.

The system employed by the 200,000 phoney joint venture companies in Russia works with matching simplicity. Goods or services are ordered by the Russian or East European organisations from their 'subsidiary' businesses in the European Union. Either the invoices for those orders are greatly inflated, the difference being the amount of money to be laundered, or the invoice is totally false, representing the whole amount that is being washed. Either way, the dirty proceeds, as a paper or wire transfer, can be legitimately sent to the West and shown as a debit in the accounts of the ordering company. The true value of whatever is imported is quite immaterial: if there is a loss on its sale in the East or anywhere else where the false invoicing system is used, this is an acceptable business expense, compensated a hundred times over by the profit gained in the first place from drugs and arms sales or other organised crime activities.

Currency exchanges and brokerage houses – extensively used by launderers – are two financial institutions particularly targeted by the 1991 EC Directive with which all member states have had to comply by national legislation. Currency exchanges negotiate large cash transactions – buying, for cash, foreign currency bank drafts to open overseas accounts is a laundering favourite – and until the 1991 legislation were poorly regulated: many firms kept the sort of 'backs of envelopes' records derided by Inspector Saltmarsh, if they bothered to keep any at all. The openness to abuse – and the lure to money launderers – is obvious from just one statistic. Through the London foreign currency exchanges *alone* $303 billion is traded *every day*! Under the British Criminal Justice and Public Order Act record keeping has to be of audited accounts standard, but some finance intelligence specialists doubt the commitment of exchanges strictly to comply with the regulations. It will, I was told, need prosecutions to convince them the legislation has teeth and that the authorities are determined to enforce it.

There is an equal government determination in England to invoke the law as it governs brokerage houses which, until the Criminal Justice Act, were more widely open than a barn door for organised crime to drive through. All that was needed was the assistance of a well-rewarded, willingly co-operative broker. Once such a financial expert was suborned, there was virtually no obstacle to money moving freely anywhere in Europe or the world. Through brokerage houses – regulated differently in practically every country in the EU – stock or bonds can be bought, for cash. The ownership can be registered in any fictitious name or shell company. There is little or no registration necessary for bearer bonds. Here again it has been suggested to me that penalty-imposed cases need to be brought before brokers will be convinced that money laundering legislation is seriously intended. As in so many other instances with so many other crimes, legislation – if of varying effectiveness – exists. What is lacking is its enforcement.

After placement and layering, the ultimate integration occurs when once-dirty money is put into a facility or business that is equal to the original investment. Recoverable on sale, this continues to generate substantial profit, compounding and increasing the value of that initially illegal investment. Sometimes the choices are as bizarre as the Yakuza purchase of luxury leather products in Paris: the Cali brothers, Gilberto and Miguel Rodriguez Orejuela, amused themselves on one occasion by gaining control, through a confusion of shell companies, of practically every mussel bed in Spain, from which virtually all such molluscs are farmed for the dining tables of Europe. Business properties are by far the most preferred facilities – witness the banks to which the Moscow mafia have been guided by their Italian mafia mentors who have perfected such infiltrations in the principality of Monaco. The Japanese Yakuza have bought heavily into the London property market. Casinos, with their uncheckable cash flow, are another favourite. Again the Italians have taught the Russians the value of gaming houses and the Cosa Nostra and Camorra and 'Ndrangheta use those in Moscow. At the time of writing the Russian capital has fifty-nine casinos, as many as Las Vegas. All are mafia-dominated and act virtually as currency exchanges. Hotels, too, are considered solid money-producing investments: an extremely complicated consortium of Japanese companies owns for eventual hotel conversion, one of the most prestigious and at one time controversial properties in the very heart of London. Nursing homes and clinics feature on the property buying list: I believe – but cannot prove – that such clinics are being put by the Neapolitan Camorra to what I have already referred to as the most appalling use it is possible to conceive, illegal organ transplants.

The Italian mafia have, in fact, spread very substantially across the now unrestricted border into France. So much so that the two countries have agreed on joint anti-mafia cooperation.

Too late, according to people to whom I spoke in both countries. As it is most certainly too late to stop the highly sophisticated laundering operation available in the most luxurious money haven in the world.

CHAPTER EIGHT

Rien Ne Va Plus

All tax havens and bank secrecy enclaves reflect the luxury of the wealth they feed off and generate. But Monaco is the glittering jewel in their crown. Uniquely it has a prince to wear it. And princesses with matching, if slightly tarnished, tiaras. To the mafias of Europe – and beyond – Monaco is viewed not just as a jewel but as a welcoming beacon. They swarm to it, like moths to a light, to launder their money through its ultra-convenient, ultra-discreet banking system: not infrequently the money couriers openly present themselves carrying cases packed with cash.[1] There are suggestions impossible to substantiate that Princess Grace invited the Mafia in, before her death in 1982.

Certainly the Italian-born late husband of one of the princesses had business links to the Mafia, like so many Monagasques. All that is publicly necessary to form a shell company behind which anonymous Godfathers operate is the sponsorship of just one resident of the minuscule, one mile square principality – only the Vatican, whose bank was also used so successfully by the Mafia and the murdered Roberto Calvi, is a smaller sovereign state – associated with that company. Matchbox-sized company plaques are tacked, like medals to the victors of crime, on the sun-whitened walls of the buildings and offices of La Condamine and Fontvieille, the commercial and business districts neatly bracketed on the one side by Monaco Town, on the rocky outcrop dominated by the sugar-pink palace of Prince Rainier, and by Monte Carlo on the other.

High society had rooted itself here long before Princess Grace, then a princess only in Hollywood, made the movie of that title, with among others Frank Sinatra. It is an idyllic, £9,000 a square metre paradise of unashamed wealth and comfort, of £1 million-plus yachts and Rolls Royces and Ferraris. Of dethroned kings and their consorts, princesses by title or profession, and of the most famous casino in the world. Surroundings, in fact, in which it is difficult to bring a mundane word like laundering to mind – until you remember that this sort of laundering is anything but mundane.

Monaco, of course, denies it emphatically and consistently: nowhere in the principality did I find one person who would acknowledge, openly or otherwise, even the possibility of a criminal presence using facilities for that or any other purpose. This unwillingness did not extend into France. The President of a French Parliamentary Commission into Mafia infiltration of their country insists that the principality is 'certainly a financial base' for organised crime, particularly for the Neapolitan Camorra.

Monaco is the staging post. Having been 'integrated' into front companies, the Mafia money flows westwards along the Côte d'Azure to make more money. A Nice property agency which refused to be identified calculates that sixty per cent of property purchased on the Riviera is in the names of companies, not their actual human owners. 'You expect me to question a man who wants to buy a thirty or forty million franc villa with cash! Why should I? It's not illegal.' The companies covering Mafia activity buy mansions and hotels, and attempt to buy casinos, hoping thus to acquire both the legitimate value of the property and, in one washing cycle, the facility to continue laundering even afterwards through the cash-generating gaming tables.

The Republican mayor of nearby Menton, Jean-Claude Guibal, has prevented the takeover of the town's casino by a company of which he did not approve, and, since October 1992, has insisted that Italian property developers seeking to invest or build in the town, which virtually forms the border between Italy and France, produce an Italian magistrate's certificate guaranteeing they have no Mafia connections. It is a doubtful precaution. Just as the Mafia 'buy' Monaco residents to front their laundering companies in the principality, so they employ French lawyers and accountants to hide their involvement in the property purchasing or developing businesses in France.

Judge Thierry Jean-Pierre, who headed a French government division monitoring large scale economic and financial criminality before becoming a Euro-MP in 1994, explained the difference between how organised crime established itself in Russia, America and Italy and how it had insinuated itself into France. In those other countries it was involved in perpetrating crime. In France, it was solely interested in investing the wealth gained from crime. 'Here the laundering rings are prospering before our very eyes . . . currently the Mafia considers France to be a land of welcome, but not an area where they can exercise criminality at a high level of concentration.'[2]

France's Parliamentary Commission was not the only indication of French alarm at the invasion of organised crime. In March 1994, there was an anti-Mafia conference at Aix-en-Provence, regional capital of the Var, considered so important Judge Liliana Ferraro travelled from Rome to attend. Her French counterpart was Michel Debacq, a former investigatory magistrate in Marseille – home of the traditional and active French mafia – who had earlier been seconded to the Italian capital to be the anti-crime liaison between the two countries.

The conference, originally intended to be kept secret, ended with all too familiar, depressingly unenforcable undertakings between the two country's fractious agencies to improve their non-existent cooperation by the greater sharing of intelligence, to make extradition easier, and to increase their efforts to impede money laundering. It had opened four days after the contract killing less than fifty miles away of Madame Yann Piat, a National Assembly deputy for the centre-right Union for French Democracy, the UDF. Madame Piat had been the vice president of the Parliamentary Anti-Mafia Commission and an outspoken attacker of the Mafia – French and Italian – and of corruption in the South of France.

President of that Commission was Francois d'Aubert, the MP for Mayenne, in Normandy, and a member of the same political party as Madame Piat. The Commission had already laid the hopeful groundwork for the assault against organised crime pledged at the Aix conference. It recommended the creation of special investigating magistrates' courts throughout France – in Paris, Lyon or Grenoble, Douai, Caen or Rouen as well as Aix –

and the introduction of a law modelled on the 1965 Italian Mafia-connection legislation already used by the mayor of Menton. There was also a suggestion to widen the scope of France's money laundering statutes – currently restricted entirely to drugs, excluding every other money-making crime – under which, according to Professor Raufer, no-one has ever yet been successfully prosecuted.

Whether there will ever be an effective tightening of the laundering laws depends upon that much-quoted necessity, political will. I didn't find much evidence of it, during my travels and researches anywhere in France. Sometimes even the opposite. Nor did I find any evidence of internal police liaison, far less of the necessary cross-border harmonisation.

It was Professor Raufer[3] who first surprised me, in a rain-lashed Paris office that seemed a million miles from the sun-soaked Riviera, by suggesting French authorities were prepared with Gallic practicality to tolerate an illegal cash-flow across the Italian border and along the Côte d'Azure, in order to benefit the economy. Francois d'Aubert put it much more candidly.[4] 'France is thrilled to see currency coming to Monaco – never mind if it's in cash, because it helps with the balance of payments. So the French Banking Commission, in theory qualified to supervise the sixty or so banks and financial establishments in Monaco, turns a blind eye and leaves them to recycle what is obviously dirty money. On the other hand the Monagasque authorities pride themselves on their local legislation to combat laundering, well-meaning in its intention but in reality not applied, due to the lack of supervision provided by the French authorities and due also to their basic curiosity when faced with people carrying cases of dirty money.'

Forty per cent of the economic activity in Monaco is generated by those banks, in which there is an estimated[5] £6 billion available on deposit at any one time.

Not unnaturally, as I have already emphasised, the accusation of being a Mafia Mecca is angrily refuted by Monaco's authorities. A government spokesman I contacted over the telephone, who refused to be named – refusing also to explain his reticence even though in this instance there was neither any personal danger, nor was he saying anything controversial – at first argued it was impossible to hide shareholdings in corporations registered in the principality: there was an open register of public limited companies. When I pointed out I was not talking of *public* limited companies, the government spokesman reminded me that while private companies, *sociétés civiles particulières*, remained just that – private – share movements were traceable. But was there any reason for the authorities to investigate the activities of a Monaco-registered, Monagasque-run company buying businesses or property in France or anywhere else in the world? No. So where was the check? They had laws. How were they enforced? To the satisfaction of the principality. What about the satisfaction of the French and their critical crime Commission? There were ongoing discussions with the French, with whom the principality had excellent relations: Monaco did not accept many of the conclusions of the Commission. Which ones *did* they accept? That was not a question he was qualified to answer: legislation *has* existed on the statute books in Monaco since the end of 1992 criminalising money laundering, said my anonymous spokesman, whose impatience at my enquiries extended to refusing to tell me the precise name of the finance division he represented. The principality wished to co-operate fully with the French authorities, he added. Of course there was a political will to prevent Monaco being used by organised crime: that was an impudent question. The language difficulty made it impossible to continue the conversation, he complained. Could I visit his office personally, with an interpreter? The telephone was replaced before I completed the request. Over a period of five days I made unsuccessful attempts to make a reconnection, to anyone who would speak to me.

France's Anti-Mafia Commission report was regarded in Monaco as very impudent indeed, naming as it did among a litany of identified mafiosi – although without directly accusing him – Stefano Casiraghi, the former husband of Princess Caroline of Monaco.

One of those Mafia figures it did accuse was Mario Contini, a fellow Italian with whom Casiraghi had extensive business interests, particularly in the construction industry actually within the principality.

The details of the Contini-Casiraghi projects, hidden within Monaco's secret banking system, have never been publicly disclosed. Nor will they ever be. The French Commission labels Contini as 'one of several people known to have committed serious offences in Italy and suspected of having Mafia connections'.

As well, of course, as having connections with the omnipotent, all-concealing masonic movement: in this case the most concealing of all, the state-overthrowing P2 itself.

The intricate linking of Casiraghi, Contini and P2 was traced for me in a zinc-topped, stand-up bar in the Opera district of Paris[6] where wine came in tumblers, by the government official who was the first of many in France to talk to me only under conditions of total anonymity. And confirmed by an official of similar rank in Rome,[7] regrettably under matching restrictions. The Italian meeting was also in a bar, close to the Piazza di Popolo. Both locations struck me as falling very far short of the surroundings in which to discuss a member, albeit by marriage, of Europe's oldest reigning dynasty, despite the assurance from my Italian informant that Casiraghi would have felt at home where we were.

The open-faced, darkly handsome Stefano Casiraghi came, after all, from a seemingly rich although extremely private Italian family. His father created the original family fortune manufacturing heating and air conditioning equipment in Milan. After graduating from the city's university, Casiraghi set up a real estate business there. He opened a retail export firm. And prospered. With the profits from his own companies – assisted by family wealth – he became a financier. As such, he met Mario Contini.

Contini, older and thicker set but just as darkly handsome, was the more business-orientated of the two. And he worked hard to cultivate their association for its business advantages when Casiraghi married Monaco's Princess Caroline, already embarrassingly four months pregnant, in December 1983. It had to be a civil ceremony because the Vatican refused to annul her previous, twenty-eight-month marriage to French playboy Philippe Junot, whom she had legally divorced in 1980.

After his marriage Casiraghi officially restricted his business activities to that of being a financier, an activity carefully disguised by the publicly portrayed persona of a speed-loving playboy: his wedding present to Prince Caroline was a £150,000 Ferrari. The discretion which governed his commercial life fitted perfectly in Monaco. The secrecy of the state's financial system – even more absolute than usual because of his place within the ruling royal family – hides totally the beginning or the extent of his connection with Mario Contini. But the official who drank with me in Paris dated their partnership from as early as 1984 and thought it involved more than two companies.

Nineteen eighty-four was the year Casiraghi achieved world

ranking level in powerboat racing. In 1985 he set a world speed record for his class on Lake Como, in northern Italy, and in 1989, off Atlantic City, New Jersey, won the world offshore powerboat championship.

Out of the public eye Casiraghi privately – very privately indeed – pursued his business activities with Mario Contini. The fellow Italian prospered as well, if not as publicly, as Casiraghi. Contini had been the first of the two to move from Italy, supported at the beginning of his entrepreneurial career – as Casiraghi had been – by family money: in Contini's case it was from his father's hydro-carbon factory in Genoa.

He made his business base in Lausanne, Switzerland, another country where it is possible to set up discreet companies, although not as secure from official scrutiny as those he formed with Casiraghi in Monaco. As well as the necessary home in Lausanne, Contini purchased a villa in St Jean-Cap-Ferrat, the most exclusive of the exclusive millionaire retreats on the Riviera and a convenient drive in a Ferrari or Mercedes – Casiraghi's was white – from Monaco.

Through an intricate chain of companies in Lausanne, Contini acquired an interest in the Mandelieu casino, in which the French gaming authorities significantly had refused to allow fruit machines because of 'lack of openness' about the casino's capital structure. Another string of Contini's Swiss companies were connected with a superlative golf course at Taulanne, in Provence: one of its many boasts was that it had the biggest clubhouse in Europe.

Yet another Swiss company with which Contini was linked was Zenith Finance, whose president was another Italian, Florenzo Lei Ravello. Lei Ravello, who lives in Switzerland, is recorded on Italian police files as having Mafia associations. His was also one of the names found on the membership lists of Licio Gelli's P2 lodge during the 1980s investigation: in March 1980, an international arrest warrant was issued against him in connection with an Italian government financial scandal.

That warrant has never been executed, despite Lei Ravello's known presence in Switzerland and his frequent travels to France. A frequent destination during Lei Ravello's trips is Contini's villa at St Jean-Cap-Ferrat.

I understand[8] that Stefano Casiraghi visited the villa of his Monaco business partner at least twice when Lei Ravello was a house-guest. I further understand[9] that Lei Ravello was there on 3 October 1990, watching the world championship offshore power-boat race in which Casiraghi was defending the title he won the previous year. On that day – the second of the championship – Casiraghi's boat, *Pinot di Pinot*, hit a freak wave directly off St Jean-Cap-Ferrat and flipped, at 125mph. Co-driver Patrice Innocenti was thrown clear. Casiraghi took the full impact as the five ton catamaran smashed into the water and was then carried down with it. He died instantly.

It was the second occasion in eight years that Monaco was to be plunged into mourning as the result of an accident to one of its beautiful people. The first had been in September 1982, with the death of Princess Grace. The circumstances of that death are confused, and have fuelled over succeeding years so much speculation – even that it might have been a Mafia killing – that in April 1993, French judge Jacques Bidalou suggested a fresh enquiry. Prince Rainier let it be known he did not wish another investigation.

The accepted facts are that on the morning of 13 September Princess Grace was travelling with her seventeen-year-old second daughter, Princess Stephanie, back to Monaco from the Rainier holiday home, Roc Agel, at La Turbie in the Alps Maritime. The car was an eleven-year-old Rover 3500. Approximately three miles from the border, the car went out of control on a hairpin bend, somersaulted several times down a 120-foot ravine and ended against some trees in a farmer's garden.

Conflicting accounts began almost at once. The palace announced Princess Grace had suffered a broken leg and a fractured rib and collar bone, but was not in danger. Her condition was 'satisfactory'. Her daughter had a bruised vertebra.

A further palace statement said the accident had been caused because the brakes of the old car failed. The Monagasque police blamed brake failure. Two British Leyland engineers were sent from England to examine the wreckage. But a French lorry driver who had followed the car down the hairpin road said the Rover began to zig-zag just before the crash and then drove over the edge 'like an arrow'. No brake lights came on. And the farmer in whose field the vehicle ended, Cesto Lequiro, said he got Princess Stephanie from the front seat and Princess Grace from the back. The palace emphatically denied that Princess Stephanie had been driving: that would have been illegal in both France and Monaco, where the minimum driving age is eighteen.

The day after the accident, Princess Grace's condition deteriorated. At 9.30 p.m. she died. The palace said the cause of death was
an intra-cerebral vascular haemorrhage. But within twenty-four
hours Dr Jean Duplay, Nice's chief neuro-surgeon, said Princess
Grace had suffered a cerebral stroke while at the wheel of the car
and that Princess Stephanie had frantically tried to apply the
handbrake to stop it plunging into the ravine. Dr Duplay also
denied Princess Stephanie was driving. The palace said Dr
Duplay's account was the first they had heard of Princess Grace
suffering a stroke *before* the accident. Or of Princess Stephanie
struggling to stop the car with the handbrake. After their
examination, the two British engineers declared the brakes of the
Rover to be in perfect working order.

The eventual official findings – that the accident was as the result
of Princess Grace having a brain haemorrhage while she was
driving the car – did nothing to halt the speculation that there was
another, sinister cause.

The most persistent story is that Princess Grace had been
introduced to Mafia figures after her marriage to Prince Rainier.
After initially raising no objection to their shell company and
property development investments, however, she turned against
them, in some cases making enemies who feared she would use her
influence to drive them from the principality. Which her death
prevented happening.

The accusations in the 1993 French Commission report that the
Mafia were heavily involved in Monaco re-opened that speculation
and led to Judge Bidalou's rejected suggestion that the enquiry into
the 1982 tragedy be re-examined.

In a 1993 interview[10] an official of the Monaco government, Jean
Pastorelli, angrily denied the Mafia connection through the
friendship between Princess Grace and Frank Sinatra. Pastorelli
called it 'absolutely ridiculous and shameful' and added: 'There is a
rumour which has blown out of proportion based on the fact that
many Italians have settled in the principality.'

When the same question was put to Francois d'Aubert, who
headed the Commission, he replied far more enigmatically: 'The
report makes no mention of this.'

Challenged that some of the claims in the report included the link
between Stefano Casiraghi and Mario Contini, and Monaco
turning a blind eye to the source of principality investments
running into billions, D'Aubert said: 'Our information is checked

thoroughly and confirmed. But because the Commission's activities have been secret, we obviously could not reveal our sources. I can only tell you that we have thoroughly dissected the information given to us, in France and in Italy.'

I found one personally to dissect.

From that zinc-topped Paris bar near the Polish church to the sybaritic abandonment of the verandah restaurant at the Carlton Hotel during the Cannes film festival – with stops along the way – I traced an operation that perfectly illustrates the world-spanning, octopus-like grip of organised crime.

It stretched from Colombia into at least five countries in the European Union. It began, predictably, with drugs. And ended, just as predictably, in money laundering. And where was that laundering done? In Monaco, that loudly-protesting principality of financial rectitude.

Michele Zaza was the kingpin.

He set it all up from Marseille, from which the original French Connection in heroin operated. This time the drug was cocaine, not heroin. By odd coincidence Zaza – nicknamed Crazy Man because of his murderous temper – bears a striking and appropriate resemblance to the actor who played the Mafia killer in the movie of the same name: dark hair slightly receding, thick set and swarthy, broken nose heightening rather than impairing the could-be dangerous attraction, completed by perfect teeth sculpted for the ever ready smile. My friend in the Paris bar had met him, twice. Professionally. My drinking companion described Zaza as the sort of man who expects the chair to be ready for him, when he sits. Before anyone else. For doors to be opened, both literally and figuratively. Which they invariably were. And proud of the societies he belonged to, in particular his own Mafia family, obviously: it was one he had fashioned himself. Helped, of course, by the protective Freemasons. He was amused, apparently, that the initiation ceremonies of both threatened death if secrets were disclosed. In Crazy Man Zaza's case, he might have imposed the sentence.

The Crazy Man has been described as the supreme boss of the Camorra. He wasn't. He was the *capo di tutti capi* – the boss of bosses – of a breakaway faction called the *Nueva Famiglia* – the New Family – which he personally formed in 1980. But he *did* intend to become the supremo of an organised crime syndicate virtually encompassing the world. To which ambition a mid-80s arrest, in Italy, was an irritation, nothing more: at that time the Christian Democrats were in supposed power, in reality doing what they were told by their Mafia paymasters. As were the judiciary. An official of the time, still in office, told me in Rome[11] that Zaza's attitude was one of annoyed surprise, then patient resignation. 'He said he didn't expect to be with us long.'

He wasn't.

Complaining of a weak heart – the ploy also of Licio Gelli – Zaza got himself transferred from prison to a Rome hospital, although still in supposed custody. After a week he simply got out of bed and walked away, after getting his guards drunk.

He re-appeared a month later on the French Riviera, showing no signs of illness – which he hadn't shown in Italy either – and eager to make his New Family a happy one. Its independence, however, placed him in opposition to the traditional Camorra. No war erupted. He had taken a very sensible precaution from the beginning.

That sensible precaution the Crazy Man took was to invite Carmine (The Furious) Alfieri, the most powerful of all Camorra Dons, to join his Family. At the time of the invitation, Alfieri had been in hiding for ten years and had undergone plastic surgery to change his appearance from that on police-wanted posters and photographs. With an army of 4,000 gun-carrying retainers Alfieri ruled absolutely a territory the size of Yorkshire. Police who no longer knew what he looked like judged Alfieri the richest Mafia leader in Italy, with an income in excess of £750 million a year from drugs, building rackets, arms dealing and illegal lotteries. Zaza promised to make him even richer.

It was the same promise he made to the Fidanzati Family, a Cosa Nostra clan with which he was anxious to form an alliance and so prevent any war erupting with the Sicilian Mafia. A meeting of the Sicilian *cupola*, the Mafia's governing commission, approved the link-up.

On a false passport – police still do not know the name or the supposed nationality under which he travelled – Zaza flew, via pivotal, drugs-transhipping Venezuela, to Cali, in Colombia. There he negotiated the right to handle in Europe the cocaine production of Franklin Jurado Rodrigues, No. 3 in the Cali Cartel. Jurado agreed, with the request that Zaza set up for him a secure laundering facility in Europe. Zaza assured the Colombian he already had that prime essential in hand.

The importation of the cocaine was agreed to be mainly through the porous Galicia province in Spain, which was predominantly under the control of the heavily moustached, flop-haired Benedetto (Nitto) Santapaola, Godfather of the Catania Family of the Sicilian Cosa Nostra and a member of the *cupola* which had approved the Fidanzati joining the New Family.

His professional Family established, Zaza set up home with his real family in a luxurious villa in Villeneuve-Loubet, near Nice, and registered his children in the local school. He took an office – although not in his name – in Marseille and almost immediately began that most important of Mafia activities, trying to find amenable judges who could be relied upon for help if help were ever needed. True to his promise to Jurado Rodrigues, in Colombia, he opened hidden bank accounts in Monaco, with the Banque Industrielle de Monaco (BIM). And he took a hidden but influential shareholding in a property development company named Sofextour, through which he had big money laundering intentions.

Although domiciled from legal necessity in France, Crazy Man Zaza did not sever his links with Italy. Through his merging with Alfieri, Zaza still supervised his prostitution, gambling and restaurant empire along Italy's Ligurian coastline, which reached to the very borders of Monaco. It was into the principality and his well-concealed bank accounts and companies there that the profits were channelled. Neither did Zaza abandon another traditional multi-million Mafia activity, cigarette smuggling. He used that particular business both for its guaranteed profits and also to test smuggling routes and so select the safest along which to move his cocaine.

When the cocaine began to flow some of it was refined as far away as Belgium. As well as in Monaco, he laundered through banks and financial outlets in Germany, France and Italy.

Zaza's New Family prospered unbelievably. Police, who were to recover £1 billion – mostly in cash – when the organisation was finally smashed, estimated that to be only a fraction of the income Zaza generated as the Riviera's Don of Dons. It would have been even more if the casino take-over had been successful. Which it almost was.

And that despite the fact that Zaza was in custody. He had been arrested again in 1989 and charged with cigarette smuggling: he spent the entire negotiation period in jail, on remand. Although he wasn't actually able to escape, as he had in Italy, prison wasn't a problem. Money bought the cooperation of guards and it was practically as easy to run the New Family from inside a penitentiary as it was from outside.

Zaza's group already had virtual control of the San Remo casino, just across the border in Italy: Sergio Cortes, a member of the New Family, had infiltrated himself as the casino's director of gaming. This gave the New Family *carte blanche* to wash money in the simplest way possible, accounting for a proportion of their vast income as gambling winnings, with certified documentation from the casino to guarantee the claim to any questioning tax or financial police official. But so vast was that income – other tranches of which they were funnelling into property development along the Ligurian coast – that from jail Zaza decided they needed to own another convenient gambling outlet. He targeted Menton's Casino du Soleil, closed in April 1989 by French Interior Minister Pierre Joxe after the chairman of its management company was found guilty of fraud. Ironically, at the time of the closure, Joxe had declared: 'Gambling is serving to launder dirty money from crime and drugs.'

The New Family take-over – to continue the use on account of which the casino had been officially closed – was to be by the Sofextour company, whose publicly identified front man, chairman and managing director Alexis Svereff, was the brother-in-law of Sergio Cortes, who had put the San Remo gambling establishment to such good use. Into the Sofextour account Zaza ordered £2 million to be moved to fund the initial bid: it was deposited at the Banco di Roma.

In France, casino operating companies have to be approved by a commercial court. Zaza was confident that would not be a difficulty, despite a questionable report upon Sofextour, particularly querying its income source, from the Gaming Commission: the chief judge of that court, in Nice, was Jean Bigarani, who had become an amenable friend. And so he proved to be. The Sofextour bid – approved in August 1990 – was described by Bigarani's court as the 'best presented commercially and socially'.

But it was – for Zaza and the New Family – a short-lived triumph.

Sofextour was not the only company working to acquire the Menton establishment. The Barrière Group – the biggest casino-running conglomerate in France – was also tendering. Unaware of the decision in Sofextour's favour in Nice, in Menton the mayor Jean-Claude Guibal, with the approval of both the French Ministries of Interior and of Finance, signed an agreement with Barrière, who were granted the right to manage the Casino du Soleil by the Ministry of Interior in December 1990.

Confronted with the decision of higher authority, the Nice court was forced to rescind its licensing approval for Sofextour, which it did in February 1991.

Zaza's defeat did not end there. Marseille magistrate Jean-Francois Sampieri, a fervent anti-organised crime campaigner, began investigating Sofextour. Alexei Svereff was arrested, along with fellow director Felix Santoni, a former croupier. Under questioning – during which both men wrongly accused Judge Bigarani, Mayor Guibal, and the mayor's assistant, Colette Jourdan, of accepting bribes – Svereff named as a sleeping partner Giovanni Tagliamento, a known Camorra gangster who had joined the New Family and was a known associate of Michele Zaza.

Zaza's problems continued. The French authorities began investigating the Monte Carlo-registered Banque Industrielle de Monaco (BIM) after the mysterious death of its front man director. When the bank went into liquidation, laying the accounts open to scrutiny, detectives discovered deposits in the name of Sofextour. They also uncovered the secret accounts of Zaza's Colombian partner, Franklin Jurado Rodrigues. With the Monaco accounts of Jurado Rodrigues as a starting point, Customs investigators traced a total of £36 million in drugs money – all of which was seized – from ninety-one different accounts spread through fifteen countries and tax havens. Under French banking regulations, depositors in a failed French financial institution are entitled to compensation from a guarantee fund. In the case of the collapsed Banque Industrielle de Monaco, that compensation was set at almost £48,000 per account. There were 1,600 depositors, some identified only by numbered accounts, yet out of those 1,600, less than a thousand risked public exposure by coming forward to make a claim. The rest sacrificed everything to retain their precious anonymity.

In Marseille Judge Sampieri was closing both the case and Sofextour, with investigations spreading throughout the South of France and beyond. He began issuing international arrest warrants, upon which other countries could act. The special Italian unit, the Direzione Investigativa Anti-Mafia (DIA) became involved. They initiated a Europe-wide hunt, codenamed Green Sea, for people accused by Judge Sampieri, linking them with other organised crime figures on their own most wanted lists: in May 1993, Green Sea swept through the European Union like a tidal wave. Perhaps the most important arrest was that of Carmine Alfieri, the man without a police face, who was seized near the Italian city of Nola. Crazy Man Zaza was arrested at his villa at Villeneuve-Loubet. Zaza's chief lieutenant, Dante Sacca, had already been sentenced to ten years' imprisonment *in absentia* at the same cigarette smuggling trial that put Zaza in prison during the attempted take-over of the Menton casino. Sacca's replacements, Antonio Sarnataro and Generoso del Gaizo, were detained. Giovanni Tagliamento, a money laundering expert fingered by Sofextour front man Alexis Svereff, was seized in Germany. Sergio Cortes' rule at the San Remo casino ended with his arrest there. In a farmhouse near Mazzarone, in Sicily, Benedetto Santapaola – who masterminded the Colombian cocaine importation through Spain – was surprised, innocently asleep in bed with his wife, when police swooped.

Operation Green Sea put out of business the most important multi-national organised crime group to have so far crossed the border from Italy, and begun operations in France.

The Riviera still has its own indigenous organised crime syndicates prepared to kill and terrorise, creating mob rule in the sun. Few are prepared to stand up to them. One who attempted to do so, French MP Madame Yann Piat, was murdered. Another – an Englishman – is actually claiming millions in compensation because of the inconvenience.

CHAPTER NINE

The French Affair

The coastal development looked like a perfect scheme. Perfect for everyone. Perfect for the European Union which saw it from Brussels as precisely the sort of joint venture between nations that the EC had been created to foster with millions in economic regional aid. Perfect for the second largest town in the Var, La Seyne, rapidly dying after the closure of its once-thriving shipyard. Perfect for the national government in Paris, anxious to revitalise an area with an unemployment rate exceeding twenty per cent and rising. Perfect for the English consortium which planned over ten years to spend £120 million creating a combined pleasure and business complex on a sea world theme: a *marepolis*.

But most perfect of all for the local Mafia. They thought.

It became anything but perfect, however, when they encountered a wealthy, implacable British entrepreneur who refused to quit, who has totally out-manoeuvred them in their efforts to gain control of the project, and who is using French law against them in a way they never anticipated. Which they don't like.

Melville Mark was seventy-two years old when we met,[1] not in the South of France which he talks of with a poet's passion for beauty, but in the grey-skied London suburb of Clapham Common, Shangri La to shantyland. He didn't intend to give in, he insisted. Or give up. The local mafia had misjudged, perhaps for the first time. He knew their reputations and what they were capable of. But some*thing* or some*body* had to give way, and it wasn't going to be his consortium. Certain people should have realised that. He'd been warned by French friends he could be murdered: he accepted it could happen. Which didn't mean he was stupidly brave. He preferred to think of himself as realistic. If Popes and American Presidents can be shot at, so can he. If the Mafia made their minds up, they could do it. If it happened, there were names he'll scrawl 'with my last dying strength' to guide the police investigation.

It was in 1989 that Mark came upon the derelict former dockyard of La Seyne and knew at once it was the ideal site for a revolutionary concept suggested by his marine biologist professor son: a maritime and business complex just across the bay from Toulon. A development company called The World Sea Centre Ltd was formed. Its partners included investment company Chesterfield Properties and Urban Waterside Ltd, a firm that had earlier revitalised England's then decaying Salford Quay, and the Marmot Group, experienced in development renewal in London's East End.

The first of many surveys confirmed Mark's initial belief that no better location could be found: the site – like his consortium – had everything. What he didn't learn, until later, was the history of the area in which he intended to develop.

The story went back four years before Melville Mark and the World Sea Centre consortium arrived in La Seyne. In 1985, the shipyard – laid out by British engineers one hundred years earlier – went bankrupt. Four thousand men were thrown out of work overnight, in a town where most of its 60,000 inhabitants relied to some degree upon the dockyard. And thrown out of office, after thirty-seven years of uninterrupted power, was the communist controlled council that had failed to prevent the bankruptcy happening.

Into power in that all-important role of mayor swept Charles Scaglia – a member of the Union of French Democracy (UDF). Scaglia's first – although very far from last – act of patronage was to appoint to La Seyne's town hall, as his personal assistant, Daniel Perrin.

Perrin was a professional of an undefined profession, a man who could detect in the wind of change the faintest scent of any possible benefit, particularly if it were financial.

Melville Mark talks of the differing priorities of the various

Mafias along the Riviera. The predominant underworld activity in Marseille, for instance, is drug dealing. In the Var of La Seyne and Toulon and Hyeres, the concentration is split between local politics and the building industry, in which there are virtually limitless public funds to be milked in limitless ways.

Daniel Perrin was a professional in that field, certainly, a director of a property agency who was at the same time acting as treasurer for the electoral campaign that had brought the grateful Scaglia to power. Scaglia appointed Perrin – a virulent racist and anti-communist – to a position which virtually made him deputy mayor. It was Perrin who supervised the contracts and the financial arrangements of the town's highways and refuse collection. Who supervised the building permission for private development. And approved the contracts for council house building and their maintainence. A man who openly admitted to me his fear of physical harm if he were identified,[2] estimated that the value of 'special favour gratitude' for such contract allocations ran into millions, each year.

Perrin was arrogantly unconcerned at being publicly identified with local organised crime figures or political extremists. He was a frequent guest at a La Seyne restaurant called L'Escale, often sitting at the table of its owner, Le Seyne's Godfather Louis (Loulou) Regnier. Another close friend was Claude Noblia, who belonged to the pro-Fascist Party of the New Force, and whom Scaglia made administrator of the council's housing office. On 17 August 1986, Noblia and three other fascists were blown to unidentifiable pieces when the bomb with which they were preparing to destroy a crowded hostel for immigrants in Toulon exploded prematurely. Scaglia mourned at their funeral.

Perrin's lucrative tenure as the man who awarded business contracts turned out to be as short-lived as Scaglia's gratitude for helping him to office: having achieved that office, in order to retain it Scaglia had to maintain his friendships with more important political power-brokers. One absolutely essential friend was Maurice Arrackx, the president of the Var Regional Council later to appear on Madame Piat's 'in-the-event-of-my-death' list. Arrackx and Scaglia knew each other well. Before his election as mayor of Le Seyne, Scaglia had been secretary general – mostly involved in finance – of the Var Regional Council under Arrackx's presidency. Arrackx had other friends, of course. One, from childhood, was Jean-Louis Fargette, the Don of the Toulon Mafia whose 1993 assassination has been linked by rumour – but by nothing else – to Madame Piat.

Soon after Scaglia's election in 1985, Arrackx began extolling the unquestionable ability of a friend and former administrative assistant, lawyer Yvan Valenti: less than a year after assuming office, Scaglia obeyed the political rules and appointed Valenti his office director, a position the lawyer had fulfilled so successfully in so many other parts of the Var.

Daniel Perrin, a man who could sniff the wind of change for its advantages, could also detect when it was not blowing in his favour. There were shouted rows between Perrin and Valenti, some of them in public. Perrin succeeded in blocking a development proposal on the shipyard site by a Marseilles friend of Valenti's and rejected another shipyard plan, championed by Valenti, put forward by a company based at Fabregues, near Montpellier. But he failed to prevent the privatisation of water distribution and the collection of household refuse going to a company of Valenti's choice. Or to stop the Fabregues firm being awarded the contract for another building project. Or block the creation of an industrial complex in a suburb of Le Seyne.

The public arguments went beyond Valenti. Perrin protested personally to Scaglia at his loss of power and influence. When that appeal fell on deaf ears, he wrote letters criticising outside companies and firms chosen by Valenti to carry out civic work, paradoxically (for an expert in the system of French local government) alleging the costs were far in excess of what they would have been if their own services had done the jobs.

On Friday 29 August 1986, Perrin was approaching his home at La Seyne – just as Madame Piat was to do eight years later – when two men on a motorcycle drew up alongside, again as in the case of Madame Piat. Four bullets were pumped into Perrin's body. He died instantly. Yvan Valenti was among a number of people interviewed by the police. After an 11-hour interrogation, Valenti was released, without charge. The murder of Daniel Perrin remains unsolved.

'It's not boy scouts that we are talking about,' judged Melville Mark, during our Clapham meeting. Who we *were* talking about was Charles Scaglia, still the mayor of La Seyne and the man at the centre of Mark's dispute with the town's municipality.

Mark had received his first indication of the Mafia system by which construction work operates on the Riviera during a conversation in London in 1990 with the French representative of a subsidiary of Lyonnaise des Eaux, with whom his consortium were considering becoming involved in a joint venture. 'He said to me "have you met the little men yet?" I said: "What little men? I don't know what you're talking about." He said: "This project at some stage will meet difficulties and when it meets them you will get a visit from the little men and they will tell you they can solve things for you". I said: "Nonsense. It doesn't happen in France. Have you got personal experience of it or are you just telling me stories?" He said "I have personal experience". I ignored it. I didn't take it in.'

He was to take it in, later. As he was to take in a lot more. The initial stages of the negotiations were smooth and extremely amicable. There were no serious disagreements in the four preliminary development contracts, all of which Scaglia signed, the last in October 1992. There were meetings with the all-powerful Maurice Arrackx, who appeared as eager as everyone else to restore prosperity to the town which had once made the giant battleships for the French navy, headquartered just across the bay at Toulon. Dr Arthur Paecht, mayor of nearby Bandol and a UDF deputy at the National Assembly in Paris, offered his support, too.

But then, as the local council began clearing the disused site in preparation for the £120 million scheme to begin, Scaglia tossed in the bombshell. He declared that the development had to be extended to include a huge, multi-lane bridge that would span part of the bay to link Toulon to La Seyne. The entire scheme, Scaglia insisted, had to be re-negotiated.

On a map dominating one wall of his loft-straddling office Mark traced for me Scaglia's additional proposal. Apart from a total lack of practicality – completely destroying any commercial benefit by carrying traffic *through* the marine complex, without its being able to stop – including Scaglia's bridge would be aesthetically abominable, like giving the Mona Lisa a third eye, in the middle of her forehead.

Soon after Scaglia tried to impose his absurd bridge on the development there began the quiet-voiced telephone calls which Mark had been warned of two years earlier in the conversation about 'little men'. Mark told his persistent callers that the British group was not going to get involved 'in an exchange of envelopes, come hell or high water'.

Instead, Mark commissioned an independent study of Scaglia's proposal from the international engineering consultants Ove Arup and Partners. It cost him £30,000 and concluded the bridge would totally destroy the sea-world concept. There were eighteen separate meetings with technical engineers appointed by Scaglia. Nothing emerged to convince Mark or his partners that the Scaglia idea made any sense. The French economist and civil servant assigned to be director general of the development, Patrick Martinenq – whom Mark calls 'a totally honest man' – publicly sided with the British, and was promptly sacked by Scaglia. I have been told[3] Martinenq risks assassination for speaking out so publicly. I further understand[4] that replacement Jacques Mikaelian – a protege of Maurice Arrackx – feels professionally exactly the same as Martinenq about the bridge. But by not expressing himself so openly he has shown more political savvy – and far more realistic concern for his own personal safety – than his predecessor.

The quiet-voiced telephone calls promising to remove obstacles continued. And were rejected, as before. By now Mark had become an expert – perhaps, for some, *too* expert – in Mafia construction manipulation and was coming to believe the bridge had never been a serious suggestion. If a compromise had been reached over the bridge idea, he suspects there would probably have been another blackmailing proposal, perhaps to drive a canal through the site, anything that would block building work until that proposal, too, had been resolved. Mark likens it to gel in a tube: if it doesn't come out one end it spills from the other, under pressure.

At this tightly squeezing stage a cash figure that might resolve the bridge difficulty finally entered the telephone conversations. Mark's caller suggested that the consortium's eventual budget of around £120 million could possibly be made to include, from the French side, a public funding allocation of five hundred million francs. At the conversion rate applicable at the time that amounted to approximately £50 million. The little man who could remove obstacles pointed out there would, of course, need to be a ten per cent commission. 'So the pay-off was to be £5 million,' recalls Mark. 'We believe it was totally phoney and totally false – that there never was any public fund allocation of five hundred million francs – but it was a means of introducing the bribery figure.'

Mark is sure that by then the approaches were even more convoluted. His theory is that, having studied the development plans the British had spent millions preparing, the Mafia realised the enormous commercial potential of the scheme. So they didn't want merely a £5 million bribe – they wanted the whole project. And thought they had a way to get it. Had Mark agreed to pay the £5 million, it would have been exposed for the bribe it was. But which, it would be claimed, had never been sought: there was, after all, no proof of any demand, just ambiguous, unrecorded telephone calls. The accusation of attempted bribery would, however, give the local authorities legal grounds for expelling the British consortium.

Instead they now face the prospect of getting nothing but public exposure. Because Mark outsmarted them.

He didn't pay any bribe. But – despite being confronted by a virtual stone wall of local municipal obstruction – he didn't quit either. World Sea Centre Ltd retain an office and employees in La Seyne. They hold contracts signed by Charles Scaglia which are legally binding under French law to develop the 75-acre site. And they've issued compensation writs against La Seyne for more than £13 million.

The effect of this is potentially devastating for the Var Mafia. They can't move in on the dockyard, which World Sea Centre Ltd still legally holds the right to develop. Neither can any other Mafia-approved or dominated consortium take over. And Sea Centre's damages claim means that the financial affairs of the La Seyne municipality – the most closely guarded secret of all – have to be disclosed and examined by the Nice-based Administrative Tribunal of the Civil Service – essentially a public audit commission. Already a number of financial irregularities have emerged. On the dull grey day we met at Clapham, Mark was sending to France by messenger his responses to a number of questions from the audit commission resulting from those irregularities. Mark was well prepared to respond to them. He has maintained meticulous records of every stage of his consortium's negotiations and transactions with La Seyne. And the non-confrontational Code Napoléon system of French law is predicated on documentary investigation.

The difficulties for La Seyne's mayor are not limited to the determination of Melville Mark. In March 1994, the unimaginable occurred. Maurice Arrackx, *éminence grise*, political godfather of the UDF in general but of Charles Scaglia in particular, was defeated in cantonal elections for president of the Var Regional

Council by a candidate from the National Front, the original party of Madame Piat.

Pragmatically Mark doubts the political changes will continue long enough to bring about a substantial shift in the administration of La Seyne, although Charles Scaglia's position is weakened. But Mark is prepared to pursue his damages claim. And to wait. 'Our position is very clear and very simple. We are *there*. We have entered into binding contracts with the administration of La Seyne which we are prepared to honour. And which we expect to be honoured in return. We will not re-negotiate. There is nothing *to* re-negotiate.'

In the meantime, Melville Mark will continue to take the advice of worried friends by being careful during his frequent visits to La Seyne, although, as he puts it, 'if they've decided to do it there's not a lot I can do about it'.

Except, of course, prepare the sort of list that Madame Piat left.

Forty-four year old Yann Piat knew the dangers. Knew she had deadly enemies even beyond those she might have made from her contribution to the anti-Mafia enquiry conducted by Francois d'Aubert, which was probably the most detailed account of organised crime the Commission received. As National Assembly Deputy for the Var region of Provence, Yann Piat had been involved for years in the politics and the intrigues in the region, around Toulon and Hyères and even Marseille. So frightened people tried to frighten her. She warned a parliamentary colleague against visiting her South of France constituency because it might start 'raining grenades'. The threats had been serious: the personal worst was perhaps the tiny coffins delivered to her Hyères home with the names of her two daughters, Laetitia and Angelique, inscribed on the sides. But in an election round in March 1992, a live grenade *was* thrown at her campaign headquarters, shattering windows. She assured other MPs she was careful. Her most positive precaution was to write an 'in-the-event-of-my-death' letter to her lawyer, identifying people she regarded as enemies.

At 8.30 p.m. on Friday 25 February 1994, Madame Piat was approaching her villa, Le Mas Bleu, in a private road on the Mont des Oiseaux, in a chauffeur-driven Renault Clio when two men came up behind on a stolen Yamaha motorcycle. The pillion passenger fired one shot at driver Georges Arnaud, forcing him to stop with a bullet in the leg. With the vehicle stationary, the contract assassins pumped five more bullets into the car, most through the rear window. Two hit Madame Piat, killing her instantly.

'A nuisance,' I was told.[5] 'She was respected in Paris – regarded as brave even – but down here certain people didn't like her. Thought she was meddlesome. That's what they thought of her, a nuisance. But one to be taken seriously, of course.'

What Madame Piat meddled in was exposing organised crime. She wrote a report on drug trafficking in the Var region – which she made available to the d'Aubert Commission – and frequently accused local politicians of links with mobsters. The most meddlesome of all was her determination – which would probably have succeeded – to enhance her already established national position by becoming a local politician herself, by campaigning to become mayor of Hyères, which some French newspapers label 'the Chicago of the Midi (the South).'

Mayors of towns and cities throughout the European Union wield great power and influence – far more so than their largely ceremonial counterparts in England – but none so much as in France. Had she been elected, Madame Piat would have governed an administration of local and nationally contributed revenues, as well as possible regional allocations from the European Union in Brussels. She would have been responsible for the hiring and firing of municipal staff. Building development and business investment and expansion would have come within her jurisdiction. And with access to the records of previous years she would have been able to learn how such administration had been carried out in the past. Which would have provided her with even more names than those she already knew.

All that power – and the access to the past – in the hands of a meddlesome, anti-corruption nuisance, was a very unwelcome prospect indeed to the organised crime clans and their cooperative friends in local government offices and departments. A man with extensive experience of the construction business in the area told me, with practical cynicism[6]: 'Someone had to be killed and it wasn't going to be the well established system. What she was trying was too controversial.'

Controversy was nothing strange to Yann Piat.

She was a twice-married, strong-featured person with startling blue eyes and short black hair, with a penchant for the bright colours of designer dresses and the instinctive chic that only French women truly possess. She was actually born, illegitimately, in Vietnam, during French colonial rule: her father was killed in the battle of Dien Bien Phu, in 1954. Her mother, Luce Millet – a descendant of the French painter Jean-Francois Millet – was a mistress of Jean-Marie Le Pen, years later to emerge an international figure as the leader in France of the far right National Front (FN). Le Pen was not her father, although for a period of her life she believed him to be. The child was five years old when they first met: Le Pen took to calling her his god-daughter. The association was interrupted by his entry into politics but in 1976 Le Pen traced her and persuaded her to join his far right movement. He has never properly explained why he went to so much trouble to locate her. By the time he succeeded she was twenty-six years old.

She agreed to enter politics. They were to become her life. And they cost it. In 1977, when she started her political career as the National Front's organiser for the Toulon-Hyères district and as its secretary for the Department of the Var, she learned far more than just politics. She learned how much money could be made from kick-backs by people in authority with the power to award building contracts. And she knew the amounts, so much of them in cash, that were available. She came to know the local politicians-for-life whose re-elections always seemed automatic, and to understand the immense power – and wealth – such men possessed. But always the knowledge was gained from the *outside* – isolated scraps of information, half a story, never the whole – and that was where the local men of influence were determined to keep her. Not that in those early days Yann Piat was looked upon as the threat she later became. They regarded her as a dedicated extremist trying to gain support for an extremist party: she was tolerated more than feared. But rarely despised: the French are the most xenophobic nation in Europe and even in the late 1970s Yann Piat's campaigning to keep France for the French found receptive ears. The man who referred to her as a nuisance for her later activities thought her early political campaigning had not earned her many enemies. 'It was always the other business that was her trouble. Poking her nose in where she shouldn't.'

The effectiveness of Yann Piat's political campaigning was proved in 1986. That was the year she became one of thirty National Front deputies to enter the French Parliament under the system of proportional representation that existed in France at that time. There were many around Hyères and Toulon who were relieved at her victory, believing that she would spend far more time five hundred miles to the north, in Paris, and that in the heady atmosphere of national politics she would lose interest in the comfortable, understood-among-those-who-need-to-know way things operated in the Var. They were wrong.

A change in the electoral system was a disaster for the National Front. In the next election in May 1988, Madame Piat was the only National Front deputy to retain her seat: ironically she lost her party patronage at practically the same time. Soon after her success, the racist Le Pen made a grotesquely offensive word play on the phrase *four crématoire* – French for Nazi crematorium – by calling minister Michel Durafour '*Durafour crématoire*'. In a fierce public rebuke of her mentor and party leader, which effectively ended their relationship, Madame Piat described it as 'schoolboy dormitory humour,' adding that Le Pen had been 'maladroit'.

In October of that year she was expelled from the National Front, officially for refusing to obey voting instructions. She remained an independent for just one year. Then she joined the conservative Republican Party, one of the groups comprising the Union for French Democracy (UDF), the party of former French President Valery Giscard d'Estaing. Madame Piat was elected to the National Assembly as a representative of the Var department centred around Toulon in March 1993: it was during that campaign that the grenade was thrown at her party headquarters.

That grenade was the most positive attack against a woman who had alarmed local politicians by canvassing on an anti-Mafia, anti-corruption ticket, but there were many verbal threats, as well. They increased after she readily agreed to become a leader of Francois d'Aubert's Anti-Mafia Commission and to make available to it her independently-compiled report and information on drug trafficking and property manipulation in the Var. Rumours began, too: suggestions that in her eagerness to acquire information Madame Piat had actually become personally involved with some sections of organised crime, particularly in Marseille.[7] Those accusations intensified after the contract assassination – in the same month as Madame Piat's election success – in Italy of long-time Toulon Mafia Godfather Jean-Louis Fargette.

Fargette had been forced to flee to Italy in the early 1980s to avoid arrest after French authorities identified him as the Don of Toulon's organised crime. The exile did not prevent Fargette continuing to run his crime empire from a base near Bordighera, but his enforced absence made that empire vulnerable to take-over by a rival mafia clan. Police have been told[8] that for some years Madame Piat had been trying to discover the full extent of Fargette's crime business: and that to learn about it she had met other gangsters prepared to supply information upon which the Italians could arrest the man, and so leave his operation open for them to take it over. To the police has been put a further suggestion[9] that some of Fargette's Family believe Madame Piat betrayed their Don, setting him up to be assassinated. I believe a lot of those accusations to be part of a groundless smear campaign against her.

Madame Piat's defeated opponent in the 1993 national election was the vice president of the Var Regional Council Joseph Sercia, a rotound, perpetually-smiling man who favours pencil-line moustaches and suits made from material that has a sheen. The name of Sercia was on the 'in-the-event-of-harm' list deposited by Madame Piat with her lawyer, Sylvain Garant. The letter accused Sercia of using public money to finance political campaigns and of embezzling a £6,000 sports grant. Investigating detectives have established that Sercia knew Fargette. Despite some initial denials, they also established that Sercia knew the two men – Ipifanio Pericolo and Denis Labadie – initially arrested but later released on suspicion of Madame Piat's murder. Both Pericolo and Labadie worked for Fargette. Also listed in Madame Piat's letter was Sercia's boss, septuagenarian Maurice Arreckx, the then President of the Var Regional Council and the self proclaimed 'political godfather' of the political right which ruled the Var locally. Under questioning by police – when they called on Arreckx he was in his pyjamas – both he and Sercia denied any knowledge of Madame Piat's murder. So, too, did the third politician named in her letter, millionaire French Socialist MP Bernard Tapie. Sercia, in turn, accused Madame Piat of accepting kick-backs because she was short of money and in campaign debt: her villa, close to where she was shot, was known to be up for sale. The accusation was rejected by lawyer Sylvain Garant, who pointed out with some logic that her dead client would not have had financial problems if she were in the pay of an organised crime group.

The killing of a national French politician – a previous one had been that of Prince Jean de Broglie in 1976 over a business dispute – forced the government in Paris to abandon its customary aloof lack of interest in crime that took place so conveniently far away, down in the south. Police reinforcements were moved into Toulon from

Paris and Marseille and Interior Minister Charles Pasqua publicly vowed there would be no cover-up. Few people with whom I discussed the Piat assassination were impressed by the minister's promise. 'Cover up what or whom?' questioned one.[10] 'What's to hide?'

A huge amount is the answer.

And an exasperated, hard-headed British businessman could be far more successful than Monsieur Pasqua in exposing the politically-motivated chicanery that Madame Piat fought so hard against. Even to the death.

CHAPTER TEN

There's Something in the Air

In Europe's first Industrial Revolution of the nineteenth century, that 'something' was smoke belching from factory chimneys, accompanied by the deafening roar of machines. People could see it and understand what it was. It was tangible.

Not so in the second industrial revolution, which is as much industrial as it is technological and which has had – and goes on having – a profound effect upon the European Union's 340 million inhabitants. But people can't see or hear a thing and the majority affected by it – which is *everyone* – only vaguely understand it. In fact, because it's so intangible European law-makers have had difficulty evolving satisfactory legislation to confront its inevitable money-making corollary, crime. Several countries in the Union still haven't although in February 1995, the European Council of Ministers agreed the text of a draft Directive that will still take more than a year to be finally adopted. And yet again there will be insufficient harmonisation, opening as many law-breaking loop-holes as have been closed.

The only section of society that, with familiar predictability, has fully understood the advantage of such technology is once more organised crime.

The computer – and the microchip that makes it work – have revolutionised not just Europe but the world, making a truism of the global village cliché. Computers were crossing frontiers in milliseconds long before the European boundaries came down in January 1993.

Social security and health data is stored in them. Population and census details are recorded in them. Telecommunication relies on them. Companies and governments and ministries communicate through them. Scientific research is conducted with their help. Universities and libraries entrust their knowledge to them. Crime – and the names of its amateur and professional practioners – is logged in them. Banks, insurance companies, finance houses and credit card companies are dependent upon them. Supermarkets and stores are run by them. Car engines work and are monitored by them. Ships sail and are navigated by them. Computers operate the controls of airliners far more than their human pilots, and air traffic is conducted by them. They took man to the moon, are the brains of space shuttles, and ensure that satellites stay in orbit properly to receive and respond to the instructions other computers relay from earth several miles below.

And none is totally secure from unauthorised entry, abuse, alteration or manipulation.[1] It's bonanza-time for the bandits of cyberspace. They're not called cyberspace bandits, though. They're called hackers.

Hackers – computer literate intruders who *do* understand the mysteries of the microchip – have broken into America's National Aeronautics and Space Administration, into the Pentagon (providing the inspiration for a hit movie), into the Los Alamos nuclear research centre, into the Ministries – that of Defence, in Britain – of several Europe Union countries, into the European Space Agency installation at the Max Planck Institute at Heidelberg, and into several NATO installations, both in Europe and America. At least two of those NATO entries, during the Cold War, are believed[2] to have been masterminded by the KGB, employing European hackers.

Because of the fear of losing customer confidence, financial institutions refuse to confess their losses – and the fact that there is no EU law requiring them to do so – the monetary loss is incalculable but is estimated in billions, Europe-wide.

The intrusions are not always with the direct intention to steal money. Just as valuable – in some cases much more so – is the confidential or top secret information that can be accessed, read and copied, either for substantial resale to company competitors or to create other databanks, for personal use and the sheer enjoyment of possessing what shouldn't be possessed. Blackmail is an easy and frequently unreported crime: I believe[3] that several European supermarkets have paid substantial sums of money to prevent their computer systems being rendered inoperative (the technical term is 'crashing') by an unknown hacker holding them to ransom at the touch of a single key on an untraceable keyboard. Near perfect forgery and counterfeiting is just as easy. As it is easy, too, for anyone – including a child – to summon on to their VDU whatever sort of pornography takes their fancy.

The Paris-based Organisation for Economic Co-operation and Development was one of the first organisations to acknowledge the dangers as well as the benefits created by computers. In a guidance document[4] it warned: 'Society, including business, public services and individuals, has become very dependent on technologies that are not yet sufficiently dependable. All the uses of information systems . . . are vulnerable to attack upon or failures of information systems. There are risks of loss from unauthorised access, use, misappropriation, modification or destruction of information systems, which may be caused accidentally or result from purposeful activity. Certain information systems, both public and private, such as those in military or defence installations, nuclear power plants, hospitals, transport systems and security exchanges offer fertile ground for anti-social behaviour or terrorism.'

Hackers are fond of arguing[5] that by breaking into computer systems and leaving their calling cards they perform a valuable service in alerting the lawful owners and operators their systems are insecure. That illogical argument is frequently extended to include an insistence that there should be no block or barrier upon the exchange of information.

Of course information should be shared and exchanged, as widely as possible: the sooner the EU gets a proper Freedom of Information Act the better democracy will be served. But I do not believe there is a sustainable argument that freedom and exchange of information should extend to the research and development upon which a company has spent millions and upon which its viability depends. Or to personal medical or financial records.

The miracle of the microchip is the speed, measured in millionths of a second, at which it can function. It is the hacker's basic tool. The others are simple: the computer containing the chip and a connected modem that can link into a telephone system, providing access to the outside world. That access is rarely, if ever, acquired through the hacker's own number: the cost of travelling electronically around the globe to play Peeping Tom would be astronomical and make it easy for the hacker to be traced. Before any hacker starts his serious work he enters the system of one of a number of companies or subscribers to which he has already gained access, so that all the charges go against someone else's account.

It is possible to write a programme that, once connected through a public telephone system, can scan – it's called 'number crunching' – *every* number listed in the directories of cities the size of London, Paris, Rome or Berlin. And electronically to identify every telecommunication number feeding an on-line computer, to be stored on disc for later search and possible entry. Passwords, to gain access to the connected systems, can sometimes be guessed at or calculated from random searches – again conducted at split-second speed – or learned from what are known as bulletin boards.

There are two sorts of bulletin board, the legitimate and the illegitimate. Both are similar to the directory and message centre that forty years ago, before computer utilisation began, was customarily covered in green baize and fixed to a communal office wall for information like internal telephone numbers and company news to be displayed. The only difference now is that electronic bulletin boards are no longer hung from walls but suspended in cyberspace, the technical term for the intangible infinity through which the intangible products of computers are held or move. Computer bulletin boards are still only supposed to be read by those authorised to receive their information, but in the age of the determined hacker bulletin boards are virtually open books. Incredibly, quite often, the passwords and security over-ride codes the hacker seeks are listed on the legitimate bulletin boards: *the major factor making computer crime one of the easiest and safest of all illegal activities is how few precautions are taken by companies and operators to protect their property.*

Once a bulletin board has been opened up for hacker inspection, it becomes available for all on an illegal bulletin board, maintained and constantly updated *by* hackers *for* hackers. Any newly dis-covered and interesting computer number, password and security code is listed. So are the numbers to dial – and to charge against the company through which the call is routed – for hundreds of pornographic movies, magazines and still photographs. As well as the numbers of stolen credit cards, against which it is still known to be safe – from the hacked-in checks made into the credit card companies' systems – to charge purchases. And to match stolen or intercepted PIN numbers against stolen or intercepted bank accounts and telephone chargecards and credit cards. And newly discovered and interesting computer numbers, passwords and security codes, which usually aren't necessary after the first intrusion: no experienced hacker quits a penetrated system without leaving his own permanent entry password, giving him – and often every subsequent illegal bulletin board reader – unlimited and uninterrupted access in the future. And because the hacker installs his password with his own programme, which the system's genuine users don't know about and therefore have no way of accessing, they remain unaware that there's a spider in permanent residence in the middle of their information web: his same concealing programme erases any trace of entry once the hacker disconnects or 'logs off'.

The crooked hacker can 'live' undetected for as long as he wants in the systems where there is an ongoing advantage in remaining anonymous. In, for instance, a financial network he can milk off infinitesimal and therefore unrealised amounts, building up from pennies a potential million-plus bank account, often in a country other than that in which he – or the unwittingly providing institution – operates. Or he can live in a hi-tech or technological development company whose ongoing research he wants continuously to read, copy and sell on to an eager – even sponsoring – competitor. Or in a medical institution or hospital whose records might provide blackmail material.

At other times, boastful hackers go very public, announcing their spider-like presence, occasionally to demonstrate the serious intent of a blackmail demand, more often maliciously to prove they're cleverer than their victims. They do so by introducing what is generically called a 'virus', a programme which, once inserted into a system, replicates itself over and over again and contaminates every other system with which it comes into contact through the communications network to which it is linked. A 'bacterium' is a software programme specifically designed to crash a computer system by blocking it: it repeatedly reproduces itself to the point of overload by filling to the brim the system's capacity, finally jamming it completely. Then there's the 'worm', which wriggles unseen through cyberspace along a network from one computer to another, erasing information intermittently as it goes. And finally there's the 'logic bomb' which is a programme that lies dormant until activated by the hacker or by some timing device to explode – electronically, not physically – to wipe out every file the victimised system contains.

And each and every one – virus, bacteria, worm and logic bomb – is usually hidden in a Trojan Horse, named with historical aptness after the commando-concealing wooden beast inside which the Greeks, according to mythology, infiltrated well-defended Troy. Upon entry into a system, the Trojan Horse seems at first benign: its true purpose only becomes apparent when – like the logic bomb – an inbuilt programme releases its destructive commando codes.

A Trojan Horse infiltration by a brilliant but mentally unstable university graduate made worldwide legal history on several levels between 1989 and 1990.

Dr Joseph Popp attempted the world's biggest ever computer blackmail – some estimates put the eventual profit at £4 billion had it succeeded – and was the first person to be extradited under specific legislation to combat computer crime.[6]

In December 1989, from an address in the London district of Kensington, Dr Popp advertised in computer magazines for sale by a company named PC Cyborg Corporation a programme entitled AIDS Information Introductory Diskette. An accurate figure of how many of these discs he sold and distributed to medical facilities, hospitals and banks is unknown, because of his later genuine mental inability to cooperate with investigators: the sample criminal charges – eleven counts of blackmail – refer to 10,000 but I understand[7] there were hugely more than that. The AIDS programme – setting out, among other things, the ways and the risks of contracting the disease – operated perfectly and informatively at the beginning: Popp had a degree in anthropology from America's Harvard University and worked for the World Health Organisation. The trigger that opened the secret trap-door to Popp's Trojan Horse was the figure one hundred. At the hundred and first use of the instructional disc, the viruses started to emerge, just like the night-raiders of Ulysses in the Greek fable. Programmes began to block and crash. And couldn't be found to be reinstated. When the system teetered at the brink of total collapse an apparent licensing agreement appeared on the display screen. If a fee – the dollar equivalent of £225 – was paid in favour of PC Cyborg Corporation to a box number in Panama, an antidote would be sent to cure the virus infection and restore every programme. If no money was paid, the system died.

Because the crime was perpetrated in the United Kingdom, it was investigated by Scotland Yard's Computer Crime Unit. Because Popp was an American – his address was traced to Willowick, Ohio – they liaised extensively with America's FBI, who in February, 1990, arrested Popp in Cleveland. From preliminary questioning – when Popp was still believed mentally capable of responding to questioning – it emerged that he had devised the AIDS-containing Trojan Horse to avenge himself after being turned down for a transfer within the World Health Organisation to a department dealing with the killer disease. It was never fully discovered how many companies and institutions paid the blackmail demand to PC Cyborg, (which was, in fact, a non-existent company), or how many lost their systems entirely.

America complied with a British extradition request and Popp was sent for trial on the blackmail charges by Bow Street magistrates. By the time he appeared before Southwark Crown Court, Popp's mental condition had deteriorated to such an extent that he wore hair curlers in his beard as a protection against radioactivity. He was judged unfit to plead. The case was never proceeded with and Popp was returned to America, for psychiatric treatment.

There was nothing bizarre in the computer-image appearance of the late-East German leader Erich Honecker when his thin-faced, bespectacled picture abruptly – and unwelcomely – came on to hundreds of VDU screens throughout Berlin on 13 August 1994. That date was the 33rd anniversary to the day of Honecker's construction of the Berlin Wall which had once divided the city, and an unknown computer hacker had decided to implant a virus commemorating the event. It arrived complete with the national anthem of the now non-existent East Germany and a message threatening to destroy computer programmes 'by order of the Council of Ministers of the German Democratic Republic'. The second message boasted: 'Honni's last revenge – I'll be back.' A programme had to be written to cure the Honecker virus, which ironically – by appearing all over Berlin – had in effect united a city he had so successfully separated during his lifetime.

The inconclusive outcome of the prosecution against Dr Popp was yet another, although in this case legally unavoidable, frustration for Scotland Yard's undermanned computer squad.

Their main and continuing frustration stems from the refusal or reluctance of British financial institutions to report computer intrusion or misuse. Fear of embarrassment from the subsequent publicity was the primary cause given to an investigation by Britain's Department of Trade and Industry[8] by financial institutions for not reporting computer intrusion. That same investigation found English companies surprisingly ignorant of the legislation existing specifically to combat computer crime.

During my researches I repeatedly heard[9] it regretted that European computer laws, where they existed, did not have the mandatory reporting requirements that are law in many American states. It is, however, the British legal view that the reporting of computer crime should *not* be compulsory: with very few exceptions, there is no legal requirement under British law that serious crime must be reported – it is not a legal requirement, for instance, in the case of murder or rape – and the opinion of both the English and Scottish Law Commission is that to include such a requirement in British computer legislation would be anomalous.

Dr Deborah Fisch Nigri, a Brazilian-born lawyer who gained her Doctorate of Philosophy in law specialising in computer crimes and who has studied the phenomena worldwide, told me[10]: 'There are far more unreported than reported cases, because financial institutions prefer to absorb their losses rather than risk their integrity and reputations by admitting they can't – or don't – properly protect themselves. We don't know – nobody knows – the full extent of computer crime, in Europe or anywhere else. The term, within the computer business, is that it's a dark figure. Which covers the number of unreported cases that supersede those that are reported.'

Dr Fisch Nigri has heard of cases of computer crime going as high as £2 billion. Bradford L. Smith, from the law firm Covington and Burling which acts for a European Union consortium of computer supplying firms grouped within the Business Software Alliance, puts[11] the cost of just software piracy alone in Europe at £4 billion a year. 'And that's a conservative estimate.'

Some British police computer crime units try to alert businesses to the dangers of hackers using a 'war game' scenario. The script has a nation-wide chain faced, an hour or two before closing on a Friday night and with its stores crowded with shoppers, with a demand for between £10,000 to £20,000 from each branch. The threat is chillingly simple: the computer which controls the item-by-item additions and the opening and closing of their tills has been entered and is no longer controlled by check-out operators. If the supermarket doesn't pay up, the virus will jam the tills, making any further shopping impossible. The financial loss would run into hundreds of thousands – less, in fact, than the demand – and the goodwill loss among turned-away customers would be in-calculable.

So smoothly rehearsed was the episode that the lawyer who described it to me is convinced that the police were re-enacting a real life situation – perhaps one of several – which never became public but which was able to serve as useful practice for any managerial staff who might be caught up in the next genuine situation. 'The purpose was to establish a recognised chain of decision-making command, to avoid any delay or prevarication. While acknowledging the recurrent risks of giving in to blackmail, the executives argued their paramount need to retain customer goodwill and confidence in a fiercely competitive market and insisted their right to pay. The immediate agreement by police officers involved further convinced me it was the re-enactment of a genuine situation. Their matching insistence was that they be immediately involved, not kept out of the picture until any money had been handed over. Their view, in this particular set of circumstances, was that the blackmailer would most likely be a disgruntled or recently dismissed employee with some knowledge of the computer system whom it would not be too difficult to discover, following normal police investigation procedure.'

The problem of computer crime is that it is still so new and continuing to evolve that, although pan-European laws have been put on to member state statutes by Conventions and Directives[12] most are inadequate.

Computers hundreds or even thousands of miles from the actual scene of the crime perpetrate theft, embezzlement, larceny, forgery, counterfeiting, blackmail, pornography, paedophilia and even murder, by the intentional alteration of medical or hospital records. So that any prosecution – once a victim has complained – usually involves a mixture of new laws and old, many enacted before the invention of the microchip. The sheer distances possible, crossing any number of frontiers, present formidable difficulties from the start for any international lawyer. If a criminal in one country commits a computer crime in another and deposits or uses the result or profit of that crime in a third, which of the three possesses the jurisdiction to initiate a prosecution? That's practically a cliché question for European Union lawyers, but remains – and will continue to remain – unresolved because of the principle of subsidiarity, the sovereign right of member nations to comply with the European Union's legally-binding protocols only according to national interpretation.

The principle of subsidiarity – for which British premier John Major was the most strident advocate during the ratification of the Maastricht Treaty – has actually created the very opposite to what was intended with the European Union's newest crime-fighting body specifically formed to achieve legal harmonisation. Which is the last thing it's got with the very weapon it's supposed to use, the computer. Like so much else in the European Union, it will take years to achieve.

Europol is Germany's crime-busting baby. The creation of a Europe-embracing police system was personally proposed and pressed into creation by Chancellor Helmut Kohl. Until it received its legally founding Convention it existed in vague limbo – for months it didn't even have a permanent building from which to work and was housed in single storey huts in Strasbourg – with its operations restricted to the centralised gathering and dissemination of European drugs intelligence. Although it will encounter fierce opposition stretching over a period of years from the police, enforcement and intelligence agencies of the member states, Europol will eventually become the Union's FBI: when we met[13] Bonn's Interior Ministry junior minister Eduard Lintner was forthrightly honest when he said that the close-to-reality nightmare of organised crime overwhelming Europe would 'compel us to take this step and to overcome the reservation'. With that operational function still a long way off, however, Europol will remain no more than an intelligence co-ordinating unit.

All fifteen countries forming the European Union have followed the legal requirements of the Council of Europe's 1981 Data Protection Convention and passed nationally-binding laws governing the use – and the access to them – of computers and their information.

But no computer legislation in any one of those fifteen countries is entirely compatible with another. Which results, according to a senior Scotland Yard detective[14] who has studied Europol from its now permanent site at the Hague, in 'yet another of those bloody daft European situations that makes people wonder if there was any point in joining a union in the first place'. Every country has its staff at The Hague, supposedly receiving from and adding to – from individual national sources – information held in the centrally-pooled databank. Except that they aren't allowed to. Some countries permit much more personalised information to be held than others. And for varying periods of time. And restrict its dissemination. Or don't restrict its dissemination. The nonsense is that police officers who are supposed to be fighting with the most modern means possible – the computer – daily run the risk of *committing* crime under their national data protection laws if they try to do the job they have been sent there to do. It's total lunacy, like so much else in the Union.

That, as the British detective rightly complained, is a Euro-nonsense. But one which, in time, can perhaps be corrected by an adjustment to national or European-binding legislation envisaged in the February, 1995 ministerial accord. A far greater problem is the police use of computers themselves. All European, national and international law enforcement or governing agencies – police, customs, immigration, intelligence service – operate and talk to each other by computer.

I have spoken to officials from each such agency – in every case in more than one European country – during the preparation of this book. Without exception each assured me that their particular system is unbreachable and therefore not at risk from criminal intrusion, manipulation or destruction.

I was offered similar assurances from specialists and companies thriving on developing anti-virus and penetration protection techniques. I saw systems that claimed to be attack-proof switch themselves off at the touch of an intrusive computer button or apparently disintegrate before my eyes at the moment of access. I saw stored information mathematically encrypted – by computer, of course – into gibberish letters and figures and symbols with the guarantee that no two encryptions were the same (a one time pad, in intelligence parlance) and therefore totally secure against unauthorised viewing. I had explained to me, at length, how hackers would finally be defeated if computer users adopted a protective system developed by America's most top secret intelligence organisation, the National Security Agency. The Clipper Chip is a microcircuit that encodes information from a key-holding sender which can only be unscrambled by the simultaneous use of a second, separately held key in the hands of a receiver.

I was equally assured, by a matching number of experts and specialists, that an absolutely guaranteed, one hundred per cent, totally secure, untamperable computer programme or system did not exist. The technological brilliance that created the computer might achieve such a programme one day. But not yet. It was even suggested to me[15] that a company working to perfect the eventual failsafe computer protection package faced the very real danger, during its period of research and development, of being unwittingly entered by a dormant spider virus, the function of which would be to read and keep abreast of such development in order to circumvent or defeat it, the moment it came on line.

Because of the frequent total ignorance of victims that they have been penetrated, combined with their embarrassed reluctance to admit it's happened when they do find out, no investigatory or monitoring agency in any of the fifteen European Union countries is able to confirm a definite or extensive involvement by organised crime.

Yet those same agencies[16] are totally convinced that every mafia group uses fraction-of-a-second computer transfers for their multi-billion laundering throughout the financial markets and tax havens of the world. I am satisfied – without being able to offer that always necessary empirical evidence – that the criminal organisations that have recognised one obvious advantage of modern technology for their laundering activities have not remained ignorant of all the others: not just the money-making as well as the money-washing potentials, but also the capability to erase or amend those records – criminal or otherwise – they feel necessary to adjust. The flexibility and mobility of frontier-skipping technology, with the absolute minimum chance of pursuit or detection, is the stuff of mafia wet dreams.

There's the stuff of other wet dreams, too, equally difficult to detect and practically impossible to stop: computer pornography. At the time of writing only one country in the European Union – the United Kingdom – has enacted legislation[17] criminalising some, but not all, electronic pornographic techniques. Few others are likely to bother, either through disinterest or from recognising the practical impossibility of enforcing such legislation.

The unpreventable techique, simply explained, is the digitalisation of photographic images which can be electronically transposed on to a video disc or a CD-ROM, an optical compact disc, and then transmitted along the telephone line connecting the computer. Any pornographic picture or image can be put on to a video, using the digitalising system. It requires only an optical scanner to pick up the original picture and a computer paint programme, an electronic version of an old fashioned artists' kit, to alter or vary the image as required by the pornographer: putting the face of a child on to a body not its own, for example, to make a prosecution totally impossible under existing European law.

In April, 1994, West Midlands police announced the breaking of a worldwide paedophile ring using the Interlink computer network to which, through government bodies, businesses and universities, an estimated 20 million people in one hundred and sixty countries have access.

The digital transmission on to computer screens of hard core pornography over a telephone line – which makes it intangible according to law – is not covered by Britain's new Criminal Justice Bill, despite demands for it to be included before it was voted into law in 1994. Those demands followed a case in March of that year in which a thirteen year old boy who had watched a digitally-relayed pornographic film was accused in a Wrexham, North Wales, court of trying to rape a girl of six. It was this case which focussed public attention on the fact that telephone-transmitted computer pornography was available – and watched – in the majority of British schools and was freely available to any computer-literate child with a system in his bedroom.

A British Home Office expert on telephone transmitted pornography told me[18] it was virtually impossible for any enforcement or monitoring body in the United Kingdom – or any other European Union country – to prevent such material being watched. 'There's only one way in which it can even be hindered at best, and then – objectively – only minimally; that's by the exercise of parental responsibility. No-one else but a father or a mother can monitor what their children receive and watch upon personal computers. Which is not this or any other government abrogating responsibility. It's being what I said – objective. If it means parents spying on their children, then that's what it takes. It is, after all, for their own good.'

The same technique that produces computer-graphic pornography virtually indistinguishable from live performances on traditional porn and paedophile movies is the same used for matchingly perfect forgery and counterfeiting. Using what is technically called Document Image Processing, passports, stock certificates, birth and marriage certificates, driving licences, immigration cards, purchase orders, drug prescriptions, credit card receipts, cheques and banknotes of every denomination in every European currency can be – and are – transposed by an optical scanner into digital images, which can then be reproduced by a laser printer or a professional type-setting machine into a copy impossible for anyone but a total expert to identify. The only difference between a counterfeit banknote and the real thing is the special, metal-strip paper incorporated in many of the genuine articles. Similarly, computer-literate college and university students can – employing the facilities of their own academies – record on a disc their own poor or even failure rated results and in minutes, with the use of an altering electronic paint kit, award themselves the highest passes, with Honours or Distinction. Many do.[19]

As will be seen later, it is technology of such undetectable excellence that is increasingly used to smuggle illegal immigrants from Asia and the former Eastern bloc into the European Union. The Czech Republic's Dr Vandas complained during a Strasbourg encounter I had with him[20] that his country had neither the technical expertise nor the trained border control personnel even to begin to try any interception. Hungary's Dr Bartok said the same.[21] At that time, some months before I had heard similar assessments from criminologists in Western Europe about the losing battle against organised crime, Dr Bartok said: 'Modern criminals are too sophisticated for us, with what we have available, to make any sort of impact.'

An important part of that criminal sophistication is the use of one of the several miracles of the computer age – the ease of instant communicating over distances of thousands of miles – to operate from what are technically called 'hacker havens', which operate on the same legal immunity principle as tax havens in money laundering schemes.

Inadequate though much of the computer crime legislation is in Europe, it does exist. As it does – with the addition of mandatory reporting requirements – in America. In Asia and the Eastern bloc, on the other hand, restrictions or legislation are virtually non-existent. And it is from these areas of the world that the cyberspace manipulators are increasingly attacking Europe, with as much ease as if they were installed in a house in the same city as their target.

And those targets do not stop at computers with VDU screens. It is now technically possible – still over distances of thousands of miles – to hack into another revolutionary electronic development, the fax machine.[22] The hacking equipment is the same, a computer or a computerised fax machine. Once having knowledge of the number connecting it to the telephone system, an intruder can enter the fax system and instruct it to send to him copies of all the documents held in its memory – including its memorised customer or recipient directory – and to copy all outgoing files. The intruder avoids detection by electronically disabling – while he is dis-embowelling the fax of its information – the automatically recorded lists of incoming and outgoing messages such machines make.

Hans Nilsson, the Council of Europe's expert on computers and the European law, says[23] the amount of time he has spent with technical experts has convinced him that with just a computer and a telephone link a hacker can operate practically unhindered anywhere in the world.

The most famous recorded case of hacker intrusion is that of the Chaos Computer Club, so named, according to its formation documents legally registered before Bonn enacted a computer misuse bill, in order to prove that as far as security is concerned, 'chaos reigns' world wide. Throughout most of 1987 the Chaos hackers – ninety in all and mostly operating from their dank and cluttered headquarters at 85, Schenckestrasse, Hamburg – roamed the globe, reading at will whatever they chose to access on VAX computers manufactured by America's Digital Equipment Corporation: a lot of it was top secret nuclear material.

Through the French communications network Transpace or the German system Datex-P, over 100,000 Vaxes in 56 countries – including all those in Europe – were interconnected: Chaos could enter anywhere they chose. They chose a lot. The NASA system alone linked 1,600 computers worldwide to information on space research, nuclear physics and molecular biology. One of the connections was to the US atomic research facility at Los Alamos, New Mexico. Scientists at CERN, another nuclear research centre in Geneva, uncovered the presence of hackers in their VAX computers before the arrival of investigating French police and admitted sometimes 'talking' to the intruders on their screens. It was the Swiss scientists who gave the lead to Chaos operating from Germany. Through Interpol liaison the French – who initially met

German resistance to their investigation – discovered Chaos had raided installations throughout Europe, Scandinavia, America and Japan. Because of the threat to national security – and the potential for a national catastrophe if one of the hackers chose to alter some of the nuclear programmes they were accessing – the DST, the French counter-intelligence organisation, was called in.

When the French police and intelligence officers, with belated German cooperation, raided 85, Schenckestrasse, they found £600,000 worth of computer equipment. There was also a list of access codes and passwords four hundred pages long. And a hundred sheets of classified information taken from NASA and Star Wars programmes.

There were three principals controlling the Chaos Club, Wau Holland, Steffan Wernery and Reinhardt Schrutzkin.

In a defiant statement[24] after their detection, the Chaos Club fell back on the hackers' cliché to insist that they had entered the systems to prove the 'unbelievable weaknesses' in the security systems. Wernery, a computer journalist, said: 'You don't leave your car in the car park with the ignition key on the dashboard. Why leave secret information on a computer that can be broken into?'

CHAPTER ELEVEN

Snuffed Out

Children are being, quite literally, snuffed out. This crime gives the most obscene of paedophilic pornography its name: snuff movies. In them children – thankfully drugged, although only minimally, to relax and make them more amenable to what is done to them by the adult performers, not to ease their physical agony – are put through every type of depravity child sex perverts can imagine, before they are finally murdered. And all the time the camera runs. Children are preferred by the perverts, but some-times filmed orgies conclude in the death of a participating whore. The first such film – entitled *Snuff* – was shot in Argentina in the late 1970s.

Although Detective Superintendent Michael Hames, at the time of our meeting[1] head of Scotland Yard's Obscene Publications Squad, says his unit has never seized or seen a genuine snuff movie – the culminating murder has always been declared faked by technical experts – British detectives believe several were made in England by a paedophile group the ringleaders of which were later jailed. One of the charges upon which a Swiss national was extradited in 1994 from Amsterdam to Zurich was attempting to murder – on film which he shot and which features him – a 14-month-old baby girl by administering electrical shocks to her naked body: he has refused to answer police questions about the disappearance of nine children in the vicinity of his Swiss home. A

British sex therapist had talked of seeing a genuine snuff movie in Amsterdam. In a pornographic video shop bordering Amsterdam's Achter canal I was told[2] there was for sale every variety of child sex films 'including animals. There's a good one with a dog. It's American. America makes the best stuff.' What about snuff? Maybe, but it would cost. How much? How much was I prepared to pay? £1000? Not enough. Name your price then? At least £5000, because 'this stuff is special. Very special. You and your friends will like it: watch it for a long time.' Could I see some of it in the viewing cubicles at the back of the shop? What about the money? Surely he didn't think I would walk about Amsterdam's red light district carrying £5000 in cash: I'd bring it tomorrow. When he saw the money, in cash, maybe I could see the film. 'You'll enjoy it.' A different man was on duty when I returned to the Achter canal the following day, with £300 in cash and a hopeful bargaining argument that £300 was all I was prepared to part with to watch a brief excerpt of the promised movie. The new salesman didn't know anything about a snuff movie. There hadn't been anyone else in the shop the previous day: he'd been working there, like he was today. He didn't think I was properly interested in what they were selling. If I was, why didn't I buy something? If I wasn't, why didn't I piss off? I couldn't cause any trouble for him. He was allowed to sell what he did. Everything was legal. Foreigners like me who weren't proper customers were a fucking nuisance.

His obviously too talkative colleague of the previous day was right about America, according to experts[3]: American organised crime – linked to its mafia outlets in Europe – is a leading supplier of child pornography, for export to the European Union.

It is impossible accurately to record how many children are bought or stolen for the trade: if there was a recognised source for such a figure enforcement agencies and child welfare groups could follow it. But in a Norwegian report[4] to the Council of Europe, based on worldwide research, estimated the figure at 1,000,000 a year. And that calculation came before the rise of the East European mafias after the collapse of communism: today that number has risen by many thousands as a result of the buying and kidnap possibilities available in all the former Soviet bloc countries. During my visit[5] to Strasbourg for the European Council of Police Unions, Czech Interior Ministry official Dr Jiri Vandas described sexual exploitation of children of both genders and young women in his country as one of their most serious crime problems. 'The younger the better, it seems. European sex pedlars are operating in Prague. Some woman cross into Europe willingly, for what they believe will be a better life. But children don't. They simply vanish.' Part of the evidence on the extradition indictment for attempted murder against the Swiss computer software expert Rene Osterwalder alleged a plot to bring kidnapped or purchased children into Switzerland from Romania for a snuff movie. The children's bodies were to be destroyed in an acid bath after their filmed murders. Two fifty-litre barrels of sulphuric acid were found by police in Osterwalder's chalet near the Alpine village of St Ursanne. It was impossible to determine medically or forensically if particles of flesh found in one barrel were human or animal.

The Norwegian investigation quoted a Defence for Children International estimate that the yearly income from child trafficking and exploitation was $5 billion. Of that $1 billion was spent by child sex perverts in America, the world's largest market. As well as exporting through US-based Mafia families, America also imports huge quantities from the mafias of Europe. Superintendent Hames told me FBI undercover agents were asked to pay £6,500 to watch a snuff movie they wanted to buy, as evidence, during an investigation into an American paedophile ring.

The principal child pornography film-making countries in the European Union are the Netherlands, Germany and Portugal. Latin America and now the Eastern bloc are not the only child sex suppliers for those films. The market is just as extensive in Asia. Children are smuggled by Triad groups into Europe from Thailand, the Philippines, South Korea and Sri Lanka.[6] In 1990 all four countries – and Taiwan – agreed with the United Kingdom, Switzerland, the United States, Germany and France on joint action against paedophiles. After a Bundeskriminalamt investigation had proved that German child porn film-makers were travelling frequently to Asia – particularly to Sri Lanka – to make paedophile movies on location, the Bonn government passed legislation that abusing a child of any nationality was punishable in Germany.

The Norwegian criticism of the liberal attitude of some European countries was echoed to me later by Superintendent Hames, who at one stage chaired Interpol's enforcement committee on child pornography. When Interpol's unit was first established some countries in the EU – although Hames did not name them I know them to be the Netherlands and Denmark – did not even refer to sex films and videos featuring children as pornography. They called them child erotica. That virtual acceptance has now changed. Child pornography legislation exists in every one of the fifteen EU countries although the strictness with which those laws are enforced varied considerably from country to country. In the video emporium close to the Achter waterway where I was briefly offered a claimed snuff movie, there were videos openly on display clearly featuring children.

It is a fact confirmed by the evidence of films seized throughout the world that paedophiles abuse boys, rarely girls: an exception to this general rule was Rene Osterwalder, in whose ground-floor Amsterdam apartment at 14a, Doogbak (with a view of a children's playground) were found videos featuring him not only with the 14-month-old baby girl but with another girl of four.

Britain's Scotland Yard – who had earlier smashed a European-wide distribution network for pornographic film and still pictures known as the Paedophile Information Exchange – confirmed in July 1990, their investigation into the making of several snuff movies over the preceding six years in their search for twenty children, some as young as six years, who had disappeared in England without trace. They set up and widely publicised a special telephone number which informants could call with an undertaking that whatever they disclosed would be treated in total confidence. An appeal was directed particularly to anyone who might have been involved in the making or processing of a snuff movie. One such witness would have been a 19-year-old youth known only as Andrew, who made a tape-recorded confession to the National Association for Young People In Care, in which he admitted being taken to Amsterdam in 1988 to film, in a warehouse, twelve men successively raping a boy of twelve. According to Andrew, the child was subsequently beaten with chains and killed by being run over by a motorcycle. The body was disposed of in a canal. Officials of the care association doubted Andrew's story until he was attacked by two men outside the London home of one of its officials. The youth disappeared before he could be interviewed by police. He has never been found.

The investigation, codenamed Operation Orchid, had begun after statements made by two of the four members of a paedophile ring known as the Lambs to the Slaughter group who were jailed at London's Old Bailey in May 1989, for the manslaughter of a 14-year-old rent boy named Jason Swift. He was paid £5 by each of the four to take part in a homosexual orgy in a council flat in Hackney, London, in November 1985. He was drugged with Valium to relax him and make it easier for the men to inflict upon him sexual activities the details of which I will not recount. The men climaxed their excesses by strangling the teenager. Before dumping his naked body in a copse, the four thoroughly washed it to remove any evidence forensically to incriminate them. Although police believe the killing was filmed, the video has never been found, although during Operation Orchid they were told a copy of the film of Jason's murder was in circulation in Amsterdam. Another film believed to have been made was of the killing of six-year-old Barry Lewis, whose naked body was found five days after that of Jason Swift. This film, too, has never been located.

As a result of what they were told by the two paedophiles, detectives went painstakingly through a list of 100 possible victims – all young boys – snatched or paid for sex by the gang. In some of the cases the detectives only had the vaguest idea of the identities they were seeking: the gang were never interested in names, only young bodies. Police narrowed their list to twenty and thought that at least six of them had been filmed as they died. But not one film was ever discovered and Operation Orchid was finally discontinued.

One of the four men jailed for the killing of Jason Swift – a man who later received two separate life sentences after he admitted killing Barry Lewis and a third child, seven-year-old Mark Tildesley, whose body was never found – was a manic-eyed psychopath called Leslie Bailey. In October 1993, Bailey was found strangled to death in the wing of Whitemoor Prison, Cambridgeshire, that specially segregates child molesters from other prisoners: in British jails child sex offenders are a permanent target for violence. Even so prison, in fact, is a meeting place from which paedophiles plan, once they are released, child-preying groups like the Paedophile Information Exchange.

Superintendent Hames – who believes there should be community-based treatment and rehabilitation centres after prison terms – talked to me of released or unconvicted paedophiles arranging child-sex orgies to celebrate the end of a jail sentence for friends, sometimes on the very day they walk through the prison gates. Hames was enthusiastic at the provision in the 1994 Criminal Justice and Public Order Act for DNA samples to be taken and stored from all convicted sex offenders. The DNA databank will supplement all sex registers, but particularly the directory of the 3,000 known paedophiles which is held both by Scotland Yard and the Paedophile Register at Britain's National Criminal Intelligence Service. 'I believe they should all be on life licences, so that wherever they go they have to report their whereabouts to the police and the central records should be maintained of where they are living and crucially what they are doing for a living. Paedophiles are among the most dangerous of all criminals because they destroy children's lives. They scar them for life. I believe in the liberty of the subject but I also believe that liberty should not equal licence and even more so when we are dealing with children. If somebody has sex with children then the price they pay for that compulsion is that they are registered and that we keep a track of their whereabouts, to stop it happening.'

The first-in-the-world DNA record system, which began to be established in April 1995, will by the end of the century contain an estimated five million entries and have cost £20 million to create. Those entries will extend beyond sex offenders to include genetic information on other criminals convicted of serious offences.

Apart from the 1994 provision, Hames is bitterly critical of other, already existing legislation to combat obscenity and pornography in the United Kingdom, describing it as a mish-mash operated through a labyrinth of separate acts. It is not, for example, an offence to possess hard core pornography of any sort, providing it does not feature images of children. And a prosecution even in those circumstances can be difficult if the face of the child is superimposed upon a body not its own, a simple and frequently used film technique.

The United Kingdom follows the successful concept evolved by pornographers. Importing from America or Holland or Germany master videos – out of their cassettes little larger than ordinary rolls of film – and copying them by wiring a battery of VCRs back to back can earn a comparatively small-time pornographer millions a year, upon which no tax is paid. Whenever the Scotland Yard unit raids a suspected maker or distributor of obscene material, they are accompanied by Inland Revenue and VAT inspectors. The penalties possible under the British tax laws are far harder and more effective than are possible under its varied obscenity legislations.

Hames and his squad have viewed pornographic films featuring every sort of human depravity. While repeatedly insisting British detectives have never located a technically confirmed snuff movie, he conceded: 'We have got examples of children being bound, gagged, hooded, whipped, beaten and buggered. It would have been possible, obviously, for them to have been killed during these encounters.' Every enquiry involving an abused child is investigated. Of paramount importance is tracing the child, who is invariably in need – sometimes in desperate need – of psychological therapy.

There is an enormous pyschological strain also upon the professional investigators of child sex. 'We keep an eye on each other, to the extent that if someone were to be either unsuitable from our viewpoint or they didn't particularly want to carry on with this work, then there is no embarrassment on either side if they stop: it's understood that it is very difficult work and an officer would go to other duties. Everyone is affected to one degree or another. It's how you actually handle the feelings that you have with what you are seeing and hearing that is important.'

Professional psychiatric and psychological help is available, if the strain becomes too severe. Within months of our meeting Hames suffered a heart attack. He retired from Scotland Yard in 1994, to become managing director of a company established to vet adults seeking to work with children. That year a decision by Metropolitan Commissioner Sir Paul Condon to scrap the Obscene Publications Squad was rescinded after parliamentary protests.

Hames – with a pan-European overview derived from his Interpol links – found remarkable the development towards extreme and grotesque physical violence and mutilation in adult blue movies. Severing of genitals – judged to be simulated – was commonly portrayed. Screaming women were filmed with nipples and every bodily oriface impaled. Bestiality was not infrequent. Coprophilia – the fetish involving human excrement, sometimes being eaten, at the moment of defecation – was a familiar subject.

The litany added a new dimension to the danger of being a prostitute, male or female. But since the ending of the divisions between East and West Europe there is no shortage of supply. In Amsterdam they arrive – often kidnapped – by the van load.

Anna's story is typical of the trade.

CHAPTER TWELVE

Love for Sale

At least she called herself Anna. And she hadn't been brought to Amsterdam with a van load of other girls to be sold, although she had heard of women who had. She'd come by car ('A Mercedes. I'd never imagined a car like that.') from Warsaw, which she pronounced with a final 'a' in the Polish way, *Warszawa*. But her home wasn't there. It was in Blonie, which was quite close. There wasn't any work there and her mother was a widow and the family needed money. Anna told me[1] she'd worked as a waitress, in a café near the Vistula, quite close the Syrena Bridge. There was a room at the back where she lived, and on her day off she went home. In the summer they set tables and chairs on the pavement outside the café. It was very nice. A lot of tourists used it. That's how she'd learned English, from foreign tourists. And how she'd met Pieter. He'd come regularly, every day, usually at lunch-time and on the third day he said he came especially to see her. 'It excited me. Of course I had boyfriends. I wasn't a virgin. But he was the first foreigner to show any interest. He's very good looking . . . I think that even now, after everything . . . and had beautiful clothes. He never wore the same thing twice and he always left an enormous tip, which he said was for me, not to be shared with the other girls.'

That week, which by Anna's story had been a year and a half before we met, she hadn't gone home to her widowed mother in Blonie. 'He took me on a boat trip, on the river. He'd brought a scarf, already in a box. It was silk. He said he'd bought it in Germany – the shop address on the box was Berlin – on his way to Poland for his girlfriend back home but that now he wanted me to have it. He took it back later. That night we ate at the Intercontinental and after dinner we went to the nightclub there. That's when I told him I wanted to be a singer, because there was a singer in the cabaret. When it got late he asked me if I really wanted to go back to the room behind the café or whether I would like to stay with him. It wasn't until then that I realised he was living there.'

Anna didn't go back to the café. 'It was fantastic, like a story. He had wine brought to the room, real champagne, and he asked me to sing for him. I was embarrassed but I did, just a little, and he said I was very good. He said he had friends in show business in Holland, in clubs and that if I liked he would mention me to them. I didn't really believe him, although I didn't imagine what he was really doing. I thought he was just trying to impress me. He was a marvellous lover. Fantastic. But then I didn't know at that time how often he did it. He's slept with everyone he's brought to the West. Says he doesn't know how many fucks he's had, he's lost count. He still fucks me now, sometimes.'

She thought the fairy tale was over when Pieter left, two days later. Never imagined she would see him again. But she did, within a month. 'I couldn't believe it when he came into the café. I decided he really was interested in me, which of course he was, although not for what I thought, that he loved me. It was just like before, at the Intercontinental, and in his room he showed me several photographs of him with people in clubs. That was when he told me his job was supplying nightclubs. Which I suppose it is, really, although not with the sort of furniture I thought he was talking about. He said he'd mentioned me to them and one was prepared to give me a try, if I was interested. I suppose you could say he was honest. He said that I might be expected to sit with customers at the club to begin with, until I'd established myself as a performer. But only to drink and make sure they drank a lot, to make the bill big. Nothing more. He said the money would be good, thousands of zloty more than I was getting at the café: more, even, than I got on the black market exchanging dollars I sometimes got as a tip.

'Of course I was interested. And to be honest I knew I would probably end up as a hostess, not a singer. My voice isn't that good. But I never thought I'd end up like I am now: it genuinely didn't occur to me. I thought just being in a club would be the work I'd do: that I'd be with Pieter at night. that's what he said. That we'd live in his house, which was very old and was on one of the canals.

'I told him I wanted to but I didn't have any papers, no passport. There aren't very many people in Blonie who've got a passport. He said that was a problem, although not in the way I feared it would be. He said his friend in the nightclub would only hold the job for a little while, as a special favour to him. That we'd lose it if we didn't go at once. And then he said it *wasn't* a problem: that he knew the way. We'd go *without* papers. It was easy: no-one ever stopped a European-registered car in the West – there weren't any frontier checks any more – and he'd never been stopped at the Polish border, either. All Poland and any other Eastern country wanted now was Western currency. He'd take me to keep the meeting with the nightclub owner and we could sort out the passport business later. He had a friend who could get me what he called an artist's visa.'

So Anna went, although her mother was against it. 'I told her about the money. What a difference it would make. Pieter was very nice to her. He took her chocolates and told her when we settled down – that's *exactly* what he said, when *we* settled down – she could come to visit. That he'd make all the arrangements.'

They weren't stopped on the Polish border, which they didn't attempt to cross at a small, out-of-the-way frontier post but at a busy crossing she remembers at Kostrzyn, on the Oder River. 'He told me later that's how they do it, all of them. A small post might take an interest but not the ones where the traffic is heavy and has to be kept moving.'

In Berlin the soon-to-end fairy tale romance continued. They stayed at the Kempinski, on the Kurfurstendamm. Pieter bought her a new dress ('Red. I still have it.') and they ate that night with two other men. 'They both said I was very pretty and I would be very successful. I asked how they could say that if they hadn't heard me sing and they laughed. I didn't see the joke at the time.'

Anna remembers it being a long drive the following day, to get to Amsterdam. She asked Pieter if they would break the journey but he said there were business reasons to get back to the Netherlands. It was very late when they arrived. There *was* a house by a canal quite close to the central rail terminal. Anna's impression was that it didn't really seem like a home: there was hardly anything personal about it, no photographs or mementoes: scarcely any pictures on the walls even. She thought she would enjoy making improvements, making it lived-in. They hadn't stopped to eat, since lunch, but there was nothing in the refrigerator. She was hungry but didn't complain. She wanted to keep things wonderful and she certainly wasn't going to appear a nag or discontented within minutes of entering his house. She admits to fantasizing, during the drive, that they would marry. It wouldn't matter, though, if he didn't suggest it. She was happy enough for them to live together. It struck her that he wasn't as attentive that night as he had been every night before. He didn't attempt to make love to her. Anna decided he was tired, after the drive. She certainly was. It would be all right the next day.

But it wasn't. 'It was like we were strangers. Not just that he didn't know me but that he didn't like me.' He left her alone in the unlived-in house for most of the day. Anna remembers being very hungry and searching cupboards as well as the refrigerator, without finding any food. 'I was frightened to go out without Pieter. I didn't know what to do. I didn't have any money. Pieter had paid for everything. I hadn't needed money: hadn't thought about it. When he came home, very late, I asked him what was wrong: why things were so different. He said things had to be different. I didn't understand what he meant. My stomach hurt from being so hungry. I said I wanted something to eat but he said there were things we had to do first. We seemed to drive around and around a lot. I was completely lost and frightened, because he wasn't friendly any more. He left the car near the big church, the Dam, and we walked to where all the girls and the clubs are. I thought we were going to the club his friend had, but we didn't. We just walked around and looked at the girls in the windows and at the clubs, but we didn't go in to any, just looked. I remember Pieter asking what I thought about it but not what I said. All I could think about was how hungry I was: it must have been almost midnight and I hadn't eaten since the previous mid-day and then not much: we'd just stopped on the road because he was in such a hurry to get back. I was very close to crying. I did a little, when I said could I please have something to eat. He said he was taking me somewhere. We got back into the car and went to another house near a canal, I don't know which one. There were three other girls there. One was younger than me, the other two about the same age. The youngest one had a bruise on the side of her face. And Jig was there. That's all I've ever known him as, Jig. I don't know why he's called that. He's dark, Indonesian. The other girls seemed frightened of him. I was frightened, too. Not of him, not then. Of everything. None of it was what Pieter had said it would be like. I suppose I knew what was happening but I didn't want to think about it. I wanted to pretend it wasn't happening.'

The fairy tale pretence had run out. Pieter announced Anna was going to work the windows, like the rest of them. Not just in Amsterdam but in Rotterdam: anywhere he told her to. Anna said she wouldn't. Which was when Jig hit her, for the first time. 'He slapped me, quite hard, across the face. That's how the other girl had been bruised. It didn't matter being hit in the face then: that's the way they do it, in the beginning. Mark you so you can see what they can do. But they stay away from the face when you're working. No-one's going to choose a girl who's been beaten up, are they? So to hit you in the face damages what they're selling.'

Anna says she still refused, that first night, so Jig went on beating her, open-handed, around the face and body. 'In the end it hurt me to breathe. My tits were black with bruises, where he hit me: punched me there, not with his open hand.'

Anna was fed, at last, with bread and some meat and there was beer to drink. The timing was psychological. Pieter told them they had to work, as he said, if they wanted to eat. He would be fair to them, not like a lot of the others who ran girls and took all their money: he'd leave them with enough. He wasn't a slaver. But if they tried to cheat they'd be beaten by Jig, who liked doing it: beaten far worse than they'd been so far. And if they cheated a second time, he'd throw them out. None of them had any papers, so they'd be arrested by the authorities. Deported, in disgrace, as whores.

So Anna became a window girl.

I found her in an alley off Monnstraat, close to Amsterdam's Nieuw Markt, one of a line of five girls dressed in suspender belts and scanty pants and skimpy bras to look seductive, which none of them did. They looked what they were, meat on display. I went to Monnstraat twice[2] to hear Anna's story, which came disjointedly, not in the chronology I have told it, although the words are hers. I paid £60 on each occasion, for thirty minutes of her time. Jig – or one of the minders working for him – would have noted my entering her cubby-hole from the cafés or the bars nearby from which they constantly monitor the girls they run, and Anna had to produce payment from every client. She would have been beaten if there hadn't been any money to account for my visits. Thirty minutes was the maximum I could stay, on both occasions. 'A fuck doesn't take that long. I can say you were nervous.' Anna said she was twenty-eight but I estimated she was ten years older. She'd believed it when Pieter had said she was pretty, because she'd wanted to: she was a pleasant, round-faced woman whose only real attraction was what seemed naturally blonde hair, which she wrongly wore in schoolgirl plaits. She was very heavy, her breasts pendulous and her thighs heavy and fat-pitted. The sheet on the couch upon which she worked was creased from previous use on both nights I was there, but was clean. The smell was the damp staleness of a room – this stall was minuscule – never aired, overlaid with a scent that vaguely smelt of roses. In the matter-of-fact tones of the sex marketplace Anna priced the tariff. It was £60 for straight sex. Fellatio was £75, cunnilingus £80. She always insisted on a condom – during fellatio as well – even though a lot of the clients offered more if they didn't have to use one. Girls like herself, from the East, often didn't bother, which was why men liked them. She'd thought at first that was why I asked for someone foreign. She worked every day and guessed she serviced twenty to thirty men during each session. She'd appeared in three blue movies, one all lesbian. In the lesbian film, the girl with the bruised face that first night had been her partner. She'd turned out to be Polish, too: Anna thought from somewhere near Leszno. She hadn't seen her for a long time now, which was sad. Anna had liked her. 'People come, people go.' She wouldn't have agreed to appear in 'bad films. You know, really kinky.' Or in sado-masochism. She thought Jig had. He liked hurting people. Being hurt.

There was a sad fatalism about Anna: the sort of dull acceptance that comes before finally letting go. It was letting go even to talk to me, which I was surprised she did, exposed to the violence she described so easily. Five other girls whom I'd approached, offering to pay for a conversation, not sex, hid behind an inability to speak English when I made it clear, before parting with any money, that I wanted to talk about girls coming from the East.

Anna's reaction, after a momentary hesitation, had been to shrug and say why not. Towards the end of our final session, on the second day, those shrugs were very frequent. Life wasn't bad. Pieter had kept his promise: she was allowed to keep the equivalent of maybe £100 a week, which few of the other girls did. And she didn't have to pay any rent for her room, which she said was near the Ooster Dock. She really was very lucky. She sent money home regularly to her mother in Blonie, although her mother had obviously never come to Amsterdam, after all. Jig hadn't hit her for a long time, even for nothing, which he'd done sometimes in the early days. He was rough in bed, though, when he slept with her. Which he did sometimes, although not lately. Pieter was still good, in bed. When he fucked her, he usually gave her cocaine. And there was always *niederweit* in the coffee houses. She did that a lot, most days.

I'm not sure how many lies Anna told: hers was a story with no corroboration. Maybe she just exaggerated a little, to make it sound more sympathetic: romantic would have been Anna's word. I don't believe she was surprised to end up selling sex, although perhaps she didn't expect to do it from a shop window. Or that she was allowed as much as £100 by her pimp. But it made her appear less gullible if she claimed she got some reward. Her estimate of up to thirty men a day – even if thirty minutes is the maximum session – was probably an exaggeration, too, making her seem more attractive than she really was, compared to the others in the window assembly line. If that really was the daily number of men with whom she had sex of one variety or another, her £100 a week was precious little reward. Only once did she show any animation and that was irritation. Of course she couldn't tell me where to find Pieter. Or Jig, either. She didn't know, not any more – they always came for her when they wanted her or to collect her money. But she wouldn't have told me, even if she'd known. How else could I have found them, if not from her? She'd told me they ran other girls: at least ten she knew about, so how could my approach be traced to her. 'Don't be stupid! Someone saw you come in! I told you that!'

Anna's story of entrapment – virtually by kidnap – into sex slavery is typical of others I heard, second hand, from sources throughout Europe. It is, in fact, less dramatic than some of the other accounts. And the Netherlands is not by any means the focus of the trade: it was the country in which I chose to research it in more detail than elsewhere in the Union, because of Holland's reputation – not totally deserved – as the sex mecca of Europe.

Eduard Linter, Parliamentary State Secretary to the German Minister of the Interior, identified[3] prostitution as one of the country's biggest problems. And I know the Bundeskriminalamt have told Britain's National Criminal Intelligence Service that in Germany alone there are 10,000 women – some under 16 – who have been kidnapped or duped from the former Soviet Union to work in the skin trade. Jurgen Maurer, head of the BKA organised crime division[4] said the trafficking was organised by the German-based mafias of Russia and the West and both he and Eduard Lintner talked of prostitutes hopefully lining the roads leading to the German frontier posts from Poland and the Czech Republic, plying for trade from the West. The traffic is not exclusively from the northern countries of the former Soviet bloc: they are the main but by no means the only suppliers. The gun-running mafias of the dismembered Yugoslavia, the Ravna Gora chief among them, deal heavily in kidnapping women and children – male and female. The Serbian Ravna Gora have snatched both Muslim and Croatian women and children, to sell in the European Union.[5] Dr Janos Bertok, a Hungarian Ministry of the Interior official, told me[6] the Budapest authorities believed Hungary was a preferred shipment route – to loop further north through the Czech Republic – rather than going through either Austria or Italy. 'We have made a few arrests. Far too few. But the smugglers think they stand more chance of getting into Germany through my country and the Czech Republic.' Dr Jiri Vandas, from the Republic's Interior Ministry[7] agreed. His country had so many problems of their own to solve it was difficult to combat those that began outside its borders, although kidnapping to put women and children into sex slavery was a terrible crime and they obviously did everything they could to impede it. The officials of both countries conceded they were on the smuggling route from another sex-supplying country, Romania. After the collapse of communism there in 1989, there emerged the horror of appalling baby farms. Hundreds of babies and children – a huge number mentally subnormal – were discovered abandoned in squalid orphanages: during our conversations and correspondence[8] Amnesty's Dr Jean Claude Alt isolated Romanian unofficial adoption societies as one of his main concerns in Europe as a source for stolen organs. The abandoned young of Romania, where in the early days of freedom from communism virtually no controls or regulations governed what happened to their infants, became the prey of European pederasts. It was from Romania, according to the Swiss prosecutors of Rene Osterwalder, that he intended importing the star of his snuff movie, whose body was to be disposed of afterwards either in an acid bath or by being fed to his pet piranha fish.

Henk Klein Beekman runs the Flamingo sex club in the Dutch

town of Apeldoorn, fifty miles southwest of Amsterdam, and is the chairman of VER, the organisation formed in 1992 to defend the interests of Dutch sex clubs and as a lobbying group for parliamentary change on brothel legislation: under the illogicality of Dutch law prostitution is legal but running a brothel is not. A bill to legalise brothels failed before the Dutch Parliament in 1993: one of its provisions would have forbidden non-European Union girls from working in Holland.

Two hundred sex club owners belong to VER. Klein Beekman recounted stories[9] of vans pulling up outside his members' clubs, full of women from Eastern Europe. The van driver and their minders were mafia: Russian and he thought Polish, with local gangsters fetching and carrying, doing what they were told. 'My people are invited on board to take their pick. As many as they want. Literally a meat market. The women just sit there, waiting.' The price quoted was the equivalent of £2000 a woman. Sometimes the vans weren't full, just one or two girls. None of the girls have the proper immigration papers, which their suppliers argue as a benefit: the women are trapped – as Anna was trapped – unable to run away or cause any trouble. 'Anyone who refuses to buy is asked if he wants to stay in business. It is pointed out it is a great offer, which can be repeated as many times as necessary because there's always a supply and one which shouldn't be rejected. Anyone who does say "no" is a fool, they say.'

The VER organisation recommends its members against getting involved in the flesh trade from the East. Klein Beekman believes the Eastern mafias are trying to undermine and then get control of the entire European sex club business not just in Holland but in Germany and Spain and France as well. Their strategy is to force their East European girls on to the clubs until the local girls are driven out. The clubs will then become totally dependent on the East European supplies of new girls ('customers like change, not the same faces or the same bodies: variety is what it's all about') and when that happened organised crime could – and would – take over the whole business. In 1992, a Russian mafia gang – believed to have been Chechen, although the crime was never solved – firebombed the Paradiso Club in Haelen, southern Holland, when owner Huub Bemermans refused to pay £2,000 for a girl they offered for sale. The ongoing deal the Russians proposed, after the initial purchase, was that Bemermans kept half her earnings and paid the other half to them. There was never any discussion about any money for the girl. Klein Beekman told me his members are frequently threatened with violence if they refuse to accept a sex slave, particularly by Russian or Polish mafia. It is hardly surprising that, confronted with such pressure, some have caved in and bought. The only sufferer, after all, is a frightened, often totally bewildered girl.

Klein Beekman insists women should only work in his organisation's clubs of their own free will and should come from within the Union, as the failed brothel legalisation proposed. 'I think for them to be terrorised into doing it is a very bad thing for everybody.' Appearing to find nothing illogical about his next statement, in a country where running a brothel remains illegal, Klein Beekman insisted that his relations with the police were 'very good. I have protested, to the very top level and they are taking the protest of me and my members very seriously.'

Compounding the apparent illogicality of Holland's sex laws, its prostitutes, who can legally operate although the majority work in illegal brothels, are subjected to regular medical checks, the concern about AIDS – a factor in the sexual demand for younger and younger uninfected partners – predominating over other sexually transmitted diseases. They also have their own trade union. Professor Jan van Dijk[10] says: 'It's much more under the control of Dutch municipalities than in Anglo-Saxon countries.'

He conceded, however, that the entry into the sex market – like their entry into every other type of crime – of the East European mafia was imposing a great strain upon traditional law enforcement. The gangs of the former Yugoslavia were particularly violent, terrorising the sex clubs and nightclubs right across the country. Based on intelligence from CRI, the Dutch Criminal Intelligence Branch, correspondent Mark Fuller identified[11] Rotterdam's Milliardaire Club as the fulcrum of a European network of women trafficking from the East. The Milliardaire network stretches throughout the entire European Union – and to countries beyond – and operates clubs particularly in Holland, Belgium and Spain. In 1991, charges against the three men who run the Milliardaire operation – Robert van Engeland, Marc Verbesselt and Ferry van Acker – of forcing girls to become prostitutes collapsed when a number of Asian girls went back from Holland to the Philippines before they could be questioned by defence lawyers. The three had denied the charges.

The Milliardaire network has been named by vice squad detectives as having forced 3,000 girls to become whores over a six year period. CRI estimate over 11,000 of Holland's 30,000 prostitutes are brought in from the East. Once installed in brothels, sex clubs or working as window girls, their income – for their pimps, not for themselves – can be as high as £500 a day.

Britain's National Criminal Intelligence Service believe[12] that by the middle of 1993 girls had been brought – willingly, not forced – by Russian mafia gangs from Eastern Europe to work in the London sex market. The gangs were not positively identified, but they were believed to have Chechen connections.

The daily income for the boys and youths imported from the East can reach £500 a day also, although the homosexual business in Amsterdam did not appear to me to be as efficiently organised as the female sex trade. The homosexual centre in Amsterdam is the Paardenstraat – a relatively short walk from the sex emporiums and Anna's windowed cell – and is increasingly stocked by Romanian boys. According to Gert Tezing[13], who counsels young gays for the Amsterdam council-funded Streetcorner Work Foundation, the number of Romanian boys far exceeds those brought in from any other East European country. But there is substantial trafficking as well in boys from the Czech Republic, Slovakia and Poland.

During our Strasbourg meeting[14] Dr Vandas said Prague had growing concern that now there were border freedoms between the once divided Europe, gay men from the West were travelling to the republic on organised sex tours, as they once did to Thailand and Sri Lanka. The boy sex trade in Prague was concentrated around the Zborovska and Petrinka areas of the city. In Germany alone the BKA[15] estimated there are more than 1,000 boys – some as young as 13 – taken each year into the West by organised crime gangs to be male whores.

A considerable number end up starring in films the showing of which is sometimes difficult to define as a crime and even more difficult to stop. They're beamed in by satellite and can even get on to the bedroom video screens of pubescent teenagers computer literate enough to scan the world's sex-and-violence offerings in seconds.

The United Kingdom was caught almost literally with its trousers down when an indulgently plump, easily smiling bankrupt named Mark Garner began transmitting hard core lesbian and homosexual porn into Britain in 1992. Mr Garner had studied a typically fudged, please-everyone-and-offend no-one Brussels draft directive and had realised its money-making potential. British government lawyers attached to the Department of National Heritage, the supposed governing body, had studied the directive, too, but entirely missed its pornographic possibilities. The directive, signed by every country in March 1989, stated that a television programme made in one EC member state could – irrespective of its content – be transmitted via satellite to any other member state, without obstruction or interference. In 1991 the European Directive on Transfrontier Broadcasting became Community law in Britain, superseding the country's Obscene Publications Act and making meaningless any objections from the Britain's TV censor body, the Broadcasting Standards Council.

Garner, who admittes his wife wouldn't allow his pornography into their Manchester house, was in business. He'd already formed a company named Continental Television. Garner applied for and got from Netherlands PTT, the government owned telecommunications network, a licence to broadcast on the Europe-spanning Eutelsat 11-F1, one of eight satellites co-owned by the telecommunications organisations of thirty one countries. He could not connect with the satellite from Holland, however: Continental Television was not a Dutch-registered company. The broadcasts were transmitted from Denmark. Within a year, Garner claimed a viewing audience of 25,000, each of whom paid £47.25 a quarter for the decoder necessary to unscramble the signal to see their porn movies. They also had to buy a satellite dish and pay £100 for it to be adapted to receive Eutelsat 11-F1 programmes.

Garner's station was called Red Hot Dutch.

There was uproar not only in the British parliament but throughout Europe – including protests from the Vatican, one of the 31 Eutelsat sovereign state owners – when a newspaper[16] exposed Garner's exploitation of the woolly-worded, legally binding Commission protocol and the incompetence of British parliamentary lawyers in not realising the opportunities it created for people like Garner.

Garner insisted that no-one but an adult could receive the material because it could only be viewed by those who possessed a decoder.

Which, after four months of prevarication by the National Heritage Department, turned out to be the weapon Britain used against Continental Television. Under an obscure provision in the 1990 Broadcasting Act allowing it to proscribe any television channel offending good taste or decency, the government banned the sale of the transcribing decoders. After the decision was upheld by appeals to the British High Court and the Court of Appeal, Continental Television announced they would seek a judgment from the European courts.

Garner's argument that his pornography would be kept from children by the need for a viewing decoder was derided by a number of outraged commentators in a general debate throughout the country about controls of material appearing upon British television. That debate arose after the horrific murder of two-year-old toddler Jamie Bulger in February 1993. At the trial of the two 11-year-olds who had lured Jamie on to a railway line and battered him to death, there were defence suggestions that the two youngsters had been influenced by scenes from a horror movie entitled *Child's Play 3*. Such films became known in Britain as 'video nasties', movies in which the concentration and content was more upon horror and violence than it was upon sex, of whatever variety.

British Home Secretary Michael Howard responded ineptly, initially rejecting demands in April 1994, from parliament that the country's censorship laws be tightened. He made a U-turn, a familiar manoeuvre for him, when confronted by an open revolt by eighty of his own MPs. They threatened to support an amendment, proposed by anti-pornography campaigner and Liberal Democrat MP David Alton, which would have introduced new measures into Howard's flagship law-and-order legislation, the Criminal Justice Bill, then going through Parliament, and would probably have brought it down. Alton was persuaded to withdraw his amendment upon Howard's undertaking to take action after all. The Home Secretary, lamely, claimed his measures were tougher (being 'tough' and 'cracking down' on crime are among Howard's favourite expressions) because he introduced jail sentences. Such penalties were not included in Alton's amendment.

In its government-revised form, the Justice Bill, which became law in the Autumn of 1994, enables a sentence of up to six months to be passed upon shopkeepers who rent 15 and 18 year-rated videos to under-age children. The penalty rises to two years for anyone supplying banned videos to children. In addition to the legal moves, the Home Secretary instructed the licensing authority, the British Board of Film Classification, to tighten its existing 15 to 18 ratings. The BBFC were also told strictly to observe statutory guidelines established to ensure that children were prevented watching videos likely to cause psychological harm or those presenting 'an inappropriate model for children'.

Three months after the Home Secretary's addition to his Justice Bill, the all-party Home Affairs Committee produced a report[17] that was ordered in the clamour after the Bulger murder. The committee found that *Child's Play 3* had been wrongly linked to the case but said violent videos already on release in Britain – an estimated 25,000 – should be re-examined and in some cases banned.

They concluded that filmed horror and brutality could corrupt youngsters and lead to crime. They reached that decision although conceding that none of the witnesses called before them had been able to provide an example of someone having committed a crime as a direct result of watching a video nasty. Academic research on any correlation was, they further conceded, inconclusive. 'We do not believe that, because video violence is one among many causes of violent crime, it should be ignored. We believe that there is some evidence to support the common-sense view that videos do have some corrupting influence upon the young, which may lead some vulnerable children into crime, and we support steps taken to deal with this issue.'

Urging public involvement in the video debate, the report recommended a six month transitional period for film censors to collect public complaints about the 25,000 movies already in circulation. They considered that any attracting significant criticism should be re-examined and re-assessed by the BBFC.

Sir Ivan Lawrence, chairman of the committee, recognised in remarks after the publication of the report that there was an element of civil liberty and an individual's freedom of choice in the discussion. Nevertheless, his committee felt the government were being 'too timid' about already circulating videos.

Although the committee were considering videos of violence and horror, its concern about the corrupting influence of what the very young see on their television screens applies equally to every variety of sexual pornography. Paedophiles often show their infant victims films and pictures of adults having sex with children, both to persuade the often confused child it is an acceptable practice, and to arouse themselves before perpetrating a fresh assault.

The Criminal Justice Bill already had – quite apart from the video nasty additions – provisions aimed at such paedophile films, intended both to extend and tighten the Obscene Publications Act against film and computer technology being used to make such sex movies and to prevent their makers escaping prosecution through technical loopholes. Included in those provisions are penalties against films in which one child's face is transposed upon the body of another – or of a willing participant who physically might appear to be a child – and against what are known as pseud or quasi videos. These movies do not, in fact, feature flesh-and-blood people or children. Film graphic technology is now so advanced that an animation feature can be created – using drawings – which appears to star live people.

Some makers of such films advertise in computer magazines throughout Europe. The Criminal Justice Bill enables British police to move against such distributors if they operate within the United Kingdom. For the first time there are now powers of immediate arrest which will prevent a pornographer remaining free to warn others – or his paedophile clients – and so enable them to destroy incriminating material. Police are powerless, of course, if the distribution address is, or appears to be, outside the United Kingdom. A common marketing ploy for British porn distributors[18] is to sell through an accommodation address or box number from countries like Holland or Denmark: the reputation of both countries as purveyors of the hardest of hard core material is considered an added inducement to buy. The order, together with the purchasing money, is relayed back to the English supplier who has the pornography ready and waiting in England but who has protected himself from detection through a European intermediary.

Such an arrangement makes it extremely difficult for British police to follow the distribution trail to achieve a successful prosecution.

There is an additional method of distributing pornography which can be watched by children who have not achieved puberty or even reached their teens.

All they have to be is computer literate, which the majority of children in the European Union now are. From the privacy of their own bedrooms, in which their personal computers are usually kept, they can dial bulletin boards – directories and access number guidance obtained and offered for subscribed use by hackers –

anywhere in the world to view, and copy, any and every sort of porn film. Copied diskettes are frequently viewed on the computers of the schools in which teachers have taught their pupils the necessary technology, in the normal course of computer lessons; one estimate[19] is that such material is available and watched in one school out of every three in England.

A Home Office specialist[20] on the subject admitted: 'It is virtually impossible to stop.'

Just as most organ transplant crime is impossible to stop.

CHAPTER THIRTEEN

The Body Snatchers

Private clinics and hospitals have several advantages for the organised crime groups of Europe. Such groups, cloaked by shell companies layered upon shell companies and administered by unimpeachably correct nominee directors, own such establishments in France – particularly in the south – and Italy. It has also been suggested to me[1] they exist in Germany.

All, on the surface, are perfectly managed and operate to the highest standards, complying with every health, hygiene and medical regulation, to avoid attracting any unwelcomed official attention to what they do unofficially. And as properly-run establishments, they provide a good and continuing legitimate income from the original money-washing investment that purchased them in the first place.

Which, to organised crime, is the first advantage.

And then, inevitably, there are drugs. What better concealment and conduit for drugs can there be than premises where drugs are in daily and bona fide use? Hospitals and clinics additionally have laboratories, where some refining can take place, although this is limited because of the risk of detection: the production of heroin, for instance, gives off an identifiable smell. Hospitals and clinics can also legitimately purchase some of the chemicals used in the refining of drugs, although again such purchasing is limited: one of the few practical ways law officers track drug refining in the

European Union is by a close and cooperative liaison with pharmaceutical companies that make their ordering records available.[2]

But there is still, to organised crime, a further advantage.

There is the horrifying abuse to which clinical facilities can be put: the removal of organs from sometimes kidnapped, sometimes bought-for-cash children and young adults, for transplant in those same clinics and hospitals into desperate and dying people, often unaware of the identity of their donor. As they are unaware that sometimes the donor dies in order to provide the organ they can afford to pay a huge price for.

The practice is known about. It has been exposed several times in the European Parliament, on the last occasion[3] by a then incumbent MEP who is himself a doctor. It caused an uproar in two of the countries – Brazil and Italy – publicly named.

Despite vehement demands, no harmonised, European-wide legislation, condemnation or code of practice to outlaw the body-robbing and murder has been enacted. Nor will it be, for years. If ever. Which, for such crimes, would be incredible were it not for the never-to-be-forgotten fact that we are discussing the supposedly harmonising European Union in which disharmony reigns.

Incredulity that no Community action has been taken was obvious in the voice of Professor Leon Schwartzenberg, the French transplant surgeon and former MEP whose report, which the European Parliament adopted, disclosed the worldwide organ-by-theft-and-murder trade that the United Nation's Secretary General itemised at the 1994 crime conference in Naples. 'It is fantastic, that nothing is being done. Or will be done. Totally fantastic,' Professor Schwartzenberg told me a year before Boutros Ghali drew worldwide attention to the trade.

As fantastic, in my judgement, as the explanation given by parliamentary officials in Luxembourg and Commission experts in Brussels for doing nothing. None of them feels – to use their Eurospeak word – they have the 'competence' to introduce a directive which the fifteen member countries would have to adopt. The Eurospeak excuse was defined for me by a Dutch official at Luxembourg as meaning Brussels can't decide how to categorise the maiming and mutilation and murder for their organs of victims often mentally sub-normal (to the further advantage of the mafias, the mentally ill are more trusting, less inclined to ask questions).

Was it, the Dutchman asked, an ethical matter? Or a social one? Or then again, a health subject? Competence was always such a difficult problem, so hard to resolve. And there was also the stumbling block of subsidiarity. The disillusioned Dr Schwartzenberg had the subsidiarity argument put to him, to explain the lack of action by the European Commission in Brussels. He was unimpressed by it.

He should not have been. Twice before – as long ago as May 1979 and then again in April 1983 – the parliament asked the Commission to create a legally binding directive on transplant systems throughout the Community. Brussels did nothing. And when Dr Schwartzenberg's report was debated in Strasbourg in September, 1993, the Irish Commissioner for Social Affairs, Padraig Flynn, warned the meeting that Brussels' powers were so limited that the Commission had no authority to propose legislation. Having once more disqualified itself from any responsibility (or *competence*, to maintain the Eurospeak), the Commission thought parliament's best – in fact its *only* – hope was for the human rights sentinel, the Council of Europe, to introduce a revised convention on organ donations that the member states of the European Union would then have to adopt. Parliament still called upon Brussels to introduce a code of conduct against the body snatchers. In reponse to which demand, yet again, Brussels took no action whatsoever.

Since that time those body snatchers continue, unhindered, to buy or kidnap children from impoverished Third World or East European environments. Or bribe the administrators of hospitals for the mentally ill, in those same countries, to give them any-time access or possession of trusting, unsuspicious inmates. Which means, with terrifying but unavoidable logic, the unhindered continuation of maimings and mutilations and murder. It is not restricted, even, to the living. The trade in transplants extends to unborn foetuses[4] killed and lifted from the wombs of unsuspecting or paid, desperate-for-money mothers.

In his report Dr Schwartzenberg invoked the analogy of Nazi Germany. 'This trafficking is all the more monstrous where it involves killing people to remove organs which can be sold at a profit. To deny the existence of such trafficking is comparable to denying the existence of the ovens and gas chambers during the last war.'

Which prompts a further question. Most of the European

nations fought to defeat Nazism: shouldn't they act with similar determination to eradicate little less than the slavery and medical abominations so conveniently relegated from today's awareness to yesterday's of Auschwitz and Belsen and Buchenwald?

Of course they should. That they don't indicates yet another failure of the Community to become anything more than a tariff-favoured group of conventionally trading nations.

There is a trade in human organs because there is a shortage of such organs for transplants which enable the lives of terminally ill people to be extended and enhanced for many years. The shortage is acute in one of the most successful of such operations, kidney transfers. A donor can give one and survive quite normally on the second the human body contains. Both can be beneficially transferred from people who have agreed before their demise to such a donation immediately after they are medically declared brain dead. Or whose relatives agree. A living person can donate the cornea from one eye and retain sight in the second. Or donate both immediately after death. A healthy heart or liver or lung has to come from a recently dead person: if that heart, liver or lung is to be suitable for exchange, it is usually necessary for it to come from the body of an otherwise healthy person who has died violently, usually in an accident.

Dr Schwartzenberg was bitterly attacked by the health ministries of several countries – and questioned on his methodology by some fellow professionals – after presenting his report to the Strasbourg parliament in 1993. Italy and Brazil led those attacks. When we spoke[5] Dr Schwartzenberg told me of the challenge he issued in the face of denials by those countries that such practices exist. 'I told Rome that I would welcome going on trial and for a court to decide if I was exaggerating or telling untruths. No defamation or slander proceedings have been initiated. And Brazil changed some of its adoption procedures, to give more protection to children.'

Both countries had been linked by Dr Schwartzenberg in one of several episodes listed in his report.[6]

He named as a child trafficker Lucas de Nuzzo who, between 1989 and 1992, had a total of 4,000 children shipped from Brazil to Italy, ostensibly for adoption. Of those 4,000, only 1,000 were ever traced after their arrival in Italy.

He further identified the Neapolitan Mafia, the Camorra, as one of an organised crime group putting Mexican, Thai and European children into clandestine clinics and hospitals to have organs removed.

He quoted a statement made in July, 1992, by Guatamala police spokesman Bodilio Hichos Lopez that children were sold for $20,000 to the United States as organ donors.

He cited the discovery of the corpses of ten street people – one a 15-year-old girl – in the lecture hall of the Faculty of Medicine in Barranquilla, Colombia. There were the remains of forty other corpses. 'The faculty warden knocked out the beggars with baseball bats. The victims were plunged into a coma and were not finally finished off until after the extraction of their organs, the most profitable being sold on the black market.'

He claimed that from Peru, over a two and a half year period, 3,000 children were sent to the United States and Italy. 'In Honduras handicapped children are adopted by people who sell them like spare parts. In the Indian village of Villivakkam, hardly anyone is physically "whole". They sell one of their kidneys for 28,000 rupees (£580) or go to Bombay to sell an eye.'

And he recalled that in February 1992, Argentina's Minister of Health, Cesar Ara, discovered that blood, organs and corneas had been removed from patients of the Colonia Montes de Ocan, a psychiatric hospital near Buenos Aires. The authorities could not locate or trace a total of 1,395 patients who had over a period of years been registered there as inmates.

The Buenos Aires case was investigated in a British television documentary[7] which photographed one mentally subnormal youth with empty eye sockets. His eyes, the programme alleged, had been removed for their corneas by medical staff scooping them out with a coffee spoon. The youth had been rescued by his family from the storm culvert into which he had been dumped, to die. Victims were customarily murdered, after which their bodies were left in culverts or drains. The same programme also named a Moscow-based Russian doctor trading in organs obtained in questionable circumstances. The doctor claimed association with the Eurotransplant Foundation, a non-profit making organisation attached to the University Teaching Hospital of Leiden, in the Netherlands. Eurotransplant encourages transplantation and co-ordinates international exchange of donor organs throughout Belgium, the Netherlands, Luxembourg, Germany and Austria, embracing a population of 110 million. There is also liaison and organ exchange between France and the United Kingdom: in its twenty-seven-year history, Eurotransplant has saved the lives of an estimated 50,000 people throughout Europe.

Having visited the foundation[8] and discussed the Russian's assertion with its officials, I am totally convinced that the connection claimed by the Russian doctor was manipulated by him to create an impression of professional integrity. There had been correspondence between him and the foundation but the foundation had never engaged in any exchange of organs. They have now totally disassociated themselves from the man. The spokesperson with whom I talked stressed Eurotransplant's transactions were only ever between medically recognised transplant organisations and hospitals, never individual doctors.

She had heard, however, of a trade in stolen organs by criminally-run private hospitals and clinics. The problem of blood grouping and tissue compatibility could be resolved if samples were taken in a crime-controlled clinic or hospital from a kidnapped or purchased donor to make sure they matched with a recipient before the extraction of the organ. 'We cannot say such a business does not exist. We have heard the rumours, like everyone else. The danger is that with the continued shortage it could be a crime that will grow. We do not like discussing it, because it deters genuine donors. We know, for example, there is a trade in selling organs in India, where it is not a crime. A man can keep his family for ten years on what he gets for selling one kidney or an eye: purchasers tout around villages, on bicycles, offering to buy. We believe such things happen in Latin America, too. But we refuse to have any connection with such practices. It is unethical.'

Ethics, of course, are never a consideration for the sort of organised crime revealed to the European Parliament in the debate following Dr Schwartzenberg's report. In fact, he was greeted with applause when he declared: 'Such acts must be considered as murder and the doctors who are guilty must be banned for life from practising medicine. We must fight against what can be regarded as absolute crime: that an individual be sacrificed upon the altar of the rich and powerful, because she or he is weak or handicapped.'

There was even an indication during the debate from one French MEP, Madame Janine Cayet, that the mafias were preying on the mentally sub-normal, arranging for them to be maintained on what amounted to body-farms until their organs were required.

The suggestion was based upon the experience of Dr Jean Claude

Alt, an anaesthetist who has investigated transplant crimes from the Paris-based branch of Amnesty International. In August 1993, Dr Alt was told by a doctor attached to an orphanage in St Petersburg, Russia, of an adoption approach for thirty children from an unnamed organisation in the United States. 'Any children were acceptable, even Down's Syndrome children, more commonly known as mongoloids, *except those who had heart problems.*' (my italics).

The obvious inference was that the children would be kept alive and tissue-typed until a compatable recipient sought a new organ.

I personally discussed[9] that encounter with Dr Alt, who works at the Clinique des Franciscaines at Versailles and is a frequent visitor to Russia. He admired St Petersburg's woman head of paediatrics, Natalia Nikiforova, as someone of total integrity and in no way connected with the organ trafficking into Europe from Russia. No children at her orphanage – and certainly no Down's Syndrome sufferer – had become a victim from the American approach. 'I believe organ trafficking goes on. The difficulty is obtaining empirical evidence. St Petersburg – and the taking of children for their organs – is mafia controlled.' He had been told of this by Dr Nikiforova. She had also told him that if anyone involved in the trade or who had knowledge of it talked to him – as a representative of Amnesty International – or to the St Petersburg authorities, they would be killed. Adoption certificates, allowing children to be taken from Russian orphanages, could be bought, provided the payment was in dollars: he did not know the current price. But it was an established and wide-spread business, against which there did not appear to be any law in Russia. 'Many orphanages are not run very well.'

The St Petersburg episode was not the only example provided by Madame Cayet during the 1993 Parliamentary debate. She also quoted several newspaper and news agency accounts[10] exposing what she called 'this odious trafficking'. The Greek Secretary of State for Health had ordered an enquiry into suspected organ trafficking in the country. A committee of enquiry had been convened by Congress in Honduras into the disappearance of children, some of whom were mutilated when later found. The director of a Swiss clinic in Vaud had been contacted by an organisation in Poland, offering organs from donors responding to classified newspaper advertisements offering to buy body parts.

Another French MEP, Madame Sylvie Mayer, cited a German

study quoting the 1991 European price list for organs. An eye was valued at $5,000, a kidney at $1,500 and two square centimetres of skin cost $20. She was outraged: 'The human body is not for sale. On the basis of this fundamental principal the trade in human organs should be banned.'

A United Nations Truth Commission is investigating instances of children farmed and kidnapped in Latin America for organ transplants.

Anguished mothers – some of whom, according to reports,[11] have had their babies stolen from them at the moment of birth – have provided UN officials with the locations of *casas de engorde*, which translates as fattening houses. These are shacks in San Salvador, Honduras and Guatemala to which bought or stolen children and babies are taken to be fed and cleaned of lice and infection to make them more attractive to prospective purchasers before their transfer to clandestine operating theatres. One credible report[12] quoted Victoria de Aviles, San Salvador's procurator for the defence of children, that they were aware of a 'big trade' in children for organ stealing and bemoaning the ease with which false documentation could be bought to get a child out of the country. Maria Teresa Delgado, executive director of the Salvadorean Institute for Child Care, openly acknowledged the existence of *casas de engorde*. During a twelve year civil war that did not end until 1992, the best run organisation in the child snatch-and-sell business was the Salvadorean military: a 1992 United Nations enquiry records over 9,000 atrocities for which it holds the army and government-supported death squads responsible. In Honduras children were bought while still in the womb and taken away at the moment of birth. Police spokesman Fredy Carcia Avalos identified the village of Boca del Monte as being the best known in the country for baby-farming. The farms charged £18 a month fattening and preparing a child for sale to or adoption by foreigners.

Although aware of the organ and child trafficking into Europe from Russia, Dr Alt considered Latin America the prime source of victims. He isolated the finding of the fifty bodies in the Faculty of Medicine in Barranquilla as positive evidence of its existence and told me he had personally spoken to a physician who had been offered 'four to six' pairs of eyes from the Colonia Montes de Ocan psychiatric hospital in the suburbs of Buenos Aires. 'There is no law, no safety for little ones.'

Dr Schwartzenberg echoed the intensity of parliamentary feeling a year after the debate upon his report when, during our conversation, he repeatedly referred to organ trafficking as 'utterly despicable'. Children and young adults were brought every week to Europe from Latin America and the Eastern bloc, to be kept alive until their organs were required. Then the organs were taken. And afterwards – or even under the anaesthetic – the donors were killed. The medical profession and investigating authorities were naive if they believed qualified doctors would not, from ethical, moral or professional revulsion, become involved in the criminality. Corneas could be transferred from a child to an adult: it was possible to transplant two of a child's kidneys to compensate for one that had failed in an adult. A heart or liver transplanted into an adult had to come from a donor of equivalent growth and weight. All were available, through the criminal organisations. There was a strong possibility that organs from a donor brought into Europe from Third World or Eastern bloc territories would be contaminated, risking the lives of the recipients. It was incomprehensible to him that the European Union was content to rely upon the individual laws of the member countries – obeying the concept of subsidiarity – instead of immediately agreeing a prohibiting convention or directive to which every member country would have to become a signatory.

Dr Ron Guttman is a surgeon at the McGill Transplant Centre of the Royal Victoria Hospital in Montreal, Canada, and an expert respected by Amnesty International for his balanced views on donor abuse from Latin America. Dr Guttman was sceptical[13] of how widespread organ robbery was. He insisted on dividing the transplants between what he called vital organs – heart, liver and kidney – and other donated material, like cornea, heart valves, bone and tissue. The transplant of a vital organ was a 'complex business', requiring a large medical team. He thought it would be difficult for there to be a large number of such illegal operations, for which it was necessary for so many people to be involved: one at least would protest or inform the authorities. He criticised media sensationalism about the subject, concerned, like officials at the Eurotransplant Foundation in Leiden, at the deterring effect such sensationalism has upon genuine donors. In the Strasbourg debate in September 1993, Madame Cayet had quoted a newspaper story[14] that, in announcing an official enquiry into organ stealing in March 1992, Senor Librado-Ricavar, the Secretary General of the provincial government of San Luis Potosi, in Mexico, had revealed that children were briefly vanishing from the suburbs of San Luis and were found to have had a kidney removed when they were returned to their families. Dr Guttman thought practically everyone had heard that anecdote: 'I've lost count of the number of times I've tried to follow the story through to track down a victim. I've never managed to find one yet. Not one. I remain to be convinced of a substantial trade in vital organ trafficking. There's been tissue and bone and cornea taken from corpses, in morgues. It's possible to transplant that some time after death. But not vital organs.'

Dr Schwartzenberg was familiar with the sort of doubts expressed by Dr Guttman. What happens to the thousands of children who vanish every week of every month of every year? Do they just disappear into thin air?

It is possible to provide an answer to that question, authenticated from the same forum of which Dr Schwartzenberg was a member until 1994.

Not all the children spirited away from South America or the Eastern bloc or Asia or even from their homes in Europe itself are stolen for their organs.

Those who live are still stolen *for* their bodies. There's far more money for European organised crime in child sex – in all its forms and outlets – than there is in stealing children for their organs. After all, those taken for medical use only have a one time commercial value: a child – of either gender – introduced into pornography or paedophilia, some only a few months old, has an earning potential over several years.

CHAPTER FOURTEEN

Give Me Your Tired, Your Poor, Your Huddled Masses[1] . . .

France presented America with its welcoming beacon to the world's homeless and exiled, upon which that most famous invitation is inscribed and which still greets new arrivals to the United States. But such altruism, like the Statue of Liberty itself, is now weathered by age and eroded by attitude. America has enough huddled masses of its own. And Europe never wanted them. It still doesn't. France gave the statue, not the poem at its base. There are other compassionate words in Emma Lazarus' sonnet. 'Wretched refuse' are two of them. They have no compassionate meaning in a European Union approaching its second millennium.

Those rusted clichés 'Fortress Europe' and 'Ring of Steel', so irrelevant against the organised crime overwhelming the EU, are much more applicable against immigrants and refugees. And – completing the paradox – they foster crime, much of it highly organised, much of it murderous.

In each of the fifteen states within the Union there are xenophobic, racially motivated extremist organisations and political parties that share a determination to keep their countries 'pure', free from foreigners.[2] With sickening inevitability that purification – by fire bomb, bullet, club or knife – goes beyond singling out people by the colour of their skin to include anti-semitism. For good measure, it is universally anti-Islamic, too.

None should be dismissively ridiculed as a group of isolated fanatics strutting and posturing in neo-Nazi pantomime. Each is linked by a clandestine sub-culture – even by a certain type of music, pop not Wagner – not limited to the European Union, but connected internationally as well. Many have ties with America's Ku Klux Klan. Most subscribe to the publications of America's neo-Nazi movement.

Germany vies with Austria as the most virulent. There is little to separate either from France. Britain, significantly with laws[3] making it the most unbreachable fortress country against immigration in the Union, has evolved the skinhead movement which now spreads across Europe – and even further, into the Eastern bloc – from which always come the front-line 'soldiers' in any racial attack. The skinheads – who are virtually indistinguishable from football hooligans – have their own independent sub-culture of cross-border fraternities but are often, additionally, members as well of the racially-motivated extremist groups.[4]

Until 1992, the European Commission hid behind the convenient excuse of a 'lack of competence' to avoid taking any positive steps even to monitor racism. That year racial violence erupted in several countries, the worst in Germany where the death toll included children burned to death in immigrant hostels while calmly watching town residents refused to intervene. The violence worsened in the following year. Then, responding to demands from the European Parliament, which had already issued two largely-ignored xenophobic warning reports,[5] Commission President Jacques Delors finally added – although ineffectively – race relations to the Commission mandate. He made immigration – and its abused victims – the responsibility of Social Affairs Commissioner Padraig Flynn, the man who had earlier offered lack of competence as a reason for the Commission's inability to take any action against the parliamentary-exposed body organ trade. Actually, Delors didn't allocate Commissioner Flynn's authority too absolutely, because in the executive of the EU, provable liability is never attached to the extent of it causing embarrassment if anything later goes wrong. In his letter to Mel Read, the British Labour MEP who demanded Commission involvement, Delors produced a masterful example of Eurospeak answerability avoidance. 'Much of what the Commission does within its designated working areas more or less directly affects the fight against racism and xenophobia. Various members of the Commission are responsible for these areas and there is therefore a collegiate responsibility for this amongst the Commission.'

There are approximately 20,000,000 legal immigrants in the European Union. The greatest majority, about 6,000,000, reside in Germany. There are more than 2,000,000 in France and the United Kingdom. One estimate[6] puts as high as 5,000,000 the number of illegal immigrants who have already entered the EU, with that figure rising 'practically by the hour'.

A pitifully small proportion of those trying to enter illegally do so independently. And these make up the highest proportion of those intercepted and turned back at borders. The vast majority get in on entry documents forged – close to perfection by modern technology, in those free-of-computer law havens in the Far East – by the organised Triads of Asia and the mafias of East and Western Europe.

Four main Triad groups control[7] the immigration racket through Europe. The profit was described to me[8] as 'incalculable: hundreds of millions a year'. The business is organised through a myriad of cells – called lodges – in every capital and large city, with its headquarters in Amsterdam. Godfather Lee Koon Mui operates from there as European head of the best organised Triad, 14K. The other groups are the Wo Shing Wo, the Won On Lok and the San Yee On. A fifth society, the Dai Hoon – made up of former Red Army assault troops – split from their 14K bodyguard function in the early 1990s. By the middle of the century they rivalled the four major groups in large scale people peddling.

The price for getting an Asian illegally into the European Union varies between individual countries of origin, but averages at £8,000 to £10,000 a person. Which is an astronomical, virtually impossible figure for most. And there is usually a family to be paid for, in addition. The Triad solution is simple: they accept as much as the would-be immigrant can offer, on the understanding the remainder of the debt is settled from his earnings once he reaches Europe. Those earnings will, according to the negotiations, be sufficient to pay for his family to follow.

They never are, of course. The interest on the outstanding debt is compounded weekly and even daily into several hundred times its original sum, and never stops climbing. The pressure never stops, either. Intimidated illegals can't report their torture to the authorities. Their left-behind families are as much hostages as they are, and are as subject to attack. Murder, as an example to others, is common, rarely seriously investigated by uninterested police forces – a disturbingly high proportion of French gendarmerie belong to extreme right-wing political parties. Such killings are customarily ascribed to 'Triad Wars', and so can be left to be settled between the warring Asian crime factions.

Often the only alternative for hard-pressed illegal immigrants is crime. Not all are forced into it. Some become criminals willingly, although there is always the need, initially, to repay their debt.

Many aren't willing, just totally and utterly desperate, beyond morality or reason and most of all beyond hope of escape. A wife can join her husband 'for free' – and make several enforced return trips to the family left behind – if she carries a drug consignment on every journey. And if, as well, she and her husband deliver to others or distribute themselves in their unofficially-adopted country the heroin from Khun Sa's Golden Triangle or Ayub Afridi's Golden Crescent. And there are always complimentary tickets for the children – male or female, the younger the better – as grist for the ever turning, ever pulverising pornographic mill.

A Triad specialist told me[9]: 'Once they're sucked into the whirlpool the only way is down, to the very bottom. And there they stay, because there's no way out. It's total slavery.'

To Western organised crime the Asian illegal immigrant scam – guaranteeing uninterrupted millions – is irresistible. I understand[10] the scheme is being operated identically by Russian and European mafias, working in partnership with the organised crime groups of Europe: immigrants who leave the East on forged papers immediately come under the pay-or-else control of the EU gangs they've been told will help them settle.

After the late 1992 atrocities in Germany – mirrored in several other EU countries, including Austria, France and Britain and continued through 1993 – there was a widespread expectation that the recognised racist parties would gain substantially in national and European Parliament elections in 1994.

That prediction proved to be false, except in Austria: the extreme right uniformly did badly in every other European poll. I do not believe, however, that the electoral failure of the xenophobes indicated any lessening in the fervour of the hard core support for EU racism. More worryingly, I can only see that support growing – stoked by the broader-based resentment caused by long-term unemployment.

Long-term unemployment is unlikely to diminish. Although no European government ever concedes anything seriously unpalatable to its electorate the reverse is more likely: such unemployment is far more likely to grow. And go on growing.

At the time of writing there are 20,000,000 people out of work throughout Europe, an unfortunate figure since it precisely equates to the number of immigrants. At least a quarter of the unemployed – a third of those unemployed in Britain and a half of those without work in Italy – are between 18 and 25, the most vulnerable recruiting age for extremists seeking scapegoats for their economic and social problems. Even if Europe succeeds in emerging from recession, growth rates in Germany and France and Britain and Italy are not predicted to go much beyond 1 per cent: to attain a growth rate of 2 per cent would be startling. It would take a sustained growth of at least 2.5 per cent just to *keep* the unemployment level at 20,000,000. David O'Sullivan, a senior employment advisor to the Commission, has been quoted[11] as saying that a European growth of 3 to 4 per cent, which he called 'extremely optimistic', would do nothing to lower the total of those out of work in the Union. The Paris-based Organisation for Economic Cooperation and Development warns[12] – but is unheeded – that the problem is of the European Union's own creation. Over a twenty-year period, every country in Europe has entwined even deeper and more expansive strands into its social security nets, oblivious to the fundamental changes in an increasing technology-led, changing world economy. While unemployment has inexorably increased, because of that technological change, so have wages and social security contributions for the more highly qualified. This has led to European business becoming less and less competitive on a world scale, which in turn has quickened the downward cycle, to further unemployment, demanding increased social support. A comparative study[13] by American business writer and consultant Alan Friedman showed that between 1970 and 1990, the US economy created 38,000 jobs, while during the same period, only 10,000 new jobs emerged in Europe.

To restore its competitiveness, European industry and business needs to restructure. Any restructuring, in the short term – a 'short' term that could last as long as four to five years – will *cost* jobs, not *create* them.

Furthermore, a blood-letting overhaul of private industry would not be sufficient, by itself. The only sustained employment growth in the past ten years has been in state industries and institutions. Without exception, every state industry in Europe is over-staffed. For any government to consider slashing state employment would be electoral suicide. Just as it would be suicidal for any government to reduce state benefits. So none do. Or will.

The potential for employment unrest being fanned into racial terrorism, to the enormous profit of the criminal fraternity, does not end with the basic inability of European government and private industry employers to adjust to world economic and technological reality. Yet another factor emerged from the signing of the Maastricht Treaty to be enshrined in the Single European Act: a worker's right to freedom of movement across EU borders.

That freedom was interpreted by the fifteen nations – and most particularly by Britain and France – as being strictly limited to nationals of the member countries, to the exclusion of non-EU workers. This interpretation allowed the French government to insist upon separate work permits – with the clear implication of their being refused – for Moroccan workers employed by a Belgian company which won a demolition contract in France. The Belgian firm appealed against this provision to the European Court at Strasbourg, which in August 1994, ruled it illegal, under European law, provided such workers were genuine immigrants, legally employed. EU law takes precedence over sovereign law. So the Strasbourg ruling makes it possible for European firms to employ cheap unskilled workers from North Africa and Turkey and so undercut tenders of companies paying higher wages to nationals of their own country.

Arguably, the possibility of that occurring on a large scale is unlikely. But for it to happen at all would hardly lessen the resentments of the 20,000,000 already workless in the EU.

So powerful are the attractions of organised skinhead crime that in 1992 and 1993 townsfolk in Molln and Solingen stood by to watch flames engulf Turkish families. Eight – men, women and children – were burned to death. Five of them died in Solingen. Twelve more 'guestworkers' were slaughtered in Germany in 1993, bringing to seventeen the number of immigrant murders that year. It put Germany at the top of the 1993 racist murder scoreboard. After forty Hitler-guilty years of open door welcome to the tired and poor seeking sanctuary, Germans firmly turned the key in the lock.

Bonn took its legal role model from London, too, as its neo-Nazis took their skinhead lead.

In copying Britain's 'no win' asylum legislation, Germany went further than simply enacting a law, however. It actually changed its post-war, 1949 constitution to enable it to turn asylum seekers back at its borders if it judged them to be under no political, religious or ethnic persecution. Interior Ministry Minister Eduard Lintner[14] referred to this change as a matter of necessity. 'We were being overwhelmed, coupled with the movement of Germans from the former communist East. It was impossible to sustain.'

Also, in 1994, Bonn tried to stem the violence by banning some, although not all, of its most violent neo-Nazi movements.

The most successful extreme right group in Germany is the *Republikaner Partei* (REP), led by Franz Schonhuber. In January 1989, it won 11 seats in the then West Berlin city parliament. Within two months, the *Republikaner*'s neo-fascist rival, the *Nationaldemokratische Partei Deutschlans* (NPD) gained seven seats in Frankfurt. In June 1989, the *Republikaner Partei* polled 2,000,000 votes, which gained them six seats in the European Parliament in Strasbourg. In provincial elections the REP established a presence also in Cologne, Dusseldorf, Geilenkirchen, Stuttgart, Mannheim and Karlsruhe. Having established itself as a legitimate electoral party, the REP became eligible for more than £6 million in state funding. It was able to draw additional finance from its membership of the Group of the European Right in the European Parliament. One analysis[15] of its formative years pays begrudging tribute to its strikingly skilful Germany-for-the-Germans nationalistic propaganda. That same analysis dismisses any suggestion that the reemergence in Germany of the extreme right was a fringe irrelevance, citing surveys[16] that found strong police support for the REP. 'In Bavaria, for example, more than 50 per cent of policemen declared support for the REP while in Hess more than 60 per cent of officers expressed similar loyalties. In addition the REP now has serious backing in the (then) Federal Republic armed forces with more than 1000 serving soldiers in party membership. The demands for a strong Germany are obviously paying dividends.'[17]

The REP's leader, Franz Schonhuber, a one-time television journalist, had been a volunteer in the Nazi Waffen-SS, and when his party began achieving electoral success he proclaimed that Germany was still under occupying powers. And in addition to the wartime Allies – the USA, the USSR, France and Great Britain – he added the Central Council of German Jews. As well as espousing much traditional Hitlerian ideology, REP officials proposed that carriers of the AIDS-producing HIV virus should have their genitals tattooed, and that a disused nuclear power plant at Wackersdorf be turned into a labour camp for the REP's political opponents.

A European Parliament enquiry[18] judged the REP's growth to be at the expense of another extreme right party, the *Deutsche Volksunion* (DVU), led by Dr Gerhard Frey. And that was although Frey's ownership of a press empire had enabled him to mail 24,000,000 homes during the 1989 European Parliamentary elections. In that election the *Deutsche Volksunion* combined with another neo-Nazi organisation to form the electoral group entitled *Liste D* (D for Deutschland). The starting point of the *Liste D* manifesto was virtually verbatim that of the REP: expulsion of all foreigners. Sample slogans proclaimed 'Germany for the Germans' and 'Germany First, then Europe' and 'Proud to be German'.

Frey blatantly used – and uses – his press empire (the lead title of which is *Die Nationale Zeitung*) to revise and 'correct' Germany's Nazi history. It takes re-writing Nazi history to the absurdity of denying that the Holocaust ever occurred. British writer David Irving, also a committed apologist for the Nazi past, is reverently and constantly promoted through Frey's publications, and with reciprocal gratitude Irving performs on DVU platforms.

Both the REP and the DVU – which are fiercely antagonistic towards each other – deny any link between themselves and extreme neo-Nazi groups such as the *Freiheitliche Deutsche Arbeiter Partei* (FAP) and the *Nationalistische Front* (NF), both of which were banned after the terrorist outbreaks in 1992 and 1993. A European Parliamentary investigation[19] claimed, however, that thugs from both proscribed groups acted as stewards at meetings of the established parties.

When Germany banned the German Workers' Freedom Party and the National List at the end of February, 1995 – bringing to ten the number of extreme right wing groups outlawed since 1989 – monitoring officers at the Bundeskriminalamt forecast a risk of underground terrorist groups being formed by the supporters of such organisations.

The German Constitution contains specific and admirable anti-racist provisions.[20] Judged objectively against the xenophobic record of the country over the past decade however, these are virtually ignored by the authorities of every land (State), as well as by those responsible for administering federal law enforcement. And by a bitter paradox, the chief targets for racial violence in Germany are precisely those foreigners who have done most to contribute to the country's admittedly now much-strained post- war economic success, the Turkish *gastarbeiter*. They are almost 2,000,000 *gastarbeiter* in Germany, some second or even third generation people who, despite constant attacks, regard themselves as more German than Turkish. They speak German, they think German, they *are* German. But they will never *be* German, no matter how many generations pass. Ethnic origin governs German citizenship. For two years investigative journalist Gunther Wallraff assumed the identity of 'Ali' to become a *gastarbeiter*. His shaming exposure of the total reality of what it means to be a 'Turkish' worker in Germany, in a book and accompanying film entitled *The Lowest of the Low*, gained him critical acclaim and admiration. More lastingly it gained him numerous defamation law suits, death threats and an official tap on his telephone. So consistent was the pressure upon him that Wallraff himself became a refugee, moving from Germany to the Netherlands.

The second of the two European Parliament investigations into EU racism[21] discovered strong cross-border ties between the National Fronts of both France and Britain. Of the two, that of France presents the most public – even smiling – face. British fascists are far busier out of the public gaze, integrating world-wide neo-Nazi ideology into an international criminal movement.

The best known racist leader in the EU is France's Jean Marie Le Pen, one-time mentor of the murdered French MP Yann Piat. Le Pen, an overweight litigious limelight-seeker with pugilistic inclinations (he hurries to sue against allegation of Nazi-type racism and is fond of posing in boxer strip, complete with gloves) not only leads France's *Front National*. He also heads the Group of the European Right in a Strasbourg Parliament that is concerned at the presence in its midst of such democratically elected fascist bigots. On behalf of that group Le Pen sought from the European Court of Justice in Luxembourg a ruling that would annul the decision of the parliament to investigate fascist racism and xenophobia in the Community. He lost. The court ruled his application inadmissible. Furthermore, a French court at Nancy in June 1993, decided it was not libellous for a publication to have described him as 'the spiritual son of Hitler'. Those – and other –

legal setbacks have not diminished Le Pen's eagerness to seek court judgments that he has been unfairly pilloried in the media.

Despite the failure of the Front National (FN) to achieve its predicted gains in the 1994 elections, the movement has in France a more substantial electoral support than any other extreme grouping in Europe: in the French presidential elections in 1988 against Francois Mitterand, Le Pen genuinely shocked the country by polling 14.4 per cent of the vote.

One of the investigations into European fascism[22] that Le Pen tried to prevent determined: 'Racism has seduced many people in France and is there in abundance, notwithstanding the efforts of numerous anti-racist movements.'

The hate doctrine of Le Pen and his party is equally divided between Jew and Arab and finds a receptive audience the length and breadth of the country, most welcomed of all in the south. In May 1990, 34 tombstones in the cemetery of Carpentras, near Avignon – where French Judaism was founded – were vandalised and the corpse of a man buried two weeks earlier was removed from his grave and mutilated. For the first time since the Second World War a French President, Francois Mitterand, took part in a 200,000-strong silent protest procession in Paris against these outrages. There were similar marches through ten other French provincial cities. There were, of course, no representatives against a resolution deploring the Carpentras desecration that was passed on 17 May 1990, by the European Parliament.

With growing unemployment in France – and the coming into office in March 1993, of a Gaullist government far short of Le Pen's extremism but whose Interior Minister, Charles Pasqua, nevertheless advocates a France for the French policy – by the mid-90s the xenophobia was concentrated against immigrants from the Maghreb, the countries of North Africa. And of all those immigrants, the citizens of Algeria, who often were fleeing its revolutionary fundamentalism, were particularly subjected both to unremitting police scrutiny and to racial assault and abuse from FN supporters. In fact, it was frequently difficult to distinguish from which of the two supposedly opposite sides the harassment was coming. There was no difficulty in interpreting one official action. In September 1994, the Foreign Ministry announced the setting up of a new centralised visa service for Algerians, at Nantes. All applications from Algeria had to be scrutinised there. Only 'recommended' Algerians would be eligible to enter the country.

This measure was rendered legal – at least in the eyes of those carrying it out – by the terms of a new immigration law presented by Pasqua in June 1993, with the intention, in his words, of achieving 'zero immigration'. This new legislation was additional to another statute change, making it more difficult for an immigrant to take French citizenship, and to France's decision – using the excuse that it was concerned about a drug influx from the Netherlands, via Belgium – to maintain border controls with its neighbours by not joining the Shengen Agreement. When Pasqua's anti-immigration proposals – which included increased police controls, making marriage to a French citizen more difficult, tighter restrictions on political asylum and withholding social and medical benefits to anyone without valid residency documentation – were put before the French cabinet, the head of the French immigration monitoring agency, Pierre-Louis Remy, resigned in protest.

Remy was not the only objector. France's Constitutional Council, which examines all new legislation to ensure it accords with the constitution of the country, amended eight of the 51 articles in the new law: one was the clause that would have given mayors the power to refuse to marry foreigners to French citizens if they suspected the union was one of convenience, entered into simply in order to gain residency rights. That rebuff was not Pasqua's only setback. A month earlier the Council had decreed France could not, after all, remain aloof from the border-easing Shengen Agreement. It stated that, according to the constitution, international treaties took precedence over national legislation.

During my researches, which took me on five separate occasions to areas of France of widely differing attitudes and cultural outlook, I was struck by how easy French people universally found it to lay the blame for all their ills at the door of Arab immigration and foreign workers. Like the Turks in Germany, foreign workers had been welcomed in the 1970s for their contribution to the economic growth of France, with the implied promise that it could become their adoptive country. I was a guest at a dinner party in Paris in June 1994 – a social occasion, which I shall not therefore identify – at which two university professors whose intellectual integrity I admired in all other conversations insisted, beyond any persuasion to the contrary, that not only was it essential to achieve zero immigration but also to repatriate legally resident immigrants even if they had lived in the country for many years. They'd benefited from France, as France had benefited from them in the

1970s: it had been an even exchange and now they should return to their own countries 'where they belonged'. It was the North African Arabs who were destroying the country's youth, with drugs. It was the North African Arabs behind all the serious crime.

At another meeting[23] during that same visit to Paris, criminology professor Xavier Raufer assured me there were throughout France one hundred arab ghettoes, mainly concentrated close to the industrial cities and areas, which were positive 'no go' areas to any of the nation's police forces. At a conference of world mafia experts nine months later, again in Paris, a French police observer doubted that number. He thought the figure far nearer five hundred.

Officially there is no such thing as a 'no go' area anywhere in Britain, Scotland or Wales. All such a claim does is show civil authority's preference for sticking its head in the sand. The reality of the situation is that there are such districts and areas in every part of the country, although not as many as even the most conservative estimate of those in France. One assessment[24] put the British number at around forty: of that, fourteen were in London. Virtually all were ethnic minority ghettoes with drugs as a common currency, wired by an underlying current of constant racial tension. Some are listed by the British Medical Association, whose security guidelines to doctors making house calls within them recommend asking for police escorts and never carrying medical bags which might contain drugs or syringes. Before going on emergency calls into Manchester's Moss Side, fire and ambulance crews wear body armour. If police venture into Wine Alley, in Glasgow's Govan district, there must be two men in the police car with a second vehicle on standby to rescue the first, if it is attacked. In Ferguslie Park, in nearby Paisley, there were eleven murders in a twelve-month period. Police tested knife-resistant vests. On the Pennywell Estate in Sunderland, stoning any police who dare enter is a game known as 'Brick the Squaddie'.

The geographical spread of such areas provides a fertile, country-wide breeding ground for racial violence, on the back of which organised crime prospers. In March 1994, Britain's Labour Party – anxious to wrest the electorally attractive law-and-order gimmick from the Conservatives – published official figures from 42 of the country's 43 police districts proving a doubling of racial abuse and attack in the preceding five years. In his evidence to the Home Affairs Select Committee investigating racial attacks and harassment, Peter Lloyd, Minister of State at the Home Office, estimated there could be as many as 130,000 such incidents a year. Labour leader Tony Blair – who was shadow Home Secretary when he disclosed the doubling statistics – guessed that as only a small proportion of incidents were ever reported, the truer figure was between 150,000 to 200,000 a year.

In the second of its two investigations[25] into Community xenophobia, the European Parliament found the United Kingdom had what it called 'an intolerably high level' of racial harassment and violence. Asians were the main targets, ahead of Afro-Caribbeans. And as in every other country in Europe, there was a parallel upsurge of anti-semitism. Racism in Britain's armed forces was a fact, although not official policy. 'Some elite regiments remain totally white.'

The Strasbourg investigators found similarities between the National Front of Britain and that of France, although the British movement lacked the French electoral support. With a membership estimated at only 1,500, the British National Party (BNP) looks for recruits in schools, through which it distributes racist and anti-semitic stickers. Additionally, there are videos and sound tapes and a book club, which enables it by a legal technicality to circumvent the law against distributing racial material. There are also two blatantly racist publications, a monthly magazine named *Spearhead* and the *British Nationalist*, a monthly newsletter.

The printed word is the sinew that holds together and gives strength to far right and racist movements of the EU. The British fascists produce *Scorpion*, the journal to which all the others in Europe subscribe. *Scorpion* is produced by German-based Michael Walker, an associate and friend of Alain de Benoist, in France, and Robert Stuekers, one of the foremost racist disciples in Belgium. Under the aegis of *Scorpion*, international gatherings of extremist political groups are held twice yearly. European parliamentarians believe that the *Scorpion* group is active in forging association with racists in Russia and the former Soviet bloc countries. And where racism flourishes, organised crime is never far behind.

In their second examination of xenophobia in the United Kingdom, MEPs[26] declared: 'Institutional racism is prevalent in British society and ethnic minorities continue to be discriminated against mainly in the justice system, in job opportunities and in recruitment into the police and army.'

The report claimed that the proportion of black people taken into police custody was twice that of their proportion of the population. Three years later, official figures released by Britain's Customs and Excise revealed that half of all passengers searched at ports and airports were black, even though official statistics proved that more white than black people tried to smuggle and that three times as many whites as blacks were found to be carrying drugs. A Customs spokesman, trying to explain the figures, told a British newspaper[27] that blacks more often carried large quantities of drugs – as professional 'mules' for UK-based traffickers – while whites usually only had small amounts for their personal use. The implication was that, despite statistics to the contrary, blacks were responsible for bringing more drugs into the United Kingdom than whites.

The European parliamentarians[28] described as 'most worrying' the growth not just into Europe but into the former Soviet bloc of the skinhead movement, born in Britain in the 1960s. Wryly, its report commented: 'Britain has an appalling record for exports in recent years but in one field she has done remarkably well, namely in spreading the racist and violent sub-culture of the skinheads.'

It would be easy to dismiss that sub-culture, but for the abundant evidence of its racial perniciousness. The shaven-skulled, swastika-daubed image of a T-shirted youth screaming racial hatred is universally recognised, from San Francisco to St Petersburg. Their operating manual, *WAR* – organ of the US neo-Nazi White Aryan Resistance Movement, of which the *Führer* is Tom Metzger – carries in every edition telephone and fax numbers of fraternal hate movements in Europe. The slogans of their hatred form the lyrics of their own esoteric music, called Oi, a mutation of punk and heavy metal. Its purveyors are a group formed around the band Skrewdriver, whose leader, Ian Stuart Donaldson, is a scion of respectable British middle class society.

Their concerts provide the meeting places for international skinhead gatherings, where they perform as recruiters for the American Ku Klux Klan. Their records and tapes are distributed worldwide by a company named Rock-a-Rama Records, based in Bruhl, Germany. There have been several unsuccessful attempts by the German authorities to close down the distributors. As well as leading Skrewdriver, Donaldson – covertly supported by the British National Party – produces a skinhead manual of his own, *Blood and Honour*. The merchandising of their products brings in an income estimated[29] in Britain alone to be worth in excess of £1,000,000.

British skinheads are so indistinguishable from football hooligans that the term is virtually interchangeable. So concerned was the United Kingdom at the connection that a specific monitoring unit was established in the National Criminal Intelligence Service. It has compiled a list of 6,000 active hooligans, the majority of whom have links with fascist organisations and outlets. During the build-up to the 1994 World Cup in the United States, NCIS liaised closely with America's FBI after it was learned that British hooligans planned with skinheads in the United States a series of violent disruptions in many of the various cities in which the games were played. The joint intelligence cooperation, which led to many unannounced preventative measures in America, foiled the planned rioting. An indication of the criminal profit at the disposal of such groups came from the NCIS discovery that the British ringleaders commuted between London and New York by Concorde.

The official investigation into the European Cup disaster at Brussel's Heysel Stadium, in Belgium, on 29 May 1985, uncovered evidence that fascist-motivated football hooligans had been involved in the rioting that cost 41 lives and injured 350. After an English neo-Nazi group calling itself Combat 18 – taking the numerals of its title from the initials of Adolf Hitler (A-1, H-8) – fermented another bloody football riot in Dublin in February 1995, Scotland Yard set up a monitoring unit additional to that already existing at the National Criminal Intelligence Service. And in their report[30] on European racism, the Strasbourg parliamentarians claim that Scandinavian skinheads travelled, via Britain, to Northern Ireland for paramilitary training.

The laws restricting and governing immigration and refugee access into Britain are tougher than in any other country within the EU. Which, it became clear in the early 1990s, looked to London for a lead on how to construct its anti-immigrant barriers. When increasingly overwhelmed Germany finally closed its previously wide open door to anyone who sought asylum, it was Britain's legal example it followed. And it was Britain which presented – at one of those closed, unreported gatherings of European Interior Ministers – the series of measures which were to create the Fortress Europe that is such a joke to organised crime.

One of Britain's proposals, adopted by the Community, was that any refugee or asylum applicant refused entry at the border of an EU country should be returned to any intermediary transit country. Both Dr Vandas, from the Interior Ministry of the Czech

Republic, and Dr Bertok, from the Hungarian ministry, complained during our meetings in Strasbourg that the Community was imposing intolerable burdens upon them, seeming to expect them and other bordering countries to turn themselves into initial buffer states against would-be entrants. No former Eastern bloc country had the facilities or experience to do that, insisted Dr Vandas. 'The Community policy, in which we have no say whatsoever, virtually makes us host countries to people we don't want and who don't want to live among us. They want to travel through, that's all. We don't even know the majority are in our country, in the first place. But when they are turned back at a Community border it's better to live with us than to go back to where they came from originally. We simply cannot cope. We are buried under our own problems: there's no room or allowance for those of others.' He estimated there might be as many as 150,000 illegal immigrants in limbo, in the Czech and Slovakia Republics.

Poland was the first of the former Eastern bloc countries to try to erect barriers of its own to avoid being a no-mans-land for lost people. By the end of 1993, entry into Poland from Romania, Bulgaria and most of the other former Soviet bloc countries was only possible for people able to produce an officially-recorded invitation from a Polish citizen. The pressured Czech Republic was quick to follow, including in their restriction Ukrainians and refugees from the former Yugoslavia, thousands of whom *have* been accepted within the EU. Before the positive action by Warsaw and Prague, the Czech republic hosted a crisis meeting attended, in addition to representatives from Warsaw, by interior ministers from Slovakia, Hungary, Austria – even though within two years it was to don the immigration-restricting corset of the EU itself – and Slovenia, in order to harmonise immigrant policies and agree on joint action against people-smuggling organised crime. Justifiably fearful at this insular, ethnically-driven erosion of the principles of the 1951 Geneva Convention on Asylum, the United Nations High Commission for Refugees (UNHCR) issued a protest statement. 'In the rush to set up new barriers to economic migrants many legitimate applicants for asylum will be hit. We can understand the concern of the governments in question, but there is a great danger that the basic right of asylum could be jeopardised.'

Responding to the criticism of Britain's attitude, the then Home Secretary, Kenneth Clarke, said[31]: 'I have always prided myself on liberal views on race relations, immigration and the need to have an open society. But that has to be combined with clear rules on immigration, on asylum and definite enforcement policy to make sure the rules are accepted. We have to have a sensible, liberal system of controlling the numbers of people that can sensibly be absorbed by our economy and public services.'

While publicly proclaiming its liberalism, Britain also urged the deepening of a further moat around Fortress Europe. An EU proposal had been for its fifteen members to recognise a single Euro-visa to control non-residents' access. The issuing of such a visa would depend upon a person not being on a central computer register compiled from lists of undesirable visitors, immigrants or aliens in the individual records of each of the fifteen countries.

Insufficient, claimed Britain, arguing that freedom of movement through the Community once a Euro-visa holder had crossed one border gave terrorists and drug traffickers access to every country.

Each individual country, the argument continued, should additionally be able to maintain the separate right of refusal. Such a principle was supported by a report from the House of Lords Select Committee on the European Communities in August 1994 – a report that was labelled a policy based on racial discrimination by Claude Moraes, director of the Joint Council for the Welfare of Immigrants.

The European Parliament investigation,[32] upon which I have heavily drawn during this section, discovered racist, xenophobic support – and formalised parties and movements through which to express it – in virtually every single country in the EU.

It described as 'meteoric' the rise in Austria of the *Freiheitliche Partei Österreichs* (FPO) led by Jorg Haider, who proudly boasts that his parents were Nazi and whose considerable personal wealth derives from the possession of forests expropriated from their Jewish owners in 1940.

Throughout 1992 Haider organised throughout the country a national petition – virtually an unofficial referendum – to stimulate parliamentary debate of his xenophobic suggestions. One of Haider's proposals was to insert into the Austrian Constitution the insistence that 'Austria is not a country of immigration.' Another proposal would have reduced all foreign workers to second class status by making them carry special designating identity cards.

Right wing extremism in Belgium feeds off the Flemish and

French speaking divisions of the country. The *Vlaams Blok* (VB) is a force in Flanders and preaches union with Germany and has links with the violent *Voorpost* (Vanguard) organisation. Although banned as illegal, there exists clandestinely an organisation called *Vlaamse Militanten Orde* (VMO) which in the 1960s and 70s formed association with the major terrorist groups in Europe: it once offered the Ulster Volunteer Force £50,000 worth of weaponry if it would launch a bombing campaign against Jews in Britain. The UVF rejected the deal. Flanders also supports the *VMO-Odal* group and the *National Front Vlaanderen*.

Several small fascist cells in the French-speaking section of the country come under the umbrella of the *Front National*, while the skinheads and soccer hooligans in the country make up the *Parti des Forces Nouvelles* (PFN). Some members of the VMO and the PFN have swallowed their linguistic and separatist differences to form *l'Assault*, which carries out racial attacks in Brussels. *L'Assault* also actively recruits skinheads and has a close working relationship with the French chapter of the Ku Klux Klan.

In Denmark the *Dansk Nasjonal Socjalistisk Bund* drew its blatantly Nazi ideological inspiration from ex-Auschwitz SS officer Thies Christophersen, author of *The Auschwitz Lie*, who settled in Denmark to avoid arrest by the German authorities. The *Fremskridtpartie*, which gained impressive although unsustained victories in the Danish parliament in the early 1970s, is avowedly racist and the European Parliamentary report acknowledged: 'The general view of observers in Denmark is that in the last few years racism has become a more serious and pressing problem and conditions are becoming more favourable for a growth of the extreme right.'

In Italy the right-wing extremism remained a continuous post-war presence in parliament through the *Movimento Sociale Italiano* (MSI), led until his death in 1988 by former Mussolini minister Giorgio Almirante. A number of men listed on Italian police records as leading terrorists during the 1960s and 1970s belonged to MSI: Massimo Abbatangelo, jailed for his involvement in the 1985 bombing of an express train near Florence, later became an MSI member of the Italian parliament.

For the 1994 elections which ended Italy's First Republic, the MSI changed its name to the *National Alliance*. Leader Gianfranco Fini banned skinhead supporters from greeting him with the Nazi salute (although he still allowed himself the famous judgment that

Mussolini was 'the greatest statesman of the century'), and gained sufficient electoral approval to be invited by Silvio Berlusconi to join Italy's brief first ruling coalition of the Second Republic. For the first time since the war, fascists in Italy were given cabinet portfolios. France's Francois Mitterand publicly expressed the disquiet other EU leaders and governments felt.

Although small in terms of membership numbers, the far right *Centrumdemokraten* (CD) party of the Netherlands has parliamentary and local council seats, giving it a voice in the government of the country. Its leader, Hans Janmaat, has criminal convictions for racism. Members of the *Jongeren Front* have similar convictions. The *Actiefront Nationaal Socialisten* is the Dutch wing of a banned German neo-Nazi organisation (ANS): one of *Actiefront*'s leaders, Eite Homann, was a sometime bodyguard for the late German neo-Nazi Michael Kuhnen. Another, Et Wilsink, is part of the European fascist liaison link with the British National Front.

Anti-immigration and anti-semitic parties found a listening audience after the collapse of the Berlin Wall among East Germans readily prepared to accept that job opportunities and housing they believed to be theirs were being filled by foreigners and Jews. Recruits flocked to the *Republikaner Partei*. So they did to Michael Kuhnen's *Deutsche Alternative*. The skinhead movement grew with them.

Racial and religious hatred expanded throughout the East. In Romania – whose gypsies, with sickening irony, are subjected to racial attack in Austria and Germany – assaults on Jews and vandalism of Jewish cemeteries and synagogues reached the level of what religious leaders described as pogroms. In 1990 the country's Chief Rabbi, Moses Rosen, publicly warned that Romania's 20,000 Jews risked terror campaigns reminiscent of war-time Nazism. And shortly afterwards, in the capital Bucharest, there was formed an organisation known as *Vatra Romanesca*, which is virtually identical to the wartime Iron Guard movement which collaborated with the Nazis and took the major responsibility for rounding up Romania's Jewish population for extermination. *Vatra Romanesca*'s published programme promised violent struggle against racially impure minorities and gypsies in Hungary and Germany as well as those within its own borders.

Democratic Forum, the predominant political party in Hungary is led by men who publicly make anti-semitic statements. Istvan Czurka openly blames Jews for the difficulties Hungary has experienced since the Second World War, and Jewish property in Bucharest, Debrecen and Tab has been vandalised. A skinhead movement liaises with those of Britain, Austria and what used to be East Germany.

Strasbourg politicians discovered links between neo-Nazi groups in the United States, like US Third Way and LaRouche, and with fascists in Poland. In Poland, racial hatred is directed more towards Russians, whose country once dominated it, than to minorities: the Jewish population of the country is, in fact, very small, following the efficiency of Nazi extermination in the Second World War.

The Jewish population of Russia is, by comparison, huge and faces pogroms from the fascist Pamyat movement, whose election manifesto literature in Moscow and St Petersburg called for the 'de-Zionization' of the country and for a legal ban on Jews occupying government jobs.

Links exist between Pamyat and extremist German organisations like Fatherland. Pamyat is registered as a legal political movement in St Petersburg, as the Republican People's Party of Russia. According to the Strasbourg enquiry[33] it is closely guided in its racism – and how to implement it – by the British National Party.

It is also into such racial climates – which exist and flourish in every country to the east of the Community's formal borders – that religious and racial refugees who fail to satisfy the stringent European Community requirements are returned.

It's not only European immigration requirements that are stringent. In response to a haphazard, uncoordinated awareness of the true extent of organised crime's encroachment in Europe, police authorities demand ever more liberty-eroding legislation, singing with one voice the hymn that if people want protection from crime they must be prepared to sacrifice some of their freedoms. The refrain runs something like this: 'What has an honest man got to fear?'

The rejoinder to which is, 'everything'.

CHAPTER FIFTEEN

The Take-Over

The intended victim of an IRA take-over, a man whom I know socially, is an entrepreneur, someone who has tried and failed several times. A man who, like many entrepreneurs, wants to try again.

This time he has the patented right to the manufacture of a product that could be revolutionary. To specify it here in the detail in which it has been explained to me would identify him to men in Northern Ireland about whom he has talked to me at length and on several occasions.

Were he to be identified, he would risk – more perhaps than anyone else who has spoken to me in conditions of total anonymity – serious physical danger. He has no doubt that the men he dealt with represented the IRA.

I limit myself, therefore, to describing the product as a recognised derivative of a natural resource but created via a breakthrough process. It would have world-wide applications throughout the leisure industry. It could also be extensively employed in worldwide civil engineering projects.

Considering its ultimate profit potential, running into multi-millions, the initial development and factory building or acquiring costs are small, well under £3 million. But earlier unsuccessful ventures have exhausted his personal capital and left him, in the eyes of banks, with an uncertain track record. From the end of 1992 and throughout most of 1993 he approached every major English bank for the necessary finance: at that stage the intention was to establish a factory and manufacture in England. He failed to get either interest or backing from any of them: each told him they needed a substantial commitment from elsewhere before they would become backers. At the end of 1993 he approached the Northern Ireland Development Board, in London, with the idea of tranferring the entire operation to Ulster. There was a series of meetings with two officials. At last there was interest, even enthusiasm. A detailed presentation was made.

Two weeks after that presentation, the entrepreneur received a telephone call from a man with an Irish accent. He gave a name – which I have but which obviously I will not publish because it would identify my informant – and called himself an agent. Later he called himself a financial consultant. He knew, in some detail, of my informant's plan to open a factory in Northern Ireland. During that initial call he suggested a possible location, which I will not publish beyond saying that it was somewhere in Londonderry.

When the man was asked how he knew about a discussion my acquaintance believed had been restricted to the Northern Ireland Development Board in London, the caller said he had 'lots of friends in the right places'. The Northern Ireland Development Board has, of course, staff in Belfast.

The caller then described his suggested Londonderry village location as being very similar to the hamlet in which my informant lives, in the south of England. There was even a reference to the similarity in the number of houses in each. The sons of my acquaintance would be very happy there, his caller assured him. So would his wife. 'It was very obvious I had been completely checked out in England. There was even reference to certain regular trips my wife made. My sons, too. The prospectus prepared for the Development Board hadn't included that sort of information. It didn't form any part of it: didn't have to. There was a file on me.'

The caller advised the entrepreneur to press his formal approaches through the Development Board as far as possible but stressed that before making the final, detailed financial application ('he knew every step of the procedure'), my acquaintance should personally visit Northern Ireland, in order to have the formalities completed for him, by the man on the telephone. 'That way I'd get every last penny it was possible to get from the government.

Unless it was done by those who knew how to do it, people missed out on what it was possible totally to get.' With the backing of a government body, fresh approaches could then be made to British financial institutions ('he said he knew them all and how to do it') to get the full and necessary building and manufacturing costs.

One official with whom the Englishman was dealing at the Development Board in London, a man who has since been transferred abroad, although still representing the British government department encouraging industry into Ulster, was especially enthusiastic about the overseas sales potential of one particular manufacturing possibility. He said a certain market area was huge for one of the leisure applications of the product and that they'd fall over themselves to buy. The United States was to feature in later conversations with the Irishman, both at long distance and during a later personal meeting.

I planned to accompany my acquaintance on a visit to Northern Ireland, purporting to be someone attached to the company that has been formed to make and market the product, but at the last minute, when final arrangements were being made, there was an insistence that the entrepreneur come alone. There was no need, he was told, for anyone else to be involved at that preliminary stage.

The arrangement was for the caller to come to where my acquaintance stayed in Ulster: there was no address at which my Englishman could locate him. The caller, a man with unusually long hair, was accompanied by two other men. One of these conveyed the impression of being a lawyer, but all three appeared to have some legal knowledge or experience.

The initial caller remained the spokesman. If the entrepreneur worked through them, his grant application to the Development Board – from whose allocation all other finance would be generated – was guaranteed. So was the unimpeded construction or acquisition of a factory: there wouldn't be any problems 'from the troubles'.

The discussion extended to the possibility of the factory being built in the Republic of Ireland, where it could attract European Union finance. That was still possible, the man insisted, if they built in Ulster, through the system operated by Brussels to pump regional aid into deprived areas of the EU. A further advantage, if they took that course, was that London would have to put up additional cash: they were supposed to match any European grant, pound sterling for pound sterling.

There was a lot of talk of the financial benefits to be gained from Brussels. There was, for instance, an extension of the aid system by showing interest in Eastern Europe. 'I was told I could get substantial amounts of money from Brussels if I apparently set up in Eastern Europe – Poland was the country specifically mentioned – a distribution outlet or company for what I intended to make in Ulster. That was the word used; *apparently*. I didn't query it and as the conversation continued, I didn't have to. The idea was to qualify for the development grant by establishing a company in, say, Warsaw and having cards and letterheads printed: an office wasn't absolutely necessary, just an accommodation address. It was also essential to visit the British embassy and establish contact with the trade department and counsellors, to give the impression of *wanting* to do business. Having got the money, it was quite legitimate to "decide" to trade in Eastern Europe wasn't viable.'

The money-raising possibilities didn't end in Brussels. There were, promised the Irishman, investors in the United States prepared to put money into either northern or southern Ireland if they were convinced – 'and he was sure he *could* convince them' – that the product was worthwhile. 'It all seemed childishly easy and I said so. He agreed with me. He said he'd set up quite a few businesses simply following the rules and regulations. Nothing was illegal.'

The discussion then got to what fee or benefits the long-haired man required. 'He said that of course there would be a fee, worked out on a percentage basis. But they required something more than that. Upon my existing board there would have to be voted a non-executive director, chosen by them. I didn't at first find anything particularly difficult about that. Then he said that after a period of satisfactory trading – and he kept stressing the success of that trading was absolutely guaranteed: those were his very words, *absolutely guaranteed* – to build up substantial profits and reserves, the company would buy me out. My other directors, too. There'd be enough money for us to live in luxury for the rest of our lives. Other directors would, of course, be brought in to replace us. They'd have a hugely profitable company and we'd be rich. He described it as a perfect business arrangement.'

The London-based official at the Development Board did not know of the man when told his name. When I contacted the board, I was told individual cases and applications could not be discussed. How then could the entrepreneur's application – and his telephone number – have been discovered by an 'agent' in Northern Ireland? 'We have no knowledge of what you are talking about.'

My acquaintance and his fellow directors, not unnaturally, didn't agree to the proposition being put to them. At the end of 1994, they abandoned any thought of trying to develop their enterprise in either Ulster or the Republic. 'Of course while I was in Ulster we talked about the troubles. I was told, by the men I was dealing with well before there was any announcement of any peace process that the conflict would end. But only when all the people who mattered were satisfied they had got everything they possibly could out of London.'

Which leaves the question: when are all the people who matter in Northern Ireland – Loyalists as much as Republicans – ever going to be financially satisfied? A limited answer is never. In the name of their individual and opposing causes they have become experts in crime, and now there's far too much money involved.

CHAPTER SIXTEEN

The Golden Goose

The denials were strident from both Republican and Loyalist alike in Northern Ireland that their competing and equally violent campaigns of terrorism, murderously criminal in themselves, were never, ever, funded by crime. Support *always* came from dedicated, freely-contributing sympathisers. Crime was not simply anathema: the terrorists claimed it was so totally unacceptable that their individual vigilantes, fulfilling a function the civil authorities were incapable of performing, scoured it from their battleground streets with summary justice. In a comparatively small, six county United Kingdom province that prostituted Christianity in the name of religion,[1] their crime-fighting crusades had the virginal purity, according to them, of a Renaissance allegory.

Which was – and is – total and utter nonsense.

Those denials and public-spirited posturings have always been lies. For two-and-a-half decades, Republican and Loyalist terrorism in Northern Ireland sustained themselves from crime. The terrorism may end. The crime it generated won't.

Over the twenty-five years since the current troubles began, in 1969, their terrorist practitioners have come to understand the full implications of the aphorism that crime pays. Long before the most recent peace process began, in December 1993 and throughout 1994, a substantial proportion of the money derived from criminal acts has gone not to the terrorist organisations in whose name they were committed,[2] but rather into the pockets of the terrorists. The offshoot of the campaign to gain freedom from British rule – or, conversely, to remain loyal to London – was the development of crime into a goose laying golden eggs for terrorism and terrorists alike.

From the 1969 beginning each terrorist group in Northern Ireland created structures both to commit money-raising crime and to extort protection money from regular criminals and criminal gangs before allowing them to continue their illegal operating.

It didn't end there.

That extortion – both implied and direct – reached out to involve virtually every member of the public in Northern Ireland. Imported London-style taxis plied unofficial but regular bus routes throughout Belfast: the fare was cheaper than a bus ticket and the service was better, delivering people to their door. It actually made sense to use the service: occasionally, if the official bus companies protested too loudly or too often, a bus or two was burned out, as an example. Every building project in every major town accounted on paper for a phantom workforce far in excess of what was necessary for whatever was being constructed, in order to provide the kickback for 'permission' for the project to be erected. The British imposition of identity cards for Northern Ireland building workers did nothing to eradicate the practice. And after buildings were completed, the payment had to continue if they were not to be bombed to the ground and the process started all over again.

Existing supermarkets and pubs and bars and hotels paid protection money to avoid being bombed or burned out: Belfast's Europa Hotel holds the record for being the most often and frequently bombed hotel in the world, and a once superbly-preserved example of Victorian pub design and architecture directly opposite had its front blown out simply because the demanded protection money was delivered slightly after the stipulated deadline and an example was considered necessary for other tardy payers.

Possibly the greatest lie of all was always the insistence of both the IRA and the Loyalists that their condemnation of illegal drugs as a menace threatening Irish life extended to their physically punishing dealers and driving them from the streets and housing projects of Dublin and Belfast.

The complete opposite was the truth.

Both terrorist groups extracted levies from drugs dealers in northern and southern Ireland in exchange for allowing those dealers to trade. Which was only part of the terrorists' drug-provided income. The IRA in particular gained large sums of money from the heroin abundantly supplied by the most fanatical of all Middle East terrorist countries, Iran.

The opium poppy has been cultivated and used in Iran since the eleventh century. When they overthrew the last Shah the ayatollahs preserved the poppy fields which, until that time, had actually been under the control of the Shah's Pahlavi family. The ayatollahs, like the Shah before them, recognised the financial power of heroin. For the Shah it had been a big earner and also had served the 1,000,000 addicts in the country during his reign. For the ayatollahs, heroin provided the finance to help spread Islamic Fundamentalism worldwide.

Before becoming a grateful recipient of Iran's drugs money, the IRA, waving the flag of liberation-seeking freedom fighters, was an equally grateful recipient of cash, arms and killer technique training from Middle East terrorist states responsible for murderous attacks upon the West, one privately-boasted coup of which was the 1988 bombing of the PanAm jumbo jet over the Scottish town of Lockerbie, with a total death toll of 270 people.

Before the end of the Cold War, according to Russian President Boris Yeltsin, the IRA sought, and probably received, weapons from the terrorist-fomenting Soviet KGB.[3] Involved in the negotiations with Moscow, through Irish communist Michael O'Riordan, were veteran Republicans Seamus Costello and Cathal Goulding. They were associates of IRA founder Joe Cahill. In 1942, then aged 21, Cahill was sentenced to death for his involvement with five others in the murder of a Belfast policeman. He was reprieved, serving instead seven-and-a-half years in jail. In 1973 he was arrested in the Irish Sea aboard an arms supply boat from Libya – the IRA's weapons supplier before Iran – and jailed on smuggling charges for three years.

Those convictions made him ineligible for a US entry visa. On the eve of the IRA ceasefire proclamation on the last day of August 1994, America's President Clinton personally overruled any legal bar to Cahill entering the United States. So it was that a convicted murderer and terrorist arms smuggler entered America and achieved the maximum propaganda for what the Republican movement hailed, in suitably Mafia-style vernacular, as a peace offer the British government couldn't refuse.

While the murder campaigns have been reduced or suspended – and in the Northern Ireland situation any sustained reduction or suspension must remain uncertain – there can never be any hope of non-terrorist crime lessening. Indeed there is every expectation of it substantially increasing in the future, and becoming more organised, just as violent but more profitable, without the cosmetic need to attribute its rewards to nationalistic or loyalistic aims.

Sir Hugh Annesley, Chief Constable of the Royal Ulster Constabulary, actually issued a public warning[4] just a month before the IRA's response to the December 1993, joint London and Dublin declaration for permanent peace. And he allied one warning with another. Basing his judgement upon intelligence analysis, Sir Hugh predicted not only that it could take as long as two or three years for the violence to 'broadly stop', but also that he did not expect the paramilitary organisations to disband. Instead he believed those organisations would turn more completely to general crime, including illegal drug importation – with Ireland so conveniently placed on so many producer-country trafficking routes – and dealing. And such a switch, in the opinion of Sir Hugh, would not be limited to the nationalist groups. The Loyalist paramilitary factions would, he forecast, form rival and potentially murderous groups, fighting over crime turf as they had once fought over the division of their country.

I have been greatly guided[5] in the preparation of this particular section of this book by someone privy to highly classified intelligence of the sort upon which Sir Hugh based his warnings. Terrorist violence on the streets of mainland Britain might cease, I was told, but not in Northern Ireland. 'The targets will change, that's all. Which, as far as the British army and London are concerned, is a very definite step forward. But the extortion will continue, with the innocent of both sides suffering.'

Extortion, under threat of physical harm, death or the destruction of property, has been the major criminal activity of all extremists on either side in Northern Ireland for twenty-five years, and according to intelligence analyses to which I have had access[6] it will remain so. It was as a warning that expected tributes and honour should continue to be paid – and paid promptly – to paramilitaries that Dublin's most flamboyant traditional organised crime Godfather, Martin (The General) Cahill, was shot dead in Dublin in August 1994. So keen were the various groups to claim credit – and appear to be maintaining the law and order that the recognised police were unable to impose – that even the Republican INLA initially boasted they'd carried out the murder. They hadn't, although they'd wanted to: Cahill had burned down a safe house they'd tried to establish to conduct their extortion business in the south of Dublin, which was Cahill's territory.

The IRA were acknowledged the true killers, both by the Garda and the crestfallen INLA, after they had insisted that the hit was rightfully theirs. They further insisted it was an assassination to cleanse Dublin of the city's leading drug trafficker. Which was the familiar lie. Cahill did deal in drugs – like he dealt in every other sort of crime – and in the past had paid off the Republicans[7] in order to stay in business. But his closest ties were to the extreme loyalist Ulster Volunteer Force, who were as quick to deny any association with the mobster as the Republicans were to claim his murder: it was to the Loyalists that Cahill had contributed a substantial percentage of his profits from the 1986 robbery of eleven art masterpieces from Russborough House.

The intelligence expert with whom I discussed the future of Northern Ireland considered Martin Cahill's execution an indication of how violence would develop in the province, in the event of permanent and lasting peace being reached between the Catholic and Protestant terrorists and their supposed political leaders. 'It'll remain, like it's always been, a battle over territory but the cause will change. In the future it'll be turf wars, like mobs have always fought anywhere in the world. Each and every side has got every sort of weapon it needs: and they've got well-established and guaranteed sources of re-supply whenever they want more. And in the case of drugs, they've got those supplies equally well set up. If you want to be totally cynical, which is an occupational hazard in dealing with Northern Ireland, what's gone on since 1969 has been an unduly protracted training course in specialised crime. And in Northern Ireland now there's the *crème de la crème*. And we're not just talking strong arm thugs and killers and murderers, characterised by the cliché of the thick-headed Paddy. The upper echelons of every terrorist movement in Ulster – and those further south, in the Republic – are highly intelligent, highly sophisticated people. The funds haven't just come from extortion and robberies. No-one will ever know how much fraud from the European Union has gone into funding Northern Ireland terrorism but if it were ever possible to discover the figure it would be staggering. It's millions upon millions. The executives of the terrorist groups know how to move money around the financial capitals of the world as well, if not better, than any executive in any financial institution. They know about laundering and numbered accounts and bank secrecy countries.'

For twenty-five years Northern Ireland has been the horrifying and particular British focus of terrorism.

After 1995 the focus – not just of the United Kingdom but for the rest of the European Union – will change, although the concern will not diminish.

If anything, it will grow.

CHAPTER SEVENTEEN

Inshallah[1]

Counter-intelligence agencies and security forces throughout the European Union universally regard the emergence and growth of extreme Islamic Fundamentalism across a vast swathe of the Middle East as the greatest threat to internal stability in each of the fifteen EU member countries. All these governments share this concern, and agree with the assessments of their individual security organisations. So seriously do the fifteen member countries regard terrorism that every one conforms – publicly at least – to an agreement banning aid to Middle East states identified as terrorist sponsors. Despite which, yet again, there is as much disunity as unity in implementing it.

So apparently concerned is the European Union with the destabilising potential of state-sponsored terrorist violence that it was made a special remit of a ministerial group originally set up to monitor Europe's drug problems. Until the signing of the Maastricht Treaty, that group was known as Trevi, after the Rome fountain close to which the group was created in 1975. Trevi was replaced by Maastricht in 1992, with a Police Council, responsible to ministers. Trevi's terrorist responsibility was transferred to this council on its formation. Before that change, I know[2] that Iran had been identified at several meetings of Interior Ministers under the Trevi banner as the most active Middle East state fomenting terrorism, both with money and weapons. Indeed, London – both privately (at closed door ministerial meetings) and publicly (with frequent emphatic statements by Foreign Secretary Douglas Hurd and other Foreign Office officials) – led the Community's political ostracisim of Iran after the late Ayatollah Khomeini in February 1989, issued a *fatwa*, an edict absolutely binding upon all devout Muslims, to execute British author Salman Rushdie for blasphemy against the Koran in his novel *The Satanic Verses*. From that moment Rushdie has had to live in hiding, protected at all times by armed British detectives.

Officials specifically assigned by the British Home Office to chart the incidences and growth of Middle East-backed terrorism have compiled a list of at least eleven assassinations in Europe for which Tehran is held responsible.[3] In addition they have irrefutable evidence – even to the names of Iranian officials masterminding the murder assignments – that the IRA was approached to supply hit men for more.

In August 1994, in an attempt to avoid the sort of indiscriminate terrorist reprisals it experienced in the mid-80s, France preferred to enrage Switzerland – and earn the contempt of its EU partners – by expelling back to Tehran two Iranians wanted for murder in Switzerland, rather than extraditing them to Basle. But France immediately had to confront the threat of just such reprisals by having to respond positively after the Fundamentalist murder of five employees of the French embassy in Algiers. In doing so Paris openly admitted that the country was facing an internal security threat from Islamic zealots.

In that same month in 1994, the politically ambitious Interior Minister Charles Pasqua was able to glory in international approbation after spiriting from the Sudanese capital Illich Ramirez Sanches, better known as Carlos the Jackal, the Argentinian-born terrorist to whom Western intelligence personally attribute 83 killings during a twenty-year bombing and murder career. The principal reason – besides cash assistance from Paris – for Sudan's co-operation with the French external intelligence service, the *Diréction de la Securité Extérieur* (DGSE), was Khartoum's eagerness to be removed from the international list banning aid to terrorist-supporting states that is maintained by Washington's State Department and America's Central Intelligence Agency. It was for that same reason that Syria, another hide-out for Carlos over many of those twenty untouchable years, let France know through diplomatic channels when Carlos left Damascus for the Sudan a year before his seizure in Khartoum on a Yemeni diplomatic passport, number 1278. The Yemen, which claimed the passport was a forgery after Carlos's arrest, is also on America's terrorist list.

Both the European Union and America regard as dangerously destabilising – not just to Europe but to the entire Middle East – a fanatical Fundamentalism that makes a *fatwa*, once issued, irrevocable and preaches that any Muslim who dies in a Holy war *jihad* will be transported immediately to paradise. A European intelligence source[4] insisted to me that such religious zealotry, with proclamations from Tehran and their mullahs being blindly obeyed, created a potential terrorist force impossible for the West to curb or stop. It was even suggested quite seriously[5] by the same source that the Gulf War's Operation Desert Storm was brought to a premature end before a final assault upon Baghdad and Saddam Hussein in order to allow the Iraqi dictator to remain in power. The rationale might appear bizarre, but a lot of analysts subscribed to it. The reasoning went that because of the murderous way in which Hussein maintains his position, liquidating his own followers as well as any opposition that his removal would have left a total vacuum. With the only thing to fill it fundamentalism imported from across the border from Iran. The position of Jordan's King Hussein was extremely tenuous during the Gulf War: the assessment was that he could have been overthrown by the same religious movement. As could President Mubarak, of Egypt. The nightmare scenario had Fundamentalists and Islamists – with which Europe and the West had no idea how to negotiate or deal – in control of the band of countries virtually girdling the Middle East and stretching down into the Persian Gulf and controlling huge amounts of the world's oil. It was far easier to leave Saddam Hussein where he was, mentally unpredictable though he might be, just as it made pragmatic sense to bolster the king in Jordan. In the case of Saddam Hussein the devil the West knew – even someone who very literally qualified for the description – was better than a committee or group they didn't know. Nor could ever hope to know.

What is regarded by Iran's fundamentalists as their guerilla army in any European *jihad* is the Hezbollah, an organisation which emerged during the Lebanese war and operates from Lebanon's Bekaa Valley as well as from Tehran itself, under the aegis of Iran's Revolutionary Guard – from which some intelligence sources[6] say it is indistinguishable. Leader of its foreign department is a girlish-voiced, heavily-bearded reclusive Lebanese named Imad Mughniyeh, whose terrorist career is even more spectacular than that of Carlos the Jackel. Mughniyeh is named in CIA files[7] as a principal planner in the suicide truck bombing of the American embassy in Beirut, in 1983, in which 241 US marines were killed. He led a group known as the Islamic Jihad, responsible for kidnapping over forty Westerners – including Terry Waite, John McCarthy, Brian Keenan and Jackie Mann – during the Lebanese conflict, and is named on a US indictment for involvement in the murder of an American during the hijacking of an American TWA plane in June 1985. In April 1988, during a Cyprus stop-over, he personally shot dead two passengers on a hijacked Kuwaiti jumbo jet after Kuwait had refused his demands to release two jailed terrorists. More recently he masterminded the bombing of an Israeli centre in Argentina, in which 82 people died, and the for once casualty-free bombing of the Israeli embassy in London, both in August 1994. He lives in heavily-protected luxury in Tehran.

As well as financing the Hezbollah, Iran is the paymaster and supporter to every European terrorist organisation, whatever their persuasion or aim: revolution is the only requirement. Those organisations have included the IRA, the Basque ETA movement, the mysterious Greek November 17 group, The Kurdish PKK, and the Corsican National Liberation Front, the FLNC.

Until its rapprochement with Israel, Iran also provided aid to the Palestine Liberation Organisation, as did the regimes of Syria, Algeria, the Sudan, Yemen and Libya. Colonel Muammar Gaddafi, Libya's leader, consistently lies when he asserts that he no longer assists revolutionary terrorism: an English intelligence source[8] believes that even after the IRA announced its ceasefire in August 1994, elements of the Irish terrorist organisation continued to receive hospitality in Tripoli. Certainly the Libyan capital is known to be the refuge of another of the world's most infamous and murderous terrorists, the operations of whom – with bizarre irony – led to the creation of the Hezbollah.

Although anti-terrorist files[9] usually list the leader of the Fatah Revolutionary Council (FRC) by his operational code identity of Abu Nidal his real name is Sabri el-Banna. A short-statured, sharp-featured, balding man he remains in permanent ill health after open heart surgery in Tripoli in 1991. Nidal's failing health has severely curtailed the activities of the FRC – already fragmented by internecine disputes – but only in 1993 did the US State

Department downgrade it from being the most dangerous terrorist organisation in the world. American terrorist records[10] list ninety outrages committed by the FRC. It was Abu Nidal's FRC whose attack on the counters of El-Al, Israel's national airline, in Rome and Vienna airports, left seventeen people dead in December 1985. And that killed twenty-one people when it bombed a synagogue the following year.

The FRC episode that was to have ironic repercussions was the failed assassination in London's Park Lane in June 1982, of Israeli ambassador, Schlomo Argov. Two days later Jerusalem cited that attempt as the reason for its invasion of the Lebanon, which proved to be appallingly misjudged. That conflict, to continue for years after, led to the formation of the Hezbollah, the terrorist organisation described by the US State Department[11] as being 'responsible for some of the most lethal acts of terrorism of the last decade'.

The FRC is a defecting faction from Yasser Arafat's main-stream Palestinian group that has now made peace with Israel. For that defection, in 1973, Arafat sentenced Nidal to death *in absentia*. Gaddafi, in another lie, claims that Nidal is not living in Tripoli but in fact is dead. That assertion – like the Sudan's cooperation in surrendering Carlos the Jackal – is made in order to gain acceptance and recognition in the West. Libya's international ostracism followed Gaddafi's refusal to hand over for either British or American trial Abdel Baset al-Megrahi and Al-amin Khalifa Fhima, the two men named by both British and US investigators as the Libyans who put the bomb aboard PamAm flight 103 that exploded over Lockerbie in December 1988. Because of Gaddafi's refusal, the UN imposed sanctions on Libya in April 1992.

Although the presence of al-Megrahi and Fhima in Tripoli most obviously links Libya to the Lockerbie bombing there is some intelligence,[12] connecting Syria and Iran to that atrocity, as well. A US Defence Department report in March 1991, named Ali Akbar Montashemi, a former Iranian Interior Minister, as the £6.5 million paymaster to the Syrian-supported Popular Front for the Liberation of Palestine for destroying the PanAm flight in reprisal for the shooting down in July 1985, of an Iranian airbus by the *USS Vincennes*. British intelligence dismiss the Iranian link as 'dud' information. Syria's President Assad, as anxious as the Sudan leader or Colonel Gaddafi to distance himself from terrorism – and for identical reasons – refuses to admit that another of the world's top-ranked terrorist leader lives in Damascus.

His religion allowing, with the addition of the traditional white beard and red cloak, the portly, heavily white-moustached Ahmed Jibril would fit perfectly into Santa's grotto in a Christmas department store. His dedication to Palestinian terrorism belies such a benevolent appearance. He and his family settled in Syria after their expulsion from Israel in 1948. Like Nidal – also born in Jaffa – Jibril is virulently opposed to Middle East peace and dismisses Arafat as a traitor to Palestine. Using the organisational expertise and training acquired during his service as an officer in the Syrian army, Jibril began his terrorist career with the hijack of an El Al aircraft in July, 1968. In 1970, he organised the smuggling of a time-bomb aboard a Swissair plane which exploded en route from Zurich to Tel Aviv. Forty-seven people died in the explosion.

The frequent gatherings of the Trevi group and the committees and councils that succeeded it convey the outward impression of a fight against terrorism in which the EU is genuinely combining. That – like the coming-together of their police forces – is a delusion.[13] One of the most flagrant examples of disunity came in the autumn of 1993, when London granted entry into England of Rashid Ghannouchi, leader of the extremist Algerian fundamentalist group *An-Nahad*, which means Renaissance. The greying, bearded Ghannouchi, a university lecturer, whose organisation is pledged to overthrow the ruling government of Tunisia, had planned attacks upon hotels in Tunisia in 1987 in which several British tourists were injured: one, Helen Strochi, lost a foot. Sentenced by a Tunisian court to hard labour for life for his part in the atrocity, Ghannouchi was freed that same year under a general amnesty to celebrate the accession of President Zine al-Abdine Ben Ali. Ghannouchi continued his campaign to replace Ben Ali's government with a Fundamentalist regime modelled on Tehran's, which predictably supported *An-Nahad* with money and arms. That campaign culminated in 1991 with Tunisian intelligence discovering a plot by Ghannouchi to shoot down the President's jet with a Stinger missile. Ghannouchi fled to the Sudan and the protection of Hassan Turabi, whose National Islamic Front won the country its place on America's terrorist prohibiting list. A Tunisian military tribunal passed, *in absentia*, a further sentence of life imprisonment upon Ghannouchi. This was known by both the British Foreign and Home Offices when, in August 1993, Ghannouchi, holding a Sudanese diplomatic passport, was granted permission to reside in the United Kingdom. Which he still does –

in a terraced house in the north London suburb of Harlesden – at the time of writing.

'Incredible and inept' was the judgement of one anti-terrorist intelligence official.[14] I understand that the criticism from Paris – tinged with hypocrisy since France had recently released the two arrested Iranians implicated in the 1990 Geneva killing of Kazem Radjavi, brother of Iranian opposition leader Massoud Radjavi – was even more forthright.[15] Paris doubted London had any serious commitment or intention to oppose fundamentalist terror. Or, indeed, whether London truly understood it.

London, never famous for its consistency, then made it clear in August 1994, that an entry visa would not be granted to Anwar Haddam, a leading Algerian fundamentalist, so that he could deliver a lecture in London. Haddem – who, incomprehensibly, is being allowed to live in Washington by the terrorist-prohibiting United States – is allied to the most extreme of fundamentalists, the Islamic Armed Group (GIA). The pledge of GIA is that it will kill all foreigners in Algeria. Officially Haddam describes himself as the President of the FIS Parliamentary Delegation to Europe and the US. The FIS is the Islamic Salvation Front, outlawed in Algeria. Its military wing, the Islamic Salvation Army, is considered by Paris to be responsible for the killing of its five consular officials in Algiers. In September 1994, French anti-terrorist officials disclosed that arms dumps belonging to the Islamic Salvation Army had been uncovered at Clichy, the Paris suburb, and at Aix-on-Provence in the South-west. Those seizures followed the arrest, five months earlier, of French-born Algerian Abdel-Hakim Boutrif on the French-German border in the Meurthe-at-Moselle department, while he was bringing into France a small arsenal of explosives, arms and electronic equipment. The weaponry had been supplied by Rabah Kebir, leader of Algeria's National Salvation Front. In the same month as the arms caches were found in Clichy and Aix, Paris deported twenty Islamic militants to Burkina Faso, in West Africa, under a 1945 law permitting the expulsion, without any legal process, of foreigners whose departure was regarded an imperious necessity for State security and public safety. Islamic fundamentalist terrorism against France escalated at Christmas 1994 with the hijacking in Algeria of an Air France airbus with 170 passengers. A commando unit of French police, the Groupe d'Intervention de la Gendarmerie (GIGN) supported by British SAS stormed the plane in Marseille.

The four hijackers who French intelligence believes intended to crash the aircraft on to Paris were shot dead. The following day fundamentalists slaughtered four Roman Catholic priests in the Algerian town of Tizi-Duzu in retribution. Warnings were also given by them that their terrorist campaign could spread to the United Kingdom.

The intelligence belief[16] is that Fundamentalist terrorism is not limited by Tehran to co-ordinating Islamic revolutionaries in the Middle East or Europe. Iran seeks international revolution.

To achieve that it even hosted a conference of every European terrorist group. As a gesture of solidarity with their freedom fighter philosophy, the hosts made a particular point of driving all the delegates along a road bordering the British embassy. Once named after wartime leader Winston Churchill, by the time of the procession the road had been renamed Bobby Sands Avenue, after the first IRA hunger striker to starve himself to death in Belfast's Maze prison in protest at not being allowed special privileges.

The conference was convened in November 1993. It was held – symbolising the success of at least one revolution – in Tehran's Feirouzi Palace, once a residence of the late Shah's family. Delegates stayed there. There were a lot of them. Western intelligence positively confirmed the attendance of the IRA, ETA, representatives of Abu Nidal's group, the Popular Front for the Liberation of Palestine General Command and the Japanese Red Army. There were, of course, a large number of Hezbollah. The delegates were welcomed by Muhsin Reza'i, commander of the Iranian Revolutionary Guards. The revolutionary representatives debated a strictly limited agenda: Iran's plan to fund a terrorist assault against the West that was little short of a *jihad*.

Virtually every major EU capital – London, Paris, Bonn and Rome were specifically listed – was to have been a target for bombing and assassination. So well documented and verified was the 1993 intelligence[17] that European Union anti-terrorist organisations for a period worked together in brief and unprecedented co-operation – 'just like the FBI we're all waiting for'[18] – to thwart the attacks. The combined action avoided the European-wide chaos that was Tehran's intention.

British intelligence record the first contacts between Iran and the IRA, back in 1981. That was the year an Iranian diplomat travelled for the first time to Belfast, to attend the funeral of Bobby Sands, now hailed in Iran as a martyr. That first visit was closely followed by another, by Hojatoleslam Hadi Ghaffari, the Iranian cleric, dubbed the 'machine-gun mullah' by British newspapers, who had personally gunned down sixty pro-Shah officials during and after the revolution that brought fundamentalist rule to the country. From Ghaffari came a quickly-accepted invitation for a Sinn Fein delegation to attend the revolution-encouraging Conference of World Movements in June 1982. Sinn Fein reciprocated with an invitation for Tehran to attend their annual conference in Dublin. It too was quickly accepted.

The IRA needs £5 million a year to operate: the ceasefire of August 1994, did not lessen its operating costs. Iran made it clear, during the early eighties, that it was prepared to provide the bulk of that operational budget, irrespective of what the Republicans raised through their organised crime operations. According to defecting Iranian diplomat Dr Mir Ali Montazam – one time First Secretary and chief legal adviser at the Iranian embassy in London – the paymaster for this IRA funding was the 'machine gun mullah' Hadi Ghaffari. Montazam told British intelligence debriefers that Ghaffari directed the activities of Iranian agents between London, Dublin and Tehran. He also operated a fund, in which an average of £4 million was constantly maintained, through the bank secrecy haven of Jersey, in the British Channel Islands. That fund was financed by selling off, at a fraction of their proper value, art treasures conservatively valued at £24 million, with which the former Shah had decorated his London embassy. Montazam's debriefing mentions his being shown gold bars and stacks of currency – the proceeds of the art treasure sale – in the London embassy by Abdollah Zeefan, an Iranian Foreign Ministry official. Five years earlier Zeefan, then a student, had been one of the militants who stormed the American embassy in Tehran and took fifty-two American diplomats hostage.

Montazam's account confirmed that the Iran funding of the IRA was well-established by the time Gerry Adams, leader of the IRA's political wing, Sinn Fein, personally went to Tehran in December 1987. His trip followed a visit, earlier that year, by two IRA emissaries to Beirut in a failed, publicity-intended effort to negotiate the release of Irish hostage Brian Keenan.

Over the six years following Adams' visit – during which he also tried, and failed, to secure Keenan's freedom – European intelligence charted a series of meetings throughout the European Union, between Republican terrorists and Iranian officials and the

Hezbollah. Among the capitals listed on intelligence records are Bonn, The Hague and Paris. Each were attended by men carrying Iranian diplomatic passports. Their usual accreditation was to the Ministry of Information and Security (MOIS), Iran's intelligence service, which is responsible for Iran's terrorist activities, worldwide. Ghaffari took part in several of those meetings. So did Ali Reza Hakkikian, who headed the MOIS office in Bonn until 1993 and Vahir Attarian, who replaced him.

According to British intelligence,[19] the MOIS Bonn office is the headquarters of Iranian intelligence and terrorism. It specifically operates throughout the European Union, targeting opponents of the Tehran regime. One terrorist gathering was hosted in the German capital in 1993 by MOIS official Amir Hussein Taghavi, creator of the scheme to utilise Iran's considerable heroin production to finance terrorism, at the same time as Iranian Security Minister Ali Fellahyan was signing an official cooperation agreement with German government officials. Hussein Taghavi is regarded by those same British intelligence sources as the head of all Iranian terrorism in Europe. London made a diplomatic protest to the agreement signed by Ali Fellahyan, and vainly reminded Bonn of the supposed EU unity against Tehran brought about by the *fatwa* against Salman Rushdie.

Those series of European meetings culminated in November 1993, with the terrorist summit at Tehran's Feirouzi Palace. And at a fringe session of that summit British intelligence has established[20] that the IRA were asked to assassinate fundamentalist opponents in return for cash and weaponry support from Tehran.

That summit – and the assassination session it generated – took place while other IRA representatives were conducting the secret negotiations in Dublin and Belfast that led to the December 1993, declaration from Downing Street and the 1994 ceasefire agreement from the Republican movement in Ireland.

There were three people named on the Iranian hit list presented at the Feirouzi Palace. Tehran wanted killed ex-President Abolhassan Bani-Sadr, who was living in French exile, Javad Dabiran, from the opposition People's Mujahedin Party, who was living in Bonn, and London exiled actress Farzaneh Taidi, who had appeared in *Not Without My Daughter*, a 1991 film recounting the attempts of an American-born woman to recover her child kidnapped by her Iranian husband and taken to post-revolutionary Iran.

It was not, according to my information,[21] the first time the IRA had been involved in discussions about murder with officials of the Tehran government. An earlier murder conversation occurred soon after the 1979 overthrow of the Shah. Then, not as well-trained or organised as they were to become, MOIS officials sought guidance from the Republicans as to how their own assassins could kill exiled Iranians.

Names on the hit list then were General Fereydoon Jam, brother-in-law of the Shah, Shapour Bakhtiar, the last prime minister under the Shah's rule who was murdered in Paris in 1992, and Ardeshir Zahedi, a one time ambassador to Washington.

In return for IRA agreement to carry out the assassinations requested in 1993, Tehran would have provided a formidable arsenal of weapons and equipment. This included communications and listening devices, the much sought-after Stinger surface-to-air missiles, sufficient Semtex to restore the Republican's Libyan stocks depleted by their bomb outrages on the British mainland, Israeli-manufactured Uzi machine guns and ammunition, and pistols.

There was also a cash incentive: almost £350,000 in genuine American dollar notes, plus a further £4 million in expertly forged counterfeit American currency. Such forgeries had earlier been provided by Tehran to all its terrorist group clients, with a double-pronged purpose: it was a cheap and convenient way to underwrite revolution and it was also a direct attack upon the currency of the supreme infidel country, the United States of America. Billions of brilliantly-faked dollars were printed by Hezbollah on what is technically known as an intaglio press, the type used by genuine currency producers. Because such presses do create genuine notes on genuine currency paper – the American counterfeit had the raised lettering of the country's normal bills, although the paper was not correct – the location of each intaglio is listed by Interpol at their Lyon headquarters. That list shows an intaglio press was supplied to the Shah of Persia before his overthrow. British intelligence[22], who confirmed that London was one of several European capitals frequently flooded with such money, believe that the press is being used either in the Hezbollah stronghold of Lebanon's Bekaa Valley or in a known factory in Tehran's Takhtee Jamshid suburb.

The IRA did not immediately reject Iran's request for hit men to take out Iran's identified opponents. It was not until February 1994 – two months after the parallel and secretly negotiated peace-seeking declaration had been made by London and Dublin and was in the lengthy process of being considered by Sinn Fein and the IRA – that Tehran was told that the IRA would not accept the murder contracts.

By then the SIS, Britain's external intelligence service, alternatively known as MI6 – and through them the Foreign Office – had virtual chapter and verse of the IRA's attendance and its side-room murder discussions with Hezbollah. That intelligence was greatly supplemented and confirmed with wall-implanted devices by eavesdropping on the Iranian embassy overlooking London's Hyde Park – bugging that was publicly protested against in May 1994 by Iranian President Ali Akbar Hashemi Rafsanjani. What was not known – the most vital but missing piece of the jigsaw at a time when peace was being discussed by other IRA negotiators – was what the Republican response had been.

The way the dilemma was resolved – and Ulster peace was kept on course – is a copy-book example of superb intelligence coupled with equally superb diplomacy, justifying every penny spent on espionage.

With the full knowledge of British premier John Major, to whom it is ultimately responsible, SIS leaked sufficient of what it knew about the November 1993, terrorist gathering in the Feirouzi Palace for both Tehran and the IRA to realise that their contact, and their discussions, were totally blown. The outlet chosen for the leak was selected with consummate skill. Britain's information, identifying Amir Hussein Taghavi as the architect of the drugs-for-guns-for-assassination scenario, was planted, via the usually-despised Greek intelligence service, in the Athens-based newspaper *Elephteros Typos*[23], which the SIS amusedly point out translates as *Free Press*. The cleverness of the SIS in choosing Athens was that it additionally showed they knew that Greece – and its indigenous and highly successful terrorist group, November 17 – was an active conduit between Iran and the IRA.

The account in *Elephteros Typos* enabled Douglas Hogg, Minister of State at the Foreign Office, to quote press reports – conveying the impression that the information had only limited connection with Britain's intelligence services – of long-established connections between Iran and the IRA when he summoned Iran's Charge d'Affaire, Gholamreza Ansari on 28 April 1994, 'to convey our concern and to request an assurance at senior level that contacts would be immediately and conclusively severed'.

During the Foreign Office encounter Douglas Hogg presented the Iranian diplomat with details of IRA and Iranian gatherings in Dortmund and Munster, in Germany, and with the fact that Iran had on provable occasions supplied the IRA with drugs. The Athens arrest in 1993 of German national Jurgen Merz and his wife Tunza-Anet – later to be accused of smuggling substantial amounts of heroin into Britain – disclosed a smuggling operation supervised by Hussein Taghavi that had been intended to supply the IRA with £19 million worth of heroin – that could have been traded for almost double that amount at much-adulterated street level. Two months before the IRA's assassination-request meeting in Iran, Ankara's intelligence service, MIT, located a heroin shipment passing through Turkey on its way to Greece. It was to be divided between the November 17 group and the IRA.

The Iranian reaction to the British Foreign Office challenge was predictable enough. Insisting that, although he knew Hussein Taghavi by name, he had never met him, Gholamreza Anseri issued a statement asserting categorically 'there is absolutely no contact between the intelligence services of our country and the IRA. We naturally understand that any such contact would produce a feeling of revulsion in the UK but as there is none there is no need for alarm or criticism. There is not a shred of evidence to support these astonishing claims.'

The fact is, of course, that Iran isn't ashamed, just irritated at the international embarrassment and ostracism that results from its being too publicly disclosed as the paymaster to terrorism.

Which it continues to be, supporting and supplying Europe's other terrorist groups, one of which is listed on intelligence files in both the EU and the United States as the most successful of any operating in Europe in the last twenty years.

The reason for that doubtful accolade is not based on the number of murders or outrages committed by Greece's November 17 organisation over those two decades, but upon a phenomenon unknown in any other terrorist group or recognised crime syndicate.

During that time the November 17 organisation has never been successfully infiltrated by undercover agents. It has never suffered a defection. There has never been an arrest of any of its members, even though assassinations are frequently carried out by business-suited killers who don't bother with any disguise or concealment.

Nor has any forensic clue ever been left at the scene of its outrages to lead investigators to its leaders. The bulging files of Greece's grossly inefficient anti-terrorist squad are mostly filled with the rambling proclamations phrased in outdated Marxist rhetoric that follow every November 17 attack. A British anti-terrorist official[24] familiar with Athens' attempts to fight the group described as 'pitiful' the intelligence assembled on November 17. 'If they threw away the political pamphlets, which they might as well do because they're useless as an intelligence source, they'd be left with hardly enough to distil on to three or four sheets of A4 paper. And that doesn't come from investigatory material: most of it has been copied from newspapers reports after a November 17 attack and commentator's guesses or opinion of what the organisation is all about.'

This disgust is echoed by every other anti-terrorist organisation within the EU and – since Greece joined the Community – in more diplomatic terms by the interior ministers of other member states at private ministerial gatherings.

While the criticism of the Greek authorities is totally justified, it should be made clear, for complete objectivity's sake, that a number of other intelligence agencies have both individually and cooperatively failed to discover anything about the Greek terrorist group. The first victim of November 17 was Athens' CIA station chief, Richard Welch. From the moment of that killing, in 1975, the CIA have tried to penetrate November 17. For twenty years the need to find Welch's killers remained at the forefront of its agents' activities in Greece. The majority of what little forensic material has been collected from the scenes of outrages has been sent to America to be examined by CIA and FBI laboratories. After the murder of US naval attache William Nordeen in 1988, President George Bush offered a £250,000 reward for information about the November 17 assassins. It produced nothing. President Bush then initiated – and President Clinton has continued – a training programme for Greek anti-terrorist officers at the FBI's academy at Quantico, Virginia.

Over the years Greece extended pleas for help. The Israeli secret service Mossad – acknowledged the world leader in anti-terrorist expertise by its intelligence contemporaries – became involved. So too – after Greece's entry into the Union and criticism of its failure from the interior ministers of the other states – did the intelligence and terrorist services of France, Italy, Germany and the United

Kingdom. Turkey, a frequent victim of November 17, contributed the efforts of its intelligence unit, MIT: it was the Turks who established the presence of November 17 at the November 1993, terrorist conference at Iran's Feirouz Palace, and who identified the heroin trafficking link between November 17 and the IRA, from their interrogations of intercepted drug dealers. But although Ankara learned much of the Tehran terrorist summit – including the IRA representation – it failed positively to discover the identity of a single November 17 terrorist.

An intelligence officer[25] involved in some of that liaison claimed that it was hard to compare the huge worldwide effort against this one relatively small insurgent group to that of any other anti-terrorist organisation. 'They should have been rolled up and buried years ago. History.'

But they aren't. Despite this massive and rare concentration of continuing attention, November 17 remains untouched and unbroken.

The terrorists took their name from the date when the junta of military colonels who overthrew King Constantine of Greece in 1967 sent tanks in to crush an uprising of Athens Polytechnic students. Twenty students died in the brutal suppression. One of the few agreed intelligence assessments reached by the Greeks without help from anyone else, is that November 17 began as, and continues to be, an ultra-left-wing organisation of well educated men: the killer of Richard Welch politely asked, in perfect English, for his wife to step aside before firing his .45 pistol (November 17's trademark) into the American, and immediately afterwards spoke to Welch's driver in educated Greek.

To that profile, over the years, has been added the fact that it seems to be insularly Hellenic. Opposed to NATO and Greece's membership of the European Union (whose offices have been bombed), and fiercely anti-American (three US citizens have been murdered and many more wounded), November 17 is clearly resentful of the presence of US military bases in the country and strongly distrustful of Turkey, with which it disputes the occupation of Cyprus. Furthermore, since all the outrages during its twenty-year history have been committed in and around the Greek capital, its members probably live closely in or around Athens.

There are other constituents to the profile. To have remained so consistently impenetrable, November 17 must be a honeycomb of connected but nevertheless separated cells, with known identities strictly limited throughout: some European intelligence agencies[26] believe that no true identities are ever used, only codenames. Its original revenge-seeking student founders must now be in their forties, so the assessment is that they are outwardly respectable professionals or businessmen – witnesses invariably describe the assassins or the bomb planters as being well-dressed, as if briefly interrupting their journey to the office. And there is an unresolved suspicion in which Washington joins the European agencies[27] that to have survived undetected for so long there has to have been tacit official protection. Turkey has publicly made the accusation that Athens was conniving with terrorism, although the main thrust of that particular complaint was Greece's alleged assistance to the PKK, the Kurdish terrorist group fighting for independence from Ankara[28].

Apart from the acknowledged presence of PKK figures in Greece, all suspicions of official complicity in any form of terrorism are based upon entirely circumstantial but logically pursuasive arguments.

November 17, espousing Marxist ideology, emerged with Richard Welch's killing a year after the colonels had been swept from power by the strongly Socialist Pasok party, headed by Andreas Papandreou. A substantial number of officials put into power by Papandreou during the once briefly interrupted administration that followed, had been either students or belonged to resistance groups living in Paris during the junta's rule. There are unsubstantiated suggestions that some members of those resistance groups were trained in Palestinian terrorist camps in the Middle East: there was almost a diplomatic rupture between Athens and Washington when an American ambassador came close to suggesting there were ties between Papandreou's administration and Abu Nidal's extremist breakaway Palestinian terrorist movement.

Greece joined the European Union not through any pan-European ideology but through sheer economic necessity – and has since been amply rewarded by its fraudulent misuse of EU aid systems. November 17 consistently claim that their attacks upon EU premises and agencies are protests at the austerity measures imposed by Brussels as a condition of Athens' entry. Greek opinion polls, with equal consistency, show a lack of interest if not open opposition to the EU, just as they show tacit admiration for November 17. Another contribution to the unhelpful profile of the organisation is that its actions invariably reflect in extreme form the views of ordinary Greeks. There was, for instance, some Greek public disquiet when the United Nations backed the Bosnian Muslims in preference to Serbia, a country the Greek Orthodox Church favours. November 17 then, hardly coincidentally, attacked UN offices in Athens, and only a torrential downpour, which caused the remote control firing mechanism to malfunction, prevented anti-tank rockets being fired at a British aircraft carrier, *HMS Ark Royal*, that was on station in the Adriatic providing air cover for the Muslim-aiding UN forces.

With the total failure, over two decades, of the world's most sophisticated anti-terrorist and intelligence organisations to locate the tiniest chink in the armour of November 17, the only hope of the EU investigators[29] is that the breakthrough will finally come when an erosion in Greek public approval produces a disillusioned informer.

Another of Europe's insurgent groups is, however, on the brink of collapse, brought to that point as much by the rejection of the people for whose independent Basque homeland it purported to be fighting as by anti-terrorist and police offensives – including at one time even raids by a murderous vigilante squad which operated with tacit official endorsement: State terrorism against urban terrorism.

GAL is a Spanish acronym for the Anti-Terrorist Liberation Group. Files collated by investigating French magistrates[30] chart its progress from as far back as 1983. Those files, which are still open, describe the official, but secret recruitment and training of French underworld hit men and criminals to carry out summary justice on members of the Basque separatist movement, ETA, against whom the Spanish authorities had insufficient evidence for a legal prosecution, or who consistently escaped Spanish arrest by slipping over the border into the safety of France. The land claimed by the Basques extends through the Pyrenees forming the natural barrier between the two countries. Reflecting the impossibility for any two European countries to co-operate over practically anything, Madrid has actually accused Paris of refusing to move against identified leading members of ETA, resident in France. France in turn has accused Spain of obstruction whenever Paris *does* initiate an investigation. Meanwhile, against the gunmen of GAL – which appeared to cease operations in 1987 – twenty-seven assassinations are recorded.[31]

Suspected official links between GAL and Madrid began to emerge in 1985. On August 5 of that year two motorcycling assassins gunned down Juan Maria Otegui, a Basque activist and member of ETA's Bilbao commando – their terrorist units are known as commandoes – in France, where he believed he lived safely, as he drove home from his genuine job in a furniture factory. He was GAL's thirteenth victim. Four months later, French police arrested four members of the Marseille Mafia in connection with the killing. Under interrogation they named Georges Mendaille as the man who had recruited them into the GAL vigilantes. Georges Mendaille had been a soldier in the French Foreign Legion and was a former member of l'Organisation de l'Armée Secréte, (OAS), which in the 1960s fought a terrorist campaign of torture, assassination and bombing against the Front de Libération Nationale (FLN) in a failed attempt to keep Algeria as a French colony. In the vigilantes' possession were two photographs of Ortegui, marking him as their target. The instructions for the assassination – written on the back – were provably the handwriting of Mendaille,[32] who had made his permanent home in Spain. Even so, Madrid refused an extradition request for Mendaille filed by French examining magistrate Christopher Seyes, based upon the French Mafia evidence.

Seven months later a GAL hitman attacked the Batxoli bar in Bayonne, the favoured residence-in-exile in south-west France of the ETA ruling executive: by ironic coincidence Otegui's wife, Kamela, and his daughter, Nagore, were both seriously wounded in the attack. Paola Fonte, the quickly-arrested gunman, disclosed under magistrates' questioning that he had been enlisted into GAL in Lisbon by Portugese secret service officer Mario da Cunha.

The French authorities officially sought help from both Spain and Portugal. Lisbon uncovered the fact that Cunha was operating for – and under instructions from – a man called Jose Amedo. Enquiries by Spanish magistrate Baltasar Garzon, who I was later to meet in Paris at a global mafia conference, established that Amedo was a Spanish intelligence officer and a leading figure in GAL. And that Georges Mendaille worked for him as a recruiter. In 1991, Amedo was jailed on charges of financing mercenary killers.

The Spanish Interior Minister Jose Barrionvevo refused Garzon's perfectly legal request for access to a special fund from which GAL and its killers would have been financed. The Spanish parliament and the Socialist government of Felipe Gonzalez also refused to authorise an enquiry into GAL and its alleged secret government connections. France's disgruntled Christopher Seyes and Spain's officially obstructed Baltasar Garzon both protested bitterly at these impenetrable Spanish obstructions and pointed out the coincidence that GAL's vigilante killings and bombings should have ceased in 1987, just at the moment when the demands for a government enquiry reached their height. It was to be almost a decade later before Baltasar Garzon linked the Gonzales government with his GAL enquiries. In December, 1994, Garzon ordered the detention of the former Director of State Security, Julian Sancristobel, on charges alleging attempted murder, illegal diversion of public funds and illegal detention.

The refusal of the Interior Ministry to allow Garzon access to its special projects fund was strongly defended at the time by Rafael Vera, appointed Spain's anti-terrorist chief when Felipe Gonzales came to power in 1982. Vera, in office for the next thirteen years, is credited with bringing ETA – a Basque acronym for Basque Homeland and Liberty – practically to its knees. In February 1995, Vera was arrested on Garzon's orders. The charges alleged the organising and funding of anti-terrorist death squads. Within hours of Vera's detention, Ricardo Garcia Damborenea, leader of the Socialist Party in the Basque region, was detained on similar charges. At the end of the month Luis Roldan, the vanished former head of the Civil Guard whom Spanish authorities want to question in connection with the disappearance of £25 million of public funds, was arrested in Laos. Roldan is also believed to have information about the fund that financed GAL. Within days he was brought back to Madrid. Which then had to admit that the document upon which Roldan had been extradited had been forged.

Vera attacked ETA on several fronts and at several levels. Prison regimes for convicted ETA men were harsh and unrelenting: Amnesty International[33] has protested about prison civil rights abuses both to Madrid and to the European Court of Human Rights after Rafael Vera became Spain's anti-terrorist chief.

One Vera innovation – successfuly employed by Giovanni Falcone to splinter Italian Mafia clans – was to disperse convicted terrorists throughout island jails, away from the mainland. Under Spanish prison regulations it is legal to tape record meetings between prisoners and their lawyers. From those recordings, Vera learned of the particular effectiveness of his separation policy. In one eavesdropped discussion ETA mass murderer Juan Ignacio de Juana Chaos, jailed for twenty-five killings, complained his movement had cast him aside.

Vera learned also that the lawyers were acting as conduits for terrorist information and support. Several were arrested.

On another level Vera encouraged Madrid to introduce into the Basque Country a Basque-speaking indigenous police force, the *Ertzaintza*. He didn't hesitate to meet and speak with ETA terrorists leaders, face to face, and did so on three separate occasions in Algeria, the first time in 1986, the last in 1989. Present at these meetings were not only leaders of the terrorist 'army' but representatives of *Herri Batasuna*, its political wing. By the time of that last meeting, *Herri Batasuna* had been as isolated from other Basque political movements as the terrorists it represented: under what is known as the Pact of Ajuria Enea, signed in 1988, those other Basque parties renounced violence. A peace accord was very close at Vera's 1989 Algeria meeting: it was blocked by the French-based ETA ruling executive.

It was at that meeting – and as a result of the ruling executives' intransigence – that for the first time an 'old' and 'new' ETA emerged, a split that became more pronounced in the following years.

The 'old' were the original founders, who had fought against General Franco's refusal to grant the Basques independence and who actively sought peace: Eugenio Etxebeste, the revered ETA leader more commonly known by his *nom de guerre* Antxon, in a public letter from his permanent exile in the Dominican Republic wrote, that the group was 'in a cul-de-sac whose only way out led to an abyss'.

The 'new' were the later recruits, pursuing terrorism for terrorism's sake. Like many in the IRA, with which the Basque group were closely allied through active arms-supplying contact, the new faction enjoyed the proceeds of the constant crime that kept ETA in existence.

Like the IRA throughout both Ulster and Ireland, in the Basque Country ETA ran a strict regime of organised extortion, openly referred to as a 'revolutionary tax'. Some industrialists and businessmen in the Basque Country paid as much as £5,000 a month in protection money.[34] Those who refused either had their premises or products destroyed or were kidnapped and held ransom for much higher figures. In 1994 it cost the company and family of businessman Julio Iglesias Zamora £1,500,000 to gain his freedom. Earlier Juan Antonio Arruabarrena, proprietor of a large pastry combine, publicly announced he was moving from the Basque Country to Zaragoza rather than continue paying 'revolutionary tax'. The *ertzaintza* later recovered a £25,000 pay-off Signor Arruabarrena had already handed over.

In late 1992 and early 1993 – working at last in fragile cooperation – police and intelligence agencies of France and Spain seized virtually the entire governing executive of ETA in a luxury villa close to Biarritz. Within a week the movement's quartermaster, Pedro Gorospe Lertxundi, had been surprised at ETA's main armaments dump and arms-manufacturing factory in Anglet, near Bayonne, and two days later Rafael Caride Simon, Madrid's most wanted ETA terrorist, was taken without a struggle – or a chance to draw the gun stuck in the waistband of his trousers – in a bar in Toulouse. In November 1994, Luis Martin Carmona, known as Kolo, and leader of the Vizcaya commando and ETA's second-in-command, Felix Alberto Lopez de la Cale, whose *nom de guerre* was Mobutu, were seized. I understand[35] that following this startling series of successes – Vera's best ever – ETA formed a new executive based in and around Paris, where they felt less exposed than in Bayonne and Biarritz and Toulouse. But security sources believe[36] that ETA's active commandoes have dwindled from hundreds into just double figures. Their violence has risen as their strength fell: death throes, I was told.[37] In October 1993, their gunmen shot dead General Dionisio Herrero, chief of Spain's Air Force Medical Corps, outside his Madrid home, and nine months later they assassinated Lieutenant General Francisco Vesguillas, Director-General of Political Defence, by exploding a huge bomb alongside his car as he drove to the Defence Ministry. Those killings brought to more than 750 the number of people – including women and children –assassinated by ETA over its twenty-five year history. The people of the Basque Country finally became sickened. A rally demanding the release of Julio Iglesias Zamora turned into a massive anti-ETA demonstration. An estimated 80,000 people –nearly half the Basque population – marched through San Sebastian wearing blue lapel ribbons to signify their opposition to the movement. A counter demonstration organised by *Herri Betasuna* attracted only 38,000, wearing green support ribbons.

Basque Socialist Party chief Ramon Jauregui predicted that 'sooner, rather than later, ETA and their hirelings will be nothing more than a sad page in the history of this country'.

Another prediction made with even more confidence[38] was that – as in Northern Ireland – the Basque Country's terrorist remnants would become full-time organised criminals. Furthermore, robbed of any political excuse, that crime will spread – like the ETA leadership – across into France.

CHAPTER EIGHTEEN

Art for Art's Sake

The crookedness in the European fine art and antique trade is the whitest of white collar crime, conducted for the most part in the surroundings of luxurious drawing room gentility or museum serenity. And it is rated by the *cognoscente* as the most preferred of all the other well practised illegalities. I have been assured even by those who police it that the chances of a real professional getting caught are almost nil. I have been further assured by dealers and collectors that some European auction houses pay little more than barely moving lip service to their highly vaunted respectability, integrity and honesty. One specialist named a specific establishment – which I won't, for legal reasons – as being virtually always aware of 'wrong' articles passing through its salesrooms.

An aristocratic dynasty with links to the British Royal family have even fallen victim to auction house deception.

I understand[1] that in their stately home there is a suite of furniture guaranteed by impeccably documented provenance to be the work of one of Britain's most famous eighteenth century furniture makers which is substantially – although brilliantly – faked.

And its owners are totally unaware how they have been robbed.

Were the suite to be offered for sale that provenance – written proof of its origins, together with recorded opinions by experts to its authenticity – would allay any doubts that it is genuine. Such doubts would be unlikely, so perfect is the faking.

It was a consummate and well planned scam, I was told.[2] But by no means totally unique. 'With the amount of money there is to be made – and is *being* made every day – this sort of thing is virtually inevitable. The difference here is that the victims are particularly well known. What happened could be regarded as a case history, from which others can – and should – learn. And by "others" I mean the professional art criminal as well and as much as the dealers. It is quite a classic.'

The collection, of fourteen pieces, has been described to me as one of the finest, totally genuine examples of the work of a famous furniture maker whose designs dominated the stately houses of the rich and aristocratic throughout much of George I's eighteenth century reign. His work commands enormous saleroom prices two hundred years later. This particular suite, bought from the maker himself, was installed in the family seat relatively close to the furniture maker's birthplace, where it remained until 1990, when it was decided that it needed complete renovation. I understand tenders were sought, via intermediaries, from several restorers. It was finally sent to a prominent firm whose name I have but cannot publish for legal reasons.

There was, of course, no reason for the authenticating provenance to accompany the furniture. That, at all times, remained with the rightful owners.

My information of what happened to the genuine suite comes from one of the restorers involved, although the man talked to me only through an intermediary.[3]

Before any attempt was made to start the renovation, the suite was examined in the most minute detail by the team assigned to work upon it. Close-up photographs were taken from every angle, to ensure a totally accurate record. Most specifically, any particularly identifying blemish or mark peculiar to any piece in the set was noted.

All the exterior carvings and decoration that could be detached from the carcase of each and every piece were then stripped off and painstakingly copied. Each design incision was measured for it to match identically the original, and the wood used dated as nearly as possible to the period of the original manufacture, cannibalised and saved from restoration of other eighteenth century furniture, although not that from the original creator's own workroom. Every mark and blemish incurred during the suite's two hundred and fifty year history was carefully replicated.

Of the original furniture only the carcases and a few pieces that could not be removed remained when it was returned to its owners. Everything else was a re-attached copy. But it would have needed the expertise in the particular work of the original maker even to begin to question its authenticity – guaranteed anyway by the retained provenance.

Meanwhile, the genuine exterior carvings and designs were attached to faked carcases of suite pieces, created again mostly from earlier cannibalised eighteenth century wood. But the fakers protected themselves against the virtually non-existent chance of discovery by intentionally making slight changes in the suite, thus avoiding the accusation that they had counterfeited a specific set of known furniture, although it was still passed off as a true example of the work of the famous maker. My intermediary informant does not know who purchased the copied hybrid set or where it is now, but the price paid would have been enormous. The most likely destination is the United States of America, sufficiently far away to remove entirely any risk of awkward questions.

At the time when the genuine suite was stripped, the price of antiques was high; my informant – a dealer and restorer himself – estimates that had it been put into a salesroom it could have reached 'anything up to £1,000,000 at auction'. The retained provenance could still achieve a fortune for the present copy, if it were ever put upon the market. 'The people who stripped it made a killing. They got paid top dollar for the restoration and renovation, and ended up with enough provably genuine work to make another complete suite. And all that remained real at the end was the original provenance that never left the owner's possession.'

In any case, it's comparatively easy to manufacture a provenance sufficient to support a sale even through one of the prominent London auction houses and certainly by any of the minor establishments anywhere in Europe.

The method used to obtain such authentication is extensively employed by the complete fakers of the furniture and was explained to me by a dealer[4] who accepted – while not condoning – it as an everyday practice in the fine art and antiques milieu. And he reminded me that it was necessary to know the tricks of the trade in order to avoid being caught by them.

The basic necessity is simple – a genuine but old catalogue. I have a fairly typical one before me, as I write. It is from an early 1900s sale conducted by one of the most famous English auction houses, and it is a far more substantial document than the familiar catalogues of today, actually bound in hardback covers. But the illustration plates are greatly inferior to today's colour photographs on heavy art paper: there are not very many, they are uniformly black and white and they lack practically any identifying detail. The written descriptions of the lots, however, are specific and lengthy. This is what makes such catalogues invaluable to fakers who actually attend old book and manuscript sales in search of them.

The faker chooses a written description of furniture not accompanied by any illustration, and manufactures the piece according to the listed specifications, paying particular attention to the wood, its age, and the glue and fastenings of its supposed period. Care is taken to ensure the piece is a middle-of-the-road article, with no claim to any especially high value or rarity: the intention always is to avoid any special attention and most definitely any publicity. The aim is to sell quickly and well, not to capture headlines by trying to pass off a fake Hepplewhite or a Sheraton or a Chippendale.

The last stage in the manufacture of the fake comes when the description from which it has been made is cut from the original catalogue and stuck somewhere on the piece, as a successful bidder might have done. The paper and printing ink of the catalogue before me is, of course, that of the period of the early 1900s when the auction took place. The 'ageing' that would have occurred had a description cut from it actually been attached to a piece is easily achieved by brushing with weak coffee and then, while still wet, being left for maybe a fortnight in a dealer's normal storeroom with other middle-of-the-road furniture for dust motes to adhere.

The final part of the deceit involving the catalogue would be to write to the still existing auction house enquiring if they did indeed sell an item described in it – which of course they did – in their sale of the specific date. All London's leading auction houses maintain meticulous records of sales. Their reply, confirming the sale, would complete the provenance.

Fakers benefit, I was told,[5] from the accepted fact within the trade that rarely does any antique of any description have a full and complete provenance, up to and including its original sale document. 'We're talking of items hundreds of years old: that's why they are *what* they are, antiques. Over that sort of history things are lost or mislaid or simply not kept. So provenance is customarily piecemeal. A good auction house would probably be suspicious if a provenance *was* complete.'

There are 4,500 listed auction house companies throughout the world[6] but the international antique trade is dominated, financially, by just four London houses – Christie's, Sotheby's, Phillips and Bonhams. Through those four pass, in cash terms, seventy per cent of the world's antique business. Each year those cash terms run into billions. All are fiercely protective of their names and reputations and take exhaustive care – particularly through an organisation to which I refer in detail later – to ensure the legal ownership of every single item passing through their hands.

Although he refused a personal interview, Paul Whitefield, deputy chairman of Bonhams, wrote[7]: 'While we are fully aware of the not uncommon problem of stolen works of art . . . we do not have any direct experience of the market, and the illegal manipulation of it, of fine art by international organised criminals.' Colin Reeve, the knowledgeable chief security officer for Christie's, was confident that the system of registration and documentation followed by his company reduced to the absolute minimum the possibility of faking, forgery, and the moving of stolen art or money laundering by professional art criminals through any of Christie's salesrooms. 'The most important thing is our name and we have a moral duty to ensure that if you want to sell or buy through us you are not going to lose any money over it.'[8]

Reeve did not, however, attempt to minimise the extent or scale of crime in the art world, although he derided my suggestion that the profit coming from it was close behind that of drug or arms smuggling. From the Watch Lists of stolen art sent to him every month by the seven police authorities in Britain who have an arts crime officer or squad – such is the low priority put upon art robberies in Britain that none of the other forces bother with a specialised unit – Reeve calculates there are 40,000 identifiable pieces of art stolen, each month, in Britain alone. The figures are roughly comparable to those in at least four other EU countries – Italy, France, Spain and Greece – but are exceeded in several of the newly liberated Eastern bloc countries. The value of paintings and fine art objects alone stolen worldwide is put at £3 billion a year[9] and that is only the commercial value at the moment of theft. Stolen property comes free. Any resale price, therefore, is all profit – as is what is made from the always strongly denied ransoming back, by insurance companies, of an item upon which those insurance companies might otherwise have to pay out millions. Or what is quite separately and additionally made from faking and the forgery.

With the 1993 lowering of internal borders, the European Union is now an open door – and an open shop – for stolen art objects moving in every direction. 'Have you ever seen anywhere a Customs officer at any of Britain's ports or anywhere else who has stopped a man and said "Where did you get that picture or that bit of porcelain? I want to check on the stolen property list," ' demanded Reeve. 'They don't have stolen property lists; they aren't connected to the Arts Loss Register. They aren't connected to Scotland Yard – they don't even *talk* to Scotland Yard from what I understand. If I stole a piece of art and wanted to take it with me anywhere in the world I'd stick it in my suitcase and go without the least bit of worry. Even if my suitcase was opened they wouldn't recognise it. They wouldn't stop me and they wouldn't ask me about it. The Customs and Excise have their own job. They're interested in drugs. Or if you've got three bottles of Scotch instead of two. But if you have a stolen piece of Meissen or a small picture, no way. The chances of an art criminal getting caught are nil.'

While the risk of such art criminals being detected remains low – most certainly while they are physically transporting their wares around Europe – the possibility of the stolen object being eventually located has increased by the creation of the organisation to which Reeve referred, the Art Loss Register.

A unique association, headquartered at London's Grosvenor Place within burglar alarm sound of Britain's biggest repository of fine and spectacular art, Buckingham Palace, the Arts Loss Register was founded in January 1991, as a computer-centralised international database for stolen artistic treasure. The four dominant international British auction houses are shareholders. So is Lloyd's of London, whose insurance syndicates are vulnerable to enormous pay-outs on unsolved or unrecovered robbery. Another shareholder is the International Foundation for Art Research, a charitable organisation based in New York which for sixteen years prior to ALR's creation kept details of some art thefts on a card index system: that carded record, containing approximately 35,000 items now listed in ALR's database, formed a percentage of the Foundation's equity when it joined the London system.

The Art Loss Register now lists 650,000 stolen art objects – ranging from traditional paintings, furniture, ceramics and jewellery to garden statuary – arms and armoury, stamps, classical cars and musical instruments, and valued at over £500 million. Its log of stolen property is increasing at the rate of 2,000 items a month. It is, said James Emson, a retired army brigadier now managing director of ALR, 'growing like topsy'.[10] The computerised material is recorded in several ways. There is the statistical case information; what the article is, where, when and how it was stolen, plus the name of the investigating officer or force, its police record number and the name of any insurance company involved. The most detailed description possible is given, not only in expert terms but also in the phrases and descriptions of the reporting police official. Finally – using the technology of computer imagery and reproduction so often used for the wrong purposes in computer crime – a perfect image of the stolen article is put onto the database, an image capable, through technological wizardry, of being sectioned and enhanced to show up the smallest identifying detail, down to a peculiarity in an artist's signature or a crack in a piece of porcelain.

All Emson's staff are history of art graduates and all worked, prior to joining the Art Loss Register, for one of the big four auction houses, giving them an expert's background in their particular subjects. Before any major sale in any of their London or European salesrooms of any antiques or fine art, those big four submit their catalogues for comparison against the ALR's computerised database, to ensure they are not offering for sale a stolen item. More than £14,000,000 of stolen art has been recovered this way since the art register's 1991 inception.

Impressed by the undeniable success of ALR, the top three hundred auction houses in the world are now submitting their sales catalogues by electronic mail to London for similiar vetting, prior to auction or sale, via a New York company set up specifically for that purpose. New York's Metropolitan Museum checks the ALR's records before making any purchase. So does the California-based Getty Museum. America's FBI is a subscriber. Scotland Yard's re-formed Fine Arts Squad uses ALR's database, and the major insurance companies in each of the fifteen EU countries subscribe to it. So do the majority of European police forces, and also Interpol, the international police liaison facility linking 179 countries worldwide. In 1994 an ALR branch office – additional to the office already in New York – was established in Italy, where more antiques and fine art exists than in any other EU country and which is considered to be at greatest risk from Mafia-organised theft. Italian police files of over 200,000 stolen works of art have been logged on the London computer system, for world wide monitoring.

Aware how much and how many national treasures are being looted from all the former communists satellites as well as from Russia itself – and of the art plunder by the Serbians in the split-up Yugoslavia – Emson has recorded art heritage robberies also, at the request of national governments.

It was through James Emson that I was introduced, by telephone in Zagreb, to Madame Branka Sulc, Director of the Croatian Museum Documentation Centre, a woman trying to record for later recovery thousands of treasures and artefacts taken from Croatian churches, galleries and museums by Serbian forces. She told me[11]: 'They have taken enthnic cleansing to every obscene level possible. The world thought it was bestial enough for them to rape Croatian and Muslim girls, to impregnate them with Serbian babies. But the world does not know what they have done to our artistic and national heritage. They have plundered and pillaged every museum and church they could occupy and picked them clean of every treasure they possessed, like a vulture picks clean a defenceless body to its bare bones. But they didn't even leave the bones. After looting everything possible, they dynamited every building they could, razing them to the ground. Sometimes they even took away the stones, so that the cleansing would be so complete no trace would even remain of what once stood there. The destruction is catastrophic and irreplaceable.'

Madame Sulc had produced, in several European language, bound documentation[12] in which she records in great detail the plundering of individual places and buildings. In one year – from 1991 to 1992, 42 galleries and museums were attacked – some totally destroyed after being looted – by Serbian forces.

Madame Sulc has recorded 245 historical or cultural sites overrun and pillaged by Serbian forces during a period from April 1991 to December 1992. Of that number, twenty-eight were razed to the ground, thirty-three were burned down, eighty-three were partly ruined, and ninety-two were seriously damaged. As well as the looted museums and galleries, nine archives and twenty-two libraries were sacked for their contents, before the buildings were destroyed. Museums, galleries and churches untouched by war were dynamited once Serbia gained control of them. Everything movable was looted. The contents of the gothic church at Vocin were taken away by the truck-load before the church was blown up: the monastery of St Philip and Jacob in Vukovar was sacked of everything it held. A total 35,000 art objects and treasures were snatched from the Vukovar Museum. One of the most complete collections of work by Croatian authors of the 19th and early 20th century was also taken, as well as the archive of Yugoslav Nobel Prize winner Professor Lavoslav Ruzicka. 'The cultural heritage of Vukovar was requisitioned and taken as booty to Belgrade and Novi Sad in violation of all international conventions under the direction and supervision of the Ministry of Culture of Serbia and with the assistance of the conservators and curators of the museums of Belgrade and Novi Sad and of the Institute for the Protection of Cultural Heritage of Serbia. The pillage was proclaimed by the Serbian media to be an evacuation.'[13]

Among the art treasures listed as missing by Madame Sulc were seven paintings and twenty-four sculptures by one of Croatia's most famous modern artists, Ivan Mestrovic, hailed by Rodin as 'the greatest phenomenon among sculptors'. Mestrovic, who died in 1962, was the foremost portrayer of Slav peasantry. He exhibited at the Metropolitan Museum of Art in New York and was elected a member of the American Academy of Sciences. In June 1994, the entire treasure trove was discovered[14] in the basement of the 13th century castle of Knin, a town designated by the Serbs as the capital of their 'Krajini Republic'. It was undamaged and under the protection of a castle caretaker named [15] as Budomir Milojko, who was also described as the head of the self-declared republic's Institute of Cultural Monuments. During a newspaper interview[16] Milojko made it clear that the Mestrovic treasures would be held until the Croatians agreed to return art the Serbians claim they have looted, and until 'the world recognises the Serb Krajina Republic'.

Madame Sulc believes the Republic of Croatia, which has emerged from the break-up of the former Yugoslavia, has the right to demand the return of all its national treasures and patrimony under binding international agreements[17] ratified by Yugoslavia when it existed as a country. To achieve that, when the war between the rival nations finally ends, she has lodged her documentation of pillage with Interpol at Lyon, through the organisation's bureau in Zagreb.

James Emson is cynical about the likelihood of a total recovery of the Croatian heritage. Much, he believes, has already gone into the European fine arts market to raise money for 'bullets, beans and benzine'[18].

The former Yugoslavia is not the only ex-communist country to be raped of its art and artefacts by expert and organised gangs. And Emson is just as doubtful about the chances of much of Eastern bloc art being restored to its rightful national owners.

The Czech Republic's Dr Vandas told me[19] his country's artistic patrimony was 'haemorrhaging' across its borders into Western Europe. 'It's well coordinated between our criminals and those in the West who have the necessary knowledge and well established structures to know and dispose of what they acquire: now that our borders are open, they arrive with art experts on what are nothing less than shopping expeditions, with the exception that they don't buy, because the articles aren't for sale. They steal, instead. They go to galleries and churches, making their choices, and then return to the west ahead of the theft, to find their purchasers sometimes ahead of the item being stolen. We thought we had suffered enough loss of national treasure, from the plunder by the Nazis. This is practically as bad.'

During a later meeting[20] Dr Josef Valek, from the Czech embassy in London, told me that more than 15,000 items of Czech art, valued at £24 million, have been computer listed as stolen, for western markets. A special art squad has been formed in Prague, to enforce the regulations in the Czech republic which ban the export from the country of any artefact or art work older than fifty years.

All listed items are duplicated on the Art Loss Register in London, in an attempt to staunch what Dr Vandas has accurately called a haemorrhage of fine art from the East to the unscrupulous auction houses and dealers of the West. That haemorrhage flows also from Hungary and Poland. During the same Strasbourg meeting[21] at which I met Dr Vandas, Hungary's Dr Janos Bertok insisted that the pillaging of his country's art heritage rivalled that of his Czech neighbour – which the listening Dr Vandas did not dispute – with the additional factor that Budapest was a major conduit of stolen art from Russia. 'As with every form of criminality, we are not equipped to combat it. We get advice from the West, by whose organised crime groups we are being victimised, on how to intercept drugs or stop illegal immigrants but very little on how to retain and protect our national treasures.'

Poland too is a conduit for stolen art from Russia, according to a

Polish Interior Ministry official.[22] Moscow-based lawyer and criminologist Evgeniy Lyahov confirmed the exodus of art from his country along the Polish route: Russian art of every type and description, said Lyahov,[23] was a target for Russia's mafia groups. In a single weekend in November 1993, 42 icons were discovered in three trains travelling from Moscow to Warsaw. 'It is being stolen and brought into the West by the lorry load. It is supposed to be a cynical joke of exaggeration that there are more icons in the West than there are in Russia. But it isn't a joke or an exaggeration at all. It is virtually true.' So huge and well-organised is the stealing that juggernaut trucks are the only effective way to ferry it through Poland and into Europe. Germany is the entry point, as it is for most of the Moscow mafia's activities. It is, said Lyakov, 'a properly conducted and established business, headquarters in Moscow or St Petersburg, with branch offices in Berlin or a city in what used to be East Germany, with associated companies – mafia groups, in this case – working with them on a daily basis throughout Europe.'

Emson was not surprised by what I had believed was an exaggeration, the claim made to me by a Warsaw government official[24] that a nationally-owned work of art disappeared from a Polish gallery, church or museum every ten minutes of every hour of every day. 'Both in Poland and Czechoslovakia there've been tremendous numbers of new antique shops that have sprung up. And mostly run by Western Europeans of dubious backgrounds. And they're making a fortune. Everybody makes deals, no questions asked. This stolen stuff rises like flotsam and jetsam in the trade, gaining a sort of respectability as it gains in price.' Sometimes an item was eventually identified, when it reached a certain price or a certain reputable auction house. Often it was recognised early as a treasure, snapped up by a collector, and not seen again until the owner died or had to sell to raise money.

Hungary and Poland, too, are listing their treasures with the Art Loss Register – and with the Art Division of Interpol – in the hope one day of recovering what has already been lost and to stem any further loss. 'Which is little more than a gesture and a symbolic one at that,' the Polish official said realistically. 'The people who steal it and sell it on in the first place know they're not going to get caught: it'll be passing between its fourth or fifth buyer – who by then probably won't have any suspicion it's a stolen item – before it stands the remotest chance of coming to anyone's attention. So listing it isn't going to stop the larceny: our only hope is of recovering it, sometime in the distant future.'

That hope lies not only in a stolen item being listed by institutions whose records are accepted, but also in a country's or court's understanding of what is known as good title. Which means provable legal ownership. In 1993 an EU Directive – legally binding on the all member states – was introduced requiring the return of any artwork stolen from any one of those states from the beginning of that year, providing it was classified as 'national treasure'. The normal limitation period for claims under the Directive is 30 years but the limitation period for the return of works of art taken from public collections or churches has been extended to 75 years. Under the Directive any item genuinely exported outside the Community needs a certificate or 'passport', guaranteeing its authenticity. Jacques Lang, French Minister of Culture when the Directive was issued, admitted[25] that 'too much protection would kill the art market in Europe because collectors wouldn't put up their works for sale. But if things are too liberal, national patrimonies will be dismantled. It will mean a loss of history.'

Jacques Lang's reservations are widely shared. I understand[26] there is a strong feeling among British dealers and auction houses – responsible for up to 75 per cent of the EU's art trade and as much as 90 per cent of its antique sales – that the Brussels Directive will unduly restrict a legitimate business worth an estimated[27] £4 billion a year. They believe collectors and institutions will be unwilling to buy articles that could be declared, after purchase, a national treasure that must be restored to an owner country and that the effect will simply be to create more illegal dealing – estimated[28] in England to be already worth £3 billion a year.

The Directive does nothing, of course, to help those Eastern European countries, often the worst sufferers from national heritage robbery, which are not members of the European Union throughout which their patrimony is being hawked. In addition to seeking the assistance of the Art Loss Register, the majority have now joined the Inter-governmental Committee for Promoting the Return of Cultural Property to its Country of Origin or its Restitution in Case of Illicit Appropriation, promoted by Paris-based UNESCO. They are also looking hopefully towards a 1995 conference called by the International Institute for the Unification of Private Law at which all European Union countries have been invited to ratify a Convention for the Return of Stolen and Illegally Exported Cultural Objects.

Like the EU Directive, the prime requirement for these international groups and art theft publications[29] is good title. Until January 1995 in England there existed an ancient legal loophole that actually conferred within hours of a theft, legal right of ownership upon any collectable item whatsoever, up to and including an Old Master.

This was possible through what was known as market overt. The establishment of such markets and such a system dated back[30] to before 1189, the first year of Richard I reign. The principle of market overt – known to have existed in Germany in the ninth century – was as simple as it was legally bewildering: a purchaser in a market overt obtained good title to whatever he bought between the hours of sunrise and sunset even if the seller did not own what he was selling. The Solomon-like medieval intention was to protect the victims of theft as well as the market stall seller and any innocent buyer. A legally-recorded case of 1594[31] established the sunrise to sunset protection for everyone involved in a market overt transaction: a victim discovering he had been robbed had the hours of darkness, *until* dawn, to tour the market to locate and recover whatever he had lost. If it wasn't found by sunrise – and was later sold during daylight – it became the property of whoever bought it. Under medieval law every 'open' shop in the City of London was a market overt, which in effect and practice meant *every* permanent stall. Over the course of eight centuries this had become limited roughly to 20 sites, of which the most famous – throughout Europe and particularly to every crooked dealer, fence and art thief – was London's Bermondsey Market. It was held every Friday on what on other days is a car park in Bermondsey Square, which is owned by Southwark Council.

This bizarre gap in the British legal system became known outside an arcane circle of lawyers familiar with medieval law, and the doubtful operators of Europe's antique trade in March 1993, when Jim Groves in innocent good faith paid £154 for two paintings which he later – in a black dustbin liner – took to Sotheby's, to be valued. A member of their fine arts staff believed she recognised them. The Art Loss Register confirmed, from the description that she provided, that they were – ironically – legal portraits stolen three years earlier from London's Lincoln's Inn: Thomas Gainsborough's portrait of Sir John Skynner and Sir Joshua

Reynolds' portrait of Francis Hargrave. Their true value was in excess of £140,000. The portraits are still, at the time of writing, in store at Sotheby's pending the settling of a legal dispute over the rightful ownership between Mr Groves and insurers who had already paid out before their reappearance at Bermondsey market.

Police, art recovery organisations and the more respectable European auction houses justifiably considered Britain's market overt system as a licence for thieves. In January 1995, the 800-year-old legal loophole enshrined as late as 1979 in a clause[32] of the Sale of Goods Act was repealed by the Sale of Goods Amendment Act.

Which goes, according to Christie's Colin Reeve[33], only partially towards correcting the inability of British legislation to protect art treasures from both Eastern and Western Europe. There is no legal requirement, for example, as there is France, for a dealer officially to be registered. Nor does that unregistered dealer have a legal requirement to ask a vendor where he got the item he is offering. Nor does he have to ask for a seller's name or for any means of identification: a seller can refuse to supply it, even if he is asked. 'A dealer could be an escapee from Parkhurst prison who had just done a bank robbery and is using the money to open a shop. He could quite legally and quite seriously call himself Parkhurst Escape Antiques. And it isn't – most certainly isn't – confined to a fixed shop. A person can do the same with a vehicle, in a car boot sale. The system – or rather lack of it – is a great big black hole into which almost all stolen art in this country goes. Car boot sales really ought to be regulated: they are an enormous buying and disposal source of stolen art.'

Only 10 per cent of all art stolen, worldwide, is currently recovered. One of a group of experts who spoke at length to me on condition of anonymity[34] said, quite seriously: 'Fagin never had it so good'. Without exception the experts derided auction house declarations that they had been genuinely deceived by those fakes or stolen property that were discovered in their salesroom. More than one suggested that the advent of the computerised checking system put into place by the Art Loss Register was privately regretted by some of the European establishments that had publicly welcomed it. 'The big houses, yes: they don't like being shown wanting: they're worried about their reputations. But not so the smaller outlets.'

The bigger houses have, embarrassingly, not infrequently been shown wanting in the past.

In June 1994, Sotheby's senior vice president Tisch Roberts described the faking of Wedgwood pottery in which the company had unknowingly become involved as 'the worst ceramics fraud' of the century. Wedgwood agreed with her: they exhibited some of the one hundred fakes found up to that time at the International Ceramics Fair held in London that month, as a warning to auctioneers and dealers. The fakery was discovered when London ceramics dealer Peter Williams offered avid New York collector Stanley Goldfein a Bacchus plaque believed to have been made during the eleven-year period in the eighteenth century when Josiah Wedgwood was in partnership with Thomas Bentley. Goldfein had just bought an identical piece from Sotheby's. It proved to be a fake. So did the plaque being offered, in all innocence, by Williams. The company discovered the forgeries to be the modern day work of a Staffordshire potter once employed at the Wedgwood factory at Stoke-on-Trent. He had died in 1976. His name was never released to protect his elderly widow.

Both Christie's and Sotheby's were fooled in the early 1980s by copies of ceramics actually made in a prison workshop in the style of leading Cornish potter Bernard Leach by 47-year-old Vincent Mason, who learned his doubtful skill in the workshop at Featherstone jail, in Wolverhampton, while he was serving a sentence for another crime. Sotheby's described one of his fakes as 'an exceptional and unusual example of Leach's work'. Christie's sold one vase for more than £1,000 and a bowl for £240. Bonhams disposed of two fakes for £800. During Mason's 1983 trial – with two others – for conspiracy to deceive, his pottery teacher, Mrs Cleone Abbs, described Mason as 'an undistinguished student'. The judge, Mr Justice Solomon, commented: 'Christie's certainly do not agree with you.' Later, told that Mason had gained only an average pass when he sat an O-level for pottery, Judge Solomon remarked: 'It is impossible to satisfy examiners sometimes. If his work is average, I wonder what they give a distinction for?'

Both auction houses were embroiled in one of the most unusual worldwide artistic conundrums – when is a fake not a fake? – in early 1994. The episode involved the making of bronzes and furniture, ostensibly by the late Diego Giacometti. During his lifetime the artist had lived by choice in the shadow of his artist brother Alberto – originator of the stickmen style of sculpture – and did not become sought-after by collectors until the critical acclaim of his last commission, the designing of furniture and fittings for the Picasso Museum in Paris. Although he was not believed to have produced a large body of work, hundreds of bronzes came on to the market after his death in 1985. Some were sold through Christie's and Sotherby's. In 1989 a tap on the telephone of a gymnasium suspected by Dijon police of trafficking in anabolic steroids revealed a conversation about a delivery of bronzes. Two van loads were intercepted. One was packed with Giacometti work. A dogged French policeman, Chief Inspector Denis Vincenot, discovered that the bronzes had come from the Fonderie de Port-sur-Saone, one of the foundries used during his lifetime by Giacometti to make his moulds and to cast his bronze furniture. Giacometti's will had stipulated that upon his death all such moulds should be broken. They had not been by Jacques Redoutey, director of the Port-sur-Saone foundry. During the four years since the artist's death, thousands of perfect bronzes had been cast, in moulds created by Giacometti, that matched in every detail and patina the genuine work produced from the same moulds by Giacometti when he was alive. As well as through Christie's and Sotheby's, they had been sold through a gallery in the Louvre des Antiquaries and the JDV gallery in the rue Boneparte, in Paris. A total of 25 people – including Redoutey and the Paris gallery owners – were convicted under a 1981 French law limiting original editions of art objects to eight copies and four proofs, all of which have to be numbered. During the trial French police estimated that eighty per cent of all the work sold after his death – for an estimated £14 million – as original Giacometti sculptures and furniture were fakes.

The French courts laboured long and hard – and through unsuccessful appeals by those convicted – trying to decide if an article cast from a mould fashioned by the artist himself was legally a fake: and were able to duck a definitive judgment by the convenience of the particular law under which the foundry owner, his workers and his Paris auction house outlets had been charged.

There are some unique listings in the Art Loss Register: those of items which vanished during the Second World War, most of them into the former Soviet Union. With the end of the Cold War, some art experts[35] anticipate a substantial amount to trickle back on the international art market. Those which can be identified and which are not voluntarily surrendered to the museums or galleries from which they were looted will cause 'good title' wrangles in international courts that will take years to resolve.

One such case involves a small painting entitled *The Holy Family with Saints John and Elizabeth and Angels* by a 17th century Dutch artist Joachim Wtewael. It disappeared towards the end of the 1939–45 war from the Schlossmuseum at Gotha, in former East Germany. After a brief re-emergence in Berlin, in 1987, it disappeared again until 1991. In that year Sotheby's were asked to sell it on behalf of a Panama-based company named Cobert Finance.

According to Sotheby's, who withdrew the item from sale after the Gotha authorities claimed ownership, the odyssey of the painting, valued at today's prices in excess of £500,000, began in the latter half of 1945, when it was 'acquired as a gift' by a Russian officer named as Adolf Kozlenkov, who took it back to Moscow. Upon Kozlenkov's death in 1982, it was inherited by his son, Alexander. He sold it in 1985, in Moscow, to Itela Sungua who in turn sold the painting to Mina Breslav, in West Berlin. It is not known how it came into the possession of Cobert Finance.

Lawyers Frère Cholmeley Bischoff, acting for the Gotha Museum, challenged that story. According to them the painting was offered for sale in Moscow soon after the war by two Russians – whose signed affadavits the lawyers hold – and who served jail sentences in Siberia for illegal art dealing. Frère Cholmeley Bischoff claim there never was an officer in the Soviet army named Adolf Kozlenkov and that after being smuggled out of Moscow to Berlin in 1987 in a diplomatic bag by a diplomat from the African republic of Togo, the painting was identified as having been stolen from Gotha by the Dahlen Museum, in Berlin which holds the most comprehensive list of art objects looted from Germany during the Second World War.

When they were asked to sell it, Sotheby's offered the Wtewael painting to the Gotha Museum, which could not afford the asking price. Sotheby's set the legal action in motion by alerting the museum when the Panamian company asked for the return of the painting.

There was an easier fate for part of a huge German collection snatched by Russians during their wartime advance from the east of the country. It included works by Durer, Delacroix, Goya, Veronese, Watteau and Manet and lithographs by Toulouse-Lautrec. In total the collection, owned by the Bremen Kunstverein, amounted to 50 paintings, 1,175 drawings and 3,000 prints. It was looted from the cellars of Karzow Castle, near

Kyritz, where it was being stored for safekeeping. In 1993, 101 items – valued at £14 million – were traced to a former Red Army officer by Konstantin Akinsha, from Moscow's Pushkin Museum, and Grigorii Kozlov, from the Museum of Western and Oriental Art in Kiev. The former officer kept the majority of the work under a sofa in his one-roomed apartment. Confronted by the Russian art historians, the man – who cooperated with them on condition that his identity would never be disclosed – voluntarily returned all the masterpieces to the German embassy in Moscow.

Part of the Panamanian company's case in the dispute involving the Wtewael painting is that they had obtained good title because so much time had passed since its disappearance from the Gotha Museum.

In every country but one in the European Union there is a statute of limitation – varying between five to seven years – after which good title comes to be held by the possessor. The exception is in the United Kingdom, where good title cannot be transferred on stolen goods. Through the EU therefore, but not in the UK, what is known in the trade as 'warehousing' occurs: storing stolen articles until the limitation period expires before offering them for sale.

The vast majority of what art insurance loss adjuster John Suter calls 'first division' high value art thefts are carried out by knowledgeable experts who look upon what they do as a profession and are involved in no other form of criminality.[36] They steal, in most cases to order, for an average of ten per cent of the true value of the article, with a receiver waiting to buy from them who in turn will have a prospective buyer lined up. Art detectives have no doubt Titian's masterpiece *Rest on the Flight to Egypt* already had a clandestine buyer before it was snatched from the Marquis of Bath's home at Longleat, Wiltshire, in January 1995. With the lowering of European border controls – and the fact that under British law ownership of stolen property always remains with the person from whom it has been stolen – a large amount of what is taken from English country houses, galleries and museums is shipped immediately across the English Channel. The belief[37] among professional art thieves is that France – with what is regarded as the most casual of any European Customs authority – is the easiest country into which to ferry the proceeds of their robberies, although within the country it has one of the most efficient police fine art squads.

It has been tested to the full by two of the world's biggest and

most sensational art robberies, by the particular Japanese love of
Impressionist paintings, and by Japan's most convenient good title
laws.

Japanese law favours the art thief over the art loser to a greater
extent than any other country's in the world. A rightful owner has
only two years, from the date of loss, in which to recover his
property. After that, if it has been purchased in good faith, good
title goes fully to the buyer. Article 194 of the Japanese Civil Code –
Article 193 governs the two-year time limitation – further lays
down that an innocent purchaser who is discovered to have bought
a stolen article has to be reimbursed in full of whatever amount was
paid 'by the injured party or the loser'. Which results, in the case of
works of art, in museums, galleries or countries having to buy back
their own property. Unattributably I have had Japan described[38] to
me as an 'art thieves' paradise' and a 'magnet for what's stolen from
Europe'. There was further criticism that except in rare cases, and
usually only when there is reciprocal benefit, Tokyo is uninterested
in taking on its share of the responsibility for combatting
international art crime. Thirty-four countries sent police representatives to a major Interpol conference on art and antiques crime in
Lyon in December 1989. Japan was not one of them.

Tokyo's attitude – and the fact that a number of priceless stolen
French masterpieces were known to be in Japan – threatened a
serious diplomatic and art exchange schism with Paris in the late
1980s. It was averted only by the paying of substantial ransoms and
reimbursements under Japan's Civil Code – a fact still fervently
denied by the French government and by the losing gallery, but
which I am assured *were* paid[39] – and by the persuasive diplomacy
of the startlingly attractive then head of the French art theft squad,
Commissaire Mireille Ballestrazzi. So enamoured did Japanese
detectives become with Chanel-chic Madame Ballestrazzi that they
festooned their Tokyo headquarters with pin-up pictures of her.
The pictures in which Madame Ballestrazzi was more interested
and which she took back to Paris with her were magnificent Corots
stolen to order for Japan's *Yakuza* mafia. And later – as a result of
her Tokyo visit – she was able to recover Claude Monet's *An
Impression, Sunrise* from which the whole Impressionist school of
art had gained its name.

If the Japanese gang that stole the paintings had not branched out
into local bank heists and fur robberies, I doubt Madame

Ballestrazzi would have been so successful: Tokyo wanted the criminals brought to book for crime committed on their soil, not for the art thefts carried out in France.

The first of the robberies took place during the night of 17 and 18 October 1984, from the municipal gallery of Semur-en-Auxios, north of Beaune. The five paintings[40] taken were by Jean Baptiste Corot, and were on loan to Semur-en-Auxois from the Louvre.

The robbery was planned in prison at Poissy, on the outskirts of Paris more than a year earlier, and was masterminded by Yakuza-connected Shinichi Fujikuma, who prided himself as a connoisseur of art – particularly of French Impressionists, the most popular in Japan – and who had outlets in the Tokyo underworld through the *Tosei-Kai* clan and its *oyabun*, Hiroshi Takayama.

Fujikuma was serving a sentence at Poissy for heroin possession. So were Frenchmen Philippe-Emil Jamin and Youssef Khimoun, a French national of Algerian birth. In their shared cell, Fujikuma talked of the easy money to be made selling stolen French art in Tokyo: more, even, than through drug dealing. Jamin and Khimoun, in return, described how badly protected most French art galleries were. An international art stealing gang was born.

Upon their release, Jamin and Khimoun recruited two child-hood friends, Nordine Tifra and Richard Leroy. Their release coincided with newspaper reports of a loan from the Louvre of five Corot works to the Semur gallery. It was a virtual invitation. The gallery was as ill-protected as Jamin had claimed it would be, the robbery went flawlessly, and in February 1985, the five Corots were smuggled undetected into Tokyo by Jamin and Khimoun, to be handed over to be fenced by the waiting Fujikuma. Four, through Yakuza channels, were bought by private collectors. The fifth, *Boy Wearing a Cap*, was bought in good faith by Kenji Takeichi, owner of the Edobori gallery in Osaka.

Jamin and Khimoun returned to France to split their profits with Tifra and Leroy. The paintings remained undisplayed and, although there were unofficial suspicions that Japan, with its fascination in French art, might be involved, there was no positive confirmation. Those suspicions heightened within the year when, on 27 October 1985, an armed gang, their faces covered, burst into the Marmottan gallery in Paris, forced the few visitors to lie face down on the floor and stole several Monet canvasses, including *An Impression, Sunrise*. Tokyo maintained there was no underworld indication that the Yakuza had been involved in either art theft.

That insistence was questioned when the Japanese daily newspaper *Mainichi* claimed Paris had twice offered to buy the paintings back from Japan. *Mainichi* based their story upon an account given by a ransom-negotiating journalist who used the name Takanari Takeda and delivered photographs of the stolen Monet paintings to the French embassy in Tokyo.

Official French denials of any ransom or reimbursement negotiations were as strident – and still are now – as those of the Japanese. Yves Brayer, curator of the Marmottan gallery, said a ransom was out of the question because the Monet work was not insured: the gallery could not afford the premiums. He did, however, concede that soon after the robbery he received several anonymous telephone calls. 'One from a young woman, with a perfect French accent, who tried to blackmail us for the insurance . . . but there is nothing to prove that this anonymous call was in any way connected with the so-called Japanese network.'

In 1987 Mireille Ballestrazzi was appointed Commissaire – the French equivalent of superintendent – of the *Office Centrale pour la répression des Vols d'Oeuvres et Objects d'Art*, more conveniently abbreviated to the acronym OCRVOA. Already lionised by the French for being the youngest ever person of either sex to have achieved, at the age of 22, the rank of Commissaire, the stunning classics graduate from Lille University had already commanded a CID division before being put in charge of 35 other officers in the art theft squad.

By the time Madame Ballestrazzi, married to an army officer and the mother of two children, took over OCRVOA, the presence in Japan of the Corot paintings from Semur-en-Auxois was beyond question. And beyond recovery claims from the galleries also, because the two year time limitation had expired. As it had expired with the Monet paintings, as well. There had already been diplomatic pressure for their return by Paris, through the French embassy in Tokyo. Madame Ballestrazzi's predecessor in the arts squad had also gone to the Japanese capital to try to retrieve them, but unsuccessfully. One of the many denials is that on their first visit OCRVOA detectives were involved in ransom negotiations in a Tokyo hotel with members of the Yakuza – with Japanese police as sideline observers. Although I understand from my informant that such discussions *did* take place and that one suggested figure got as high as £21 million, they finally achieved nothing.

On 9 November 1987, Madame Ballestrazzi took her squad to Tokyo for the second time. Circumstances had changed since the unit's first visit. The previous year – at around 8 a.m. on 25 November 1986 – there had occurred what the Japanese media described as 'The Robbery of the Century'. In the very centre of Tokyo, Fujikuma's gang, which had arrived in the city earlier that month from France, ambushed a security van outside a branch of the Mitsubishi Bank. Watched by a bewildered rush hour crowd – which did nothing to intervene but was able to provide eye witness evidence later – the armed bank robbers escaped with almost £1.5 million. It was Japan's biggest bank robbery. Tokyo police felt humiliated by the ease with which the robbery had been conducted: they had, in Asian terms, 'lost face'.

Although the robbery had gone perfectly, the escape did not. The gang left several clues, including clothes with Made in France labels and banknotes littered with fingerprints. Some of those prints matched police files on Shinichi Fujikuma, who was already being hunted quite separately for stealing £123,000 worth of furs from a Tokyo store in 1985. Other prints, of Nordin Tifra, Philippe-Emil Jamin, Youssef Khimoun and Richard Leroy, were recorded in French police files. Madame Ballestrazzi had a bargaining position: French help in identifying the Mitsubishi Bank robbers – to enable the Tokyo police to announce the solving of the crime – in return for Japanese cooperation over the art thefts. Someone familiar with the case at the time told me[41]: 'It was an advantage she used brilliantly. And she had to be brilliant. Not only was she initially confronting the traditional resistance of the Japanese, but she was a woman not just in a male-dominated society but in a totally male-dominated police environment.' An essential part of that brilliance was for Mireille Ballestrazzi always to appear to defer to her Japanese counterparts. 'She manipulated everything and everyone and the Tokyo detectives never realised what was happening,' said my informant.[42] 'They just asked when it was all over for her photograph to hang up.'

Madame Ballestrazzi had another advantage. Shinichi Fujikuma was in Tokyo police custody on the bank and fur robbery charges. And he wanted to talk. Throughout November and December of that year, Madame Ballestrazzi sat in Fujikuma's cell, piecing together the details of the Corot theft and the pictures' disposal. I have been told[43] that she was also aware of the financial arrangements to obtain their return. I have not been able to obtain a corroborated figure for what was paid to get them back – although Kenji Takeichi, owner of the Osaka gallery, demanded his full purchase price of £35,750 – but I understand it was considerably less than the once-mentioned figures that had run into millions. And not all came from Paris. I was assured[44] that a proportion of the reinstatement money was contributed by Tokyo.

Madame Ballestrazzi flew back to Paris with the Corots, but without the Monets stolen from the Marmottan Museum. She did, however, have a clue: a photograph of *An Impression, Sunrise* that had been shown by Yakuza salesmen around Tokyo's exclusive Ginza's galleries and even, during ransom approaches, to the French embassy. In the photograph Madame Ballestrazzi did not concentrate upon the paintings themselves, but upon the surrounding background against which they had been taken. She had the prints subjected to the most minute forensic examination. It took a further three years for the patient but determined Frenchwoman to match the background visible in the photograph to a location. She was aided finally by taps on telephone conversations between Japan and the French island of Corsica.

On 4 December 1990, Madame Ballestrazzi led OCRVOA detectives to an apartment in the southern Corsican resort of Porto Vecchio, from and to which conversations with Tokyo had been monitored by eavesdropping telephone authorities. The apartment belonged to a barman named Donatien Comiti. In it police found photographs matching those which Madame Ballestrazzi had brought back from Tokyo three years earlier. Comiti took them to another, empty apartment in which nine Impressionists from the Marmottan gallery, including *An Impression, Sunrise*, were found. All were undamaged. Because Corsica is a French colony, there was no question of good title preventing their immediate return. A special plane went from Paris to retrieve them.

The owner of the empty apartment in which the paintings were found, Dona Comiti, was initially charged with handling stolen property until police accepted she had stored the Monets under duress, threatened by her barman relative.

The finding of the paintings in Corsica confirmed a definite link between fine art theft and the financing of terrorism. Such links had for years been recognised by European anti-terrorist agencies. As long ago as 1986, for instance. Ireland's arrogant organised crime Godfather, Martin Cahill, had masterminded the theft from the Russborough House home of Sir Alfred Beit of eleven priceless masterpieces – including works by Vermeer, his contemporary Gabriel Metsu and Goya – and had sold them, for a fraction of their estimated value, in Amsterdam and Istanbul, from which they were later recovered.

CHAPTER NINETEEN

Back to the Future

The opening scenes of Italy's Second Republic had about them all the elements of a Hollywood soap opera. To mixed, often hostile, reviews they ran for eight months before achieving a suitably cliffhanging climax. The sequel promised to become the sort of long-running drama so beloved of soaps.

The plot contains every cliché in the script-writer's almanac. The setting is a country of ancient elegance and culture (Italy) pushed over the brink of political collapse into chaos by gangsters (the Mafia) and by cosmic corruption (of and by practically everyone). Political leaders and elder statesmen (including three former prime ministers) are accused of every crime.) A pernicious secret society (outlawed Freemasonry) cloaks the activities of another pernicious secret society (the Mafia again), both of which find justification in the risk (greatly exaggerated, but then a lot of facts in this script read more like fiction) that re-born communists will gain the power that has been kept from them for almost fifty years, often at the urging of a third pernicious secret society (America's CIA).

Enter the hero, a dynamic boy-made-good figure of charm, charisma and welcomed promises ('There will be a new Italian miracle'). Modestly born (his first job was crooning Nat King Cole classics on a cruise liner) he is now a multi-billionaire: befitting the soap opera scenario he owns the country's three commercial TV stations (as well as a lot of other things) and is married to an actress of stunning beauty with whom, from a first night seat in the stalls, he fell in love so deeply that he rushed backstage to tell her. His first wife was at home at the time.

The storyline for the first series runs as follows. Disgusted and dismayed by the rot of Italian government, this man (reverentially referred to as *Il Cavaliere*, the knight) who had no experience whatsoever of politics (very arguable) formed a party (named after a supporters' chant at Italian soccer grounds: he owns a football club), created an election campaign and in just three months performed the promised miracles by coming to power.

Within months the critics were slating it. Our hero was officially told – while hosting in Naples an international UN conference on organised crime – that he was under official investigation for corruption. Rather than face inevitable defeat in a Parliamentary vote of confidence in December 1994, he resigned, demanding fresh elections which he was confident he would win, thus bringing on to the Italian political stage, if not to the television screens he controls (and which he refuses to surrender), the sequel to the previous year's melodrama.

The first electoral achievement in April 1994, of media tycoon Silvio Berlusconi had indeed been remarkable. Into the thoroughly disgraced arena of Italian politics he brought the mechanisms of ruthless big business survival. He abused his control of television. He contemptuously dismissed his own past links with outlawed freemasonry and crooked politicians. And achieved an electoral majority ensuring – he believed – that he would be a coalition ringmaster in the country that invented the circus, an arena in which, since the Second World War, most of the political clowns have cried all the way to the bank.

Berlusconi's party is Forza Italia. The words form the supporters' chorus from the terraces for the national football team: its most appropriate translation is 'Go for it, Italy!' It's also the battle cry for A.C. Milan, the football club Berlusconi owns. It perfectly sums up Berlusconi's political message – delivered with Big Brother regularity from his TV stations – that the time had come for the discredited old to be replaced by the exciting new. There was no chance of Forza Italia doing this alone, in a country where all parties, whatever their titles, are always an amalgam of every imaginable political view. And particularly not after an election in which, for the first time, 75 per cent of the vote had been for individual candidates – the first past-the-post British system – with only 25 per cent coming from the old party-not-candidate proportional representation system.

Under the same reformed voting system, in June 1993, municipal elections had produced two guidelines for Berlusconi. The first had been the success of the Democratic Party of the Left, a new name for Italy's communist faction. For 45 years CIA manipulation – plus millions of American dollars pumped into the right wing coffers of their opponents – had kept the communists comfortably on the sidelines. Now, suddenly they were a threat. Berlusconi's concern was that a similar general election surge towards the Democratic Left, which is committed to nationalisation, could seriously endanger his lucrative TV monopoly. Communists, under whatever name, had to remain in a minority position.

The second guideline for Berlusconi was the success in his homeland around Milan of the Northern League, a party of scarcely concealed racism led by the crude-mouthed Umberto Bossi ('Ours is the party with a hard-on') who preached the division of Italy into a federation splitting the business-rich north from the financially draining, Mafia-corrupted, indolent south.

Berlusconi perceived that an alliance between his party and Bossi's would seriously disadvantage the Democratic Left. The coupling of Berlusconi and Bossi was a doomed marriage of practical convenience. Bossi, whose later desertion from the coalition was to bring Berlusconi down, claimed the media magnate represented nothing better than the old corruption. Berlusconi, with unwitting prescience at the time, called Bossi untrustworthy, dangerous and as unpredictable as a wounded boar. Bridesmaid at the uneasy ceremony was bespectacled, Yuppie-smooth Gianfranco Fini, ('Mussolini was the greatest statesman of this century') who tactfully stripped the black-shirts off his skinhead supporters, banned their stiff-armed salutes and brought back from the political wilderness of four decades Italy's despised fascists under the banner of the National Alliance party.

Ill-matched as they were, Berlusconi and Bossi did marry. Or at least cohabite. And called themselves the Freedom Alliance. Their platform was a Thatcherite-model programme (a revered photograph of Margaret Thatcher dominates Berlusconi's office wall) of tax and state deficit cuts, higher pensions and lower state spending, which economists found difficult to add up.

In the general election of March 1994, the Freedom Alliance gained 42.9 per cent of the vote, achieving an outright majority with 366 in the lower Parliament, the House of Deputies. They were only six seats short of a majority in the upper Senate.

One of Berlusconi's first post-election undertakings was to create a 'new Italy'.

The old Italy had crumbled under the finally insupportable weight of cronyism, graft, the Mafia, manipulating secret societies and murder. There were fifty-one governments – plus a non-elected caretaker administration – in the First Republic, dating from the end of the Second World War until 1993. These government turn-arounds, like the corruption, became so established that they were jeered at as being 'revolving door' administrations. Throughout almost five decades, power remained predominantly with the Catholic-approved, CIA favoured Christian Democrat Party. Within a week of his coming to power, however, Berlusconi was negotiating for support in the Senate, where he lacked a majority, with members of the centralist Popular Party, which was the new name for what remained of the Christian Democrats. The other party that had spent so many years in the revolving door were the Socialists. With whom Berlusconi has had a much longer association.

When Berlusconi graduated from Milan University with a law degree he entered the construction business. His most spectacular development was Milan 2, a landscaped township of high priced flats, tree-lined walkways, a sports complex and a lake virtually attached to the original city. It could never have been built without the influence an important Socialist friend who persuaded the civic authorities of Milan to vary their zoning regulations. In the 1970s Berlusconi began establishing his three television stations, which grew over the next twenty years to be watched by more than 45 per cent of the country's viewers. For much of that time, although there existed in Italy a law forbidding such a monopoly, it was never enforced.

This is hardly surprising perhaps, since Bettino Craxi, Italy's prime minister from 1983 to 1987 and dictatorial leader of the Socialist Party until he was forced to resign amid allegations of corruption, extortion and violating the laws of political party financing, was one of Berlusconi's closest friends. Craxi was best man at Berlusconi's wedding to actress Veronica Lario and is godfather to their daughter, Barbara. It was Craxi who persuaded

Milan to change its zoning requirements and whose government did not enforce the television monopoly law.

The period from the 1970s into the 1980s were the formative, golden years for Silvio Berlusconi. Through his holding company, Fininvest, Berlusconi, whose university thesis had been on marketing and publicity, took control of the country's biggest advertising agency, Publitia. He bought the firm which publishes a third of Italy's magazines and a quarter of all books. His film library rivals any in Hollywood. There is a supermarket chain. And music publishing and insurance firms. And, of course, the Milan football club. Today Fininvest has a £6 billion a year turnover, and its bank debts exceed the equity of its 320 companies.

Having discussed the Berlusconi triumph with a number of long-time Italian political observers and commentators[1] I am persuaded that Berlusconi's meteoric election success benefited from the experienced political wisdom and guidance of Bettino Craxi.

Berlusconi dismisses such suggestions as smears put about by – who else! – the communists. He did the same when Milan magistrate Francesco Saverio opened an investigation into allegations that Marcello dell'Utri, head of the Publitia advertising agency, had links with the Mafia. Communists were again blamed by Berlusconi when his brother Paolo – who runs the construction division of the empire – was briefly arrested a month before the 1994 election on suspicion of bribing both Christian Democrat and Socialist politicians with a £440,000 commission to clinch a property sale: the judiciary and the press that revealed the allegations were involved in a 'communist plot'. In July 1994, arrest warrants were re-issued for Paolo, after Salvatore Sciascia, Fininvest's tax director, had told investigating magistrates that it was Berlusconi's brother who authorised bribes to the country's tax-probing financial police. The communist plot was invoked again when police raided the Milan and Rome offices of Forza Italia investigating illegal freemasonry.

Berlusconi *did* belong to the crime-concealing P2 masonic lodge. His membership number was 1816, issued under a code, E.19.78, on 26 January 1978. The membership card assigns Berlusconi to group 17, with a document file number 0625. A receipt for Berlusconi's initial subscription – number 104 – was issued on 5 May 1978, for the lire equivalent, at that time, of £50. It was a friend – whom I believe to have been Bettino Craxi[2] – who had asked him to join, but despite these membership documents Berlusconi denies any active involvement in P2. With doubtful self-mockery he says he was so outraged when the membership documents arrived at his magnificent 18th century villa at Brianza to find the lodge described as a Guild of Masons – to which he considered himself superior as a property developer – that he threw everything into the dustbin. Berlusconi's and his Rome office adamantly refuse to discuss anything of Berlusconi's P2 membership.

An essential part of Silvio Berlusconi's campaign – and an important element in its success – was the constant polling and testing by his publicity division of public opinion, to which he constantly responded. A repeated finding was that the public was wearied by the daily media recital of crime and its high level perpetrators. And wearied most of all by *tangentopoli*, bribesville. Indeed, one of the most surprising results in the election that brought Berlusconi to power was the virtual collapse, nationally, of the anti-Mafia La Rete movement. Its failure to gain MPs was greater where it was expected to achieve most, in Sicily, where its founder, Leoluca Orlando, had only months before been over-whelmingly elected as mayor of Palermo. La Rete's most notable casualty was Nando Dalla Chiesa, the son of one of the Mafia's most famous victims. He was so disillusioned by what he considered a combination of voters' apathy and lack of support from within La Rete that he resigned from the party. Dalla Chiesa told me when we met[3] five months before the election: 'People are so shocked by the criminality of their rulers in the past they say no, it can't be true. It has to be an exaggeration. They think it is impossible for me to make a rational judgement because of my father's murder.'

The polls showing a public lack of interest, similar to his own, in government corruption, led Berlusconi to make the first serious error of his administration when he personally issued a decree – which he humiliatingly had to rescind – freeing over 2,000 corruption-accused politicians and businessmen whom he declared to have been wrongly treated by over-zealous investigating magistrates.

One of the magistrates he labelled over-zealous was the totally honest and totally fearless Judge Antonio di Pietro. The exposure of *tangentopoli* that ended the First Republic began in Milan, earned the title of the Clean Hands Operation and was led by di Pietro. So popular is this son of a peasant farmer that T-shirts emblazoned with his name became a fashion fad in the early 1990s. Indeed, in 1993 he was declared the most popular man in the country in one national opinion poll. That was not, of course, the opinion of the hundreds of Mafiosi he jailed: he worked and lived under a permanent, 24 hour guard, and has at least five separate Cosa Nostra death contracts out upon him.

It was di Pietro whom Berlusconi first asked, when elected, to be his Justice Minister. Di Pietro refused and later issued the arrest warrants for brother Paolo. He also announced the investigation of Berlusconi's political partner, Umberto Bossi, in connection with Italy's biggest political bribery scandal. And approved the official investigation warning given to Berlusconi at the Naples crime conference. Within a week of that warning, Berlusconi's Justice Minister, Alfredo Biondi, ordered a government inspection of di Pietro's office. Di Pietro then caused a sensation by resigning, in protest at official obstruction and interference. It was, said his resignation letter, his last action of dedication to justice. He was doing it 'with death in my heart'.

After Berlusconi's resignation and the resulting turmoil, di Pietro refused to comment upon suggestions that he envisaged a new career for himself in politics.

President Scalfaro tried to quell that turmoil in January, 1995, by appointing banker Lamberto Dini to head a stopgap technocrat government pending new, mid-1995 elections. With Berlusconi spokesman Jas Gavrouski indicating a month later that Berlusconi was tiring of his brief foray into politics – which contrasted with evidence that Berlusconi was gearing himself and his media empire for the contest – Gianfranco Fini, whose National Alliance Party at its January, 1995 inaugural congress declare its past fascist doctrine replaced by a Liberal Democrat mandate, emerged the favourite as Italy's next democratically elected premier.

Corruption is not the only charge levelled at Italy's political leaders. The story of one politician is a case history of the octopus-like entanglement in which the Mafia, freemasonry and corruption exist.

CHAPTER TWENTY

The Man They Called Uncle

Giulio Andriotti *was* Italian politics. He was the rock upon which the Christian Democrat Party of Italy was founded. He was its icon.

No other European statesman served his country longer, almost fifty years. No other European statesman held more ministerial portfolios during that period, a total of thirty-three. Seven were as prime minister. Margaret Thatcher was still a student at Oxford when he became Italian premier for the first time: she'd gone as Britain's leader before he held the office for the last.

He knew five Popes. And every Vatican cardinal. Every world leader. Every head of state.

They weren't, however, the only people he knew. There were Mafia people whom he kissed, in the traditional form of respect. And who called him *lo zio*, 'the Uncle', in returning that respect. As well as crooked judges, who adjusted sentences according to his bidding. And grandmasters of hidden masonic lodges where he met such people and made such arrangements.

Andriotti's unprecedented political life is a matter of public record. So, incredibly, are the alleged facts of his even more unprecedented secret life. *Because* of that political career. It culminated, after those thirty-three ministries over almost half a century, with Andriotti being elected a life member of the Italian Senate, which accorded him permanent immunity from criminal prosecution. To get that immunity lifted to enable a complete investigation to be carried out – and following the European 'guilty until proven innocent' Code Napoleone legal system under which all the evidence is studied before charges are preferred – magistrates had to disclose to a special Senate commission all the accusations made against Andriotti during their nine-month preliminary investigation. This they did at the beginning of 1993: there was a 246-page master file summarising documents that filled a crate. After considering the evidence, the Parliamentary Commission removed Andriotti's protection, describing the decision as 'the best we could have taken in the interest of the country'. Luciano Violante, at the time President of the Parliamentary Anti-Mafia Commission, insisted that bringing Andriotti to trial to answer the charges alleged against him was 'an act of duty'.

Andriotti took to Italian state television[1] to proclaim his innocence. 'I am not an angel or a half-sinner. Maybe I am a full sinner. But not in politics or in respect of the Mafia. In these I am more than an angel.'

It will be for the courts to decide. It is possible they will never do so. Andriotti was 74 years old when the accusations were laid against him in 1993. Italian justice is the slowest in the European Union. Ten years could be the earliest any case comes before a court: longer by half again if each charge is contested and argued along the way, which it will be. Findings of the Court of First Instance are re-examined by the Court of Second Instance, which frequently reverses lower decisions. Verdicts of the second court are subject to varying stages of appeal.

All of which is virtually academic. The charges have been laid. The most serious is that he is an inducted member of the Mafia, a charge officially levelled by Palermo's chief public prosecutor, Judge Giancarlo Caselli. In March 1995, Andriotti was ordered to stand trial on that mafia-association charge. The hearing was scheduled for September of that year. It is expected to be deferred. In the week in which the trial was announced, the mafia assassinated ten people in Sicily. One was the nephew of Tomasso Buscetta, a Mafia supergrass and one of the main witnesses against Andriotti.

The bulk of the supposed evidence linking Andriotti with Italian organised crime comes from *pentiti*, former Mafia gangsters who have turned supergrasses to mitigate prosecutions or sentences.

Andriotti, a slightly hunched, bespectacled, always courteous man of dark suits and quiet voice who really does look like a favourite uncle, insists that no court can believe the word of such men, since their daily lives involved lying and cheating as a matter of course.

That has never been the view of General Carlo Alberto Dalla Chiesa, appointed the anti-Mafia Prefect of Palermo after he successfully smashed Italy's Red Brigade terrorists. Or of Italy's anti-Mafia crime chief Judge Giovanni Falcone. Or of his successor, Judge Paolo Borsellino. All three men relied heavily upon *pentiti*. It was the evidence of such witnesses upon which were based the Italian 'Maxi-Trials' of the mid-and late-eighties, which led to the jailing of hundreds of mafiosi who faced their accusers through the bars of specially built courtroom cages.

All three of the judges who trusted the word of *pentiti* are dead, victims of Mafia assassination. Every *pentiti* – close to five hundred, all living in various parts of the world under permanent protection – has a Mafia death sentence upon him. The eight who gave evidence against Andriotti did so in affadavits to investigating magistrates who sometimes travelled to their hide-outs rather than risk bringing them back to the danger of Italy.

Not all the sworn evidence against the Uncle comes from supergrasses whose honesty can be challenged. Most explosive of all are Dalla Chiesa's secret diaries which the accusing magistrates possess, of which Andriotti was unaware until he was confronted by them. And the sworn evidence of one of Dalla Chiesa's sons, Fernando, who testified to his father telling him how Andriotti 'went white' at being told of the diaries and what they contained.

The general's other son, Nando, told me Christian Democrat politicians knew his father's killers and that when his father arrived in Sicily to take up his position as prefect, he soon realised the servants at both his official home and his office were Mafia spies.

It was to take another eleven years before Nando Dalla Chiesa made his public accusation to me. It was allegedly confirmed, independently, by two of the eight Mafia informers all of whose testimony linking Andriotti to the Mafia was put before the Senate immunity commission. Some was also placed before the Parliamentary Anti-Mafia Commission. One man is the most famous of all *pentito*, the overweight, asthmatic Tommaso Buscetta, once a member of the Cosa Nostra hierarchy in Palermo. Buscetta, rarely appearing without heavy-framed dark glasses or the added padding of a bulletproof vest, and always within a phalanx of shoulder-to-shoulder guards, was the first Mafia Man of Honour to break the code of *omerta*, the vow of silence by which mafiosi are supposed to live. Another was Francesco Marino Mannoia. Both men now live under permanent protection in America: there is no conceivable protection that would keep them alive in Italy. The poisoning in his Italian prison cell of Mafia financier and P2 member Michele Sindona, who had not even agreed to cooperate with investigators, proved the Mafia's powers.

It is Mannoia's testimony, made publicly available and in full to the Italian Senate, that directly places Andriotti at a meeting with the Cosa Nostra *cupola* in Sicily. And sets out for the first time the Mafia's use of freemasonry. According to Mannoia's evidence, Andriotti's Mafia connections were cemented in the late 1970s, when the Cosa Nostra's *capo di tutti capi* was Stefano Bontade, subsequently killed in a Mafia dispute over heroin trafficking. Bontade was a member of a masonic lodge. It is not named in Mannoia's affadavit but I understand it to have been a Sicilian offshoot of P2.[3] According to the witness, the Cosa Nostra Don knew 'that in such a way he would be able to have important contacts which would increase his power and his personal prestige'.

The important masonic contact Bontade made was with Salvatore Lima, Andriotti's protégé and the island's Christian Democrat leader, its MP and later its representative to the European Parliament in Strasbourg. This encounter led to Lima becoming a fully initiated Man of Honour in the Matteo Citarda Family. For the Cosa Nostra it was a staggering success. It gave them a permanently open door to the highest of the high in the ruling Italian government. And an influential presence within the non-elected administration in Brussels and the Strasbourg parliament of what was then the European Community.

It was Lima who guided the clever leaders of organised crime to the receptive leaders of Italy.

The eagerness of that reception was chillingly clear from what Gaspare Mutolo, another of the eight *pentiti*, alleged to the Senate. 'The most powerful political reference point for Cosa Nostra was Senator Andriotti.'

As if he were describing polite arrangements made over cocktails in an exclusive club – and in many ways the Mafia is indeed the most exclusive club in the world – Mutolo called it 'a peaceful cohabitation and exchange of favours between Cosa Nostra and part of the political world of which the Andriotti conduit was an essential component.'

According to the filed depositions, Andriotti's first known personal visit to the Sicilian *cupola* became necessary when Piersanti Matterella, the son of a respected Mafia politician, turned his back on both his personal and underworld Family by announcing a campaign in general against the Mafia as an organisation and against its influence in particular within the Christian Democratic Party, of which he was the island's president. For the Cosa Nostra it was more than a declaration of war. It was a test of their carefully cultivated and tended connection to the Christian Democrat leadership. One to be used, they decided, as a demonstration of which – the Mafia or the government – was the more powerful.

Mannoia records that the *cupola* conference was held in a hunting lodge in the brown, sun-hardened Sicilian hills overlooking Palermo. Behind shading shutter windows were open, to catch whatever breeze there was to cool the lodge. It would have been comfortable to be without jackets. But unthinkable. This was a meeting of the ruling commission of the most completely organised crime entity in the world. Respect was everything, at such an echelon. And this time the country's prime minister was attending, so jackets were worn. And tightly knotted ties. It was Stefano Bontade who had demanded the presence of Italy's prime minister. Who had come, as ordered. He was not the only dutifully attending politician. Salvatore Lima was there, as well. So, too, were two other leading mafiosi: Antonio and Ignazio Salvo, who were cousins and who, according to the much later accusing magistrates, were to become very close to the Italian leader, particularly after Lima had to be used as an example.

None of the testifying *pentiti* actually attended the meeting to hear what was discussed or decided. They were the outside people, the arrangers kept in the villa grounds. But when Piersanti Matterella was assassinated shortly afterwards, they knew what the conference decision had been.

Mannoia claims he was a witness to a later *cupola* gathering which Andriotti attended. It was hot again. It was a business meeting, as such meetings always were, so everyone had to dress for business. This time it was in a walled and gated villa, blinds closed over open windows as before, for discretion and to shade the rooms. Mannoia was one of the people in the grounds, along with many others: the protection provided for the Mafia hierarchy – and their very important visitors – was always good.

'When we heard the horn of a car sound we rushed to open the gate,' Mannoia says. 'The car drove in and the gate was closed immediately after it.'

It was a bullet-proof Alfa Romeo, with blackened windows completely concealing its occupants. Giulio Andriotti was one. So were Antonio and Ignazio Salvo, who had chartered the private aircraft that had flown the Christian Democrat leader from Rome to a shielded-off part of an airstrip at Trapani.

Andriotti paused momentarily, looking first at the villa and then beyond, around its protected setting, when he got out of the car. He was dark-suited, like everyone else. Bontade was at the villa door, with the rest of the *cupola*: for everyone to welcome Andriotti was a sign of respect. Andriotti had come to them again, after all. Courtesy had to be shown in return. All the smiles were brief: not part of any ritual, except that of respect.

The meeting lasted for about forty-five minutes. Mannoia remained in the garden but believes the meeting in the villa became heated. 'I clearly heard shouts coming from inside.'

Andriotti left the meeting first, hurrying into the armoured Alfa Romeo to be taken back to the private plane on stand-by at Trapani. Stefano Bontade was talkative, pleased with the encounter.

He had told Andriotti, 'We are in command in Sicily and if you do not want to wipe out the Christian Democrat party completely you have got to do what we say. If not we will take away not only your votes in Sicily but also in Reggio Calabria and all southern Italy. You can only count on the votes of the north.'

Independent corroboration was to come of that mafia stranglehold. Late in 1994 former Palermo City councillor and self-confessed Cosa Nostra member Gioacchion Pennino told investigating magistrates on the island that in Sicily the Christian Democrats were virtually a 'Family' of the Mafia. According to Pennino's evidence Antonio Salvo always referred to Andriotti as 'Uncle Giulio'.

At the time of the Palermo 'clarification' meeting Andriotti was under pressure to bring in anti-Mafia legislation. Bontade said he had warned Andriotti against the introduction of such laws, 'otherwise other serious things will happen'.

Other serious things did happen.

Before the Senate cleared the way for the Andriotti proceedings, Tommaso Buscetta had testified earlier to the parliamentary anti-Mafia commission of a political 'entity'. But on that earlier occasion Buscetta refused to identify the 'entity'.

Something very dramatic occurred to persuade Buscetta and other *pentiti* testifying against Andriotti to change their minds. It was the televised appearance on the first day of his trial, more than a decade after the Sicilian meetings they described so vividly, of the most recently identified *capo di tutti capi* of the Cosa Nostra.

Salvatore (Toto) Riina had been present at those Sicilian meetings. After the death of Bontade – and others who succeeded him – Riina, who is a near double for Hollywood actor Rod Steiger, murdered his way to complete control. He killed – or had killed –most of Bontade's successors. At his September 1993, trial – at which he was sentenced to life on a charge of just two killings – he was said to have been personally involved or implicated in 500 more. Two of the murders were of Judges Falcone and Borsellino. Another was that of the rebellious Piersanti Mattarella.

So effectively did Riina use the televising of his trial to frighten and reassure those outside the courtroom that the prosecutor at one stage accused him of attempted intimidation. In another trial, in Reggio Calabria in May 1994, from the dock, Riina specifically named three judges in what Buscetta later insisted had been a death sentence. A month later, in Paris[4] I personally asked one of those judges, Giancarlo Casilli, if he was frightened by the threat. Mafia assassination was the risk judges like himself faced, he said: he accepted it. Because it was such a risk, all the judges worked in groups, not singly, so that if one were killed the others could continue their prosecutions. 'Of course I am concerned but it does nothing to alter my determination to go on opposing the Mafia.'

It did nothing to intimidate Tommaso Buscetta, either. Or Gaspare Mutolo. They understood better than anyone the real messages Riina was sending out when he claimed that he knew no politicians. Mutolo translated what Riina was really saying. The most feared Mafia Don of all time wanted to take over control of every Mafia clan in Italy as well as some of the Colombian Cartels, and so become the most powerful gangster in the world. Accordingly he was reassuring the watching politicians that there would be no embarrassing disclosures by him or his Corleone Family. At the same time, he wanted those politicians to 'move' again in the Mafia's interests. Mutolo believed that if Andriotti had not been publicly named by himself and others, the ongoing Mafia investigations would have been officially blocked. Buscetta believed the same. He told the Senate committee: 'The entity of whom I spoke before the anti-Mafia commission is Giulio Andriotti.'

In their application to the Senate, for the lifting of Andriotti's immunity from prosecution, the investigating Palermo magistrates made extensive references to the Dalla Chiesa diaries. There were daily entries up to the day before the general died. Yet again the Mafia had used their favourite assassination method. The general's wife, Emmanuela, was at the wheel of their Fiat when two assassins pulled up alongside on a motorcycle. Seconds before they began spraying the vehicle with bullets from a Kalashnikov rifle, Dalla Chiesa threw himself across his wife, to try to protect her. He took most of the fire, but she was hit sixteen times. Their totally inadequate police bodyguard, in a following car, was also killed. In the diaries there are accounts of several meetings between the general and the Christian Democrat leader, Giulio Andriotti, whose recollection of these meetings, when questioned, varies substantially from what Dalla Chiesa recorded. The magistrates comment bluntly: 'It can be ruled out that the general would have written falsehoods in a completely personal document.' In one entry the general reveals that before accepting his appointment as Prefect of Palmero he told Andriotti he was unconvinced of the Christian Democrats' anti-Mafia commitment. The general writes that he felt 'isolated' by the politicians from whom he believed he deserved support. He also reports Andriotti's response to the complaint, which appears to have had no relevance to the conversation they were having. Andriotti's answer was to refer to a New York contract killing of a Mafia *capo* named Pietro Inzerillo, after which coins were put into the man's mouth. This is a symbolic Mafia act by which they signify the penalty imposed upon someone who has broken the code of *omerta*.

Over a decade later the Palermo judges translated Andriotti's reply. In their opinion it was possible 'to hypothesise that the Honorable Andriotti wished to introduce a message that (Dalla Chiesa) should not exert himself too much in territory where the interests of the Cosa Nostra crossed with the Masons and compromised politicians.'

There was a meeting between General Dalla Chiesa and

Andriotti on 6 April 1982, a month before he officially took up his duties. In his entry for that day, the general records telling Andriotti he intended to ignore any political pressure and to charge all the Christian Democrat officials in Sicily with Mafia involvements, about which he knew everything. That 6 April meeting was the one at which the general later told his son, Fernando, that Andriotti had 'gone white' after learning the extent of his knowledge.

General Dalla Chiesa survived in Palermo for five months. He pursued the Mafia, like investigators to follow, through their money laundering and bank accounts: the day before he died he had obtained from the Finance Ministry a report on the tax and financial affairs of more than 3,000 suspected mafiosi, many linked to Andriotti's party. That investigation died with the general.

Other evidence died with other killings. A 1979 murder had been that of investigating journalist Mino Pecorelli, proprietor of a weekly, *Osservatore Politico*. Pecorelli specialised in exposing government secrets. He was an active member of P2, through which he had many contacts with Italy's intelligence services. Also in P2 were a number of secret freemason politicians. I understand[5] that it was one of those politicians – whom Pecorelli closely questioned – who first warned Andriotti there was going to be an embarrassing personal exposé in *Osservatore Politico*.

There had been an ominous additional warning in a previous Pecorelli article. In it the journalist claimed that the Italian terrorist group Red Brigade were not the true organisers of the sensational kidnap murder of Christian Democrat grandee Aldo Moro.

Moro, a small, balding man, had a political pedigree rivalling that of Andriotti, having served five times as prime minister before his kidnap in April 1978. The abductors demanded the release from Italian jails of all their fellow terrorists in return for Moro's safe release. The Christian Democrat party, dominated as always by Andriotti, refused. On 9 May 1978, Moro's body was found. He had been wrapped in a blanket and stuffed into the boot of a tiny Renault car, which had been sprayed by a machine pistol.

Andriotti led the Christian Democrat mourners at Aldo Moro's funeral the following day.

In that last article before his murder – shot in a car, typically as he was about to drive away from his office – Pecorelli claimed the Moro kidnapping had been for political reasons, not primarily those of terrorist idealogy. Nor planned by Red Brigade terrorists.

Pecorelli was planning to follow up that claim with a cover story, but was shot before he could write the exposé. It was the information upon which Pecorelli intended to base his article, plus more gleaned over the intervening three years, that made the colour drain from the man's face when General Dalla Chiesa – in fatal misjudgement, as it transpired – told Andriotti on 6 April just how much he knew. And what he intended doing with the knowledge.

One of the most devastating secrets I understand Pecorelli possessed[6] was that during the Aldo Moro kidnapping the Mafia offered to free the politician from Red Brigade captivity, believing that to do so would be a quid pro quo expression of gratitude for all the favours the Christian Democrat Party had extended to it. The discussions – in secluded villas in the Sicilian hills – were short lived. They ended abruptly when an unnamed Don – whom I believe[7] to have been Salvatore Riina – told another whose identity has not been suggested to me: 'You haven't understood. Top politicians in his party don't want him freed.'

Giulio Andriotti was at the pinnacle of those top politicians, manipulating everything and everyone.

The order that Mino Pecorelli should be assassinated before he could disclose the secrets of the Aldo Moro killing was relayed through cousins Ignazio and Antonio Salvo. At one stage in their relationship with Andriotti they were known as 'The Messengers'.

Andriotti insisted during a twelve hour interrogation in Rome on 16 December 1993 – after his immunity has been removed by the Senate – that he did not know, nor had he ever known, Ignazio or Antonio Salvo. Magistrates promptly confronted that denial with a photograph taken in June 1979, of Antonio Salvo at a Sicilian gathering of Christian Democrat functionaries, with Giulio Andriotti at their centre. It had been taken by Litizia Battaglia, a Palermo photographer and by 1993 an anti-Mafia La Rete MP. The incriminating occasion had been a dinner during an election campaign at the Hotel Zagarella, a resort on the outskirts of Palermo owned by the cousins. In further confrontation, the magistrates produced statements confirming the meeting from Vito Ciancimino, a former mayor of the Sicilian capital subsequently jailed for Mafia affiliation. Ciancimino and the manager of the Hotel Zagarella testified that Andriotti and Antonio Salvo spent a considerable time together, much of it walking or sitting alone in the hotel gardens where nothing they discussed could be overheard.

Andriotti persisted in his denial of any friendship or sinister association. Antonio Salvo had been someone to whom he had been introduced during the convention. He'd had no idea of Salvo's identity. Neither Mafia cousins could be questioned. Antonio was dead of natural causes, before Andriotti's December 1993 questioning. Ignazio had been assassinated by the Mafia the previous year. Had he not been, Ignazio would have been interrogated on a much more sensational episode alleged by another *pentito*.

Ignazio Salvo's answers could have made that December examination even more traumatic for Andriotti. As it was Andriotti remained apparently calm and unshaken throughout the confrontation, even when brought face-to-face with Baldassare di Maggio and accused of having given a Mafia *capo* the kiss of respect. 'Totally untrue,' he insisted.

Di Maggio was the newest and most highly valued of the *pentito* giving evidence from personal experience. Di Maggio, astonishingly, made possible the arrest of Riina who – despite outstanding arrest warrants – had lived contemptuously and openly in Sicily for twenty-three years while officially listed as one of Italy's most wanted men.

For a lot of that time di Maggio was Riina's driver, physically closer to the 'boss of bosses' than almost anyone else in the Corleone Family, upon which Mario Puzzo's *The Godfather* was based.

At the very end of 1992, di Maggio was arrested on minor charges. Instead of remaining silent and waiting for his release to be arranged, which would have been hardly more than a matter of form, di Maggio panicked. He demanded to see a carabinieri officer and offered a deal. In return for freedom from prosecution –plus a reward supposed[7] to be about £250,000 – di Maggio offered to tell the police how they could catch Riina. It was an offer the authorities couldn't refuse.

There is a set of traffic lights on the Avenue of the Sicilian Region, a run-down suburb on the outskirts of Palermo. Every morning there is a rush hour jam at precisely that spot, the traffic bottlenecked in swirls of dust and fumes. Di Maggio had sweated and cursed there for years, he told police: Riina liked to travel at that time, when there were a lot of cars and trucks around. He believed that the mêlée gave him cover, although he was so sure of his political protection after so long that this was scarcely necessary. But if there was now no longer any political protection, those traffic lights were in fact in the ideal place for an ambush.

On 15 January 1994, police blanketed the area. The few in uniform kept out of sight. The rest were plain clothes, crowding the sidewalks with pedestrians: all were carabinieri or anti-Mafia units. A van packed with electronic equipment was the central command point for unmarked radio cars tucked away in the side-streets, forming a complete circle into which they hoped Riina would drive. A helicopter was already airborne before the congestion formed into a jam, too high overhead to attract attention but linked to the mobile command centre if aerial pursuit became necessary. It didn't.

Riina kept to his routine that January morning. Police waited until his Mercedes was blocked by cars and lorries, totally unable to move, before swooping. Encircled, Riina didn't panic. He spread his arms in a gesture of bewilderment at the guns and machine pistols pointed at him and said: 'What do you want with me? I'm not a criminal.'

'We know you are. And *who* you are,' replied an arresting officer.[8]

Riina meekly outstretched his arms to be handcuffed. The man implicated in 500 murders was unarmed. It took two hours longer than usual to clear the traffic jam. The arrest brought personal congratulations from Italy's President Oscar Luigi Scalfaro to the police involved.

The information leading to Riina's arrest earned di Maggio the criminal immunity he demanded and the £250,000 reward. But there was more to come. Under further detailed questioning, Di Maggio talked of taking Riina on 20 September 1987 to the Palermo home of Ignazio Salvo: the collusion between the Mafia and the island police was such that Riina, well known as he was, could walk freely and unmolested through a carabinieri cordon whenever he wanted.

Di Maggio had more to say than that even. The most incredible allegation of all was that Riina's visit to Ignazio's home was so that Andriotti could meet him. Di Maggio witnessed everything, he assured the magistrates. And what he saw was Andriotti, who was then serving one of his seven terms as prime minister, kiss Riina in the traditional Mafia greeting. It was, testified di Maggio, the accepted form of respect between mafiosi. The alleged evidence of The Kiss – and its implication – supported claims from yet another *pentito*. Leonardo Messina testified Andriotti was actually *punciuto* – initiated – into a Mafia Family.

It was Messina who identified Andriotti by name as the man able to fix or reverse any lower court sentence upon a Man of Honour through the one time President of the Italian Supreme Court, Judge Carrado Carnevale.

Before being transferred from the Supreme Court in 1992, the studiously bespectacled, balding Judge Carnevale had overturned upon appeal – usually on highly technical legal grounds – more than four hundred Mafia convictions imposed in lower courts. So frequent did these sentence reversals become that Italian newspapers picked up the nickname by which Judge Carnevale was known in Rome's legal circles and began using it. The nickname was *ammazzasentenze*. It translates as 'sentence killer.' A year after Carnevale's transfer, Italy's Supreme Council of the Judiciary – the country's highest legal authority – began an enquiry into his reversal decisions. The judiciary council's was the second such examination. Judge Falcone had begun one before his Mafia assassination in 1992.

Within the Mafia, according to the evidence, it was accepted that there was a precise guarantee that Andriotti could 'adjust' court decisions. The chain of command was traced through Salvatore Lima to Andriotti to Judge Carnevale. And when the judge was officially transferred with him went the Cosa Nostra's very special relationship with the highest court in the land.

The arrogant Cosa Nostra *cupola* believed that Andriotti could have prevented the judge's transfer. They had already decided Salvatore Lima was not functioning as effectively on their behalf as he should have been doing. A *cupola* decision was therefore reached[9] that a very forceful reminder of the power and expectations of the Mafia was necessary. Salvatore Lima, a disposable asset, was shot in Palermo during an election campaign in March 1992. This killing was specifically directed at Andriotti. In Mafia terminology, it was to 'denigrate' the Christian Democrat leader by showing him how easily the Cosa Nostra could carry out the threat allegedly made during that much earlier hunting lodge conference that Andriotti had travelled to Sicily to attend: clearly, whenever they wanted, the Cosa Nostra could wipe out the Christian Democrat party by taking away its electoral votes.

Andriotti emphatically denied all the allegations made against him. His lawyer filed a sixty-six page rebuttal and Andriotti added to it with a personal nine page defence. The basis of Andriotti's total denial of each and every detailed accusation was that he was a victim of a Mafia conspiracy to discredit him, and that the ex-Mafia *pentiti* were by definition incapable of telling the truth. Their evidence, therefore, should be totally disregarded.

That had been Andriotti's insistence from 3 April 1993, the day he disclosed for the first time that he had been served with *avviso di garanzia*, a court document required under the Italian legal system officially advising him he was under investigation. Andriotti pointed out then that during his administration several effective anti-Mafia laws had been enacted and added: 'I should have expected their vengeance and in a way it is better that it should be this rather than the *lupara* (a wolf gun, which is the traditional killing weapon of the Mafia).'

In the protestation of innocence Andriotti filed with the court, he argued that it would have been impossible for him to attend *cupola* meetings in Sicily, constantly surrounded as he was by anti-terrorist security. Andriotti's statement insisted: 'I was never without surveillance even for a single moment of the day.'

But in May 1994, Palermo judges disclosed that their investigations had discovered from police records that on that September 1987, day when it was claimed he kissed Riina, Andriotti was without police escort or protection for the specific four-hour period during which their encounter was said to have taken place.

Andriotti's lawyer, Odoaro Asceri, argued there was no basis in law for any charges to be formally brought against the Christian Democrat statesman: everything was based on hearsay and rumour, with no evidence of fact. 'The methodology of the investigation appears clearly distorted by a pre-conceived theory, inspired by the anxiety to obtain from those interrogated confirmation of the prejudice that Senator Andriotti collaborated "not occasionally" to protect the interests of Cosa Nostra at a national level.' By making all the allegations public, as they had done, the magistrates had trampled on justice.

Giulio Andriotti is not the only Italian politician in Italy's First Republic against whom allegations of corruption and membership of secret organisations have been levelled, just its most famous. Before the First Republic's final, ultimately unmourned demise, two other prime ministers resigned in the face of such accusations and 253 MPs and disgraced ministers were warned they were under investigation. Extra legal staff had to be recruited to the Justice

Ministry and magistrates' divisions merely to handle the paper-work.

As Leoluca Orlando told me[10]: 'For many years Italy didn't have a democratic government. Crime ran it.'

With the weakness of governments in Eastern Europe, faced with the superior wealth of co-ordinated mafias, it is not an exaggeration to suggest it is a situation that could recur elsewhere on the European continent. And there's always the masonic movement there to help.

CHAPTER TWENTY-ONE

Il Big Bang

All explosions have fall-out. That which followed the end of Italy's First Republic had the proportions of an atom bomb: it will take years – even beyond the year 2000 – for the dust to settle.

And the irony is that the detonator was little more than a squib.

Physically Mario Chiesa isn't big. He looks the clerk-like administrator he was, a narrow-shouldered, always eager-to-please man who basked in the reflected glory of his very occasional, very brief encounters with the god-like figures of Italy's Socialist Party. But he *did* meet them and when he did they told him how valuable his work was as a fund raiser and organiser in Milan. And they meant it. Chiesa was loyal and industrious: a totally committed party person who could be trusted. In return for that trust, he showed not only loyalty but also unquestioning admiration: reverence even. The party leaders *were* his gods. What they did, he did. Or tried to. How could something be wrong, if they did it? Theirs was the system he knew so much about and he was part of it. A small part, admittedly. So Mario Chiesa, the tiniest of cogs, wanted only the tiniest amount of oil.

The bribe Mario Chiesa accepted from a firm seeking the cleaning contract for a Milan old people's home was just £3,200.

It destroyed Italy's two leading political parties, with almost half a century of revolving door government virtually shared between them. It destroyed hundreds of politicians and businessmen, also –

some literally, when they chose suicide to court humiliation – and decades of masonically-linked, Mafia-tainted corruption.

And the entire collapse took just two years.

It was in February 1992 that the then deputy Milan prosecutor, Judge Antonio Di Pietro – yet to become the hero of T-shirt and waistcoat fads – traced Mario Chiesa's financial records[1] with his computer expertise and found the pitifully small £3,200. Given Chiesa's position in the local Socialist Party, the affair was scheduled as a routine examination: production of the proof, the inevitable confession, the usual contrition, a court appearance making headlines for maybe one or two days in the local Milan newspapers. And then forgotten.

But Chiesa, like others in the future, panicked. In his desperation to avoid a prosecution he abandoned the loyalty and discretion for which the Socialist leaders had praised him. He talked about the system that was to become known as *tangentopoli*. And insisted that the Socialists weren't the only party operating it. The Christian Democrats shared in it too: all Judge Di Pietro had to do was ask Roberto Mongini, the Christian Democrat party leader in Milan. So Di Pietro did, after incarcerating Mongini in Milan's San Vittore jail for seventeen days. Initially reticent, on the eighteenth day Mongini talked as well.[2]

The *tangentopoli* system was staggering both for the amounts of money involved and the simplicity of their allocation. Although that allocation varied according to the voting strength in each city – a total of thirty townships were finally investigated – in Milan, where it was first uncovered, the cake was cut with fifty per cent going to the Christian Democrats and twenty five per cent each to the Socialists and the Communists. *Every* business involvement in *every* state or local municipal project, enterprise or development had to be bought with bribery, to the party and to the people in power who awarded the contract. The 'commission' was normally five per cent of the contract value, but again it varied from town to town. The bribe was usually built into the over-estimated cost of the project which meant, ultimately, that the state was being systematically robbed. But not all the money went into party coffers. Millions were siphoned off – to establish personal fortunes – into numbered bank accounts. One of these accounts containing one such personal fortune – known about by leading Socialist Party officials – was linked to secret masonic lodges.

According to court evidence[3] publicly filed under the Code Napoleone, Bettino Craxi, the Socialist Party leader, former Italian prime minister, former Euro-MP and friend and advisor to the country's initial Second Republic premier Silvio Berlusconi, was one high official in the know. Confronted by that and other accusations, Craxi, a towering, balding Milanese frequently depicted by Italian newspaper cartoonists as a black-shirted Mussolini because of the autocratic way he controlled the Socialist Party, resigned the leadership. A year earlier he was being confidently tipped to become Italy's President: a sycophantic 'court' was in regular attendance in his luxurious permanent apartment suite in Rome's Hotel Raphael. Now, in the initial weeks of his disgrace, people spat at him in the street and shouted 'bastard' if he ventured out into the open, and he fled Italy for the safety of a luxury villa in Hammamet, in Tunisia. He was still there in July 1994, when he was sentenced, *in absentia*, to eight and a half years in jail for complicity in the fraudulent bankruptcy of the Banco Ambrosiano.

Another knowing Socialist was claimed to be Justice Minister Claudio Martelli who, until a week before the allegation was made against him, had successfully campaigned to establish himself as the front runner to succeed Craxi – who was already discredited by accusations of other financial manipulations. It was Martelli who, when in power, had completely blocked investigations into masonic and Mafia infiltration of the European Union by anti-corruption judge Dr Agostino Cordova. And it was Martelli again who prevented Dr Cordova from being promoted head of the Parliamentary Anti-Mafia Commission, and from getting the appointment as Naples' public prosecutor. When the evidence was deposed against him, in February 1993,[4] Martelli, denying every accusation quit both his office and the party: briefly he went to London to take a course in economics.

The evidence in question – linking both men to numbered Swiss bank accounts and secret masonic lodges – was laid by Silvio Larini, a friend and one time most trusted confidant of Bettino Craxi.

Larini himself had fled Italy at the end of 1992, after being named in Di Pietro's widening investigation into political corruption, and for several months wandered from hide-out to hide-out in Switzerland, France and the islands of the South Pacific. In February 1993, he returned to Italy and surrendered to investigators.

The story Larini told was mind-boggling.[5]

He admitted that his had been the name – concealed by the Swiss banking system – under which a special purpose numbered account was opened at the Union des Banques Suisses in Lugano. The special purpose was to hide any incriminating connection with the Socialists. Into it was channelled millions upon millions of lire paid over the years in bribes to the party and its leading officials.

Going into detail, Larini said there was one particular deposit of £4.9 million personally made by Roberto Calvi, before his flight to London and his murder, beneath Blackfriars Bridge. The £4.9 million was not Calvi's own but came from P2 Grandmaster Licio Gelli. It was the 'commission' owed in gratitude for a £50 million loan in 1980 from the Socialist-controlled State energy conglomerate ENI, in order to keep afloat Calvi's Mafia-and-Vatican entangled Banco Ambrosiano. The £50 million was one of several loans which enabled the bank to continue trading – and building up even greater debts and perpetrating even greater frauds – for another two years. Larini, an architect who is associated with the company that technically owns the Hammamet villa in Tunisia constantly used by Craxi, testified that Martelli – as well as Craxi himself – knew about the Swiss account. Larini made available to the investigators all details, including a substantial number of bank statements.[6]

The explosion had graduated from the squib to the nuclear.

It was not, however, the first that the probing magistrates had heard, either of the £4.9 million bribe or of the Banco Ambrosiano, the name and shadow of which hovered over so much of the *tangentopoli* and virtually all the leading political parties throughout the 1980s. There were already incomplete references to the £4.9 million in papers seized in raids upon Gelli's Tuscany villa. But the Gelli documents made up only half the jigsaw. It was Larini's evidence that filled in sufficient to form a picture.

Larini's testimony went further than the £4.9 million payment. Also funnelled into the Lugano account, he alleged, were millions in kickbacks from the contract to build the Milan underground. And those millions were not destined for the party. They were personal, for Craxi himself.

Just as the giant ENI conglomerate – a State-owned enterprise providing just under half Italy's energy demands with an annual turnover in the region of £20 billion – was traditionally considered a private fiefdom shared by the Christian Democrats and the

Socialists, to be manipulated for personal and political benefit, not for the benefit of the country and its people.

That arrogant misuse culminated at the end of 1993 with the beginning of a legal process likely to take years: maybe, even, as long as the probe into the half century of Giulio (The Uncle) Andriotti's secret political life.

The process was described at its beginning in Milan by Di Pietro – an essentially shy man who shuns personal publicity and prefers his do-it-yourself-workshop to jewel-bedecked first nights and is not given to exaggeration – as the 'father of all corruption trials,' involving the 'mother of all bribes'.[7] It had already cost the lives of two of Italy's most flamboyant and internationally famous industrialists – as well as others – and the disgrace of yet another former Italian Prime Minister, Christian Democrat Arnaldo Forlani. Less than a year before his public exposure as a taker of bribes Forlani had narrowly failed to be elected President of Italy. He would have achieved that highest of high office, in time.

He won't now.

The rightfully labelled 'mother of all bribes' amounted to a single cosmic payment of £62 million. That was the kickback approved by Raul Gardini, international world class yachtsman and Admiral's Cup challenger, the silver-haired patriach of the Ferruzzi family dynasty which could perfectly have fitted the helicopter and private jet image of America's *Dynasty* and *Dallas* soap operas.

The bribe was divided, strictly according to the understood rules of *tangentopoli*, with more than half going to Craxi and his Socialists. More than twenty five per cent of the remainder was accepted, according to the filed evidence, by Forlani and his Christian Democrats. The remainder was split between the conniving smaller parties that made up the ruling coalition.

The bribe was intended to extricate Gardini from a disastrous attempt in 1989 to wrest from Fiat chairman Gianni Agnelli the mantle of Italy's most successful industrialist. The richly-born Gardini resented the wealthier Agnelli referring to him as *il contadino*, (the peasant).

If Italian television ever makes a soap based on the Ferruzzi family – which they might, although now it would be a story of humiliation rather than of glittering triumph – the character that was Raul Gardini would need no scriptwriter's improvement.

Gardini, accustomed to the comfortable riches of a substantial land-owning family, had entered a world of unimaginable wealth and power when he married Idina, the daughter of Serafino Ferruzzi, whose real life dynasty, from its headquarters in Ravenna, controlled a vast commodities, grain and cereal empire. There were 2.5 million Ferruzzi acres of agricultural land in Italy and the United States. The Ferruzzi ranches in Argentina covered thousands of acres. The Ferruzzis travelled always by private helicopter and personal jet, with fleets of cars on constant standby, and lived in ancient but luxurious palaces – Gardini's was on Venice's Grand Canal – attended by uniformed and white-gloved servants.

For twenty years Gardini was always at the right hand of his father-in-law and mentor. There was no aspect of any operation of the multi-million conglomerate that Gardini did not know better than the managers employed to run them. Serafino Ferruzzi had a son of his own, Arturo. Raul Gardini succeeded his father-in-law both in control of the empire and as the family patriarch. Gardini never denied the legend that when the family was gathered after Serafino's death he told them 'You must decide now if you're willing to let me do things my way and give me total control. Or if, instead, you just want to remain a wealthy provincial family.'

By that time Gardini had acquired another, more flattering nickname. It was *il corsaro*, (the pirate).

The Ferruzzis chose to have a pirate at the helm. It was, initially, a wise choice. At one stage in its history, Ferruzzi – under Gardini's guidance – became Italy's second largest industrial group, beaten only by Fiat. Gardini achieved this by breath-taking corporate nerve. From 1985 he acted like a true pirate, embarking on a corporate raiding scheme to acquire stock in the Montedison chemical giant: by 1987 he had forty-two per cent of the group. Ferruzzi-Montedison was born. No-one then could have guessed the true financial cost. Gardini certainly wasn't going to tell anyone.

Raul Gardini didn't want to be second best. He wanted to be *the* best. And to solve a certain secret problem at the same time, the enormous debts built up by the corporate raiding that had given him control of Montedison in the first place. The way to achieve both, he determined, was to form a joint venture group between Enichem, the chemical subsidiary of the state-owned ENI petro-chemical conglomerate, and his Montedison group. He opened negotiations with ENI president Gabriele Cagliari. And, of course, with the necessary Socialist and Christian Democrat leaders whose approval had to be obtained, both publicly but more importantly – and more expensively – in private.

Approval was given. Substantially bought, of course, with private contributions: a witness at a later magistrate's examination talked of money being carried to grateful recipients in suitcases.[8] The new company, named Enimont – an acronym created from letters taken from both founding organisations – came into being in 1988: Montedison held forty per cent of the shares, giving the ENI group control. One of Gardini's first actions was to try to solve the problem no-one knew about by transferring a major portion of his corporate raiding debts into the accounts of the new joint venture.

From the start, Enimont was a business disaster: Raul Gardini appeared to have lost his Midas touch. But he most certainly hadn't lost his pirate's instincts. With stunning audacity – and the promise of a £62 million bribe, duly delivered, to the politicians who would have to agree – he proposed that ENI buy him out. Which they did, in November 1990. And actually gave him a profit on the deal by purchasing his shares at a grossly inflated valuation.

It was not until two years later, after Mario Chiesa's blurted explanation of his own minuscule £3,200 'commission', that Milan's Antonio Di Pietro began following the Socialist Party money trails to 'the mother of all bribes'. Gabriele Cagliari, ENI's president, was arrested in early 1993 and thrown into San Vittore jail. An arrest warrant was issued for Guiseppe Garofano, chief executive of Montedison, who fled. It took a long time – almost three months – for the magistrates to extract sufficient evidence from Cagliari to support charges against Gardini. Then, on 20 July 1993, Gabriele Cagliari suffocated himself to death in a bathroom of the San Vittore prison.

Meanwhile, Garofano had been arrested in Switzerland: under questioning he broke much more quickly than the former president of ENI and described exactly how the Gardini bribe had been divided out: £32 million to Bettino Craxi, nearly £15 million for Arnaldo Forlani. Garofano insisted that Gardini had personally ordered the creation of a slush fund, specifically to pay off politicians: he had, insisted Garofano, simply been obeying orders.

There was finally enough to justify criminal charges.

Cagliari's funeral was arranged for 23 July. Raul Gardini planned to attend. That morning, however, over breakfast in bed at his Milan flat, he read of Guiseppe Garofano's confession. He put a Walther 7.66mm pistol to his temple and pulled the trigger. An hour later, police arrived with arrest warrants. The charges on them were of false accounting, corruption and breach of political party financing laws. Gardini's final legacy to Ferruzzi was a £20 billion debt. The empire had to be surrendered to the creditor banks.

The first man actually to be convicted in connection with the case, financier Sergio Cusani, was jailed for eight years and fined £6,500 for channelling the bribes from Gardini to Craxi, Martelli and Forlani. Cusani was also ordered to repay the bribes he handled.

Ferruzzi was not the only Italian business giant to be sucked into the swamp of Italian political corruption. Fiat, the country's largest, was publicly identified in April 1993 as having participated, with the arrest for questioning of four directors. And the following month – ahead of any official action by investigators – Carlo Di Benedetti, the dynamic head of the Europe-spanning Olivetti electronics firm, defiantly volunteered, in an open statement to Milan magistrates, that between 1988 and 1991, Olivetti had paid £4.6 million in bribes to politicians, in order to secure government Post Office contracts. 'I authorised those payments,' declared Di Benedetti, who at present is appealing against a six-year jail sentence for being an accessory to the fraudulent bankruptcy of the Banco Ambrosiano, of which he was briefly deputy chairman. Insisting in a later statement that he was merely operating the unchallengable system every business in Italy had to observe if it wanted to survive, Di Benedetti demanded: 'Name me a single big Italian company, or international one, that has not done the same.' Di Benedetti admitted also, with disarming candour, that in order to protect his company – which had been denied government contracts when he initially refused to pay up – he would bribe again if called upon to do so.

By the time Silvio Berlusconi had swept to power, more than 1,500 businessmen, civil servants and municipal level politicians had been arrested. Those 1,500 are in addition to a further 3,000 – including 250 MPs and ministers who had traversed the revolving doors of government in the First Republic – against whom the tangentopoli probe had at that time only reached the stage of formal investigation. Italy's head of state himself, President Oscar Luigi Scalfaro, made an impassioned live television denial[10] of accused intelligence officers' claims that, during his four years as Interior Minister, from 1983 to 1987, he had received £42,000 a month from secret funds controlled by SISDE, Italy's internal security agency.

Under the labyrinthine intricacies of the Italian legal process, accusation is only the first step. Guilt or innocence is quite another, and is reached at the end of a very long road. Sometimes it is never reached at all. It won't be, in many of the cases which brought down Italy's First Republic, either through legal manoeuvring or legal fatigue. In quite a few cases – considering the age of some of the accused – the cases will close with death.

Some of those deaths may not be through old age. There are still secrets the Mafia do not want to come out in public trials. They suffered reversals in the early 1990s: now it's important they re-establish themselves. There's always the masonic movement there to help.

CHAPTER TWENTY-TWO

The Hydra Factor

The Mafia has always grown new heads when old ones have been cut off.

The most brilliant example of that was its rebirth as the monster it is today after its successful decapitation by Mussolini, who rounded up Family godfathers and incarcerated them in island jails.

Lucky Luciano achieved that – just as he achieved so much else that is feverently denied today by the country that helped him to do it and which has been vainly trying to crush his American successor ever since.

It was Luciano who, before being jailed in 1936, created the ruling Commission – with himself the *capo di tutti capi* – that forged all the American-based Families into the syndicate that operates organised crime throughout every state of the United States. And it was Luciano who saw the advantages – far more quickly than America saw the dangers of it – of cooperating when naval intelligence sought his help during the Second World War. From his upstate New York prison cell – where he was serving a maximum 50 year prostitution-running sentence – Luciano forbade theft from war supplies passing through the mob-controlled New York waterfront. Or any delay in its shipment to Europe. There were no thefts. And no delays. Having demonstrated his irrefutable power, the far thinking Luciano proposed a deal, now much denied by the American authorities: his parole in return for

Mafia help in the Allied invasion of Sicily. At the time, in the words of *The Godfather* movie cliché, it was an offer America couldn't refuse.

This deal is derided by every official department in Washington – particularly the FBI – and in every publication approved by them, but before his death I succeeded in meeting Moses Polakoff, the lawyer who represented Luciano during his 1946 parole bid: at the time of my meeting with Polakoff I was considering a book, never written, specifically upon Luciano.

Polakoff was then a very old man – he died, aged 97, in June 1993 – but mentally very astute: he thought before answering any question, a lawyer looking several questions ahead like a chess player considering several moves ahead, sometimes shifting his hand as if he were writing down the words, as well as speaking them. No episode that he recounted or date or name he gave proved wrong in the checks I was able to make, afterwards.

He obviously admired the founders of America's remarkable crime organisations: his client, Luciano, had after all been *the* organiser. As for legendary gangsters like Frank Costello and Meyer Lansky and Bugsy Siegel and Albert Anastasia: 'They would have been big in anything they did, in any business. Their business was crime, that's all.' Now they were all dead: 'like I'm going to be soon'. In those dying years, I believe, he had no reason to lie: no secrets to hide, no client's confidentiality to protect. And there was no secret about what Luciano had done in the war anyway: Polakoff thought the government's denials were dumb: his expression. It had all happened so long ago. Who cared any more? There was no longer any need to hide what had happened. It was necessary at the time. Admirable. The prostitution case was a bum rap: everyone knew that. Thomas Dewey, the prosecutor and later New York governor, had fixed it. People in the DA's office admitted as much. Luciano deserved a deal. Everyone benefited.

Polakoff's clear and carefully considered recollection was of regular messages from Luciano's cell, instructing Sicilian immigrants to New York to cooperate with naval and military intelligence. Maps were marked, identifying the best landing places around the Sicilian coastline, and the good or the treacherous ground beyond, over which invading troops and machinery would move afterwards. Safe paths and routes were drawn. And through those immigrants – 'I don't know how: it just happened. Like I said, these guys *made* things happen' – orders were relayed back to

Sicily itself, orders in Luciano's name. They told the Mussolini-fragmented Mafia, so anxious for the leader Luciano was shortly to become, precisely how to be reborn.

The official history of the Sicilian invasion[1] records one of the lowest casualty rates in any Allied landing in Europe: the British medical service prepared for 10,000 battle wounded in the first week: there were 1,517. In the first 58 hours, there was a 60 mile advance.

'They had a very special private army on their side, waiting to receive them,' Polakoff told me. 'How could it have gone wrong?'

The soon-to-die Polakoff wasn't my only source for this account of Mafia rebirth in its Sicilian cradle, later to expand throughout the rest of the world. Forty-six years after the Sicilian invasion – and five years after my fascinating encounter with the Jewish lawyer for a mob which rarely admitted Jews – I ate discreetly in a restaurant just off Rome's via Condotti with Andreas Scrosati,[2] whose dedication to the ideals of La Rete, the anti-crime party, has made him an historian of Cosa Nostra. 'Everything is true,' insisted Scrosati. There was one American flag carried by those who first came ashore on the Sicilian beaches. But many more were of another simple but very special design. Against a totally white background there was an L (for Luciano) picked out in black.

'It was the sign,' Scrosati assured me. 'The routes were prepared, the passes open. Lucky Luciano had ordered everything to be ready and it was. To the American invaders, he was an invaluable asset. To the Cosa Nostra, he was a midwife.'

One who, even if he could not be present at the actual birth – at the time he was still in a New York jail – was at least able to ensure the baby was properly nourished. On Luciano's instructions, lists had been carefully prepared. On them were recorded every Mussolini fascist and every German collaborator, precluding them from any position under the militarily supervised government installed after the successful landing. Putting communists in positions of local power was unthinkable, too. But not a problem. There were other lists. Those who'd guided the American troops ashore had ready suggestions who the occupying forces should install to maintain local government in smooth running order.

The American administrators gratefully accepted the suggestions and those chosen eagerly took up their positions. Virtually every municipal office on the island of Sicily was filled by a member or an associate of the Cosa Nostra.

'Sicily had been served up on a platter, to be devoured by the Mafia,' insisted Scrosati.

Deportation was a condition of Luciano's jail release. His expulsion from the United States in 1946 did not, initially, diminish his power as the American mafia's *capo di tutti capi*. He merely continued to influence the organisation from faraway Italy. The enforced exile did, however, place him ideally to oversee the postwar resurgence of the Cosa Nostra he had initiated from his upstate New York prison cell.

Luciano was born in Palermo. And chose his birthplace for the birth of his own doubtful memorial, the creation of a *cupola* – the sort of Costa Nostra ruling commission he had earlier created in America – that still exists, despite setbacks, in Italy today.

A coincidence stretching irony into the bizarre links the foundation of that *cupola* to Judge Giovanni Falcone, the man who, more than three decades later, tried – and failed – to destroy what it represented. And who, instead, was himself destroyed.

'This is Palermo. This is the way things happen,' I was told[3] by the man who disclosed that coincidence. 'It would have amused Luciano. I know it amused the Mafia-hunter.'

When I researched this book in Palermo, I lived at the Grande Albergo e delle Palme, on the via Roma. It is a huge, high-ceilinged, chandeliered conversion from a one-time palace of echoing rococo grandeur and now of fading, slightly frayed elegance. In 1947 it would have been better preserved, neither so faded nor so frayed: its most recent and regular clientele had been German officers who had demanded – and received – the very best during their late war-time occupation of the island. It is not known if it was this popularity with the German high command, in whose departure he had been so closely involved, that prompted its choice by Luciano – enjoying an irony of his own – but several people I spoke to thought that was the reason.

Whatever led to its choice, it was to the Palme that the saturnine, slightly paunchy Luciano summoned the Sicilian Godfathers in 1947, after an unsuccessful attempt to establish himself in Cuba, from where he had hoped to go on running America's organised crime empire.

The gathering was held in a room in which I sat forty-six years later, under the watchful gaze of someone who might have had a relative at the original Luciano conference. Now it is a bar, with a long, low table for bottles and glasses and a huge dresser beyond, for more bottles and more glasses. There were, I was told, no drinks for the 1947 meeting: wine was served afterwards, a gesture of courtesy, but during the conference Luciano decreed that everyone must stay clear-headed.

He was obeyed, of course. In Sicily Luciano truly was their boss of bosses, the man who had given them life again. There were kisses of respect and silent, uninterrupted attention to what Luciano proposed.

Which was startling, nothing less than a Mafia joint venture bringing together in a common organised crime enterprise the continents of Asia, Europe and America. Now it is a reality, but for several years after Luciano suggested it the warring, jealous local Cosa Nostra clans – like the jealous, warring police factions of today – resisted the idea of a tie-up. A member of Leoluca Orlando's La Rete staff reluctantly conceded that, in the creation and running of organised crime, Luciano was a man ahead of his time. 'Luciano could have made it happen much earlier than it has. He had the infrastructure in New York and he could have formed something similar here, in Sicily. But the Families here were too small-minded: Mussolini had curbed them and all they could think of was fighting among themselves, to gain supremacy over each other. They adopted the idea of a *cupola*, a ruling commission, but for too many years they didn't operate it properly. Judged from a criminal viewpoint they were stupid. For which, I suppose, we should be grateful.'

One man who did not consider the Mafia stupid, when he was chosen to confront and break it as an organisation, was Judge Giovanni Falcone, the man linked to Luciano by the bizarre coincidence.

A member of the Palme staff keeps a personal visitors' book of the famous and the infamous who have visited the palace. Luciano is recorded, arranging his 1947 conference. So, too, is Falcone. When he visited the Palme in late 1991, Falcone knew of Luciano's use of the hotel more than four decades earlier. The keeper of the visitors' book showed me the chair in which Falcone sat, a large, heavily carved seat. 'It was the one Luciano is supposed to have used. The judge joked that he should sit in it, too – which he did – to see if it gave him any ideas. He said it didn't but that he knew all the ideas the Mafia had anyway. To rob and steal and kill.'[4]

Part of that joking remark was fatally prophetic.

On 23 May 1992 – seven months after visiting the Palme and

using the chair that the architect of the Mafia's rebirth had used –
the greying, heavily moustached Falcone landed at Palermo's
Punta Raisi airport. He had come to spend the weekend at his home
in the Sicilian city. With him was his wife, Francesca – also a
magistrate – and three bodyguards. For security, they used a
private plane. Waiting for them was another security precaution,
bullet-proofed cars.

And an ambush.

The *cupola* that Luciano founded had decided Falcone, who
perfected the 1980s system of Maxi-trials that put more than 2,000
mafiosi in jail, should die. His movements around Rome were
watched: he was followed whenever possible. That Saturday
afternoon he was tailed to Rome airport, where the flight plan to
Sicily was filed. By the time Falcone's plane landed at Punta Raisi –
5.49 p.m. – a man called Gioacchino La Barbera was already in
place: he'd been on standby readiness for Falcone to arrive for five
days. On his cellular telephone – the call later traced from records –
La Barbera alerted two other men, Giovanni Brusca and Antonino
Goie, on their mobile telephone. They were waiting in the hills
overlooking the airport and the road culvert beneath which
2,200lbs of explosive had been primed. La Barbera filtered in
behind the Falcone's motorcade, keeping up a running com-
mentary as he drove, to pinpoint the precise position of the judge's
car. At the spot where the bomb was hidden – six minutes
travelling time after the motorcade left the airport – La Barbera
switched his phone off. In the overlooking hills, Brusca pressed the
remote control detonator. Falcone, his wife and their bodyguards
were blown to pieces. America's FBI later identified Goie's DNA
from saliva on the cigarette butts he chain-smoked while waiting
for Falcone's car to reach the assassination spot. Goie later hanged
himself in prison. Brusca and La Barbera were jailed for life.

Capo di tutti capi of the *cupola* that issued the Falcone assassination
decree was Salvatore (Wild Beast) Riina. The assassination was a
mistake Luciano would never have made: before his New York
arrest Luciano had killed the gang leader who was intending to
murder Thomas Dewey, the man who jailed him, because
Dewey's assassination would have caused too much public outcry.

Which was what happened over Falcone's murder. There was an
upsurge of public outrage, which Riina contemptuously ignored.
And went on making mistakes.

Before his death, Falcone had cooperated with journalist

Marcelle Padovani in the creation of a book based upon a long series of taped interviews. Its title – *Men of Honour*[5] – indicated the genuine respect in which the Palermo-born Falcone held the men he was sworn to destroy, and whose implacable violence he knew so well. In one section of the book he urges mafia-hunters to exercise more caution about their personal safety: most, he feared, did not fully accept how deadly the Cosa Nostra were. His death showed the sad truth of that. As did his successor, Judge Paolo Borsellino's.

Borsellino's mistake, I have been told,[6] was to make a simple call on a cellular telephone. He did so on 19 July – just two months after Falcone's killing – to tell his mother he was on his way to visit her at her Palermo home. It was bugged by a scanning device operated by the listening Cosa Nostra: it gave them sufficient time to get into position. As Borsellino's car drew up, outside his mother's house, the watching assassins detonated by radio control a hurriedly parked vehicle packed with explosives. Borsellino died at once. So did his bodyguards, one a woman.

By the time my visit to Palermo was arranged, the lack of security of mobile phone conversations had been realised, particularly by the constantly-endangered La Rete politicians and staff. 'A mobile phone in Sicily is an open radio, listened to by everyone.' I was told never to initiate a call to anyone using one anywhere in Sicily. Which I didn't. But several outgoing calls were made on cellular equipment to me. In one of which my arrival flight details were discussed. In another, they were confirmed.

I first noticed the man with the blond hair of a northern Italian at Rome's Leonardo di Vinci airport, while I was waiting for my onward connection to Palermo. He drank – only coffee – at the same small bar where I was drinking. He was immaculate, the green checked sports jacket and fawn trousers superbly cut, the paper-thin gold watch just visible beneath the cuff of the pale blue shirt that was obviously silk. The dark suede loafers were Gucci. The effect was of totally co-ordinated style topped with just the right hint of flamboyant elegance. Which made him noticeable.

I was to notice him a lot in the succeeding days.

Which, it was later decided by people I spoke to and who understood, was the very definite intention. The interest wasn't in me. It was in those I was meeting. 'If they don't want to be seen they're invisible. They *wanted* us to know, through you, how easy it is for them to learn what we're doing. Who we're seeing. To be ahead of us if they want to be. Showing they're always in charge.'

I didn't see the man board the Palermo flight. I had been in the bar at the Palme for only about fifteen minutes when he came in. There was just the two of us there. Thinking I had a coincidence here, I smiled and nodded. He ignored me. And continued to ignore me when he entered cafés in which I was drinking coffee or wine on three separate occasions, and twice entered restaurants I had chosen for lunch, totally on the spur of the moment.

My final sighting of him was in the departure lounge of Palermo airport: he was drinking coffee again. Everyone – and every official department – with whom I had meetings either in Sicily or Italy denied any knowledge of my blond-haired attendant. It was a La Rete official who first suggested who he might be representing. And why.

When I met Leoluca Orlando, he told me his ambition: 'My dream is to build a normal town. My hope is to live in a normal country. When Palermo is normal, then the easier it will be for Italy to be normal. From Palermo comes the abnormality of the Mafia linked to the politicians linked to the police and the judges linked to the masonry. To demonstrate it is possible to have a normal government in Palermo will be a revolution.'

The failure of the anti-crime party to attract its expected support in the 1994 general election deeply depressed its founder Leoluca Orlando and was the strongest factor in Nando Dalla Chiesa's resignation from the party. Indeed, some observers saw in it strong indications of Mafia-accusation fatigue throughout Italy. But during my meetings[7] with both men, each was anxious to stress his belief that the long-term establishment of their fledgling movement – it was only formed in 1990 – would build like the Liberal Democrats in England, not from the top down but from the bottom, from its municipal level. The most frequent translation of La Rete is that it means *Network*. This was not the definition given to me by Orlando. Crossing his fingers to make small squares, he likened it to 'the net in which you catch the fish. That is what we have to do, catch the small fish who will learn to trust us and to vote for us.' That trust and that grassroot support had to grow throughout Italy. Major cities would form the network, a grouping not even necessarily of the same political ideology but powerful enough to confront and determine the policies of national government. And within that plan, in the earlier local elections in November 1993, the party maintained its popularity: Orlando himself gained an astonishing 75.2 per cent of the mayoral vote and led the victory chant of *Palermo e nostra, non di Cosa Nostra* – Palermo has freed itself from the Mafia – from the balcony of the Palace of Eagles, the island capital's town hall.

The chant was premature, wrongly anticipating a similar result in the general elections to follow. Certainly, the possibility of other assassination attempts upon Orlando is as great as ever. Even so, after he became mayor (for the second time) his wife Milly and their two teenage daughters moved back into their apartment in Palermo's via Principe di Paterno. Previously he rarely spent more than two nights a month there, his family moving to avoid the type of bombs that killed Falcone and Borsellino. For the rest of the time the Jesuit-educated lawyer who additionally read languages at London and Heidelberg moved from safe house to safe house or slept in army or police barracks. No location was ever decided until just a few hours before his arrival: sometimes only minutes. 'Mine is not an ordinary life. It can't be, not any more. I cannot ever go to a restaurant with my wife or children. To a movie or the theatre. It's the price I have chosen to pay.' Whenever possible he travelled – as he still does – by helicopter. When it's not possible, his Fiat is armour-plated, its windows are toughened, bullet-resistant glass. It is not a security breach for me to identify the Via Principe di Paterno as Orlando's home: the surrounding security makes it the best known address in the city, if not the entire island. The vicinity around the apartment is sealed for about twenty yards either side: I had first to pass an army-staffed, armoured-car road block and then a further army checkpoint before even reaching the high outer gate, steel-ribbed and monitored by intercom. As well as the obvious uniformed and flak-jacketed soldiers the grounds were thronged with plainclothed bodyguards. All the soldiers – I stopped counting after thirty – carried machine pistols or automatic weapons.

He has achieved a certain philosophical acceptance of what could happen to him at the hands of a Mafia assassin – and Orlando, a swarthy man whose girth hints at his enjoyment of pasta and chianti, is certainly not averse to the international fame and local adulation he gains as the challenger of the Mafia. Some of the sound-byte phrases are obviously well prepared – he used words to me that I've since read him using to journalists – but the threat of death, not just to him but to his adored family, is real and constant and the strain shows. As well as the first sign of greyness flecking his otherwise thickly dark hair, the hands are in constant movement, gesturing and motioning. The speech is quick, the words sometimes colliding. His wife was safely absent when we met, but a daughter was home. She seemed unconcerned by the gun-toting, flak-vested soldiers visible through verandah windows on every overlooking vantage point.

It was the way it was, he explained. He'd grown so accustomed to it he couldn't really remember it being any different. There was a lot he wanted to achieve. He'd scarcely started. He hoped he would be able to finish.

'Of course I don't want to die. Who would? That would be stupid. But it could happen. I know that. I know the *cupola* decided to kill me, when Riina was *capo di tutti capi*. There were three of us on the list. Falcone, Borsellino and me. After they got Falcone and Borsellino I told everyone – all the media – that I would be next, but that the masons were as much involved as the Mafia. I know just how much protection the masons give to organised crime and I let it be known. If I had been killed it would have been proof of what I was saying. I believe I saved my life on that occasion. And now Riina is in jail, for life. But he'll be replaced. So . . .' There is a shrug – it became a familiar gesture – and a moment of reflection. The daughter – never named, just as no other member of the family is ever identifiably photographed – passed through the room.

'When I began La Rete, the security people said I was a man at risk. That is a kind of designation, the level of threat I was under from Mafia attack. But then, as the movement grew – showing how much ordinary people wanted to get out from under the pressure of the Mafia – the personal threat against me increased. So I was placed at the very top – a man in danger is the phrase they use – of people the Mafia want to eradicate.'

Italy and Sicily are not the only places where Orlando is classified as a man in danger. On one occasion in 1992, while he was on his way to Germany for a conference, the Bundeskriminalamt confirmed underworld intelligence that the Italian mafia installed in Germany intended making an attempt on Orlando's life. His hotel, further travel and engagement schedules were all switched while Orlando was still in mid-flight.

He insists that Germany is the only other country in the European Union which fully realises how well-established the Mafia is, throughout the entire European continent but in Germany in particular: shielded by masonry, of course. Never think of one without the other, he urges. That's what he always has to do, convince people that the two are connected. Secrecy hiding secrecy. Blood oaths of silence sworn upon blood oaths of silence. Germany is where the Mafias are most deeply entrenched, because Germany is now the main organised crime crossroad between East and West. And the East is where organised crime is putting down roots that may be impossible to tear up. The East is weak, and will be for a long time. Its governments and its banks and its police and its judges and its laws are weak. Those last two weaknesses Orlando views as a particular problem. One that has to be resolved: as in every aspect of organised crime, there are Italian examples of the legal erosions that can occur.

Italian legislation is based upon a Code Napoleone, which requires a magistrate's examination of all the known facts *before* a formal charge is made. After which a prosecution begins. The Code does not, however, preclude an arrest, but a charge must be proferred within six months of that arrest. If it isn't, an accused has to be released from custody. If proceedings do not start within a further six months after any charge again an accused must be freed. As he must if there is no sentence within one year of a trial beginning. And the judicial path is littered with the sort of legal technicalities and appeal paraphernalia on which Judge Corrado Carnevale was such an expert that he earned himself the 'sentence killer' label.

There are other judges with particular understanding of the intricacies of Italian law, and they have attracted so much attention that finally their governing body, the Supreme Council of the Judiciary, has announced a formal enquiry. Its conclusion, inevitably, is not expected for years.

One already arrested is former Neapolitan prosecutor Armando Cono Lancuba, who found many obstacles preventing his bringing an accusation or charge against Carmine Alfieri, whose position as Italy's richest Camorra Don and a member of the New Family organisation established by Michele Zaza was accepted by every other law enforcement official on the abundant arrest-warrant evidence available. Alfieri was, finally, brought to trial. The charge – chosen as if at random – concerned his involvement in the massacre of eight rival mobsters in a gang war shoot-out in a Naples suburb in August 1984. Don Carmine's sentence of life imprisonment was overthrown, on appeal. He was freed. Part of the appeal decision states: 'The image of the Alfieri clan has been distorted. Their unimportant police record, their limited wealth, their total legal activity as real estate brokers, appears to exclude their belonging to a Camorra clan and even more to their playing a leading role in organised crime.'

Lancuba's detention followed evidence from two *pentiti*. One of them is Pasquale Galasso – Alfieri's one time deputy – who described[8] the prosecutor as Alfieri's 'political consultant' who stage managed all the prosecutions against the Neapolitan Camorra, and named the judges to bribe for either a dismissal or a case reversal upon appeal. Part of the deposition[9] sworn by the other *pentito*, Raffaele Cutolo, says: 'Lancuba was my baby.'

One intriguing example of the convoluted maze that is Italian justice came with Judge Sergio Soichilli's verdict in April 1994, on Licio Gelli and on that most famous – or infamous – Masonic lodge of all time, P2.

After a fourteen-year official outlawing of P2, because it caused the downfall of an Italian government and had been the clandestine gathering place of Mafia Dons, their money launderers, Vatican embezzlers and coup-planning fascists – Licio Gelli chief among them – Judge Sorichilli ruled in the Second Section of the Rome Assizes that P2 was, after all, completely innocent. It had not, his judgement asserted, engaged in political conspiracy. It had not been involved in illegal activities. It had not violated state laws. And it was no longer, therefore, an outlawed organisation.

In its first life it had chosen to operate as an underground organisation: could it operate openly now? No. Prosecutor Elisabetta Cesqui – whose case against founder and Grand Master Licio Gelli had alleged all those offences – immediately appealed. Which has legally outlawed P2 again until a further decision is reached by an appellant court. Which can, in turn, be appealed to an even higher tribunal. P2's heady period of legality – the time between what Judge Sorichilli said and what Judge Cesqui said – lasted six minutes. And Gelli? The terms of his oh-so-convenient extradition agreement from Switzerland prevented his being charged on any joint indictment with the claims made against the organisation he founded. So he was untouchable. But not quite. He was sentenced to eight years imprisonment for obtaining information to which he had no right of access (state secrets from the intelligence service heads who belonged to P2, which had now been declared not to be part of a political conspiracy or engaged in crime), six years in jail for uttering false or slanderous accusations, and three years for falsifying accounts.

Seventeen years in jail then? Wrong again. Gelli's lawyer, Michele Gentiloni Silverij, successfully argued that the eight years for obtaining state secrets did not apply, because of that Swiss extradition exclusion. Nine years, perhaps? Wrong once more. Five of those years were annulled because of various pardons granted over more than a decade of hearings, findings and appeals. So it's four years in total? No. They're being appealed, so Gelli went back to supposed house arrest at the Villa Wanda in Tuscany. And in any case, by April 1994, Gelli was seventy-five years old. He is not expected to serve any time at all in any Italian prison.

Judge Carmelo Conti is on an initial list of judges whose verdicts and activities in connection to organised crime are being examined by the governing judicial body. The investigation into Conti aims to establish possible links between the man who was president of the Palermo appeal court and Salvatore Riina during the time when Riina was ultimate Godfather of the Corleone clan and chairman of the ruling Cosa Nostra *cupola*. It was during that time that Riina was named as the Don who had ordered the killing of Judges Falcone and Borsellino – charges repeated at his trial – and of General Dalla Chiesa. Riina's deputy on the *cupola*, Benedetto Santapaola – who controlled a large proportion of Europe's cocaine importation through Spain – was actually sentenced to life imprisonment in December 1987, for masterminding the assassination of the general and his young wife. That sentence was overturned on appeal. Conti is no longer a serving judge. Upon his retirement he became president of the Palermo waterboard. That organisation is under investigation – which will take years – for financial irregularities and Mafia connections.

The most intensive, and longest running, judicial examination remains that of Judge Corrado Carnevale, who not only killed sentences but attempted to re-write the Mafia-acknowledged history of the Mafia. On 25 June 1992 – just one month after the massacre in which Giovanni Falcone died – Judge Carnevale declared in a Supreme Court ruling that there was no such thing as a *cupola*, an over-all governing commission upon which sat representatives of every Family. Nor was there, according to Carnevale, any hierarchic structure in those Families: no Don giving orders to his *capo decina* to be relayed to the soldiers, or Men of Honour. This edict came during a judgement by Carnevale which annulled sentences previously confirmed by his own Supreme Court on four leading members of the commission who had been successfully prosecuted by Falcone. According to *pentito* Antonino Calderone, Falcone's assassination resulted from that initial Supreme Court confirmation. 'As long as the Supreme Court was annulling these sentences, there was no reason to act.'

On 29 June 1992, over 100,000 people travelled from all over Italy to demonstrate on the streets of Palermo against the state-within-a-state power of organised crime throughout the country.

'It was the start,' recalls Liliana Ferraro, Falcone's successor and once his deputy, who remembers him with adoring respect and who knows, realistically, that she is now just as much a Mafia target as the still surviving Palermo mayor, Leoluca Orlando. She adds, realistic still, 'Who knows what the end will be?'

Liliana Ferraro is a tiny, heavy-featured woman who colours her hair an orange-tinted red and cheats herself into thinking she's cutting down on her intake of cigarillos by breaking them in half to smoke each piece separately. As she lights one directly after the other, it doesn't really work. That's about all that doesn't work about the dynamic woman in charge of Italy's efforts to defeat the Mafia. She averages fifteen hours a day, *every* day, either at her desk at the Tiber-bordering Ministry of Justice building or travelling Europe – and America – preaching the message of organised crimes's world-wide infiltration. Her opinion concurs with that of Leoluca Orlando. Or maybe his with hers. 'For a long time – too long – people thought the Mafia was an Italian problem: limited to Sicily even. But it isn't. It's everywhere in Europe, particularly in the financial centres of Paris or Frankfurt or the City of London, where they launder their billions. And Russia. Particularly Russia. The Mafia preys on weakness and the East is weak. So they're there, organising, forming alliances. Other countries are waking up to the threat, but slowly. Too slowly.'

Liliana Ferraro is an expert on threats. Living daily with them. Making them. As the head and guiding force behind Italy's effort to confront the Mafia, she permanently faces the bomb or the bullet. Ironically, Liliana Ferraro's dedication to jailing mafiosi has in fact condemned her to the strait-jacket of *vita blindata*, a life behind bars. She can never travel in anything other than a car that is armour-plated and never without bodyguards. An extra table, sometimes more, has to be reserved for her protectors on her very rare dinner outings in public restaurants. They shop when she shops, an even rarer occurrence. They're on permanent duty outside her Rome apartment, even when she is not there, to prevent a a bomb being planted in readiness for her return. They occupy a special observation room outside her office suite: video cameras record every approach and there is a monitor in her inner sanctum.

It wasn't always hers. It was Giovanni Falcone's, before his assassination. Kept there, as a monument to the respect and affection in which she held him, is a virtual farmyard of ducks, sixty-three in total. Falcone bought each to record what he regarded as a personal mistake: *papera*, 'duck', is also Rome street argot for cock-up. A sixty-fourth would have been whatever error allowed the Mafia to know his travel plans to Sicily that fateful weekend in May 1992. Even so long after his murder, Ferraro's eyes strayed occasionally to the display, while we talked.[10] She did so animatedly, broken cigarillo following broken cigarillo, her heavy gold jewellery worn in such profusion that it sometimes clattered and clinked with a gesture or a finger-wagging point. Ferraro, who wears a man-sized watch and designer clothes matching the brightness of her coiffeur, very obviously regards herself as continuing the work Falcone initiated. Nearly every remark was qualified by the insistence that Falcone would have done this or Falcone would have said that. She knows, of course. She worked with him for a very long time, from the 1970s when Falcone took on and beat the Red Brigade. As he would, she is sure, have finally beaten the Mafia, if they hadn't killed him first. *Can* the Mafia be beaten? She thinks so. I suspect she is relaying Falcone's opinion rather than her own total conviction.

She has strengthened the infrastructure Falcone began building. It was Liliano Ferraro who devised the countrywide system of twenty-six special Mafia-prosecuting offices, ensuring each is staffed by dedicated examining judges, all working as a team. As murder-contract-nominee Judge Casilli made clear to me in Paris, the teamwork is necessary. It means an organised crime investigation does not end if one magistrate is killed: his colleagues will know the case he was working on, which possibly caused his assassination. After attending the funeral, they can continue the prosecution.

Ferraro knows the killing tenacity of the Cosa Nostra and the

Camorra and the 'Ndrangheta. It was she who personally thought of and supervised the building of the underground tunnels from the holding prisons directly into the court-rooms and the steel cages from which the hundreds of Godfathers and mafiosi faced justice during the Maxi-trials staged by Falcone. It was the only way she could think of to prevent rescue attempts to free the Dons. And to prevent the killing of *pentiti*, already-sentenced mafiosi, giving evidence against them. *Pentiti* are important, insists Ferraro: General Falcone thought so and so does she. So is uprooting those men convicted of Mafia association. Mafia leaders are no longer jailed in the towns and cities they once ran. It was too easy to go on being a Don from the inside. It has been a Liliano Ferraro policy, copied from Mussolini, to imprison mafiosi as far away as possible from their known territory, preferably on one of the distant Italian islands.

'We'll win, with the support – the will – of the people. Now there is a new attitude, a new wave of hope in Italy. It's vital not to let the old ways rebuild themselves. Otherwise there will be a rebirth.'

Which I believe there will be.

The Mafia are far – very far indeed – from being destroyed by the assault upon the *cupola*, effective though that has been. It was even suggested to me[11] that Salvatore Riina's removal might assist a rebirth: that his bloodlust for power, which caused a lot of internecine battling and killing, had been doing more to fragment the Cosa Nostra Families than the investigations of the state. Now Riina is no longer causing those internal disruptions, Italian-based organised crime can reform and rebuild.

And can continue to insinuate itself, as it has already – with its masonic helpmate – insinuated itself virtually undetected into the very heart of the European Union and the EU capitals of Brussels and Strasbourg and Luxembourg.

Why undetected? Because so few choose to see.

CHAPTER TWENTY-THREE

I Have a Right to be Blind Sometimes[1]

At the merest suggestion of legal embarrassment or difficulty, the institutions of the European Union retreat inside their burrows like night animals exposed to light. Its bureaucrats are above reproach or question, runs the denying litany. What mafia? Which masons? Baseless sensationalism and rumour, nothing more. Even to consider a response would give credibility where no credibility exists. Wrong then to say anything. Quite wrong. Sorry not to be able to help you more.

I have the names – which I cannot publish for legal reasons – of four permanent officials of the European Parliament (as well as one former official) who are members of a mafia-concealing masonic lodge which holds Tuesday night meetings in a private dining room of a Strasbourg restaurant. Some MEPs attend when Parliament is in session. According to an English MEP with long experience of Brussels and Strasbourg, one of the permanent officials named to me[2] holds high office in that lodge. And is additionally a Man of Honour, someone formally initiated into an Italian Mafia Family.

The MEP, who must also for his personal safety remain unnamed insisted[3] that within both Parliamentary committees and certain grades of the Brussels-based Commission linked mafia/masonic groups have equally divided influence. 'The masons operate on a political level, to the totally undisclosed advantage of various European countries from the capitals of which guidance comes – through connected lodges – how various decisions should be influenced. Of course conflicts of interest arise: that's inevitable. They are customarily resolved in total privacy: a concession made here for a concession to be gained later.'

Sometimes the guidance from the member countries came from the highest level. 'The *very* highest.'

The interests of the mafias are in straight profit. Over the decades since the original creation of what is now the European Union they have been extremely patient, infiltrating themselves into the institutions, particularly within the Commission. They are now in place. And able to install successors when their tenure is up.

There has been blatant pressure imposed upon MEPs when organised crime felt at risk. A Luxembourg judge who went to Italy personally to investigate a suspected fraud was knocked down by a vehicle which reversed over him, breaking both legs. His investigation was never concluded. He has never, since, been able to walk properly. During another Italian enquiry by the MEP who talked to me of the combined mafia/masonic link, he had in constant attendence – every waking moment! – a man he named as having much stronger allegiance to masonic mafia than to the European ideal. Such unremitting supervision enabled the official to know precisely what was being uncovered – and who the informants were – at every stage of the investigation, even to the private asides and remarks one committee member might have made to another. One war hero survivor of three assassination attempts – no longer a serving MEP – was split away from the enquiry team of which he was the chairman during every day of their investigation in Italy. 'Whenever I suggested going some-where or doing something, I was obstructed. I was virtually *told* what to see: where to go. The official explanation for my being parted from the group was that such an arrangement made it possible for us to do and see more. Protest? Of course I protested. I was told these were the arrangements that had been made. That the plans couldn't be changed.'[4]

The eventual report made by the enquiry team was rejected several times by the parliamentary division to which it was submitted. Its author considers it to have been emasculated by enforced revisions and dilutions. 'It was nothing less than ridicu-lous. A whitewash. There was no point in protesting: there never is. It's the system. People don't like the boat rocked in Strasbourg or Brussels or Luxembourg. Isn't that an ironic cliché, rocking boats in three cities that are landlocked! Silly remark. Boats aren't rocked, ever.'

Some United Kingdom MEPs are prepared to be identified – most of whom are, in this book – in their determination to protest against what they believe to be undue and insidious masonic influences in the inner workings of the Union. Others will identify themselves by their campaigning in the future.

What is the official response to such accusations? Total rejection. Nonsense became a word much favoured by spokesmen in the Commission and in Strasbourg and Luxembourg when I put to them such claims. There were abuses, certainly: that was inevitable, considering the size – further to increase – and the complexity of the European Union. To imagine that would not be so – to imagine there would not be instances of occasional outright criminality even – would be naive. Which they weren't. An anti-fraud division was being strengthened and given proper powers. But entrenched, organised manipulation by entrenched, traditionally organised crime or entrenched, organised secret societies? Nonsense! It wasn't possible: couldn't be possible. Absolute nonsense.[5]

A conversation I had with a Commission official perfectly illustrates the Commission's reaction to any enquiry hinting embarrassment or illegality. Mauro Giallombardo worked for the European Parliament, didn't he? Yes. Well, actually, no. He was never a proper staff employee: his official job description was that of a 'temporary agent'.

What about his private financial institutions created under the convenient secret banking regulations of Luxembourg? Nothing was known about any private financial institutions.

Shouldn't such an activity have been officially recorded? They were not able to answer that question.

What about his connection with Bettino Craxi, that disgraced, masonically-involved former premier of Italy? Nothing was known about any connection with Bettino Craxi.

Wouldn't any employment by Bettino Craxi be recorded, on an official application form for instance? They were not able to answer that question.

Not even of his once being part of Craxi's secretariat? No.

Didn't Giallombardo disappear? No. Mauro Giallombardo

went on leave on 1 February 1992.

So he resumed work when his leave expired? Actually no. Nothing was heard of him for eleven months. Then there was a letter of resignation on 11 December 1992. It was accepted.

And that was the end of it? Yes. The parliament decided there was no cause as far as they were concerned for any enquiry into the activities of Mauro Giallombardo.

That isn't the opinion of others who are still investigating the bribed purchase by the Belgian government of Italian helicopters and the *tangentopoli* in which Bettino Craxi was entangled.

Milan investigating magistrates name Giallombardo as having been in complicity with Bettino Craxi over a bribe paid to the Italian Socialist Party by a construction firm in return for a contract for work on the Milan-Serravalle motorway.[6] His complicity, according to Italian investigatory files,[7] was in channelling bribes through the discreet banking services of Luxembourg, where Giallombardo owned two luxury villas while working there for the European Parliament. His first official role in Luxembourg –after supposedly leaving the encircling entourage of Bettino Craxi in Italy – was with the socialist group in the Parliament. Later he transferred to the secretariat of the Secretary General. His payroll description was that of a researcher, a lowly rank for a man who had earlier headed the European Confederation of Socialist Parties. Job comparisons were scarcely relevant, however: Giallombardo hardly ever turned up to work at his sinecure anyway. However, an official assured me[8] that at no time during his accredited functions was Giallombardo involved in any financial activity affecting or concerning the parliament: the implication was that the Italian had neither interest nor expertise in fiscal matters.

That is certainly not the opinion of Italian investigators.[9] They have identified a myriad network of Italian, Luxembourg and Belgian registered companies all associated with Giallombardo. He set up the founding enterprise, Merchant Italia, in Milan in 1980 with assets of £3 million. Eighty per cent of stock was controlled by businesses with Italian Socialist Party connections: twenty per cent was held anonymously. Merchant Italia was, in turn, administered in trust by the Lambert Bank of Brussels. In 1990 Merchant International Holdings, a subsidiary of Merchant Italia, was established in Luxembourg. Its £2.6 million capital was made by transfer from Italy. Giallombardo was named as chairman. Giallombardo was also registered as chairman of Merchant Europe, on Luxembourg's Avenue du Bois. Merchant Europe was a subsidiary of Merchant International Holdings. Italian investigators hold documents issued by these companies for consultancy work to account for the transfer of large sums of money through their accounts.

The extensive movement of money through Italy, Luxembourg and Belgium is the focus of the enquiries being made by Belgian magistrate Veronique Ancia, who heads a bribery and corruption investigation that is enmeshed in the unsolved murder on 18 July 1991, of veteran Belgian Socialist Andre Cools, a bespectacled 64-year-old miner's son.

Cools was shot dead, with a 7.65mm pistol, by a lone gunman in the car park of Liège railway station, to which he had driven his mistress to catch a train. She was seriously wounded. Police described it as the work of a professional assassin. At the time of his death Cools was advisor to King Baudouin as minister of state and mayor of the Liège suburb of Flemalle. He had been deputy prime minister of Belgium – traditionally governed by a coalition between Socialists and Christian Democrats – from 1969 to 1973 and remained a towering figure in the country's Socialist Party. Additionally he was considered by many to be an idealist. Some even said he was honest, by the standards of Belgian politics.

That honesty, together with his short-tempered outspokenness, was the most likely cause of his death. Five days before he was gunned down, Cools told journalists he intended to make 'interesting revelations' about the Belgian government purchase, three years earlier, of forty-six Italian attack and reconnaissance helicopters. His murder prevented those revelations being made.

Many are believed to have subsequently emerged, however, as the result of Judge Veronique Ancia's ongoing investigation.

Negotiations on the Italian helicopters deal began in 1988, after Belgium's Socialist-dominated coalition government invited tenders for the helicopters. Those tenders had to be vetted by the Defence Ministry, at that time controlled by the Socialists. Against Belgian Army preference, the £231 million contract went to the heavily-lobbying Italian firm Agusta Spa, despite the aircraft's running costs being seventy per cent an hour greater than alternative French or German machines. One of the inducements offered by the Italian company was an undertaking to build in Belgium a factory, employing Belgian labour, that would manufacture the helicopters' spare parts. The factory has never been built.

Judge Ancia's report into the negotiations, later largely leaked, referred to a possible further inducement: up to £3 million in bribes through discreet banking arrangements.

Quite independent of Judge Ancia's investigation, a government commission in 1994 criticised the running costs of the Agusta helicopters, which machines, it said, did not basically deliver proper value for money. This was visibly demonstrated early the same year when government ministers had to be airlifted to areas of Belgium badly affected by floods. The flights had to be made in previously purchased French-built Alouette 11 machines: the Agusta Spa helicopters were not considered sufficiently reliable by the army high command.

Judge Ancia's report[11] alleged the technical evaluations of the French, German and Italian helicopters were 'adjusted' either by the 1988 Defence Minister, Guy Coeme, or by people in his cabinet to make Agusta Spa's tender the most favourable. Coeme publicly denied the accusation when it became general knowledge in 1994; by which time he had become Deputy Prime Minister.

Two other ministers – Guy Spitaels, Minister-President for the Wallonia region of Belgium and a former Socialist Party leader and Guy Mathot, Wallonia's Interior Minister – are also named by Judge Ancia as being implicated in the manipulation of the Agusta contract. They, too, deny any allegation of impropriety.

But Judge Ancia's summary of evidence is known [12] to contain an affadavit sworn by a former Socialist deputy premier, Philippe Moureaux, attesting that the two men conspired to ensure the contract went to the Italian firm. There is a further allegation that some of the money received in repayment for the deal was used to buy a villa in the South of France.

Before compiling her report, Judge Ancia declared publicly[13] that she believed the bribery chain ran from Italy, through Giallombardo's network of companies and up into Belgium. I believe there is a definite link with Bettino Craxi. And yet an EU official had implied to me that the Italian had neither interest or expertise in fiscal matters.

The scandal remained at the very highest level of the Belgian

Vandenbroucke resigned, admitting he asked for money secretly given to his Flemish Socialist Party to influence the acceptance of the Agusta deal to be burned to conceal its existence. At the same time Vandenbroucke confirmed he knew of a secret bank account in which his party hid the Italian bribes. Vandenbroucke was not the only high ranking Belgian enmeshed in the scandal by 1995. In February of that year demands were made for NATO General Secretary Willy Claes to resign after Claus admitted knowing of Agusta conributions to Socialist Party funds when he was Belgian Minister for Economic Affairs.

All the parliamentary officials identified to me as mafia and masonic links had served in the three European Union capitals – Strasbourg, Brussels and Luxembourg – during the time when Salvatore Lima, an initiated Man of Honour and political fixer for the Cosa Nostra, was a Euro-MP.

Lima's entire career was in politics and the Mafia: in the end the combination was to cost him his life. He joined the Christian Democrat Party in 1945, when the American occuping forces in Sicily were putting the Luciano-suggested officials into their positions of power. Lima stayed in such positions – in Palermo, where he was mayor on seven different occasions, in national politics in Rome and on the European stage – until he was gunned down by motorcycling assassins in the seaside resort of Mondello, in March 1992. He was 64 years old.

The heavily-built Sicilian with the cascade of waved silver hair was described to me by a former MEP as one of the first Mafia figures fully to realise the potential, both for influence and profit, of the EC, 'Long before he became a member himself'. In fact he became a member in 1984, eight years after he had been cited a total of 163 times as having Cosa Nostra connections in an anti-Mafia report laid before the Italian parliament. 'It didn't affect him one jot in Rome and it certainly didn't influence the way he was received in Strasbourg.' As a member of first the Italian and then the European parliaments, Lima was immune from prosecution.

True to the Mr Fixit expertise he developed in Italian politics, Lima remained in the background in Strasbourg, keeping any committee work to a minimum and rarely making speeches: there were, in fact, long periods when he didn't attend parliamentary sessions at all, although he always ensured he received his maximum allowances. He knew and mixed with the men whose

Lima remained in the background in Strasbourg, keeping any committee work to a minimum and rarely making speeches: there were, in fact, long periods when he didn't attend parliamentary sessions at all, although he always ensured he received his maximum allowances. He knew and mixed with the men whose names I have: even, I have been assured[14], sometimes attending masonic meetings on a Tuesday night. 'There was a peculiar kind of shock when he was assassinated. Not, exactly, shock that it happened: his associations were no secret. But then again that it *had* happened. There seemed an aura about him: almost that he was untouchable. That he could do anything.'

It seemed Lima thought he could do anything, too. A six month long enquiry following his death concluded Lima had assured the Cosa Nostra *cupola* he could persuade Supreme Court judge Corrado Carnevale to get the verdicts against 342 mafiosi convicted in Maxi-trials annulled or reduced. Not even Carnevale would agree to that. So the Cosa Nostra killed Lima, as an illustration to others that promises to them had to be kept.

Another high ranking official more loyal to organised crime than he was to the European Union apparently didn't wait for the Cosa Nostra to deliver their judgement on his failure.

He guessed their displeasure and delivered judgement upon himself.

CHAPTER TWENTY-FOUR

For Tobacco Road, Read Easy Street

Did Antonio Quantraro jump from the window of his sixth floor Brussels office in March 1993? Or was he pushed? Thrown even?

The initial official finding of the Belgian police was that Quantraro, who orchestrated the biggest single theft of Community money in its fraudulent history, committed suicide. By early 1995, however, doubts emerged. The police file on the 59-year-old Italian Eurocrat remains open.

Having studied the relative facts and discussed them with current and former MEPs and Commission officials,[1] I believe there are grounds for the reasonable doubt the police now have. It is unlikely ever to be resolved: no-one has discovered the crime group for which Quantraro was operating. Now he is dead, they are unlikely to.

The stalled enquiry into Antonio Quantraro's mysterious death is not the only one in which he featured.

At the time of Quantraro's death there was an ongoing European parliamentary investigation into a multi-million tobacco fraud throughout Italy, Spain and Greece. Quantraro was due to be questioned in detail on either 5 or 6 April 1993. He plunged to his death on 30 March, one week before that interrogation. Alive, he might have confessed and incriminated others – and so exposed the mafia-masonic influence within the European Commission. Dead, he never would. There were officials in Italy, Greece and Spain from whom the parliamentary investigation sought information, and from every single one came emphatic denials of criminality or of any knowledge of what Quantraro had been doing.

The only thing that was totally proved was the complete insanity of paying vast support premiums and export refunds on European-grown tobacco of such inferior quality that nobody wants it. A fact that didn't need confirmation because everybody knew it already. But the tobacco subsidy is part of the Common Agricultural Policy, folks! Quantraro's might have been the single biggest scam, but let's keep it in perspective – if anything can be kept in perspective in a discussion of the CAP which in every year is defrauded of at least £6 billion. Roll up, roll up and dip into the bran tub. Millions do. Quantraro did.

The diminutive (he was only 5'3" tall) Italian, who had four grown up children by his German-born wife, was a career European bureaucrat, attached to the Brussels-headquartered Commission for twenty-two years. On an official, low-taxed salary of slightly under £100,000 a year, he lived in an expansive house – Villa Quantraro – set in fenced and wooded grounds in an exclusive Brussels suburb. The razor-wired fence is hung with 'Entry Forbidden' signs.

For three of his twenty-two-year European career – from 1988 until 1991 – Quantraro headed the tobacco division of DG6, the Commission's agricultural directorate. He had been attached to the directorate for more than ten years. During his period of control, subsidies for virtually worthless European tobacco (dumped in the former Soviet Union or Third World African countries, because no-one would smoke it in the West) soared from £772 million a year to more than £1 billion. It was Quantraro who agreed the contracts and authorised the payments of export refunds claimed by growers and processors to bring up to the supposed world market price the cost of their unsaleable, already subsidised tobacco. Quantraro – an expert after serving so long in one division and part of whose job anyway was drawing up the necessary regulations – actually reworked some of the Community's tobacco rules to make the running of the fraud easier. The particular beneficiary of those changes was organised crime. Few, if any, records were kept by the producing countries: some of the vast amounts of money paid out were for tobacco that didn't even exist.

Quantraro, in fact, used the artificially inflated budget of the European tobacco industry for his own private, non-stop, never-losing roulette game. The other players will never be fully identified. Some, though, can be guessed at.

Soon after his arrival in Brussels in the 1970s, Quantraro made very obvious his support for the Christian Democrat Party of Italy, mafia and mason dominated, and now scandal-defunct. For six years he acted as the party chairman in the Belgian capital. Quantraro's reputation was of a solid, dependable worker: someone who could be relied upon to follow through any task entrusted to him.[3] I understand he was a member of a Belgian lodge covered by the banning edict of the controlling British authorities and during his twenty years in Brussels held several functionary positions within it.[4]

It was the merest of chances that set off the probe into a fraud so massive that the European Union's financial watchdog, the Court of Auditors, declared[5] its total cost to be virtually incalculable. A friend of Merseyside Labour MEP and anti-smoking campaigner Terry Wynn returned from a trip to Tirana in 1990 and casually mentioned he had not known that Italian-grown tobacco was being exported, in return for a substantial refund, to Albania. Wynn, a member of the European Parliament's Budgetary Committee, hadn't known it either.

One of the early findings of the investigation that Wynn initiated was that Quantraro had been in charge of the Commission's relevant directorates during the 1988-to-1990 period when thousands of tons of sub-standard tobacco cultivated in Italy and Greece under the highest agricultural subsidy system in the Community – with smaller production in Germany, France and Spain – had been sold to Albania for an additional export-refund profit.

The investigation further discovered that in 1988, when Quantraro took over the directorate, £724 million had been paid out in tobacco subsidies. By 1991, the figure had gone up to £996 million. And was continuing to rise. In 1991, following these discoveries, Quantraro was relieved of his responsibilities as tobacco supremo and transferred sideways to a nebulous post as advisor in a trade department. His £100,000 salary and all the Eurocrat benefits were unaffected by the move.

Wynn's investigation, which the Luxembourg-based Court of Auditors virtually accuse the Commission of obstructing[6], continued. Which Quantraro knew. He was advised, two years after his transfer, that he would have to explain certain matters to the enquiry. Commission officials talk[7] of his showing obvious sign of strain. He was prescribed tranquillisers by his doctor.

The night before his death, Quantraro kept a dinner date. It was with former Italian Foreign Trade Minister Vito Lattanzio, a fellow Christian Democrat. Lattanzio had been given the foreign trade post by mafia-linked Giulio Andriotti. Lattanzio refuses to discuss anything about the dinner. Belgian police refuse to give any information about what Lattanzio told them, although they imply that it helped them little.

Quantraro's immediate office staff told police they noticed nothing particularly unusual when he arrived for work the following day, 30 March 1993. He appeared preoccupied, nothing more. It was a brilliantly sunny day but he made no reference to it, merely wishing them good morning. It was just past 9.30 a.m., his customary arrival time. There were no witnesses to what happened inside the sixth floor office – which has more than one entrance – with its panoramic view of the Community institution buildings that form the very heart of the European Union. Quantraro's immediate staff told police they heard no indication of a struggle. Or even the window being opened. Police sealed the office within an hour of Quantraro's death, for forensic examination. That examination, according to police, produced no evidence of anyone else having been in the room. Police refuse to say whether or not a suicide note was discovered. I understand there was not. Witnesses from outside the building who saw Quantraro plunge to his death were unable to say whether or not there was any sign of anyone else at the window through which Quantraro emerged: the reflected glare of the sun against the glass on such a bright day made it impossible to see.

His death was instantaneous. An autopsy found only crushing injuries consistent with his having hit the ground at the optimum force of someone falling 75 feet. Any wound or abrasion sustained just before his fall would have been medically impossible to detect.

Police insist they found nothing to link Quantraro with organised crime. But their investigation was not into such associations. It was confined entirely to the circumstances of his plunging to his death from his office window. The independent parliamentary enquiry into the tobacco fraud found no connection with the Mafia, either. But then they were denied the opportunity to question Quantraro: the breakthrough in the organised crime and corruption investigations which destroyed Italy's First

Republic came from questioning suspects who confessed in order
to negotiate a better deal for themselves.

Asked directly about Quantraro's possible Mafia association,
Terry Wynn said: 'There is no evidence'.[8] Which is quite different
from saying there is no connection. The conclusion of the
parliamentary enquiry was effectively that Quantraro had worked
on his own with a group of people, forming a cartel through which
he virtually controlled the production throughout Europe of either
grossly inferior or entirely fictitious tobacco.

Long-time Brussels observers doubt[9] if one man alone could
organise such a fraud, stretching through five European Union
countries. They also point out that agriculture in Italy – the main
tobacco producing country – is virtually 90% Mafia controlled.
Their doubt extends to the idea that Quantraro acted entirely for
his own personal enrichment, quoting the often-expressed belief[10]
that substantial amounts – running into millions – were channelled
back to the Italian Christian Democrat Party. Every enquiry I
made failed to discover any documentary proof. Both the police
and members of the parliamentary investigation team were
adamant there was no evidence whatsoever of Community funds
being siphoned off to the Christian Democrats. The corruption
investigations, of which Italy, by 1994, had grown so tired,
uncovered only an infinitesimal amount of *documentary* proof of
such money transfers.

Nevertheless, one of those observers,[11] a man who has served
both in the Commission and in the parliament, who has personally
seen there Mafia-respect hand kissing, and who knows the strength
of the masonic network, finds it incredible that Quantraro would
have taken his own life for fear of punishment or imprisonment.
'That's not the way the well established system works and
Quantraro would have known it, after all the years he spent in the
Commission. His future would not have been seriously affected, if
he had been found guilty of corruption by an internal enquiry, no
matter how massive that corruption was. The Commission *always*
covers up. As they would have covered up in this case. He had
already been transferred, without loss of salary or privileges. At
worst, if the enquiry had found him culpable – which he clearly was
– he might have been demoted and asked to leave. And if he was
demoted, his pension would have been reduced. He might have
been asked to repay some of the embezzled money. So might
members of the cartels with whom it could have been proved he

was working: if, indeed, they all *were* cartels. Which I doubt. Some, maybe. A front would have been necessary, after all. But the fraud wasn't confined to cartels. I'm sure it wasn't. They had their use, nothing more. Which is beside the point, really. Demotion, a possible invitation to resign and a reduced pension. That would have been the very worst that would have happened. Certainly there would not have been any police prosecution. Which, as I say, Quantraro would have known full well. It wouldn't have even become a public embarrassment, for him and his family. So he had no real reason to kill himself, did he? Quantraro was frightened of far more than what would have amounted to a slap on the wrist. So would a lot of other people have been.'

An open complaint in the special auditors' report into tobacco irregularities[12] virtually confirms the 'behind closed doors' attitude of the Commission disclosed to me by this particular observer – the survivor of three assassination attempts during a professional intelligence career who, because of his opinions and knowledge of mafia and masonic involvement in the Community, insists upon remaining unnamed. The auditors accuse the Commission of refusing to respond to repeated requests for a separate internal Commission report on Quantraro's activities. When the Commission did make it available, after the accountants had finished their field work, it was to just one auditor, who was not allowed to make a copy. The Commission enquiry – before Quantraro's death – apparently established the man's guilt. Yet, the auditors said, 'There was no evidence of action on the part of the Commission or a member State to bring suspected wrongdoers to justice.' The official Commission reply was that they felt they had done all they could and all that was necessary. Tellingly, they said their enquiry had ended with Quantraro's death.

Two members of the European Parliamentary Budgetary Committee involved in the tobacco enquiry, Labour MEPs John Tomlinson and Terry Wynn – while refusing to speculate on Quantraro having any mafia connection – were both prepared to be identified in their vehement criticism of the ingrained Commission practice of covering up for Eurocrat wrongdoing, even if it is blatantly criminal. Tomlinson coined the following analogy and Wynn agrees with it wholeheartedly: if a person is caught shoplifting in Marks and Spencer the crime isn't resolved by their being told to put the goods back on the shelf. Both MEPs are determined – flexing the extra muscle given to the European

Parliament with the ratification of the Maastricht Treaty – to ensure there are open-court prosecutions in the future.

The system which allowed Quantraro to play his game with European taxpayers' money has been changed and the Commission believes any such fraud to be impossible in the future. And because the final settlement of accounts is made two years *after* an audited year, Quantraro's cheating – as well as the payments claimed for non-existent tobacco for which Albanian importers had been bribed to provide receipted invoices – was discovered in time for Brussels to refuse to pay to Greece and Italy their illegal export refunds. In total that amounted to £909 million. In the case of Italy – whose tobacco industry is government owned – the money had already been transferred. All countries in the European Union are responsible for policing claims within their own territory for refunds under the CAP. So it is up to Athens and Rome to investigate how and with whom the frauds worked in their respective countries. And it is for Italy to recover the money from the producers and processors who have already been paid. Having uncovered the frauds perpetrated by Quantraro while he was in overall charge of the tobacco division, the auditors are going back even further, to investigate possible irregularities during the years he was employed in the tobacco sector, although not its controller.

Terry Wynn insisted – with what to me seemed unarguable logic – that the entire tobacco cultivation policy needed changing in a Community which has officially endorsed a healthy, anti-smoking campaign. Of the 390,000 tonnes of inferior European tobacco – high in tar and nicotine content – grown each year under subsidy by the producing countries of Italy, Greece, Spain, France and Germany 210,000 tonnes is dumped on poorer, Third World or Eastern bloc countries: European cigarette manufacturers import seventy-five per cent of their tobacco in the form of the lighter, much preferred Virginia tobacco.

The special auditors' report[13] after the Quantraro fraud commented: 'Subsidies are paid for producing tobacco which has practically no market in the Community. Almost all this tobacco is exported to Central and Eastern Europe and North Africa, where there are insufficient controls of tar content and where the countries can hardly afford to cope with additional bought-in mortality and high health costs.'

The financial costs – in subsidies – are almost beyond comprehension. On the 1990 figures – those upon which the auditors' report was predicated – the CAP support for cereals was £104 a hectare. The support for tobacco was 35 times more, at £3,622 per hectare! At the time of my meeting with Wynn,[14] he put the yearly expenditure on maintaining the European tobacco industry at £1.3 billion. Which was more – in one year – than the United States of America had spent in supporting its tobacco growers over the previous *sixty* years. Nonsense piles upon the nonsense. Under agreed Commission reforms, the expenditure in subsidies was scheduled to reduce in 1994 and 1995 to £720 million. But added to that figure was a further £720 million, largely for the storage of what no-one wants for the compensation payments calculated on the final settlement of accounts running two years in arrears. Which brings the figure up roughly to what it was before the crackdown began.

It was the entry of Greece into the Community in 1981 that led to the tobacco boom and it was Quantraro's presence in its controlling directorate in Brussels that made all the fraud possible. There is no land register in Greece – or Spain – so no proper checks are possible on what tobacco is grown. Requests for proper checks in Italy, Spain and Greece have been ignored by the government authorities controlling production in those countries. None was pressed by Quantraro to meet their statutory requirements. The auditors' investigation[15] quotes a staggering example of how the payment agency (DIDAGEP) of the Greek Ministry of Finance settled its accounts with the country's tobacco board (EOK). 'DIDAGEP's subsequent checks on the authorisation of payments was unsatisfactory in so far as it was carried out on data recorded on the outside of envelopes provided by EOK, such as the beneficiaries' names and payment order numbers, which were compared to a payment list also furnished by EOK. The envelopes themselves containing the supporting documents for each payment were not opened. Under such a system the regularity and legality of payments could not be assured.'

The back-of-an-envelope system has now been banned. And the Commission, which often appears in its responses to be deriding the auditors' criticism as unjustified, made much of the fact that a large proportion of the money expended on tobacco growing was a social cost, supporting poor communities throughout Europe in which tobacco farming was the only livelihood. Wynn – and other tobacco critics – were justifiably unimpressed. If social costs had to be considered, said Wynn, it would still be cheaper to allocate the money through an outlet already in existence in the European Union – it's called the Structural Fund – to find an alternative to tobacco as a crop or to train its growers in other jobs.

Italy is the biggest producer of tobacco in the Community, cultivating 190,000 tonnes each year. And the most corrupt. The auditors talked of finding contracts dated as having been fulfilled before the date they had been signed. Inspectors whose job it was to carry out unannounced spot checks to ensure regulations were being complied with telephoned processors to ask for a car to be sent to collect them for their surprise visits.

Above it all, manipulating a budget rising to more than £1 billion a year and countenancing – even encouraging – the irregularities that made his fraud so easy, was Antonio Quantraro. Record the auditors: 'The lack of a transparent filing system in the period before 1990 rendered any review impossible.' Incredibly, it didn't improve after Quantraro's transfer, which the Commission's own internal report concluded to be necessary because the Italian was robbing the system blind, by manipulating the payments system through his cartels. The auditors's report says: 'In the period January 1990 to April 1992 Italy and Spain frequently failed to comply with the requirements of the regulations. Italy failed to comply with the reporting requirements of the regulations in 83% of the cases investigated by the Court (of Auditors) and Spain failed to comply in 75% of the cases. The information on the quality of the previous year's harvest and the average prices paid to the farmers was not provided at all by Spain and Italy. In 1991 Italy, France and Greece did not provide any or only incomplete information. With the exception of Germany, no other member state indicated the original source of the information supplied and there was no evidence that the information had ever been checked for reliability or that any such verification procedures existed.'

The Commission's reply was that the tobacco market was 'notoriously difficult' to monitor. Which was why they had abandoned the old insufficiently documented system – largely one created by Quantraro for the benefit of himself and his companions in crime – and replaced it with a new one. The implication , which I find difficult to accept, is that it can't and won't happen again. In a written reply to the auditors' exposé of how the CAP's goose had been fattened to lay its golden eggs, the Commission insisted the new rules would 'put an end to the malfunctioning encountered in the past'.

The auditors were particularly critical – justifiably so – of the total hypocrisy of a Commission-endorsed system that supported at such vast expense the cultivation of the most medically harmful tobacco in the world.

In June 1985, the Council of Ministers – the group of member-government ministers holding the appropriate portfolios of their respective countries who meet in unreported session and whose decisions only emerge in what they choose to tell their individual parliaments in open debate – approved a Community-wide programme entitled Europe Against Cancer. Its aim, promoted by two campaigns, was to reduce cancer deaths in Europe by fifteen per cent by the year 2000. To achieve that the European Union, which spends £1.3 billion a year *growing and processing* tobacco, has agreed that tobacco – particularly the varieties it pays to have cultivated in Europe – is bad for you and *shouldn't* be smoked. The Commission, which justifies its tobacco expenditure on social grounds and uses the word 'humanitarian' to describe its dumping on Eastern Europe, has put forward seven anti-smoking Directives, the Euro-speak word for a recommendation to member countries to bring in binding legislation. Six of those anti-smoking, anti-tobacco Directives have been adopted. The seventh – banning cigarette advertising – is opposed by the British government, which has only partially adopted it.

The investigation[16] prompted by the plundering of the Community's tobacco treasure chest pointed out that medical experts recognised tobacco use to be the most important preventable cause of lung cancer: one in four smokers prematurely died from lung cancer or from coronary heart disease or chronic lung complaints. Just in case the Commission had forgotten it, the auditors called the attention of the Brussels Eurocrats to a reply they themselves had provided in June 1991, to a European Parliament question on the health risk of tobacco.

The Commission said then:

'According to WHO (World Health Organisation) statistics, it is estimated that tobacco is responsible every year for the deaths of 432,000 people in the member states of the Community. Tobacco probably now accounts for at least 25% of all EEC deaths in middle age (35–69) and for at least 10% of all EC deaths in old age. Those who are killed by tobacco in middle age lose on average about 20 years each of life expectancy. The predictable annual death toll from tobacco in the major European region, which serves as a basis for WHO's estimate among those aged under 25 in 1990, is about two million by the year 2025.'

The WHO identified tobacco as responsible for about 90% of deaths from lung cancer, 75% of deaths from bronchitis/ emphysema and 25% of deaths from ischaemic heart disease. Maternal smoking during pregnancy was associated with a higher risk of premature births, retarded wound healing, extended recovery periods after surgery, and tooth loss and bone erosion.

The Commission saw no contradiction between the health risk of tobacco and their encouragement of it being grown for the greater benefit of fraudsters like Antonio Quantraro. Responding to the auditors' criticism, they said: 'Tobacco would, of course, still be consumed even if the Community withdrew its support for tobacco-growers, thus ending tobacco production in Europe: the effect on public health would be zero.'

There are many Euro-MPs who believe also that the reforms introduced in 1992 to farm support and subsidies – of which those affecting tobacco were only one part – have had a zero impact. One, John Tomlinson, even suggests the reforms had the reverse effect. 'What I fear we are going to get is the infrastructure of reforms put into place which is going to be costly: buying out excess production, set aside (a policy of paying farmers *not* to plant or grow on certain fields, to reduce yields) is all going to be expensive at the beginning, but if you get the expense without the benefits and then not having had the benefits you've still got the surpluses and with the surpluses you've still got the infrastructure for fraud then you're going to get the worst of both worlds.'

Fellow anti-fraud campaigner Terry Wynn agrees. 'CAP is a mess. And there isn't the political will to confront it. No government is prepared to stand up to its farmers.'

By the beginning of 1995 the Maastricht-strengthened European Parliament were using one of the Treaty's clauses – 13c – to set up committees to investigate illegality. And when a probe began into allegations of financial mismanagement possibly involving criminality in the Commission's tourist promoting unit anti-fraud Commissioner Anita Gradin announced that national police forces were at last being brought into the enquiries.

Within weeks of that declaration, Brussels fraud detectives raided the tourism deparment and seized a large number of files.

Two officials were suspended from duty. For legal reasons I am unable to indicate the echelon within the Commission to which the police enquiry extended.

The major activity of the proscribed masonic lodges of Belgium and France and Italy, all so deeply entrenched within the European Commission and the European Parliament, is politically to influence decisions and legislation in favour of their respective farmers. Which, in the foreseeable future, is going to do nothing to diminish the size of the CAP budget. Which in turn will go on laying golden eggs for organised crime and independent fraudsters. The official Court of Auditors agreed figure for theft, each year, from the CAP is £2.5 billion. No-one in the Commission – or, unofficially, in the Court of Auditors – disputes the more accurate figure to be £6 billion: I have even heard it put as high as £10 billion.[17]

'A way has got to be found to stop it,' insists Wynn.

There are enough examples from which to choose and learn.

CHAPTER TWENTY-FIVE

The Frankenstein Scarecrow

The idea of a joined-together Europe becoming totally self-sufficient in food supplies was one of the most understandable and logical to follow the revolutionary concept of an eventual European Union of nations existing in economic harmony and cooperation. It was considered by founding fathers like Jean Monnet and Robert Schuman long before there was any awareness of how large that Union might become: and even longer before the establishment of the EEC by the Treaty of Rome in March 1957.

The notion of a united Europe was born of war and initiated by the French, who believed that a German partner – particularly a divided one – would not invade France as it had twice in the previous thirty years. The European statesmen of the late 1940s and early 1950s looked to the future with their minds locked in the past. And one of the strongest memories of that frightening past was that the lack of independent food supplies in sufficient quantities to feed the people of Europe had been one of the Allies' greatest strategic weaknesses in the Second World War.

Although the principle of the need to work towards food self-sufficiency were enshrined in the Treaty of Rome, it was not until 1968 that a Common Agricultural Policy was formally brought into being in a Community of which, at that time, Britain was not a part.

Even critics of what, since then, has grown into a Frankenstein monster agree there was sound reason for a CAP in the formative days of the Community. British MEP John Tomlinson is one of them. 'It was a good policy when you've only got fifty per cent self-sufficiency. And seventy or eighty or ninety per cent. You could even argue it was a reasonable policy when you've just got a slight excess of self sufficiency, because the slight excess could produce buffer stocks. But it's when you've got structural surpluses of particular commodities being 120% or 125% self-sufficient that the real problem begins to emerge.'

A problem which also distorts any attempt at a logical discussion on how farmers should be rewarded. Every country in the world artificially inflates its agricultural prices with farm subsidies: Austria was compensating its farmers with support payments three times greater than those of the Europeran Union before it entered in 1995. The subsidies paid by Finland and Sweden were also greater than those allocated by Brussels.

The reality is that there are no such things as world market prices for agriculture: there is only competition between the developed countries of the world over the prices at which they dump their unwanted food surpluses upon the undeveloped countries of the world. Which, in the case of the countries of the European Union, creates another lunacy which only the double-speak Eurocrats of Brussels are brave – or lunatic – enough to attempt to justify.

Through the European Union development programmes, million of pounds are given in direct financial aid and even more in agronomy training and field instruction to numerous countries in Africa to establish sustainable agricultural bases which can go some way towards feeding their own populations.

Which is admirable.

What isn't admirable is that at the same time the Community is swamping those same African countries with its artificially-financed, fraud-promoting surpluses at prices much lower than those African farmers are obliged to change. Mali is just one of many examples of this folly. The Community is trying to develop with European money an indigenous beef industry in this land-locked, West African republic. And also is dumping on it subsidised European Union beef at 50% below the cost of Mali beef production! John Tomlinson suggested to me that in some cases the Community is practically *causing* famine in parts of Africa by undermining the agriculture of certain countries – the health of whose people, by a further absurdity, it already damages by dumping on them the Community's cancer-causing, high-nicotine tobacco.

The only real and consistent beneficiaries of the EU's Common Agricultural Policy are the fraudsters and organised crime.

Clearly, although the most popular buzzword of European Union is harmonisation, disharmony reigns. Sadly, the disharmony of the various Community institutions is only equalled by the disharmony of its crime fighting organisations.

The Court of Auditors, which is supposed to monitor a £57 billion yearly budget, considers the non-elected European Commission to be arrogant, claiming that it ignores its criticisms, particularly those involving criminality. The Commission, the permanent bureaucratic machine which is supposed to run the Community, meanwhile despises the Court of Auditors as weak and vacillating, unprepared to press its findings forcefully enough. The Council of Ministers, for its part, regards both bodies as mere functionaries of the Union, above which it aloofly holds its unreported meetings, deciding upon policies – to be fine-tuned through the Commission – which are invariably fudged later in trade-off between the various countries and their ministers. All of which obey the regulations and Directives that suit them and totally ignore those that don't. And finally, the European Parliament considers all three bodies – the Court of Auditors, the European Commission and the Council of Ministers – to be undemocratic, inefficient, sometimes corrupt and greatly in need of wide sweeping reform and redesign.

Unsurprisingly, the aforesaid three institutions regard the European Parliament as a cosmetically necessary but quite irrelevant figurehead forum, to which lip service should be paid for the sake of politeness. That is the view also of the majority of the member states.

But the European Parliament was given great powers when the Maastricht Agreement came into force in February 1992, and a number of British MEPs are committed to using these powers in their fight against Community crime, despite the obstruction of vested influence from masonic and criminal enterprises and – most incredible of all – from some member governments themselves.

One of the first results of those new powers was successfully to urge the replacement of the head of the Commission's anti-fraud division (UCLAF) who meekly allowed himself to be ordered from a meeting of the fraud-plagued agricultural directorate –

which he had every right and justification to attend – by someone described to me[1] as 'more Rambo-like'.

Virtually all the theft, fraud and regulation manipulation which siphons off at least £6 billion a year from the European Union's £57 billion budget is stolen from the CAP. Not all is stolen by organised crime. Farmers, traders and government agencies all have their snouts in the trough. John Tomlinson describes the ease with which farmers can claim subsidies for growing and refunds for exporting and premiums for importing, as the greatest incentive for crime that exists in Europe, with middlemen fiddling rules and regulations which look as if they've been designed to be fiddled.

The government agencies of Italy, Greece and Spain were all implicated by inefficiency, if by nothing else, in the tobacco fraud perpetrated by Antonio Quantraro and his cartels. A cheese and powdered milk scam that netted many millions came a close second. Not only was official complicity revealed at individual government level, but also within the financial monitoring body of the Commission itself, the Court of Auditors. For two years an official report exposing the scam was suppressed by the Luxembourg authorities to which it had been forwarded. In his disgust at the suppression, the British accountant closely involved in the investigation prematurely quit the court.

The scam was simple. Claims at the highest rate were made, and paid, for low grade cheese and milk powder produced in four Community countries – Ireland, the Netherlands, France and Germany – which in some cases were found actually to be unfit for human consumption. Some of the cheese even contained animal hair.

Among the firms were An Bord Bainne (ABB), the state-owned Irish Milk Board whose best known product is Kerry Gold, Deutsches Milch-Kontor (DMK) of Hamburg and UNCEA, a French producer.

The report[2] is a damning indictment of official connivance in financial irregularity. Its estimate of what Brussels paid to Ireland alone is put at £13 million. All the funds obtained should have by now been repaid. They have not been. No-one in the four respective countries, in the Commission or in the Court of Auditors could – or would – tell me how much has been returned. In the case of Ireland, which receives a total of about £1 billion a year in farm subsidies from the European Union, the country had received an over-payment in excess of £10 million. The Irish government has temporised, refuting some of the investigation's findings. France has refused to cooperate at all.

The auditors' report discloses that the Dublin government had not audited ABB's relevant accounts for five years, although it is their legal duty to do so under a Community law which makes member countries responsible for their farmers' subsidies. Germany hadn't bothered to examine the relevant accounts of DMK for six years. In just one year – 1989 – the two companies between them were paid £214 million. In one quoted example, ABB was shown to have claimed £25 per 100kg of milk powder more than it was entitled to, describing the powder as semi-fat when it was in fact buttermilk. In a reply to that accusation, Dublin assented that to claim for one instead of the other – and at a higher adjustment rate – showed no evidence of dishonest intent. That one transaction cost the Commission almost £1.5 million. It was in a consignment of ABB cheese, too, that animal hair was found after its export to America. Upon its rejection and return to Ireland, ABB relabelled some of it Grana-type Italian cheese and sold it to a trader within the Union, for re-export. Which he did, benefiting along the way from a fresh 'support payment' of over £100,000. Some of the cheese, I understand, went to Egypt. The Irish said it wasn't animal hair in the cheese anyway: it was microscopic rennet fibre, used in cheese production.

The Irish producers were not the only ones exporting inedible cheese at a profit. Germany's DMK received a subsidy of £584,500 for a shipment of Gouda-type cheese sent to Poland as fit for human consumption. Warsaw rejected it, as uneatable. DMK kept their export grant.

ABB tried to do exactly the same with a shipment of Irish cheddar to Singapore, for which the British Intervention Board – the body responsible for administering Community payments – advanced the export refund. ABB didn't report it when Singapore rejected the cheese as unfit. Even so, on this occasion, the Intervention Board got its money back.

The scam carried out by the French UNCEA company was more complicated. It claimed a subsidy of almost £15 million on the supply to Algeria of skimmed milk powder produced within the Community. The auditors' investigation discovered no Algerian contract for such an order. What it did discover was a labyrinthine arrangement, involving DMK and another firm in Germany, as well as firms in the Netherlands, Britain, Liechtenstein and Switzerland, to provide the milk powder for Algeria from suppliers in Switzerland and what was then Czechoslovakia. And since neither Switzerland nor Czechoslovakia were members of the Community, in fact no subsidy whatsoever was due.

When the scandal finally emerged, another irregularity came to light. Ireland was the only country in the EU whose agriculture ministry paid CAP export refunds to its own farmers. That was contrary to Community rules, which insist there should be a separate – and supposedly independent – agency.

John Carey was the British accountant so disgusted by the obstacles placed in his way in his efforts to expose the cheese and milk fraud that he resigned from the Court of Auditors. Great pressure was brought upon Carey from vested national interests within the court itself. The auditor came as close to an open accusation as he felt able in his December 1992 resignation speech to a closed session of the European Parliament Budgetary Control Committee. Scathingly, Carey told Euro-MPs: 'There is no consensus in the court that detailed, on-the-spot audit investigations at the level of individual operations and transactions are a proper task, let alone a priority task.' Then, in a direct reference to the Irish opposition he encountered, Carey said: 'A court member who is confronted by a colleague with a draft report which offends his (the court member's) sense of decorum, will be only too happy to see it suppressed.'

Carey's resentment was not directed at any of the 200 strong auditing staff. The attempts to muzzle him and his report came from the very highest level within the court and were politically motivated. So anxious were some people to prevent the results of Carey's enquiry ever becoming public that there were threats to issue damage-recovery writs, through the Irish courts. Those threats were extended to include newspapers and their Brussels-based correspondents who reported what Carey said. The episode led some MEPs to wonder if it was advisable for the Court of Auditors to be headed by a collegiate representing each member country.

There was a degree of support for this view from André Middelhoek when he took office as President of the Court in April, 1993. Making no secret of his federalist views – unwelcomed in London – the former Permanent Secretary at the Dutch Finance Ministry said that the cohesive financial future of the European

Union was endangered if oversight and administration of the CAP were left with national governments. 'There is and always has been 100% subsidiarity in the execution and control of the agricultural subsidy budget. In fact, too much power was given away to the member states. The EC should have the powers and the resources to intervene at any time to protect taxpayers' money because the member states clearly don't.'[3]

They most definitely don't.

The Court of Auditors' past reports – largely ignored before the 1992 ratification of the Maastricht Treaty – contain many accounts of ingenious scams, schemes and scandals which at first sight might appear amusing until the cosmic scale of the theft, mostly unrecovered, is realised.

The Republic of Ireland is a Community member in its own right. Northern Ireland also qualifies for agricultural and farming subsidies, being part of the United Kingdom. But farm prices, against which subsidies are calculated to bring EC producers up to the artificially high, internally fixed level, are different in the two countries. Pig farmers in the early 1990s on each side of the border made fortunes estimated in the millions, simply by driving the same herds of pigs back and forth across the frontier – particularly where it separates the salient of Monaghan that juts into Northern Ireland from the south – each time collecting a balancing rebate. Quite separately, from the frauds John Carey uncovered, as much as £70 million was stolen by organised crime in Italy, via their newly-forged links with the Russian mafia, through unwitting traders. From Italy milk powder was exported to Austria, where – as milk powder – it attracted a subsidy to compensate for the difference between the high price in the Community and the lower price in Austria, at that time still not an EU member. From Austria it was sold to the former Soviet Union. From where, within weeks, it was re-imported back into the Community. This time false documents described it as animal feed. As such it qualified for a production grant.

Russia – both before and after communism – has proved a convenient backboard against which to bounce Community fraud. In 1991 forty thousand tonnes of heavily subsidised, top quality Irish beef was sold to Italian and Germany processors, to be tinned for onward aid to Moscow. In May 1992, 180 tonnes of it was discovered by British Customs in a warehouse near Liverpool, about to be sold in England at less-than-market bargain prices.

John Tomlinson talks[4] of other scams.

When the Soviet Union *was* the Soviet Union the sale of butter to the communist monolith was banned. Every country in the Community – and every agricultural trader in every one of those countries – was required, under EC law, to observe the embargo. The provision of subsidised butter to Moscow's acolyte, Cuba, was not, however, forbidden. So Havana was the destination listed on all the documentation for a total of thirty-two butter shipments from European ports. Most usual routing – and loading – began at Rotterdam. From Holland, part-loaded freighters sailed across the North Sea to London, where they were again part-loaded. From London, they retraced their routes across the North Sea, to complete loading at Copenhagen. From where, since Denmark was then not an EU member, they were able to continue eastwards to the forbidden Soviet Union. Tomlinson asked the Commission and the auditors – to whom the scam was reported – why grants would still be paid. He was told by both that neither considered there to be sufficient evidence of fraud.

Shouldn't the Community have the right to withhold payment until it is satisified regulations have been properly observed? Tomlinson now asks. The question echoes, without answer, from the black hole into which the stolen billions disappear, never to be seen again. Just as it's impossible to see all the supposed trees in Italy and Greece upon which are supposedly grown the supposed olives from which came the supposed oil which has created a fraud rivalling that of tobacco, cheese, butter and milk.

It should be very easy to see these trees, particularly in Italy where, according to a source whom I will not identify even by the date or location of our meeting, because he has already come under intense Mafia intimidation during a parliament-initiated field enquiry into olive grove claims – farmers get £2 for every tree planted – statistically the entire landmass of Italy and Sicily must be so tightly covered by olive trees that it is questionable if there is sufficient room left for Rome or Palermo or any other major city. It has even been suggested to me that a lot of Mafia-obedient farmers who actually bothered to try to grow their fictional plantations cultivated the early plants in large pots that could quickly be moved from field to field in the event of a surprise spot check. But since I understand that the Italian olive oil inspectors mount their swoops with the same unexpectedness as their tobacco supervising counterparts who call for cars to collect them, the precaution appears to have been scarcely necessary.

Italy, of course, isn't the only olive oil producing country. Before Greece, Spain and Portugal became members of the EU the racket was to sell their oil to Italy so that it could be claimed for as Italian oil. Now they play the tree game even more enthusiastically, and the current olive oil cost to the Community totals £2 billion a year. Which is worth the bother of a few movable trees in pots.

For once, when two Court of Auditors inspectors made an unannounced visit to the port of Hamburg, Germany in May 1991, the fraudsters were caught out. The two inspectors witnessed the Russian-registered *Kapitan Danilkin* being loaded in the forward holds with wheat that was being unloaded from the aft holds. The subsequent investigation proved it to be a long-established ritual – hence the dockside carelessness – to claim grant export subsidies by docking vessels at a German port and briefly putting the cargo on German soil. The wheat in this case had been originally loaded in the French port of Dunkerque.

Grain is high on the list of CAP swindles. In June 1993, there was uncovered in Italy a Mafia-inspired fraud with a potential £100 million plus profit. Growers of pasta-making durum wheat were paid by the Italian government – which later intended reclaiming the advance from Brussels – for wheat they were, in fact, offering for sale on the world market. And at the same time silo operators who didn't have the grain were claiming the subsidies they would have been eligible for if wheat *had* been in their silos. That discovery led a year later to the unpursued arrest of Pasques Casillo, a billionaire who controls a third of Italy's grain exports, owns 62 companies, thirty freighters and the First Division soccer club Foggia. Casillo's arrest was ordered by Licio Violante, at the time head of the Parliamentary Anti-Mafia Commission. Casillo had been identified to the Commission as being involved in a scheme to claim £100 million from Brussels for a non-existent export of couscous bran to North Africa by two *pentiti*. One was that richest mafioso in Italy, Carmine Alfieri, bargaining for leniency on charges preferred against him. Italy – which, in fact, *is* the Mafia – has long been identified by the Court of Auditors as the robber baron nation of the Community: in just over one year – 1992 – the value of fraud committed by Italian farmers, traders in organised crime was put at £59 million. The court never discovered what happened to hundreds of millions allocated to the Naples area after an earthquake in 1980, except that very little went into any sort of reparation.

Anti-fraud campaigners like MEPs John Tomlinson and Terry Wynn are determined to stop far more abuses than has been possible in the past. And they believe that they at last have some chance of succeeding, despite the fact that Finance Ministers at one of their secret 1994 meetings *cut* the budget allocated to fight fraud. In the face of the seemingly illogical subsequent claims by governments that the fiscal restraints do not indicate any lessening of their commitment to fraud reduction, Per Knudsen, the new head of the fraud unit, is also confident.

Danish-born Per Knudsen has the concentrated dedication of a man determined to do his job, which is both to prevent as much as possible of the £6 billion from being stolen each year from Brussels, and to get back as much as possible of the money that eludes him.

When we met[5] in his functionally modern Brussels office Knudsen sat in front of a large framed picture of myriad pin–point colours which could have been by a leading Impressionist painter. It was, instead, sophisticated satellite imagery of Italy, identifying by reflected light, moisture content and colours, exactly which individual crop, under which particular cultivation, was being grown throughout the entire country. It represented just one of the hi-tech weapons in Knudsen's armoury. The spies-in-the-sky cost £4 million, cheap if they work. If . . .

Knudsen knows it's not enough. What he needs more than technology is national government commitment, scarcely obvious if the cash cuts to his budget are anything to go by. And there is doubt from the financial watchdogs themselves that the 1993 reforms, the first in thirty years, will do very much to halt the escalating, illegal drain of money from Community coffers, either.

Those 1993 reforms – named after Irish Commissioner Ray MacSharry, who devised them when he was responsible for agriculture – switched the method of paying the Union's nine million farmers from price subsidies to direct payments. Farmers are now paid after the event rather than before it, by claiming for the amount of hectares farmed or animals bred. But – despite outer space surveillance – accurate verification would only be possible if there were up-to-date land registers available in every one of the fifteen member countries. But there aren't such registers. And there won't be in the foreseeable future. If ever.

The Court of Auditors most definitely doesn't accept that the 1993 changes in the agricultural price structure mechanism will reduce the robbery. They believe the opposite: that what was hailed as a fraud-defeating move will instead make it even easier for the funding drain to continue. The changes were, in reality, the typical fudge that achieved nothing.

Certainly satellite imagery can make an important contribution. In one survey the cameras proved that only 1.9 million acres of spaghetti-making durum wheat were under cultivation, not the 4.2 million acres Italian growers had claimed. In another, Greek farmers were caught out asking for payment for twenty-five per cent more olive groves than genuinely existed: a satellite in space can't be seen, so the growers can't move their potted plants around quickly enough to defeat it. But there are technical drawbacks. For example, satellite imaging can't spot the difference between the vining pea and the protein pea – but the former, which people eat, had never earned a subsidy, while the latter, used in animal feed, had always been a nice little subsidy earner. So what happened? The Solomon- like decision of the Commission was that to avoid possibility of fraud *all* pea growers should in future get a subsidy of £127 an acre. A spokesman[6] for the British industry described the decision as crazy, which indeed it might seem to be, to anyone but a Brussels bureaucrat.

Britain leads the European Union league in its fraud detection rates, not because it has more villainous farmers or organised criminals than other members, but because it observes its legal obligations under EU rules more efficiently and dutifully than they. Admittedly, during the Maastricht negotiations, Prime Minister John Major and Whitehall negotiators succeeded in getting into the treaty the obligation for all member states to treat crime and fraud against the Community with as much diligence and severity as they treat crime and fraud against their national interest. Getting such obligations into the treaty is still no guarantee, of course, that they are going to be observed any more stringently in the future than others have been in the past. But at least the Court of Auditors now has the right to take to court any European Union member which refuses to supply requested information about suspected fraud or, in its opinion, consistently fails to confront crime against the CAP within its own frontiers. Additionally, under the Maastricht Agreement, the European Parliament has the power to convene proper investigative public hearings. According to Terry Wynn,[7] 'Things are going to start to happen.'

One of those things has been that the Budgetary Committee, despite financial constraints, has virtually doubled the staff allocation – bringing it up to one hundred – of the *Unite de Co-ordination pour la Lutte Anti-Fraude* (UCLAF), to coincide with Knudsen's appointment. But Knudsen, an experienced Eurocrat, wondered during our conversation if the Commission – of which the fraud unit is part, not the Court of Auditors – would actually take on the extra staff whose salaries had been budgeted for. Tomlinson said the Commission would fail to do so 'at their peril'. If at the end of 1995 – the first opportunity the budget committee will have to check – they find the Commission has not taken up the full complement, they could refuse to approve the Commission's financial report. A motion of no confidence carried by a two thirds majority in the Parliament would mean the Commission being dismissed.

Were he and his anti-fraud campaigners prepared if necessary to throw the ruling collegiate of Commissioners out of a job? 'If they don't get behind us to beat these crimes, yes.'

UCLAF is not a supra-national police force, but during our talks Knudsen did not preclude its powers widening in the future. Virtually every fraud crosses borders: the only way to claim fraudulent export and import refunds is to have a transaction – even if it is entirely fictitious – involving more than one country. So any investigation needs to be co-ordinated. Providing a central information dissemination point through a database known by the acronym IRENE (*IR*regularities, *EN*quiries, *E*xploration) is the function of the unit, and Knudsen anticipated its role expanding in the future to make it an intelligence organisation. Already his staff travel to member countries to form part of an investigatory team.

Just as an investigation is the responsibility of national agencies, so is the recovery of stolen money from organised crime or crooked traders and farmers. If a country can't get back what has been provably embezzled from Brussels-administered funds, the money has to be repaid to the Community from that government's internal budget. There is, however, a carrot dangled: if a country gets back all the stolen money its allowed to keep up to twenty per cent of it.

There is also, thanks to MEPs like Tomlinson, a network of hotlines upon which whistle blowers can call, anonymously if they so choose, to report fraud in the Community's subsidy system. Initially the Commission allocated a pitifully small sum – £160,000 – to pay fraud informers, but this was later increased.

CHAPTER TWENTY-SIX

When Two Plus Two Makes Five

Henri de Compte says he is not a Freemason and Henri de Compte must be believed. He's gone to the European Court of Justice to insist upon being believed and for well over a decade the court has found in his favour. Those who don't believe a lot of what Henri de Compte says have to be wrong, then. Which sadly means no-one is ever going to find out what happened to an elusive £52,366. Yet another disappointment for the Court of Auditors, which really would have liked to know. Disappointment, too, for those British MEPs involved in the attempted budgetary control of the European Parliament. Still, it's in the past and anyway, it's only European taxpayers' money. Also, it's only £52,366, which is minuscule by European Union standards: scarcely worth talking about. Henri de Compte must surely be fed up talking about it: he did so for more than a decade, after all.

De Compte – whose name, ironically, means *to count* in French – was never proven guilty of any fraud. He didn't *ever* commit fraud, he says. He also says he isn't a mason. For someone who is *not* a mason, Henri de Compte appears to have had a great many freemason supporters to band together in his defence when his own, personalised method of accountancy caught – by the merest chance – the attention of Parliament.

The Belgian faction of Grand Orient lodges to which de Compte does *not* belong is, with the French faction to which two former

French leaders have links, the most active of the unrecognised European brotherhoods. World masonic authority John Hamill[1] described the two as 'very politically active. Strongly Socialist'. I know – but for legal reasons cannot publish – the names of past and present Belgian members of the Brussels Commission and the European Parliament in the very highest echelons of EU policy and decision making, who are also members of Belgian Grand Orient freemasonry. As I know – but again cannot publish for the same legal reasons – the name of a leading Belgian conglomerate, with business links to a well known European bank, which uses whenever possible the masonic connections of its directors and family members to manipulate the thinking of the Commission and of Parliament. The most valuable masonic asset for the conglomerate and the bank is advance knowledge of the route along which that thinking is travelling.

A primary interest of Henri de Compte was, literally, in routes. As long ago as 1979 he was head of the European Parliament's treasury and accounts department. As such he controlled the MEPs' cash office at Strasbourg. That office paid – most usually *in* cash – MEPs for their travel and subsistence. It also advanced the substantial secretarial allowances to which MEPs are entitled. Money not handed over in cash was given in bank transfers or cheques, both of which naturally provided a paper trail recording expenditure claimed and expenses reimbursed. De Compte's operation was based in Luxembourg, but his cashiers moved between Brussels and Strasbourg too, doling out the allowances.

In 1979 Parliamentary membership rocketed with the introduction of direct country-by-country elections to Strasbourg: the representation jumped from 198 to 411 and with the accession of Greece in January 1991, the figure rose by a further twenty-four. MEPs often asked to be paid differently, sometimes a mixture of cash and cheque, sometimes all in cash, sometimes all by cheque.

To ensure he was able to meet every demand de Compte followed what is known in accountancy jargon as an imprest account, commonly recognised as an easy-to-control fixed-float petty cash system, the sort of money-in-the-sugar-tin arrangement with which office boys buy stamps and coffee and get repaid when they produce the necessary receipt.

The MEPs' imprest account wasn't run by office boys. Had it been, it might have been administered more efficiently. But it would have been difficult to get all the Parliamentary petty cash into sugar tins, no matter how many there were. When the Court of Auditors began studying de Compte's method of accountancy in July 1981, it discovered by December of that year that the imprest account stood at £4.4 million. Its maximum authorised limit was £70,000. Furthermore, the auditors found that in the course of a full year, a staggering total of £21 million was moving through de Compte's office, in more than twenty currencies and with very little proper financial control. In one of those under-statements they are so good at, the Court of Auditors complained in its first report that such a system created the danger of 'a large number of irregularities'. Claims weren't supported by invoices or receipts. Travel and subsistence money wasn't separated from allowances for secretaries and assistants. There was little or no check on chequebook stubs. Already signed blank cheques lay about in offices, conveniently ready for amounts to be filled in. Together with a number of unsupervised cheque books. There was no system of cross-checking accountancy within the office and there were never surprise audits. A total £1.7 million was entered into the accounts for a year to which it was not applicable. Some bank accounts were over-funded, others overdrawn. Parlia-mentarians who were over-paid weren't chased to pay the excess back. The Irish punt – valued at that time against sterling at 90p to the punt – was held in the same account as sterling: for some years expenses claimed in punts had been over-paid in sterling. All of which, said the Court of Auditors in another of its Eurospeak understatements, was 'unsatisfactory'.

It remains unsatisfactory, even though today much more – but still not enough – is known. All of which leaves one long unanswered question. What really *did* happen to £52,366 for which de Compte was ultimately responsible? De Compte, who has to be believed, says he doesn't know. Parliament, which spent more than fourteen years trying to find out, doesn't know either. Nor does the committee of MEPs that tried to solve the mystery and received more masonic bullying than satisfactory explanations. Neither, to this day, do the sceptical insurers of the European Parliament. Which is why they've never paid out a single penny, pfennig, franc, peseta or drachma in compensation. Nor ever will.

The £52,366 was the amount drawn – in September and November 1981 – through a Luxembourg bank in French and Belgian francs and German Deutschemarks on two cheques. It was a typically mixed currency exchange of the sort made many times before to reimburse MEPs. The only unusual aspect of the transaction was that the withdrawal was made from a deposit account at a London branch of the Midland Bank about which the European Parliament and its budgetary examiners had not the slightest knowledge. But that was not immediately to emerge. Each of the two cheques was signed by different members of Parliament's cash office. Both were countersigned by de Compte, who later told MEPs the money was given to Parliamentary cashiers on the same day as the transactions took place. Which, as far as de Compte is concerned, was the end of the matter. Part of the finding of one subsequent Parliamentary disciplinary hearing against de Compte says, in part: 'On the basis of the documents available, this interpretation (that it was given to cashiers, for disbursement) is not obligatory.' In less clogged language, that means you haven't got to believe it if you don't want to.

The £52,366 has never been found. It remains recorded in Parliamentary ledgers as a 'shortfall to be recovered'. More than fourteen years later, to the moment of publication of this book, it has *not* been recovered.

In the beginning investigators and auditors tried to get it back. And some surprising discoveries were made. Perhaps the most intriguing of which was the London bank deposit account of which there was no record in any Parliamentary documentation. It showed interest of £50,347 accrued in 1980 on a £400,000 deposit. The £400,000 transfer had been made from a current account the Parliament and the auditors *did* have knowledge of: it was one of the many officially registered holdings which held the £21 million with which de Compte paid MEPs for their out-of-pocket expenses. It had, in fact, been the suggestion of the Midland Bank itself that an interest-earning deposit account should be opened because there was so much money in the current account. The suggestion made sense; at one stage in 1980 interest rates reached 16%. Not difficult, with £400,000 in the pot, to rack up £50,000.

The Strasbourg and Luxembourg accountants might never have learned about the undisclosed deposit account or its £50,000 nest egg but for British banking rules that require cheques to be cleared against current, not deposit accounts. In fact, had the two cheques been cleared as was obviously intended, no-one would have ever known about the missing £52,366 either. The cheques would simply have absorbed the secret deposit interest, leaving the £400,000 intact and available.

But by being settled through a known current account the transactions involving the two cheques for £35,177 and £17,189 became detectable. And the enquiries commenced.

An MEP who sat upon the budgetary control committee investigating the convoluted episode told me,[2] fourteen years after it occurred: 'Parliamentary funds were used to earn thousands of pounds, which Parliament didn't sanction or know about. It doesn't matter that the capital sum was not affected and eventually returned, in full. It was crooked and it was fraud. There should have been a prosecution. But there wasn't. There was freemasonry instead.'

The President of the European Parliament in 1981 was Dutch Socialist Piet Dankerts. He had been elected specifically to put an end to the widely-held belief that to be in any way associated with the Strasbourg assembly – and best of all to be an MEP – was to get a first class, champagne-all-the-way ticket to a life of luxury. One of his first acts, in May 1981, was to transfer de Compte and his deputy away from Parliament's treasury department – laying the ground for the first of the many de Compte appeals – and to appoint an independent firm of auditors to look into the affair.

The masons of the European Parliament flocked to de Compte's support, both publicly and privately. Chief among them was Jean Feidt, the French Director General of Administration, the head of the institution's civil service and a member of a lodge proscribed by the British governing authority. His administration service – threatened in any case by a job-cutting reorganisation by the Dutch President – went on strike after a secret meeting at which another mason, a leading Parliamentary official whose presence at a strike meeting was in any case curious, claimed that de Compte was being victimised and should be defended by the strongest means possible. This threat of strike action, with Parliament literally grinding to a halt in the absence of any administration staff, caused the first disciplinary action against de Compte to be abandoned. At the time the reason for the strike threat was concealed, for the benefit of both de Compte and Dankerts, as a protest against job reorganisation.

The de Compte affair dragged on for another fourteen years. The only positive action taken against the man while he remained a civil servant was his transfer to the position of junior administrator in Parliament's personnel division. There were several attempts to reduce his A3 grading, which carried a salary of over £4000 a month, to an A7, at below £3000. But de Compte appealed every time, usually through the internal disciplinary procedures of the Parliament itself, quoting technicalities to claim he was being improperly and unfairly treated, but on more than one occasion to the European Court of Justice. In one appeal de Compte complained that a salary loss would make it impossible for him to meet the mortgages on apartments and houses he owned. It was not until June 1994, that the Court dismissed de Compte's final appeal against the A3 to A7 demotion.

Throughout those fourteen years de Compte argued that the disputed money had simply disappeared through the inefficiencies of a financial system he had been obliged to follow and to which he had objected. But in any case, Parliament's legal division could not decide whether or not proceedings should be initiated because it could not make up its mind which country – Luxembourg, France or Belgium – had criminal jurisdiction, so the police were never involved.

Parliament's insurers, Royal Belge, refused to cover the £52,366 loss: their rejection talked of 'intentional violation' of regulations and of a 'serious offence'. The Budgetary Control Committee delayed their approval of Parliament's 1982 financial accounts until 1985 – after critical reports from the independent accountants, Moret and Limperg, and the Court of Auditors – but withheld their discharge from de Compte 'in respect of his stewardship of funds up to 30 April 1982'. That was the date de Compte was transferred. Although transferred – and temporarily demoted on occasions – de Compte remained on the administration staff of the European Parliament for more than a decade after the mysterious 1981 disappearance of the £52,366. He is now retired, but because of the 1994 decision he is on a reduced pension. Although outspoken in protesting his innocence before every appeals tribunal, he declined to discuss the affair with me.

John Tomlinson was a member of the Budgetary Control Committee. He called[3] the episode a classic case of masonic intervention and protection, although he stopped short of believing Brussels and Strasbourg were run by a masonic conspiracy. 'I am not a conspiracy theorist. But I don't like the degree of influence throughout the institutions. Or secret societies being part of them.' In Tomlinson's view, Parliament had two choices over the case of Henri de Compte. They shirked both. The police should have been involved from the start, to decide if there was a prima facie case of fraud. If there was no fraud, the insurers should have been sued over their refusal to pay out.

Tomlinson supports the idea of having a register of masons within the Union's permanent institutions, which was suggested by Leslie Huckfield when he was the Labour MEP for Merseyside East. Mr Huckfield declined to discuss with me his attempt to open up to public awareness the masonic involvement throughout the governing bodies of the Community but indicated[4] that he had come under strong pressure from French and Belgian MEPs not to press the matter.

A former European parliamentarian[5] was much more out-spoken. He talked of a cabal of masons, directed from certain national capitals, that worked at every level to influence decisions in favour of countries. Brussels has the highest concentration of lobbyists of any capital in Europe – because it was regarded by businesses and conglomerates worldwide *as* the capital of Europe – but such lobbying is open, a matter of public knowledge. Masonry is not necessarily an insidious, covert influence which should be opposed: there is an English lodge in Brussels – forbidden from any contact with its European Brotherhood by the London banning – that meets and operates according to the true principles of masonry, not as influence pedlars or manipulators. But as to illegal masonic activities, like so many other abuses throughout the Community, my informant did not believe anything would ever be done to curtail them. 'Which is outrageous. It should be exposed and stopped. It puts other countries at a totally unfair dis-advantage.'

It was this man – himself a British mason – who also talked at length of the Mafia presence throughout EU institutions, particu-larly in Brussels. There was a chain, linking Mafia Families in Italy with Mafia offshoots in Brussels, Strasbourg and Luxembourg, the last having a second and third generation indigenous Italian population. There was a lot of Mafia presence and influence at the lowest grade, D-level, in Brussels. 'I've seen hand kissing there: all the signs of the greatest Mafia respect. I believe the Mafia has a strong influence upon appointments: it's possible – but emphatic-ally denied, of course – because the Commission is non-elected and staffed by citizens from member states. And I am not just talking or restricting myself to Italians: other countries have their mafias, too.' Grade C – secretaries and personal assistants – was relatively free of mafia, because that level had little practical influence. The next echelon, the executive-level, aid granting and grant awarding Grade B, was heavily infiltrated. Although he did not believe any of the Commissioners had active Mafia associations he was sure they knew of its existence and operations within the Commission: during this particular conversation I was given the name – which legally I am prevented from publishing – of one Commissioner with strong masonic connections to a lodge proscribed by the governing London body. But there was not the shell-within-a-shell concealment between Mafia and masons in the Community's permanent working bodies that existed elsewhere in Europe. In the European Union institutions the two were independent, but at the same time there was no friction: the two covert organisations co-existed to their mutual benefit. 'It's long established: an existing system. It will continue to exist, just as it will continue to be denied.'

My account of masonic and mafia infiltration of the European Union is not based upon meetings with just one conspiracy-minded man with no more than passing experience of the Community. I discussed such infiltration with a total of six present and former MEPs as well as people with detailed knowledge of the Commission and of Luxembourg and of Strasbourg: after the most specific of those meetings I asked the people with whom I talked to check and agree – and even add – to my notes. Each had worked and lived in the parliament or its institutions for four or more years. One had been in both the parliament *and* the Commission.

More than one even suggested to me, with resigned cynicism, that the European Union would *benefit* if it were officially run by the Mafia. If it were, the reasoning went, there'd be an unprecedented crackdown on the rule-bending and the perk-perpetuating. And the European Union would save incalculable millions. Despite the dedication of the far-too-few financial watchdogs, there remains no effective check on vast amounts of European taxpayers' money. Or even on how European parliamentarians spend it on themselves.

One of the main complaints of John Tomlinson – and others – concerns the perpetual movement of MEPs between Brussels and Strasbourg, which is the result of an official inability to decide which city should become the permanent site for the Parliament and all its administrative offices within the Community. This dispute demonstrates – among other things – how far away any thought of true federalism is.

In December 1992, there was a summit of Community state leaders in Edinburgh hosted by British premier John Major. At that time the construction of a new, £800 million parliamentary complex was under way in Brussels. Yet in Edinburgh the decision was taken to build, at the cost of £300 million, a new parliamentary chamber in Strasbourg, to replace the existing inadequate facilities attached to the Council of Europe building.

The working routine of the parliament – which under Maastricht has gained effective power virtually for the first time – defies understanding. Its official headquarters are technically in Luxembourg, but only its civil servants work there. For two weeks of every month, MEPs work in Brussels, in committee sessions. A third week – also in Brussels – is devoted to meetings of their respective political groups. But for the fourth week they all pack up and journey to Strasbourg to sit in plenary session. Which means that every month there is a caravan of about 4,000 parliamentarians, support staff and journalists travelling at quite unnecessary and inflated expense the 350 miles between the Belgian and French cities. Outside every parliamentarian's office sit large metal trunks, draped with their permanent security padlocks and chains, into which have to be packed materials and documents for the migration. Which is reversed when they all come back, five days later. Trucking firms with their twenty-ton lorries make millions. But the horrendous waste isn't just financial. There's a matching loss in efficiency. Under the existing system, an urgent parliamentary matter that arises on the Monday after the return from a plenary session has to wait another three weeks, until the next return to Strasbourg, before it can be properly discussed.

British MEPs have been among the most strident in demanding that the entire working of parliament – plenary sessions, committee meetings and political group gatherings – be concentrated in the one set of buildings that will be finally completed in Brussels in 1996. Predictably France, which believed the Edinburgh decision had won it a thirty year dispute over a permanent parliamentary site, led the campaign to maintain the existing system and build the duplicate chamber in Strasbourg. France openly threatened to use its power of veto to throw the Community into chaos if any attempt were made to overturn the Edinburgh decision.

It is the intention of some Euro-MPs[6] to procrastinate in the hope of preventing the Strasbourg building from being started before 1996. That is the year scheduled for an inter-governmental conference heralded as the most important decision-making gathering since the Treaty of Rome formation of the Community. If the aims of the 1996 conference are met – which I doubt – the Community will virtually be rebuilt, and much of the money-leaking, out-of-date policies – the CAP chief among them – will be reformed. With the changes, many MEPs hope, will be swept away the decision for the Strasbourg building. The European Parliament never owned the chamber in which it meets in Strasbourg. It was the property of the Council of Europe, the guiding function of which is the preservation of human rights.

CHAPTER TWENTY-SEVEN

The Rule of Law

The European Union's difficulty in confronting its all-pervasive masonically-cloaked mafias is not its lack of police forces, intelligence agencies, enforcement authorities or technical facilities.

Rather, it is the absolute opposite. There are too many agencies and far, far too many conflicting technologies. Each force has its own defensive, insularly-protective hierarchy. Each has its own mine's-better-than-yours computer system.

Few work in full cooperation with each other, even within their own countries. Fewer still liaise across their newly-opened frontiers with anything like the success of the organised crime groups already embedded deeply in the foundations of the Community.

That is not, of course, the official message to the voting population of the European Union. Leaks from crime prevention gatherings of Interior Ministers in Brussels and Luxembourg, spread with intentional frequency that most favoured of all Euro-speak words, harmonisation. The suggestion that the law enforcement bodies of Europe are coming together as one appears again, by implication if not in so many words, at the end of most international conferences, in the form of resolutions pledging joint action and pooled resources.

All of which is utter nonsense.

Even to begin to confront European organised crime there needs to be an integrated, fully operational, properly functioning FBI of Europe.

To create this there needs in turn to be genuine political will on the part of every EU government. And genuine willingness on the part of the dozens of different policing agencies of the fifteen member nations to surrender a small part of their empires.

Neither will nor willingness exists. And I do not believe that either will come until too late, until crime has proved unbeatable. Dutch Euro-MP Pieter Stoffelen and his fellow countryman Dr Jan van Dijk issue constant warnings to this effect, which equally constantly are ignored.

Only Germany – and to a lesser extent The Netherlands – is prepared to consider the possibility of a European FBI. The United Kingdom, to which the word federal in any European context is absolute anathema, certainly isn't.

French criminologist Professor Xavier Raufer, who shares the pessimism of his Dutch counterpart, predicts[1] that it will take between forty and sixty years to establish a federated European police agency. 'Until which time European policing is going to be in a terrible mess.'

In addition to sovereign police resistance and a lack of political will, Professor Raufer identifies a third obstacle to the creation of such an organisation: the conflict between the common law principles of the United Kingdom and Ireland and the various Code Napoléon systems of Continental Europe.

The two won't mix, legally. And can't mix, politically. But they have to, somehow, some way, some when.

The embryo of a European FBI exists in Europol, the concept of which – and even the name – originally came from a former British chief constable[2] but has been eagerly adopted, even kidnapped, by Germany which sees itself as the motivating and controlling nation. Unfortunately, to several European countries with memories of two world wars, any such concentration of German power erects yet another obstacle. Europol was a frail child – even a foundling – at its conception, existing for the first year of its life in the humble barrack hut on the edge of a Strasbourg field in which I found it in July 1993. At that time not only did it lack a proper home, it lacked the legal right to be alive at all. It did not, explained its engagingly forthright German executive officer, Chief Superintendent Peter Vowe, actually exist: while it awaited an establishing Convention it was merely *Project* Europol, and was entrusted solely with collating and assembling from the EU member states a computer database on drug trafficking.

Although it has now transferred to a permanent home at The Hague – where, incidentally it can't assemble its drug database because of the widely differing data protection restrictions governing each of the member countries – its establishing Convention is not due until 1995 and is by no means certain to be ratified that year. Europol's eventual remit will include nuclear, conventional arms and explosives trafficking, extortion, blackmail, protection racketeering, investment fraud, aggravated burglary, money laundering and illegal immigration. The legality of such a broad remit already exists on the EU statute book. Drugs, money laundering, terrorism and illegal immigration are all covered by Conventions and Directives that enable them to be dealt with by a single European enforcement body.

But, inevitably, there are snags. Nothing in Europe is simple. Spain, anxious to crush ETA once and for all, and Greece, eager for *anything* that might lead to a breakthrough against November 17, head the campaign for terrorism to be ratified in the Convention. The United Kingdom, with MI6 and MI5 seeking continued justification for their existence after the end of the Cold War and the fragile peace accord in Northern Ireland, adamantly oppose the inclusion of terrorism. So does France. And the trouble is, the Europol Convention specifically excludes any opt-out, by any EU country. Which means, once it is signed, that MI6 and MI5 and every other intelligence service in the Community will have to put all their terrorism intelligence into Europol's common database.

Which highlights the fact that some countries reluctance to surrender territory is only equalled by their reluctance to surrender information. Although Europol now has a permanent home and an expanded Convention in the pipeline, there is clearly still no intention – or political will – to make it operational.

Europol *will* one day become an operational FBI-type organisation, staffed by multi-lingual, multi-national detectives backed by its own forensic and scientific facilities, guided by its own international lawyers and legally able to operate in each and every country in the Union. But before that can happen at least one apparently unanswerable question must be dealt with. Who's going to be in charge?

An early conference[3] at which European Justice Ministers dared to approach the dilemma – at a stage when Europol was only being discussed as an intelligence gathering body, with no operational ambitions – ended in disarray and acrimony with the United Kingdom's then Home Secretary, Kenneth Clarke, complaining the assembled ministers had wasted hours 'dancing round the edge of hair-splitting semantics'.

As they are likely to keep on dancing for years.

In the United States the FBI's director is answerable to the President, and this is a politically appointed (but Congressionally vetted) American responsible to a democratically elected American.

From which of the fifteen – and eventually more – EU member nations would come the director of Europe's FBI?

It's no use saying that Interpol operates quite successfully under a British Secretary General, with a supporting multi-national collegiate. Despite a widespread understanding to the contrary, Interpol is *not* an operational, international police force whose investigators roam the world, solving crime. It is simply an intelligence disseminating organisation through which law enforcement agencies of 179 member countries liaise and exchange information.

For the foreseeable future each European member country will resist and resent the appointment of any but one of its own nationals as the man to head Europol. A yearly or five-yearly rotating figurehead as titular director of a collegiate of law enforcement officials from each member state might offer something approaching shared democratic control, but would surely create a warring snake's-nest of top heavy bureacracy beneath which the efficiency of any Europe-wide force would be stultified.

If, however, that structure of command were accepted as a working model, to whom would the figurehead director report? The International Court at The Hague was the suggested control while Europol remained merely a database collecting service, but clearly has no role in a working police force. The President of the Commission isn't an easy or even acceptable candidate. The power of the non-elected Commission is already resented to the degree of bare tolerance by the European Parliament and several of the governments of the individual states. Quite apart from any legal bar, the current individual and collective EU attitude to the Commission makes the appointment of its president as the ultimate supremo of Europe's FBI totally unthinkable.

Who then? A special committee of members of the European

Parliament? This notion deserves reasonable discussion, but any discussion at a summit of European leaders would be anything but reasonable. Most EU countries – with the United Kingdom stridently in the lead – despise the peripatetic parliament (except for its elections, which they regard as barometers of party popularity at home) and try to limit, not extend, its power. To award it control of an FBI is even more unthinkable than giving control to the Commission.

Such intractable problems promote among many opponents to Europol's eventual role the understandable view of Interpol's Secretary General Raymond Kendall.[4] In his view – later echoed at the United Nations' Naples conference – organised crime was a global crisis which needed a truly global organisation, like Interpol, to fight it. Europol was not and could never be such an organisation. Its role, representing the limited number of countries in the EU, could only ever be that of a sub-regional bureau of the worldwide Interpol system. Kendall described as presumptuous even the name Europol, when it did not serve all the countries of Europe, which Interpol did. Demonstrating what he considered to be Europol's limitations, Kendall cited the international investigation after the attempted assassination of Pope John Paul II in St Peter's Square in May 1981. The Browning automatic used by Mehmet Ali Agca was manufactured in Belgium, a member of the Community, and legally exported first to Switzerland and then to Austria, neither of which was at that time in the EC, before re-entering the Community by coming into Italy. Only Interpol, to which each of the four countries belonged, could have established the trail by organising liaison between those countries' individual enforcement agencies. Europol would have lost the trail, from the moment of its leaving Belgium to its re-appearance in Rome.

I do not find such an example entirely convincing against Europol: its operational function could always work in tandem with the intelligence distribution and liaising function of Interpol. But Kendall had – and still has – a bad image to defend on Interpol's behalf. Which he readily conceded.

The history of Interpol, founded in Vienna in 1923, is unimpressive. Until Kendall's appointment in 1985 – extended for a further five years after he completed his first statutory period in 1990 – a Frenchman had always been Secretary General of the organisation. And in those days Interpol was lamentably inefficient and practically universally condemned by law enforcement bodies. Delay extending into weeks – even months – was the norm for responses to investigatory questions. This was perhaps hardly surprising, since they had to be answered from a card index system initiated upon Interpol's formation in Austria, continued in a gutted condition in Berlin during the Second World War, and perpetuated upon its return in 1946 to France. Computers were still not used because, under stringent French privacy laws, it was forbidden to include on computer databases precisely those names of criminals and organised crime figures about whom it was supposed to hold records for international reference. Not that such an absurd defect worried the French administration, which preferred card indices, even if they took weeks to access. The situation was rectified by an almost equally absurd manoeuvre, by making France the head-quarters, not the host, country of Interpol, which therefore no longer needed to abide by French laws. And by putting Kendall in charge.

During his ten year secretary-generalship, Kendall has revolu-tionised the information-distribution facilities of his Lyon-based organisation, introducing constantly updated technology. 'Police people who come here are amazed at what they see. What we have here beats most national police forces in terms of technology and everything else, including the most developed countries.' Response times, for replies to information requests, are stan-dardised by code-regulated guarantee: while the official maximum still seems inordinately long Kendall insists that it be judged against the fact that Interpol deals with 179 countries through which requests have to be channelled and from which answers have to be awaited. 'The biggest problem in international coordination is the sheer mass of international criminology that we have to deal with.' A request designated 'Flash' has to be met immediately, with twenty-four hours the maximum permitted delay. 'Urgent' requires a reply as soon as possible, with a maximum of ten days. 'Routine' again stipulates a response as soon as possible, with a month the longest time allowed.

The criticism to which Kendall takes the strongest exception is that his organisation and its records can be manipulated and accessed by criminals or terrorists: the terrorist states of the Middle East are Interpol members, as are the cocaine-producing nations of Latin America and some of those in Asia heavily involved in the manufacture and movement of heroin. Kendall is adamant, however, that Interpol's data protection controls – combined with the sovereign-state restrictions individual countries can impose on sensitive information – have made such abusing manipulation totally impossible. 'Nothing can be more strict than the way in which information is controlled. We are unique in that respect.'

Facts hardly support Kendall's emphatic assertion.

Operation Green Ice was a two-year, American Drug Enforcement Administration led, seven-nation assault on the money-laundering activities of Colombia's Cali Cartels, of which the laundering masterminded by the Rodriguez Orejuela brothers was the main target: on one occasion close-to-£5 million in sequestered small denomination notes took accountants in London twenty-three days to count, to the fascination of Italy's anti-Mafia judge, Liliana Ferraro.

One of the laundering couples pursued during the operation was American-domiciled Silvia Veles-Agudelo and her accomplice, Carlos Rodrigo Polania-Camargo.[5] Polania's official position when he was not acting as financial advisor to the Cali Cartel was actually *in* the Colombian government, working in the department of the Director of Special Investigations for the Superintendent of Banking. As such he oversaw foreign currency transactions from Colombia and controlled those banks taken over by the Colombian administration. He also ran investigations into companies involved in international commerce. Which was by no means all he did: hardly more, in fact, than a useful training background for the best job of all. At one stage he was the Inspector General of Colombia's intelligence service, the Administration Department of Security (DAS). In which role he was Colombia's liaison official not just with the DEA and the US Customs, but *also with Interpol*.

That one incident demonstrates precisely the objection to Interpol which Dennis Martin, president of America's chiefs of police, expresses so openly – 'We wholeheartedly support the setting up of Europol which is independent of Interpol'[6] – and to which others subscribe but refuse to be quoted.

Germany is the strongest proponent of Europol, of which it admittedly sees itself the guiding force, if not the leader. The Interior Ministry's Eduard Lintner[7] concedes that because it involved the dreaded world 'federal' it had been a mistake to refer to Europol as Europe's FBI. 'It made the others (countries in the EU) suspicious, but as far as the subject matter is concerned it certainly would mean Europol should become an FBI type agency.

It should have executive powers. It should not just be concerned with data compilation. Europol should develop to become the European operational police agency.' Germany, being a country with a federal government system, does not have the difficulty that non-federal nations have in surrendering elements of its law enforcement to a non-national organisation. 'We just hope that the increasing international curriculum of crime will compel us to take this step and to overcome this reserve. I can only hope that it will come about as soon as possible.' Lintner made a joke of hoping to see an operational agency created in his lifetime. And another that Germany might be its chief financial contributor. But he stopped short of any jokes about who or what would be in control.

Holland's crimonology professor Dr Jan van Dijk[8] shares Lintner's hope that the inexorable growth of European crime may force governments quickly to overcome national jealousies and put Europol on an operational footing. Germany and Holland are ahead of the rest of the EU, he told me, in recognising both the danger and the need to oppose it. 'We think it (Europol) will be a big important police force much sooner than most politicians, certainly in the UK, think.' Public opinion, driven by media crime hysteria, will spur the political decisions. For politicians Europol is 'a cheap way to be tough and concerned about real values. So it is also super-attractive for politicians.'

Although Holland welcomed the establishment of Europol's headquarters at The Hague, there exists in the country a deep reservation about one inevitable consequence of its being there: the presence of German police well before the question of their gaining administrative control has been settled. I was told[9] that such are the Nazi-occupation memories of the older Dutch generations that some senior ministers in the government, while publicly approving Europol's location on their soil, privately 'hated' the idea of German police on Dutch streets. 'There is only that sensitivity towards the Germans, not to any other nationality in the Union.' And already, although under the Shengen Agreement there is provision for limited cross-border pursuit of criminals, there had been instances of German police 'over-reacting' and breaching those limitations.

The United Kingdom policeman who conceived the name and the idea of Europol is John Alderton, a widely-respected former Chief Constable of Devon and Cornwall who went on to become a Research Fellow with the Centre for Police Studies at Exeter

University. He is vehemently opposed[10] to Interpol absorbing Europol into its European Division, even though Raymond Kendall points out in his take-over argument that this division accounts for 80 per cent of his organisation's activity. Alderton's objection is founded upon his strong belief in what is democratically inviolable in law enforcement, accountability. Which he insists Interpol lacks. He also dismisses Kendall's claim that Interpol cannot be manipulated for political purposes. 'International crime is growing and governments are involved in it, particularly in South America but elsewhere, too.' Certain governments – Iran and Libya, for example – had in the past disguised enquiries that could lead them to exiled political opponents as legitimate criminal requests. Harmonised European law *had* to be enacted for a European FBI to enforce. Of paramount importance – as it was for every policing agency – was proper and full oversight. 'An openness about it all: freedom of information that's one of the greatest defences against abuses of all this power that would be entrusted.'

Alderton finds some comparisons easy between the American FBI and what is necessary for Europe. The American institution grew because federal laws, with which European laws could be equated, were not being properly or adequately enforced. And crime in the United States became much more mobile, with which there is now a parallel in open-bordered Europe.

Although accepting an eventual European FBI, Alderton does not envisage sufficient political will emerging in the countries of the EU for such an organisation to be created in less than a decade. From my conversations throughout Europe over a period of two years, I expect the United Kingdom to be the very last to agree. A British Home Office official from whom, from her close association with anti-terrorism work, some acceptance of a pan-European force might have been expected, met the suggestion by demanding[11]: 'What need is there for an FBI?' And refused to acknowledge any argument to the contrary.

Certainly one British Home Secretary foresaw the necessity for such a bureau *within* Britain, the only country in the EU that does not have a national police force. Kenneth Clarke was an enthusiastic promoter of the National Criminal Intelligence Service in his intended British policing revolution, which would have streamlined the country's forty-three independent forces into nine regional divisions. The concerted opposition of forty-three chief constables faced with losing their empires successfully forced Clarke to abandon such a visionary change. This opposition was just as successful in hampering the early development of NCIS, which in mid-1994 suffered a re-organisational upheaval, which actually reduced some of its units, as a result of unremitting county divisional and London Metropolitan police sniping.

The most common criticism was that duplication between county and regional forces and the NCIS would endanger the outcome of investigations. In the case of the United Kingdom, it was a weak charge: there are within the NCIS computer systems to warn NCIS and local force convergence.

But any discussion involving technology must be widened both to include yet another obstacle to a European FBI and to reinforce the argument for its creation. There are so many different computers operating in so many different law enforcement agencies in so many different countries on so many different systems that, if cyberspace didn't have limitless capacity the disharmony would be deafening.

All Europe's national police forces use computer systems. So do their regional forces. And their sub forces: in Belgium, for example, in addition to the three state authorities there are sixty other police units covering security, railways, aeronautics, maritime control, health, post and telecommunications, Customs and immigration. And more.[12] Every state security agency utilises them, and doesn't believe it is bound by data protection laws, which it therefore doesn't observe. Every Customs authority is run by them. Finance ministers and their fraud investigators employ them. Interpol boasts that its technology leads the world. It is in computer files that Europol enters its criminal intelligence, which the fifteen national forces do their best to collate: by computer, of course. The names of *all* doubtful, prohibited or undesirable entrants into the European Union are on the Shengen Information Service database. And because they are not part of Shengen and are therefore not supplying or receiving countries, the United Kingdom, Ireland and Denmark separately record that sort of detail on their own immigration databases.

Hardly any of these computer systems are programmed to communicate with anyone else. Two high ranking European police officials, one Belgian, the other German, quite independently complained[13] to me about the practical difficulties of even beginning to *think* of harmonisation. The German, perhaps predictably, was the more specific: 'There is *some* liaison, between Customs and the various drug authorities. But it's little more than a drop in the ocean. Certainly insufficient even to be described as the sort of cooperation there should be: *everyone* has to come aboard, not just an isolated few. There are far too many escapes, for those who want to take them. There's the convenient hideaway of data protection differences, which will take years to resolve. Then the problem of systems compatibility. Which is more years. And the language barrier,[14] which is the weakest excuse of the lot but still there. But most of all there's that ever-present lack of political will, the anti-Europe attitude.'

CHAPTER TWENTY-EIGHT

The Dirge of the Dreadnought

The dreadnought was a supposedly invincible class of warship when Britannia ruled the waves. Sometimes admirals chose them as their flagships. Sometimes, wisely, they didn't: no matter how thick a dreadnought's skin, it transpired that it could be sunk, after all.

The 117-clause Criminal Justice and Public Order Bill was the dreadnought launched by Britain's Home Secretary Michael Howard – the European equivalent of an Interior Minister – after his get-tough-jail-works-hit-them-hard announcement had been greeted with a rapturous standing ovation at the Conservative Party's annual conference in Blackpool in October 1993.

Never in the history of shipbuilding was a vessel so badly holed beneath the waterline *before* it was launched, than was Howard's flagship bill when it finally wallowed out into doubtful law.

In 1993 he brought the party conference to its feet with the sound-byte cry: 'Prison works . . . Let's take the handcuffs off the police and put them back on the criminals where they belong.' Let's indeed. At the next conference, a year later, the party faithful remained firmly seated. They were still waiting. Of the twenty-seven undertakings with which Michael Howard created so much excitement in 1993, only one had become law. That, predictably, was greatly to reduce warning cautions from police for minor offences and prosecute instead.

The abandonment of an already chipped-away pillar of English justice for more than three hundred years, a suspect's right to silence under police questioning, was the provision in the Bill most fiercely condemned by the legal profession, the judiciary and the police.

For three hundred years anyone facing police interrogation had been told: 'You do not have to say anything unless you wish to do so, but what you say may be given in evidence.'

Arguing repeatedly that silence enabled criminals to escape justice, Howard changed the whole basis of Britain's innocent-until-proven-guilty legal system, making it possible for a court to draw an inference of guilt if a person said nothing. Howard did this by replacing twenty-two easily understood words with a clumsy sixty. They were: 'You do not have to say anything. But if you do not mention now something which you later use in your defence the court may decide that your failure to mention it now strengthens the case against you. A record will be made of anything you say and it may be given in evidence if you are brought to trial.'

Howard's justification for this – supported by an erosion in a previous Justice Act[1] – that 'an innocent man has nothing to fear' was nonsense. It is precisely the bewildered innocent, frightened at being in police surroundings – perhaps for the first time – who has everything to fear. A professional criminal plans his defence at the same time as he plans his crime. Which is *before* he even commits it.

With a single voice Britain's judiciary, legal profession, police and penologists condemned Howard's change. Civil liberty groups threatened challenge before Europe's human rights tribunals.

Perhaps emboldened by the fact that, although it had been criticised in the Bar Council's response to a Royal Commission on Criminal Justice, there had been no overwhelming opposition to the earlier legislation,[2] Howard pressed on. Previous Home Secretaries deplored the right-to-silence abandonment when the bill went before the House of Lords, Britain's upper house of parliament. The Law Lords in the same chamber loudly echoed the denunciation. Howard told his peers he would re-introduce anything they cut out when the legislation returned to the House of Commons for final ratification.

The fatal damaging shot to Howard's retrogressive proposal came in September 1994, from the European Court of Human Rights, the two-tiered civil liberties tribunal in Strasbourg that, with galling irony, Howard had himself been discreetly trying to undermine for most of that year. A ruling of the lower of those tiers, the evidence-assessing Commission, brought to public awareness the fact that the famous British right to silence had in fact already been smothered by five different Acts[3] governing financial crime. Under those various statutes, fraud investigators were empowered to compel suspects to respond to their enquiries. Refusal was punishable by two years' imprisonment. The reasoning behind such fundamental encroachment was that the sort of people suspected or guilty of such crime would be highly intelligent, with access to immediate legal advice. Such an argument could, of course, be used equally forcefully against the sweeping-aside provision in Howard's new bill, removing as it does the protection from people who might not be so intelligent.

Confronted by the compulsory legislation, City of London high-flyer Ernest Saunders provided Serious Fraud Office detectives with the evidence upon which was based his prosecution in 1990 for false accounting and theft. Saunders was jailed for five years – although released after only ten months on health grounds – for taking part with three others in a price-supporting share-rigging scheme immediately prior to the take-over of brewing giant Guinness, of which he was chairman.

Upon his appeal to them, the civil liberties Commission ruled that Saunders had been denied a fair trial under Article 6 of the Convention on Human Rights because he was 'compelled to incriminate' himself. That judgement has formally to be confirmed by the higher European Court of Human Rights but Britain's legislature anticipate the confirmation to be automatic.

Despite all this, Michael Howard has steamed blithely on with legislation that will inevitably be over-ruled whenever it is challenged in the future. Which, just as inevitably, it will be whenever a conviction is obtained by it. So during the coming years English justice, once the envy of much of the world, will instead become a laughing stock, costing millions of pounds in compensation and bring about the reversal of sentences on the very people Michael Howard seeks to jail, the organised professional criminal.

Admittedly the European process is cumbersome and slow – the fault through which Howard sought to undermine it – and could take several years to endorse over-turning verdicts that the United Kingdom will then be legally obliged to accept. When it does, though, the way will be open for Saunders' conviction to be quashed and for him to claim substantial amounts in costs and compensation. As it will be for everyone else convicted under Howard's Criminal Justice and Public Order Act. And as it will be also for those convicted, like Saunders, under the financial legislation that had already been established by the five earlier statutes which, it should be made clear, Howard did not steer into law. Many of those convicted will be guilty, but will have an escape provided for them by the law. Anthony Scrivener, a former chairman of the Bar Council and a persistent critic of recent changes in British law, conveyed the near-to-unanimous opinion –and some of the despair – of Britain's legal establishment when he said: 'Michael Howard seems to have forgotten that Britain is in Europe. The right of silence will be upheld by Strasbourg and, once that happens, Mr Howard will not have done much good for crime. His legislation will simply have ensured that someone got off.'

Britain is a bound signatory to the 1951 European Convention on Human Rights. None of the protocols and provisions of that Convention, however, have ever been put into English law. Yet English law is, obviously, what must be followed and imposed by English judges, who then find it, under the European treaty, challenged – as it was by Ernest Saunders in 1994 – and reversed. Between 1983 and 1991 – with the single exception of Italy – the British government had more cases brought against it and suffered the ignominy of more adverse judgements than any other country in Europe. And in that shameful statistic are included some countries in the formerly repressive communist East.

In February 1995, Liberal Democrat peer Lord Lester QC, introduced into the House of Lords a private members' bill which by the end of that year could lead to the House of Commons finally debating the incorporation of human rights legislation on to the British statute books.

In a vain plea for the government to introduce a Bill of Rights, the Lord Chief Justice, Lord Taylor, warned[4] as long ago as 1992 that its disregard of the European Convention on Human Rights brought British justice into serious disrepute.

In a televised lecture[5] Lord Taylor complained: 'Our ratification of the Convention obliges us in the end to accept it, but our refusal to incorporate means that acceptance occurs only after a decision in Strasbourg, much delay and humiliation. It is as if we said in 1950 the well-known prayer "God make us good but not yet." The standing and reputation of our justice system becomes badly bruised.'

Later in that same lecture, criticising goverment restrictions on legal aid, Lord Taylor issued a further warning, also disregarded: 'If the rule of law and citizens' rights are not safeguarded, the result may be not only the injustice but even unrest, especially during high unemployment.'

Michael Howard's dislike of the Strasbourg court not only ostracised him from a Europe of which he in any case had no wish to be part, but also led, according to insiders,[6] to fierce cabinet disputes with Foreign Secretary Douglas Hurd, a former Home Secretary with views diametrically opposed to those of his successor.

The human rights tribunal, which is part of the Council of Europe and totally separate from the European Union, wanted to avoid delays in its adjudications, which can take up to five years, increasing to as long as ten with the addition to the 1951 Convention of countries from the former Soviet Union. Those additions brought to thirty-two the number of signatories. Under the 1951 provisions judges from every one of those countries have to adjudicate in the upper, ratifying court. At a member-country conference in Vienna in 1993 it was agreed that a 32-judge tribunal would cause an already snail-like legal machine to grind practically to a halt. The streamlining decided upon, aiming to bring rulings down to two years, was to combine the two structures into one tribunal. At the same time every European citizen's mandatory right to appeal against injustice, abuse and discrimination would be guaranteed. Thirty-one countries agreed. Britain didn't.

The view of Michael Howard – opposed by former Home Secretary Douglas Hurd – is that the right to appeal should remain non-mandatory enabling any government to prevent, if it chooses, its citizens' access to Strasbourg. Howard also argues that such rights should be subjected to regular review.

This dispute is neither the only nor the most divisive between the two government ministers. The widest separation is over the cornerstone of Britain's law and order system: prisons.

Against a mass of evidence and opinion to the contrary, the Home Secretary remains adamant that prison *does* work. 'Of course it does,' he insists.[7] 'It stops those in prison committing crimes and it deters others from committing crime.' He is an avowed admirer of the US quick-to-jail policy, despite statistics that show it doesn't reduce crime. Setting out his philosophy Howard wrote[8]: 'A new fashion has grown up (in Britain) to attack punishment as unfair, out of date and ineffective. For centuries people took it for granted that punishment deterred people from committing crime. Reward for good behaviour, penalties for bad behaviour. But since the sixties powerful sections of opinion have called all this into question. I will have nothing to do with this nonsense.'

Two very powerful sections expressing such opinions have been Howard's own party, and a much-respected Tory judicial think-tank. It is composed of members of the judiciary, civil servants, journalists (who attend on the understanding of total secrecy) and criminologists. There is also American representation. It convenes every year at Ditchley Park, a stately home in the county of Oxfordshire. The Home Secretary of the day always attends. In 1989 Douglas Hurd was that Home Secretary, and in day-long discussions he agreed with his legal advisors and policy-makers that everything possible should be done to *prevent* petty criminals being jailed. Before the conference were statistics showing that fifty per cent of adult male prisoners committed further crimes after their release. Jails, the Hurd-chaired meeting decided, were 'universities of crime'. In a later government discussion document, prisons were identified as 'an expensive way of making bad people worse.'

The United Kingdom has the highest jail population in Europe – in excess of 50,000 and growing at the rate of 450 a week – with a large number of these not even convicted but on remand awaiting trial.

In the judgement[9] of Frances Crook, Director of the Howard League for Penal Reform (the name of which had nothing whatsoever to do with the Home Secretary) 'this gross over-use of prisons is a matter of national shame'. She further accuses Howard of 'ineffective and hysterical tough posturing'. In August 1994, the League sent for a legal ruling from the United Nations a report claiming Britain that was breaking international law, under Article 21 of the UN's Universal Declaration of Human Rights, to which it is a signatory, by privatising three prisons.[10] 'The shift towards commercialisation is accompanied by an unacceptable decrease in accountability,' said the report forwarded to the UN. Also in August 1994, a British newspaper[11] disclosed that of the 40 deaths in UK prisons in the preceding eight months, eleven were suicides. The youngest was 17 and most of the deaths had occurred in young offenders' institutions: five were among remand prisoners awaiting trial for minor offences.

Harry Fletcher, from the National Association of Probation Officers, pointed out[12] with unsettling logic that if prisons really did succeed in reducing crime, the country would be dismantling jails, not busily building six new ones. Research from Howard's own department yet again contradicts him: calculated against the 1994 prison population, an additional 12,000 people would have had to be jailed to reduce crime by just one per cent. 'Research suggests that is not a cost-effective solution.'[13] John Bartell, chairman of the Prison Officers' Association, believes[14] that jail over-crowding destroys any prospect of rehabilitation, confirming the 1989 think tank's description of jails as universities of crime. In the annual report[15] of the National Association for the Care and Resettlement of Offenders director Vivien Stern warns: 'A punitive approach does not prevent crime or protect society but will instead make society more violent and less safe . . . if newspapers describe delinquent children in terms more appropriate to wild animals, then they and their families will feel that is how society regards them and respond accordingly. Within such a framework, crime and disorder can only grow.'

Condemnation comes from the legal profession also, led by Lord Woolf, who conducted a 1990 enquiry into a £1 million-plus riot at Manchester's Strangeways prison. He recommended a re-examination of drugs criminalisation, and accused the Home Secretary of policies that were 'shortsighted and irresponsible'. Prisons, he claimed, were 'a shocking waste of resources.[16]' Lord Scarman and Sir Frederick Lawton, both Law Lords, agreed.[17] Sir Thomas Hetherington, a former Director of Public Prosecutions, pointed out[18] that similar policies in America had done nothing to reduce the US crime rate. Anthony Scrivener thought[19] the Home Secretary was ruled by political dogma, and chose to ignore all evidence to the contrary. Scrivener even quoted another finding of Howard's own Home Office department. 'Most criminals are not violent and for many of those who commit them, punishment in the community is likely to be better for the victim, the public and the offender.' Expressing his own opinion, Scrivener said: 'What makes the government attitude so hypocritical is that their financial policy actually means that there is no money to prosecute hardened criminals – we can only afford to caution them. This is why we have the highest crime rate ever and less criminals going through the courts.'

Lord Woolf persisted with his attack on Howard's policies in the House of Lords in February 1994, stimulating a debate in which Labour Baroness Mallalieu, a part-time judge, declared: 'A party which is desperate to regain favour with the electorate has seized on genuine fears about rising crime and thrown itself wholeheartedly in support of the ill-informed prejudice of the "lock-'em-up" brigade within its own ranks for a bit of popularity.' Picking upon Howard's reputed interest in the opinions of Britain's popular press, Baroness Hilton sneered: 'Our Home Secretary is effectively governing by tabloid press. It is irresponsible if not immoral to follow the dictates of the media and the public's desire for revenge.'

All of which was (and is) the sort of nonsense Howard is happy to ignore. Even within his own department he has gained an upsetting reputation for ignoring – sometimes refusing to meet – his most senior advisors whose views he does not want to hear.[20]

Demanding prosecutions from the police rather than cautions, the Home Secretary declared[21]: 'It is totally unnecessary to have persistent offenders thumbing their noses at authority or, worse, bragging about the experience of being cautioned.' Two days later in another get-tough declaration,[22] he said: 'If we are concerned about the protection of the public, you cannot simply put to one side the extent to which the public are protected while people are in prison.' With continuing syntax problems Howard added: 'If you are concerned about reconviction . . . then the statistics don't really demonstrate that those who have been in prison re-offend to a greater extent than those who have not been sent to prison.' Jails were, he decreed, to be made more austere and not be 'places where prisoners enjoy excellent facilities and simply while away their time at leisure[23].' There had to be a mandatory life sentence for murder, irrespective of the extenuating circumstances – which a judges' committee[24] has suggested they are responsible enough to take into account at the time of the trial – thus properly retaining the ultimate penalty for serious and recognisably violent killings.

The removal of a suspect's rights to silence is not the only controversial provision in Michael Howard's Criminal Justice and Public Order Act.

Under the new regulations, courts were able to impose terms of imprisonment on juveniles as young as ten were, within months of the Bill becoming law, thrown into disarray in March, 1995, by the

Law Lords restoring the age of criminal responsibility from ten to fourteen. Until that ruling, the law in the United Kingdom had – as the result of a decision a year earlier by Britain's Court of Appeal – given England the lowest responsibility age in the European Union. Fourteen is the age in Germany, fifteen in Denmark and Sweden, sixteen in Spain and eighteen in Belgium.

Under Howard's Act secure detention provisions for persistent offending children between the ages of twelve and fourteen ranged from six months to two years and the maximum possible sentencing for 15-to-17 years olds was doubled. There may be convincing arguments for another Howard innovation, taking a DNA sample from every man convicted in the United Kingdom of an indictable crime, not just of rape, but it risks challenge before the human rights judges of both the European and United Nations adjudicators. Also, although just *one* fatality from an overdose of an impure or kitchen-manufactured drug is too much, so was the police power to ban 'rave' parties at which such tragedies occur. New age travellers rarely vote, so there is no electoral risk in fettering their nomadic life style with police-enforced restrictions on rock festivals. Home and property owners have every right to protection from squatter invasions, but if the UK had a better, more consistent policy towards its homeless confrontational legislation against the country's disadvantaged would not have been necessary in a Bill supposedly designed to combat serious and organised crime. The 'catch-all' Act even criminalises unsolicited windscreen-cleaning youths who pounce on motorists at traffic lights and pressure them for a tip.

Within just thirteen days of premier John Major having offered[25] yet another law and order sound-byte – a citizens' Partnership Initiative to create an 'anti-yob' culture – Howard, who had earlier declared an end to ill-judged attempts by the social services[26] to rehabilitate persistent young offenders, announced a policy of physically demanding regimes for community-based sentences. Parents were made responsible for ensuring that their children completed their sentences. If they failed to do so they faced fines of up to £1,000. And if they didn't pay (you've guessed it!) they could be jailed, presumably in one of the British prisons which Michael Howard has determined to make 'more austere'.

Like Whitemoor was supposed to be austere.

This £58 million, three-year-old prison, near March in Cambridgeshire, has within its perimeter what amounts to an inner jail, in which are held top category and violent inmates. It's called a special secure unit, which was found to be very special indeed when Judge Stephen Tumim, Her Majesty's Chief Inspector of Prisons, visited it in February 1994. Warders were waiters and skivvies, he found, hurrying to clear lunch plates upon which IRA convicts had served steak and chips to their Sinn Fein visitors. The steak had come from local supermarkets, like the lobsters sometimes featured on the menu, all obediently bought by warders given daily shopping lists. The prisoners, who were not required to work, were allowed to spend as much private cash as they wanted, in addition to a weekly allowance of £13.80, more than double that earned by prisoners in the outer jail, who did work. There was unlimited access to telephones for calls anywhere in the world, for which these special inmates did not have to pay. There was a fully equipped gymnasium. There were video facilities as well as television: warders rented the latest movies on their lobster-and-steak shopping expeditions. There were no cell searches: the prisoners were allowed so many personal possessions that the task would have taken too long.

On 21 July an alarmed Judge Tumim submitted a report to Michael Howard, warning of a 'dangerously cosy relationship' between the ten special unit prisoners and their twenty warders. In the judge's opinion, the unit was 'out of control', creating a emergency that needed immediate corrective action. It was not the only – nor the first – warning about Whitemoor that Michael Howard had received. On 1 January, Lady Olga Maitland, a Conservative MP, had visited the jail and that same month sent the Home Secretary a detailed account of the 'hotel style' regime inside the special unit. The austerity-pledging Home Secretary did nothing. On 19 September an armed robber and five IRA prisoners – one of whom, Patrick Magee, had been involved in the attempted assassination of Margaret Thatcher and the British cabinet in Brighton's Grand Hotel bombing in October 1984 – shot their way out of Whitemoor's inner compound. They had two handguns, one of which is now believed to have been smuggled into the jail in an Indian take-away meal collected by one of the waiter-warders. On 22 September a police search of the jail, prompted by the break-out, uncovered 2lbs of Semtex explosive and three detonators in a storage container, to which only warders supposedly had access, that was used to hold prisoners' belongings. The explosives were more than sufficient to have blown a hole in the outer wall, close to which the six were recaptured.

In December 1994, a report into the Whitemoor fiasco by Sir John Woodcock, the former Chief Inspector of Constabularies, called it 'a disaster waiting to happen' and itemised 64 recommendations which the Home Secretary – who denied any personal professional responsibility although conceding it was 'a dreadful state of affairs' – undertook to implement.

Michael Howard is distrusted by British police as much as he is distrusted by the judiciary. In early 1994 he inherited from his hardline predecessor, Kenneth Clarke, a report by Sir Patrick Sheehy proposing police reforms. These reforms proposed abolishing some senior ranks, and suggested that police should work fixed-term contracts in a system of performance-related pay scales based on experience, responsibility and the difficulties of the job. Not surprisingly, the Sheehy report hit a stone wall of police opposition. The Home Secretary capitulated on every contentious proposal.

He continued, however, to clash with the British judiciary in his interpretations of the law. At the beginning of November 1994, the Court of Appeal ruled that Howard had abused his powers when he introduced a new cheaper scheme to compensate victims of crime. Later the same month the High Court ordered Howard to make available to six men, who were alleging a miscarriage of justice, evidence they claimed to be in their favour that he was withholding.

Such confrontations followed a previous furore over the Police and Magistrates' Courts Bill, another flagship proposal by the Home Secretary, one of the major principles of which was an overhaul of local authorities control of their individual police forces, that would impose upon them supervisory committees of sixteen members with Home Office-appointed chairmen. Those committees had to work within objectives laid down by the Home Secretary. In what police understandably interpreted as a harbinger of job cuts – which despite official denials were *exactly* its intention – the Bill also gave the government powers to simplify Kenneth Clarke's amalgamation of forces which had earlier been successfully delayed by chief constable opposition. Other Sheehy proposals were included also.

Once again there was universal condemnation at what was seen as Michael Howard appointing himself supremo over every organisation, authority and regulatory body responsible for policing in the United Kingdom.

As they were to do later, with Howard's Criminal Justice Bill, former Home Secretaries and senior Law Lords fired salvo after salvo at the proposals of the Police and Magistrates' Court Bill. During a withering debate in January 1994, in the House of Lords,

Labour's former leader and one time Home Secretary, Lord Callaghan, charged Howard with being 'a wilful and ambitious' occupant of the office. Lord Chief Justice Lord Taylor found 'chilling' the controls Howard intended imposing on magistrates. Lord Whitelaw, a former leader of the House of Lords and a revered elder statesman of the Conservative Party, said it was inevitable that the paid chairmen of the local authority police committees would be regarded as the 'Home Secretary's men'. He was, he said, 'anxious and worried' at the power Howard wanted to assume for himself, through proposals originally advocated by his predecessor.

In consequence Michael Howard withdrew all the clauses that would have, in effect, destroyed the historic separation of the police from political manipulation. In February 1994, he declared: 'These changes will put the independence of police authorities beyond doubt. The bill has never sought to centralise control over the police, nor to threaten the independence of police authority, but there is obviously a need to remove this fear.'

The police service of the United Kingdom did not – justifiably – lose its suspicion of Michael Howard. Richard Coyles, chairman of the Police Federation of England and Wales which represents Britain's rank and file constabulary, predicted that, from the time of our meeting,[28] within ten years police strength in Britain would be decimated by cost-cutting economies into a privatised two-tiered system – to the detriment, not the improvement, of law and order. Within a year of our conversation – quite apart from station-closing economies – there was confirmation of that forecast in September 1994, when the use of civilians, very few of them sworn-in special constables, was proposed in community patrols. This absurd 'street watch' proposal created the spectre of vigilantes – earlier foresworn by Howard – and risked a depleted, over-worked law enforcement system, already sometimes unable to respond to genuine emergency calls, being inundated by well-meaning do-gooders playing Sherlock Holmes. According to Howard: 'The police cannot be everywhere at once. Street watch can provide many thousands of extra pairs of eyes and ears, passing on to the police vital information in the fight against crime. It will not in any way take the place of the police.'

By January 1995, the infighting between the police and the Home Office had forced into yet another U-turn much of the changes envisaged in a year-long Home Office study entitled *Review of Police Core and Ancilliary Tasks*.

Richard Coyles and the 126,000 policemen he represents were not convinced. They had every reason not to be. Too many of Howard's proposed funding economies had already leaked from a disenchanted Home Office. And there was that Police and Magistrates' Courts Act: one of the provisions in it Howard didn't drop was the total control it gave him over police budgets.

As he moved to exercise that control he was warned – as he had been warned before – that he was making it impossible for police in the United Kingdom to perform their legally assigned function. Which was, after all, the enforcement of law and order to which Howard was so publicly committed.

Howard's proposed economies for 1995–96 slashed police funding throughout England and Wales by tens of millions: £92 million was cut from the budget of London's Metropolitan Police alone, leading Sir Paul Condon bluntly to complain: '(The formula) may impair the Commissioner's ability to discharge his responsibilities in respect of national functions and capital city policing particularly and the policing of London generally.'

The Association of Chief Police Officers denounced Howard's budget as 'entirely untenable.'

The most obvious result of the economies was a countrywide freeze on police recruitment in 1995. London, in addition to that, risked a reduction of almost 1,500 in its number of officers. Staff cuts were as high as 17 per cent in some constabularies. The recruitment ban for 1995–96 was not, however, a new experience for the chief constables of England and Wales. Public expenditure restraints had frozen recruitment in 1994. And in the year before that. And in the year before that. In 1993 there had been the irony of South Wales Chief Constable Robert Lawrence warning that the economies threatened his force being declared inefficient by the Inspector of Constabularies: Howard himself had been born in South Wales, in Gorseinon, between Swansea and Llanelli.

In February 1995, the Derbyshire Constabulary *was* declared inefficient by Constabulary Inspector Geoffrey Dear – for the third year in succession. It needed, the Inspector found, an immediate cash injection of £40 million. A Home Office 1995–96 infusion of an extra £6 million would not, in the inspector's opinion, solve the problem.

Not only did Howard's cost-cutting proposals contradict law and order pronouncements. They also for the first time conceded that unemployment was a crime-contributing factor. Every judge, police official, probation service and rehabilitation group, as well as ignored analysts within the Home Office itself, had insisted this for years but the Home Secretary and the Prime Minister had previously just as insistently denied it.

Michael Howard's economies, eroding morale throughout the United Kingdom police as fast as it eroded jobs, came at a time when some surveys[29] estimated the total cost of crime in Britain to be as high as £20 billion a year: £10 billion of that was business fraud. Only 4 per cent of stolen property was recovered and only 9 per cent of an estimated £450 million taken from commercial undertakings was ever located. Another survey[30] put at £7 billion the annual cost of crime committed by people aged between 10 to 20, out of a total yearly loss of £17 billion. That particular survey had been conducted during a period when the government was reducing youth scheme funding by several million.

A triumphant welcome might have been expected from the Home Secretary for the announcement in September 1994, that the amount of crime recorded by the police showed a drop of 5.5 per cent, the biggest reduction for forty years.

It didn't come. The figure of 5,400,000 offences tabled by the police was more than double what it had been when the Conservative Party came to power in 1979, on a law and order platform. Cause for the reticence came in November, 1994, when the government published a survey[31] admitting that from 1987 to 1992 crime in Britain and Wales had risen by 44 per cent, the fastest increase during the same period not only in the EU but anywhere else in the developing world.

Even the police statistics for 1994 gave Howard little cause for celebration. There was no drop in crimes of violence or sex: those offences – which cause most fear and concern among the public – showed an increase of 6 per cent. The greatest reductions in those late 1994 police figures – 93 per cent – referred to property crime. Burglaries were down by 107,000, to 1,300,000, thefts were down by 8 per cent, to 2,600,000, and vehicle crime showed a reduction of 136,000, to 1,400,000.

On the same day as the police figures were made public, the Home Office itself released far more reliable statistics in its bi-annual British Crime Survey. That survey was compiled by Home Office researchers questioning in the closest detail 14,500 victims of crime on every aspect of their experience. The survey suggested crime in the United Kingdom had risen 18 per cent

between 1991 and 1993 and that for the year covered by the police –
who had logged 5,400,000 offences in 1994 – the truer figure was
18,000,000, only just over a quarter of which were reported and
recorded. For the first time the annual survey proved that, either to
protect no-claims bonuses, prevent insurance premium increases
or because they lived in such high crime areas that they felt they
would be wasting their time, people were not reporting crime.

The need for Michael Howard to fight so many rearguard
actions on behalf of his Criminal Justice and Public Order Act and
the Police and Magistrates' Courts Bill, has overly delayed his
introduction of criminal justice measures some lawyers argue are
far more important.

One of these was the much promised authority to investigate
miscarriages of justice, of which appeal courts in the United
Kingdom have found too many disturbing examples. Another
measure proposes to correct a failing in existing British law that
requires the prosecution to name witnesses that it intends later to
produce in court. Disclosure provisions result in hundreds of
guilty people in Britain escaping justice, through trials having to be
abandoned either because of witness intimidation or to protect the
lives of undercover informants. In 1994 six separate trials of Yardie
groups on charges of murder, drugs and fire-arms offences
collapsed after witnesses were terrorised into 'forgetting'. Sixty
prosecutions in which the National Criminal Intelligence Service
was involved in just one year[32], were cancelled to prevent men and
women who would have been intimidated or killed if their
identities had become known. A Bill to curb the disclosure rules –
which will be fiercely protested by civil rights groups – was
scheduled by Howard to be announced at the end of 1995 and
enacted during 1996.

Paradoxically, the disclosure rules which brought about such
miscarriages had been introduced to prevent very public abuses
that did so much to discredit British jurisprudence.

At the time of our meeting[33] Richard Coyles, the leader of the
Police Federation of England and Wales, was understandably
proud of the procession of fledgling police authorities from East
Europe seeking British constabulary advice on the establishment of
their own forces: a Polish delegation was leaving as I arrived.
'We're the best in the world: the obvious role model to follow.'
Coyles was equally quick to defend his members against accusa-
tions of perjury and dishonesty in the long litany of over-turned

convictions[34] that, in addition to damaging the reputation of British justice, have cost millions in appeal court costs and damages compensation. The majority concerned people accused of murder: one set-aside verdict was that upon Winston Silcott, found guilty for the murder of PC Keith Blakelock during a riot on a London housing estate in 1985. 'Not one British policeman brought to trial on any charge involving perjury or conspiracy to pervert the course of justice in relation to these cases has ever been convicted,' Coyles stressed. Which is true, although the entire regional crime squad of the West Midland Constabulary, many of whose officers were involved in one such miscarriage – six men wrongly jailed for the bombing of two Birmingham pubs that cost twenty-one lives in 1974 – was completely disbanded by their chief constable.

The courts' failure to convict any policeman did not impress Bar Council spokesman Anthony Hooper, either during our meeting[35] or in his substantial contributions to the Council's response to a Royal Commission on Criminal Justice. In that response Hooper wrote: 'We all have experienced examples of what appears to us as professionals to be clear police dishonesty, albeit that it would often be difficult to prove it in a criminal case against the officer. It has often been said that the dishonest police officers are merely rotten apples. Although in one sense that is true, the rottenness is not always confined to individual officers. It is too often rottenness in a squad, in which junior officers are introduced to dishonesty by their senior officers. When senior officers are involved, it seems unlikely that the dishonesty is not widespread. Nor is it likely that the officers were dishonest only in this case. An honest officer may suddenly become dishonest for one case and then become honest again – but it is unlikely.'

Despite opposition in the House of Lords and throughout the judiciary to the sort of centralised power Michael Howard sought in his Police Bill, it will be necessary for a measure of centralisation to evolve – eventually – so that a British FBI can be created. The National Criminal Intelligence Service – so bitterly opposed by regional and county constabulary – still sees itself in that role some time in the future. But there is another determined claimant to the role: the ambitious MI5, Britain's counter-intelligence agency.

Anxious to keep her 2,000 strong empire intact after the collapse of communism and the fragile ceasefire in Northern Ireland, MI5's Director General, Stella Rimington campaigned in 1994 for it to grow. She had already managed, in a blood-letting internecine war, to take over all aspects of Northern Ireland terrorism from the police-based Special Branch, so she then went on to attack its function on the Europol liaison commitee.

In a 1993 MI5 brochure – the first ever – that explained the service's purpose, Mrs Rimington acknowledged her agency's increasing role in Ulster and disclosed that 44 per cent of its resources and £150 million budget was devoted to Irish and 'other domestic terrorism'.

It was natural – and even logical – according to Mrs Rimington, for MI5's remit to extend further, taking over every sort of terrorism, and even gaining for itself a niche in the country's enforcement and interception efforts against drugs. Accordingly, in August 1994, MI5 was given – together with Britain's external service, MI6 – what was described as a support role to police in general, and NCIS in particular, in monitoring the influx of Russian and East European mafias into the country.

Officially the Home Office response to the suggestion that MI5 should become more of an FBI was to repeat an argument of Kenneth Clarke, when he was Home Secretary, that drug trafficking and organised crime had not reached the level of threatening the UK's economy, which was necessary before the intelligence agency could become involved under its authority charter, the Security Services Act, 1989. So great is the profit from organised crime and its use of Britain's financial services that it is possible for Mrs Rimington to argue convincingly against such a rejection.

And for a Home Office already starving its regular law enforcement authorities of resources and manpower to transfer policing roles to MI5, which has an already-accepted budget, would be a convenient and cost-effective way of operating under Treasury restraint.

The Police Federation's Richard Coyles implied deep suspicion when he talked[36] of a 'hidden agenda' totally to change the traditional methods and practices of policing the United Kingdom.

Part of that agenda is hardly hidden any more. If fully implemented – which every effort will be made to ensure over the coming years – such proposals as Michael Howard's pose a threat to civil liberties far more insidious than any Orwellian prediction.

Governments, using their what-has-an-innocent-man-got-to-fear argument, will, of course, fervently deny it. They always do.

CHAPTER TWENTY-NINE

A Question of Identity

It is not scaremongering to describe some of the closed-door people monitoring discussions in the European Union as Orwellian. To compare what the writer of *1984* envisaged, with what technology-aided governments can already do, is in fact to understate. They haven't achieved robotic mind control yet, but then they scarcely need to.

Constantly evolving computer technology provides the mechanism and the modern version of an identity card is its key. The Council of Europe's 1981 Data Protection Act[1] is inadequately out of date in its uneven country-by-country adoption throughout the Union providing little protection from abuse, both unofficial and official.

Once the long and wearisome road to political compromise and legal harmonisation has been travelled, properly used computer science could be a formidably effective weapon against the masonically-guarded organised crime mafias that are ever tightening their grip on the European Union.

This provides governments with a strong argument in favour of their invading individual privacy. The justification advanced to me in five[2] of the fifteen EU countries went beyond the unfearing honest-or-innocent man rationale. The sometimes vehemently added insistence was that citizens demanding protection against crime had to surrender liberty.

What was never expanded in such arguments was how *much* liberty people needed to sacrifice in this computer controlled age.

Every country in the European Union, even the United Kingdom, operates a variety of voluntary or compulsory ID schemes, either an actual card or a PIN number with the same function. In a United Kingdom traditionally hostile to carrying identity documentation, until 1994 a little realised link existed between National Insurance numbers and income tax records. In that year, however, the government introduced initiatives that I believe[3] will in coming years prepare the electorate for pervasive, intrusive and potentially oppressive legal ways by which it will be officially and unnecessarily scrutinised.

Instead of being openly called an ID card – which it is – the United Kingdom's surveillence will utilise newly-designed, credit-card-style driving licences. What about the approximate 30,000,000 – more than half the population – who don't *have* driving licences? No worries, Big Brother: there's still that National Insurance number, which will be included on another plastic rectangle – the Carecard – linking in with a nationally accessible computer database. Plans were finalised in 1994 for such cards to replace the 57,000,000 pension and benefit books issued each year. As such cards are held by the old and the socially disadvantaged – the most unlikely two groups to be covered by the driving licence listings – they will do nicely, won't they?

For each card there is a totally defensible need.

Britain's new driving licence, carrying a photograph of its holder – common practice in many countries in the world – is intended to prevent impostor friends sitting driving tests for others, and to stop licences borrowed from such friends keeping disqualified drivers illegally on the road. The new computerised medical card is intended to make it impossible for unentitled foreigners to receive free treatment – and fraudulently to obtain free prescriptions costing £30 million a year – under the UK's national health system. And also to reduce £5 billion a year social security and benefit cheating.

Their potential misuse by prying government authorities and law enforcement bodies (in the name of protecting the law and keeping good public order) and by organised crime (for fraud, theft, blackmail and financial manipulation), derives from the fact that they are not just pieces of plastic. They are smart-cards, equipped with computer chips upon which can be stored every conceivable aspect of a person's life.

When in August 1994, Transport Secretary of State Brian
Mawhinney announced the introduction of the new pictorial
driving licences, gradually from July 1996, replacing the old upon
which a signature was the only authentication, he strongly denied
any infringement upon personal liberty. He did, however, admit
that there were future 'improving' plans. It was left to his
department to concede that the eventual information on the
computer chip would 'doubtless' contain next-of-kin information,
address, occupation or job description, place of employment, all
previous driving details (including possible court appearances),
insurance details, blood grouping, allergies and organ donor
permission. It was also technically possible to add retina patterns –
a further identification technique tested in Germany and the United
States – and DNA profile. And, to make that computer bridge to
the UK's secondary ID card totally toll-free, the holder's National
Insurance number would be there, too. Through which could be
accessed the Carecard which would complete its holder's entire
medical record and history. And if that history involved any
private, insurance-paid hospital treatment it would provide an
avenue to bank records.

Although it is officially denied, I know[4] detailed consideration
was given in government committee early in 1994 for facilities to
widen the police's on-the-spot ability to 'read' smartcard licences.
It was discussed at the same sessions – two in cabinet – that decided
against a police request for an addition to the new licences;
fingerprints. I believe their eventual inclusion is another of Dr
Mawhinney's 'improving' measures. The fingerprint addition was
strongly pressed upon Michael Howard by a Chief Constables'
committee which like the Police Federation, advocates the introduction of an identity card by its proper name. The Chairman of
the Chief Constables' group, West Midland's police chief Ron
Hadfield, made no secret of what they wanted after one Home
Office consultation in April 1994. 'There is a window of opportunity here. If we are going to the expense (£500 million) of putting
photographs on driving licences then why don't we go one stage
further and put a thumb print on them as well?'

Although at that stage the government held back from including
fingerprints, I know[5] it did agree to allow the police in future to
have full access to the computer at Swansea, in South Wales, where
details are available of the 32 million drivers registered on the
records of the Driver and Vehicle Licence Authority. Prior to that,

police checks on drivers were restricted to the Police National Computer on which is logged information concerning the country's one million disqualified drivers.

At the time its files were made fully available to the police, the Swansea record centre was evaluating revolutionary technology by which it is possible, according to its inventors,[6] to isolate and track suspect vehicles anywhere in the United Kingdom. The system, based on neural network techniques which ape the function of the human brain, was perfected after scientists succeeding in programming a computer to 'recognise' any wanted registration number from pictures taken every one sixth of a second by a motorway-mounted camera.

By the time of its introduction, the police will be able to use the United Kingdom's new photograph-bearing driving licence in an equally sophisticated way. The photographs on the British licences will be digitalised and stored in computers from which they can be machine read and matched. In America a research company[7] has perfected a technique, using similar neural principles as those employed on wanted car checks, that enables a surveillance camera to photograph and digitalise twenty faces a second, and to compare them with pictures on an existing digitalised database. The process is so sophisticated it can penetrate any attempted disguise.

Simon Davies, visiting fellow of Law at Essex and Greenwich Universities, estimated[8] that by 1996 – the same year as the new British driving licence introduction – a machine developed from the American research would be capable of comparing 50 million faces in less than sixty seconds. He predicted its use in Britain within a decade, by which time every driver in the country will be faceprinted in Swansea. And not just the drivers. Motorway cameras which already have the capacity automatically to register an over-fast driver from his number plate and get his address from the South Wales licensing authority for a speeding summons will, within the same ten years, be photographing to digital perfection every car's occupant as well. The technique will also be available to every security camera in every shopping precinct, street monitoring location, bank, shop or supermarket.

The use of motorway cameras – and their contribution to a pool of personal information so vast as to be almost beyond human comprehension – does not end there. By 1998 it is intended that Britain's 2,000 mile motorway network will be toll operated. Toll fees will be automatically deducted from electronically-charged

Smartcards, triggered by a motorway sensor, which every motorist will have to carry in his car. Motorway cameras will record anyone trying to cheat by not 'charging' his card to activate the payment system: which at the same time will create a method for police forces to know when – and where and at what time and with whom – anyone is, anywhere in the country.

And not just in the United Kingdom. Within the time frame anticipated by Simon Davies there will be hugely improved liaison between law enforcement authorities, despite any unevenness of individual data protection barriers. In an opinion[9] given in 1994, Davies wrote: 'Within ten years every computer on the planet will have the ability to speak to any other computer on the planet. There will be a vast web of information and technology touching every aspect of our lives. We will need to be "recognised" by this web. We will need to establish our credentials to move within it.'

And the photograph-carrying, finger-smudge imprinted, retina-flickering Smartcard with its DNA profile will not be the only method by which a person will be identified. Already, in 1994, innovated at New York's John F. Kennedy airport and in testing operation at Amsterdam's Schipol terminals, a voluntary identification system helps frequent travellers to obtain a security clearance card bearing an electronically coded version of their palm print. If, on arrival or departure at either airport, the pressed-down palm on a scanner matches that on the pre-recorded digitalised card, there is no further security check. Unless, of course, the record is required by an enforcement agency using an investigation of a possible crime or offence to justify – even if it bothered with such justification – its access beyond the proclaimed purpose of the system.

Unrestrained access to monitoring technology can, of course, be convincingly justified by quoting occasions when such access has solved major as well as minor crime.

The two children who murdered tiny Jamie Bulger were caught by a shopping precinct security camera. So were two Harrods bombers. Police were able to place the child serial killer Robert Black in the vicinity of each of his murders by timed and dated cash withdrawals from bank dispensing machines.

The all-important caveat to such arguments is that access should not be *unrestrained*. Without a single exception, every authoritative law and order thinker in the European Union whom I met during the two year preparation of this book insisted – despite their equally unanimous recognition of the successful entrenchment of organised crime – that satisfactorily to fulfil its function and retain public confidence every police force should be governed by proper accountability.

Which amounts, surely, to stating the obvious? Or does it? Isn't it stating nothing more than a hoped-for minimum standard with the unspoken understanding of how difficult that standard always will be to attain?

From which questions, predictably emerge further caveats.

Like the fact that concern at the increase and level of crime is such that too great a proportion of the population, and far too many working policemen, acquiesce in rule-bending and corner-cutting: sometimes, even, such acquiescence descends the perilous slope that ends in miscarriages of justice, when ready acceptance is made that the law has to be broken in order for it to be upheld.

Further, it must always be recognised that *no* intelligence agency, either in or out of the European Union, with its blanket responsibility to safeguard the security of the nation in whose name it functions, observes the restrictions under which publicly-accountable constabularies and gendarmaries are expected to operate.

Indeed, to come to the final cynicism, governments themselves, despite public protestations to the contrary, not infrequently expect their intelligence agencies to perform in such ways. Legislation which might exist to stop this happening is ignored, oversight committees or tribunals certainly can't challenge the accuracy of what they are told by intelligence chiefs whose very *raison d'être* is secrecy.

Wasn't Britain's SIS, condoned by the government of Margaret Thatcher, prepared to see jailed businessmen whom they were actively encouraging to provide forbidden weapons systems to *both* sides in a Middle East war?

Can any intelligence service, set those sort of standards by politicians they serve, be expected *not* to abuse, access, tamper with and regard as an information harvest cultivated just for them, every technologically-gleaned tid-bit, irrespective of why or for what it was originally collected?

It was Richard Helms, a former Director of America's CIA – fined $2000 in 1977 for lying under oath to an agency-monitoring Congressional oversight committee – who uttered the core philosophy by which all clandestine organisations (including those in every country in the European Union) work. An intelligence agency, according to Helms, was the 'bag of tricks' for the executive.

It is only when the cat gets out of that bag – as it did with the Matrix Churchill arms embargo trial – that law-abiding citizens of the EU get a blurred insight into how governments and their permanent enforcement bodies interpret the laws and the human rights they so self-righteously proclaim they uphold and protect.

And with that blurred insight comes a warning of how endangered those rights are.

CHAPTER THIRTY

Thinking the Unthinkable

During the researches and writing of this book I have become increasingly convinced that the creation of an effective, pan-European law enforcement agency is an urgent priority. But that no proper political will exists among EU member states to form such a body. Perhaps more importantly – and obstructively – even if that will could be generated, the various national enforcement agencies are too jealous of their individual territories to bring about anything like the sort of harmonisation that is absolute essential but at the moment totally lacking. Having reached such a depressing belief, I find it difficult to offer any constructive suggestion as to how the mafias I have described might be confronted, even minimally.

Seizing their vast wealth is perhaps the most obvious way of defeating them – ideally through the proper use of computers. I personally believe there is another way.

It is the almost unthinkable step of the decriminalisation and ultimately legalisation of currently illegal drugs.

Should it really be *so* unthinkable to propose decriminalisation? If the spiral of constantly rising drug profits were broken, would that not break the back of organised crime? Doesn't the equally spiralling number of drug addicts in every country in the world need to be halted, stabilised and then reduced?

There can surely be one answer.

In 1985 I published an investigation[1] into worldwide illegal drug trafficking, in which I suggested that the possession of cannabis for personal use should no longer be treated as a crime. Except by a very few, the idea was condemned as ill-judged liberalism: the drugs scourge had to be met with 'battles' and 'wars' and 'new initiatives', which were going to cleanse society of abuse, and of the abusers and their suppliers. To even whisper the word 'decriminalisation' was to give in. Admit defeat. Unthinkable.

By 1994, however, the idea of changing this drugs policy had been advocated by the head of Interpol, by leaders of the British judiciary, by senior officers of the Metropolitan Police – including a former Commissioner – by innumerable commentators, professional treatment specialists and learned criminologists. Declaring 'We've won several battles but we've lost the war,' West Yorkshire Chief Constable Keith Hellawell announced at the Association of Chief Police Officers' 1994 conference that decriminalisation was now the policy of their association's drugs committee of which he was chairman. At their annual conference, the British Medical Association called for a report from their Board of Science to consider the 'benefits or otherwise of decriminalisation or legalisation'. The law had been changed in Italy and a British government survey[2] found thirty per cent of the UK population to be in favour of a change. Another idea I floated in 1985, to be greeted with ridicule, had been widely adopted: by 1994 sterile needles were being issued to addicts in most countries in the European Union to reduce the risk of AIDS and other infections.

I do not give these examples to promote myself ahead of time in the vanguard of radical opinion. I do it solely to show how far and by how much official and public attitudes have changed over a nine year period. Nine years from now – and I hope far sooner – maybe cannabis will be officially accepted throughout Europe, rather than unofficially as it is now, and, while I fully recognise the dangers and fully anticipate the appalled counter arguments, I trust that the decriminalisation debate will have been extended to include heroin and cocaine.

It should be. It desperately needs to be.

The stark, unarguable fact is that the worldwide policy of criminalising the taking of certain drugs (but not others) has not worked. And will never work. Ever. To continue it is pointless, a complete waste of the millions poured into it. But worse, far worse, making certain drug takers criminals is an abandonment by governments of proper concern for the health of their citizens.

The abject failure of liquor prohibition in America between 1920 and 1931 makes a tattered but valid analogy. The only effect of attempting to stop Americans drinking alcohol was to make multi-millionaires out of 1920s organised crime bosses: a Pontiac once owned by Al Capone was the jewel in the vintage car collection of the drug supremo Pablo Escobar. The only effect of trying to stop people taking drugs has been to make billionaires out of 1990s organised crime bosses.

While the drug barons grow richer the number of addicts grows larger, the misery increases and health deteriorates. I believe unnecessarily.

What I wrote in 1985 remains just as true today: 'For thousands of years people have taken substances to improve or heighten their feelings. And always will, despite all efforts to prevent, dissuade or penalise them. Some actually *need* drugs.'

So a wide range of currently illegal drugs should be available, legally, sensibly and most importantly of all, under proper medical control. Eventually to reduce, not increase, the abuse. And to reduce every sort of crime associated with it.

I am not, for a moment, proposing a junkies' charter, although I shall be accused of that by blinkered critics. I am proposing the absolute reverse – that at last governments acknowledge reality and stop using anti-drugs campaigns as a guaranteed law-and-order vote catcher. Making drug-taking illegal actually undermines that very crime-fighting commitment they claim to have, but do so very little to uphold. Which they know very well but ignore, because it is unpalatable. Similarly, they choose to ignore the true cost, in every meaning of the word, of their hypocrisy because that's unpalatable, too.

In February 1994, Labour leader Tony Blair tried to make political capital by linking the cost – in monetary terms – of drugs and crime. He asserted that drug addicts in the United Kingdom stole around £2 billion a year to finance their habits. Admittedly, there are no empirical statistics upon which to base that claim, but six months later a report by the National Association of Probation Officers did at least produce statistical evidence that half of Britain's one million solved burglary, theft and property crimes were committed by people addicted to drink or drugs. The £2 billion estimate can be supported also by Home Office figures which put the value of illicit drugs consumed in Britain at around £1.8 billion, most of which comes from crime, while cost of police and Customs efforts to enforce narcotics legislation – again a Home Office figure – is an additional £500 million.

A British drug cost figure of £3.3 billion was suggested by the Tory government in October 1994, when it announced yet another initiative, together with the totally ambiguous acknowledgement that – although they had no intention of joining it – a decriminalisation debate had merit. If drug consumption continues to be treated as illegal, such incredible costs – for Britain alone! – can only soar. The Pompidou Group's assessment of a £131 billion cost for the whole of the European Union also can only soar. And with it – going ever upwards – will inevitably rise the number of robberies and burglaries and muggings and thefts.

That's the monetary cost, inseparably linked to the growth of crime. More important, in my opinion, is the human cost. People die, mostly not from the drugs themselves but from unreliable levels of purity or from poisonous adulteration. AIDS and other infections are spread. Children – male and female – become whores. Babies are born addicts to mothers who are addicts. In the case of crack, babies are often permanently mentally impaired. Despairing addicts, uncounselled and destitute, commit suicide.

Shouldn't the whole enormous cost – in money and crime and human lives and human dignity – be halted?

If drugs were legally and medically provided – hard drugs such as heroin through clinics, and soft drugs such as cannabis in supervised 'coffee shops' as they are in Holland – there would be no reason for addicts to steal or prostitute themselves. Crime would inevitably drop, just as at the moment it is inevitably rising. Purity and strength and administration would be controlled, so there would be far less overdosing or death or sepsis.

Decriminalisation is *not* giving pyromaniacs paraffin to play with, a *carte blanche* for abusers literally to burn themselves out. Once again, it's the absolute reverse. By legally providing drugs the users would be put into a medical environment where their needs – and their problems – could be handled *completely*. An environment which would include counselling and education and advice. Most countries in the European Union regard drug abuse as a health problem. Why isn't it *properly* treated as such?

The idea will, of course, be derided by the 'lock-'em-up-and-throw-away-the-key' lobby, personified by the current British Home Secretary who in 1994 increased to £2,500 the maximum fine for possessing soft drugs, including cannabis – a measure that will be sensibly ignored by most British police forces who, like most enforcement authorities in the EU, will continue dealing with personal possession as they have for a number of years, by a caution. The immediate warnings from police and judiciary in the UK that the only effect of raising the maximum soft drug fines would be to increase the jail population with people unable to pay did nothing to dissuade Mr Howard. He remains a firm believer in incarceration, despite other and earlier warnings that the easiest place to obtain any drug of choice is in HM prisons. By early 1994, in fact, prison authorities were creating official drug-free wings in British jails for inmates wishing to escape the rampant narcotic environment to which they were being sentenced.

Certainly the concept of decriminalisation – and most definitely the merest idea of legalisation – would be anathema to the current Conservative government of the United Kingdom, although some Home Office officials privately admit the legalisation of cannabis use is only a matter of time. In June 1994, at the same conference at which Mr Hellawell revealed their decriminalisation policy and Interpol's Raymond Kendall advocated a change in Britain's drug policies, Mr Howard told the Association of Chief Police Officers 'This government has no intention of legalising any currently banned drug. To do so would be bound to increase the human and social damage, especially that inflicted on the young.'

That 30% support for decriminalisation in the survey I've referred to was *only* for soft, not hard drugs. And Tony Blair made it quite clear when he linked the cost of drug addiction to property crime that Britain's Labour Party was firmly opposed to any legalisation.

A possible change in drugs policy is widely and publicly debated in Germany, where in April 1994, the constitutional court in Karlsruhe ruled the possession of small amounts of marijuana or hashish should not be a punishable offence. Chief Superintendent Jurgen Maurer, the country's anti-organised crime chief, said the police attitude was that addicts only became criminals in order to pay for their habits and 'we have to decriminalise these people'. Frankfurt and Hamburg, both with heavy addict populations, operate what amounts to a non-prosecution policy, sometimes even with hard drugs. So do Belgium and Spain and Portugal. None – including Germany – risks voters' disapproval by actually passing a totally permissive law, although I predict Spain will be the first to follow the example of Italy. Rome's decision to allow the possession of small amounts not just of cannabis but of cocaine and heroin was taken in order to reduce its jail population. Although not full legalisation, it was an acknowledgement of what the British Home Secretary refuses to accept, that draconian laws fill jails but do nothing to reduce addiction. At the time of Italy's law change, in January 1994, it was revealed that 15,000 of Italy's 45,000 prison inmates were drug addicts. France does not differentiate between hard and soft drugs, imposes fines calculated from the value of drugs seized (in which the value of any smuggling vehicle can also be included) and has publicly stated that it intends to retain a policy of repression. There has, however, been extensive parliamentary debate about relaxation of law. One enforcement official, who talked with me on condition of anonymity,[3] suggested that the discussions were intended to encourage a referendum that would vote down any easing of restrictions 'and finally close the issue dead'. French criminologist Professor Xavier Raufer disclosed[4] that French police customarily retain five per cent of any drugs seized, particularly heroin, with which to pay informers. He saw no likelihood of any change in French repression.

Switzerland, which will eventually join the Union despite having once rejected membership by referendum, began in 1993 issuing medical prescriptions to a limited number of heroin addicts as a controlled experiment.

It is a common misunderstanding that Holland, universally condemned as over-permissive by anti-drug campaigners, has specifically relaxed drug legislation. It hasn't. What Holland does is treat drug use pragmatically.

That pragmatism extends to allowing cannabis-supplying 'coffee houses' where the availability of soft drugs is usually proclaimed by a marijuana-plant motif. There was just such a motif on the coffee house I visited[5] close to Amsterdam's main railway station. Inside there was a thick smell of what I learned later was cannabis: *niederweit*, (what the British call skunkweed). The available selection was listed, items on a menu. It was a noisy place, a lot of laughter, but not rowdy. Tina Turner was the loudest of all, singing 'Private Dancer' on the juke-box.

I joined a table occupied by a girl who introduced herself as Ingrid. Her boyfriend was Henry. It amused them and others around to have a curious foreigner at the table. I accepted their claim to be Dutch: foreigners are not supposed to be sold cannabis. It was all they ever took, they both insisted. It was better than alcohol. Ingrid said she rarely drank; Henry 'not much.' They didn't do other drugs, although they had been offered them on the streets. *Niederweit* was enough. Theirs wasn't a regular habit. Weekends, mostly. That day neither had lectures at their university. They hadn't set out intending to come to a coffee house: it had started to rain, and this place was somewhere to shelter. They thought the attitude of other countries ridiculous. Henry wanted to be an architect, Ingrid 'something with children'. Would she let her children smoke cannabis? Of course. Why not? It was better than letting them drink gin. Would I mind my children coming into such a place? No, I admitted. Well? they asked, enquiringly. And waited. I tried to buy, to test the rules. And was refused. By that time I had been singled out by a wider audience as a questioning foreigner. I am not convinced I would have been refused if I had tried to buy as soon as I entered.

When I met[6] Dutch criminologist Dr Jan van Dijk, he conceded that the coffee shop concept had 'not worked very well'. Moves were being considered to reduce their numbers, especially those close to the Belgian and German borders: too many had opened, profits were too high and they were advertising internationally, which they were not allowed to do. Dr van Dijk didn't mention Maastricht, but the city is perhaps better known in Europe for the drug situation its geographical position creates than for the treaty that was signed there. Maastricht is a cartographic oddity, so close to so many borders that just outside the town it's possible to stand in Belgium, the Netherlands and Germany at the same time. More than a thousand 'drug visitors' come every day to smoke cannabis in Maastricht: the town has almost forty coffee houses to serve the influx. Showing typical Dutch pragmatism, Dr van Dijk said: 'I don't think we can in any way prevent people from taking the train or car and driving there or to Amsterdam and buying their soft drugs. It would also be unreasonable, we think, from the German and Belgian point of view, to expect us to do that because that would really mean total overhaul of our drugs policy and there is absolutely no feeling in Holland amongst the main political parties that we should change the policy. I think everyone agrees that we want to have our own drugs policy but we don't want to cause problems for our neighbours.' In one of the most revealing statements during our discussion Professor van Dijk added: 'We are also convinced that in the year 2000 everybody (in the European Union) will have adopted our policies. So why should we change?'

Professor van Dijk considered the year 2000 to be an important date: if drugs were still criminalised at that time, the professor shared the pessimism of his countryman, Euro-MP Pieter Stoffelen, that crime would permanently defeat law enforcement.

Although technically laws exist that enable prosecution, no action is taken against anyone in Holland for possessing – for personal use – heroin or cocaine. Professor van Dijk anticipated both being properly legalised. 'Most of our chiefs of police repeatedly go public with this idea that this is what should happen.' The concept of total decriminalisation attracts little public opposition. The professor believed there was a parliamentary majority in support, as well: the only hesitation might be the political reaction from the rest of the European Union.

The need to change Britain's long-standing official attitude to drugs is gaining acceptance among influental thinking jurists and certainly among treatment specialists. Janet Parker, director of the British government's National Youth Agency, urges open discussion on soft drugs. So does Sir Peter Imbert, former Metropolitan Police Commissioner. Commander John Grieve, head of the Metropolitan Police Criminal Intelligence Branch, has called for research into the possibility of licensing users and suppliers.

Lord Woolf, one of Britain's most respected judges, has publicly expressed the most outspoken and radical opinions of all. At the end of 1993 he advocated wide ranging relaxation, linking drugs to the high cost of crime ahead of the Labour Party's warning. In a speech[7] he said: 'Should we not at least be considering whether it would be preferable for drugs, or at least some drugs, to be lawfully available in controlled circumstances, so that it would no longer be necessary for addicts to commit crimes to feed their addiction?'

The former Lord Justice of Appeal did not limit his outspokenness to drugs alone. A week before Lord Woolf's address, Home Secretary Michael Howard – who in my opinion limits any concensus of opinion strictly to views he wishes to hear – had thumped the law and order drum by announcing twenty-seven new anti-crime measures. Lord Woolf commented: 'Statements are being made that now is the time to get tough on crime. Such talk is short-sighted and irresponsible. The difficult option is to try to identify the underlying causes of criminal conduct and then set about tackling those causes.'

Concern about British jurisprudence was justified. But, insisted Lord Woolf: 'It would be a terrible mistake to squander resources on short term palliatives, window dressing, which instead of making the situation better would make it worse.'

It is upon the need to strip away the vote-catching window dressing and properly use instead of squandering the available resources that the liberalisation debate is predicated. I see relaxation of suppression as the method to encourage addicts voluntarily to go into a medical environment in which their drugs are available, although controlled: into an environment where they could be made well. Interpol's Raymond Kendall – a long-time critic of the inability to enforce Britain's drug laws – couples his call for the end of punishment with the demand that users should, instead, be forced to follow treatment in a specialised centre. Expanding that view[8] on a radio programme he said: 'I think you must have some means of getting the abusers into treatment programmes and there is a certain coercion necessary to do that.

British drug legislation and treatment programmes *are* a mess, despite a late 1994 re-examination, entitled *Tackling Drugs Together*, which promised fresh approaches and allowed itself at least to mention the dreaded word, 'decriminalisation'. Unfortunately there is a depressing lack of cooperation between the Home Office, the Department of Health and the Ministry of Education, which share the responsibility for enforcement, treatment and anti-drug advice, with a slight input – topping-up finance to rehabilitation agencies – from the Department of Social Services. The appointment in December 1993 of Privy Council President Tony Newton to chair a central drugs co-ordinating unit was confirmation of the need to sort out the confusion. Part of the new unit's function was to ensure that the £500 million a year drugs budget was well spent. Unmentioned was the fact that eight months earlier the government had made local authorities responsible for allocating as they see fit the £22 million it had previously specifically apportioned to fund 140 residential rehabiliation centres. Or the fact that local council grant reductions – later reversed – had been made for anti-drug education in schools. Seven anti-drug campaigns over a nine-year period from 1985, each costing an average of £2 million, failed to reduce the drug-taking population of the country by a single per cent. A narrow shaft of light briefly flickered in December 1993, when thirteen British MPs signed a motion critizing as 'an affront to individuals, civil and human rights' the then existing drug legislation. Mr Howard ignored them.

The problems of decriminalisation are formidable, as are the arguments against it. And there is, additionally, binding international anti-drug legislation[9] to which all members states in the European Union are signatories. Even so, if governments dare think the unthinkable and show the political will, the problems *can* be overcome, the disputes resolved and international legislation amended.

The Pompidou Group's Christopher Luckett[10] believes that the drug czars of Asia and Latin America – and after them the organised crime tradesmen – will fight, literally, rather than be put out of business. To break this stranglehold would for the first time in years correctly earn the boast of a proper, worthwhile 'war against drugs'. All the producer countries, with the exception of Afghanistan, are Western aid recipients. The threat to withhold that aid – if seen to be genuine – would be a powerful incentive for those countries to legalise their production.

Richard Coyles, chairman of the Police Federation of England and Wales, ridiculed[11] decriminalisation with an analogy. Burglary was increasing yearly, but no-one advocated the absurdity of legalising burglary. So why should drug taking be legalised, just because the addiction rate always went up? But surely that supports, rather than detracts from, the thought of relaxation? Doesn't escalating house robbery make up the greatest proportion of the £2 to £3 billion worth of crime committed every year to fund drug use? If addicts didn't have to steal to pay whatever price was demanded, property crime – burglary chief among them – would plummet.

Far too few doctors are prepared to regard drug users as people in need of medical care, despite the 1994 BMA decision to consider decriminalisation: too often the belief is that an addict's condition is self-inflicted. Medical attitudes would need to change, as they have already gradually changed so that the abuse of alcohol, a legally-available drug far more dangerous than most, is now accepted as a disease. Furthermore, the abuser of proscribed drugs is not physically bringing upon himself the cancer or the heart disease self-inflicted by the chain smoker of cigarettes, a legally available drug far more difficult to kick than heroin.[12] General practioners need not, anyway, totally bear the additional treatment responsibility of persistent drug users. The £500 million currently spent on failed prevention could fund rehabilitation centres and clinics. Such centres could just as easily be provided with money saved from their drug suppression budgets by every other country in the EU. And once they were established – and *trusted* by addicts – proper research could be conducted into the causes of addiction, and proper staff training and addict education could be carried out.

Reforming drug legislation is not the perfect answer. There isn't one. Most drugs will leave their scars. Many addicts will take a long time to learn to trust clinics, and will continue buying and suffering on the streets. Drug-related crime will not totally disappear. The Mafias and the Cartels and the Triads and the chapters *will* fight, to keep their market going. Relaxation would probably, initially, result in an *increase* in abuse. This is by no means certain, however: when English law was changed in 1990 allowing pubs to remain open all day, drunkenness did not increase. A government – better still, more than one government, each to support the other – would need an iron will if it was to pass laws sanctioning the supplying of mind-destroying crack and nose-rotting cocaine to its citizens. And it would need great courage if it was not to collapse when public opinion turned against it, which in the beginning it surely would.

But the ills and the failures would, in the end, be far less than the steadily worsening ills and the failures being suffered at the moment. The flood of illegal profits so huge that organised crime is on the brink of beating existing legal systems would finally be blocked. The unstoppable tidal wave of drugs *would* be stopped. Petty crime, the break-ins and the car thefts and the muggings, would plunge. Fewer people – most important of all, fewer young people – would get hooked.

So which is the country most likely to show the iron will necessary to evolve a drugs policy beyond Italy's prison-clearing move and Germany's tentative first step?

The Netherlands is the most obvious. And certainly it was their leading criminologist, Professor Jan van Dijk, who confidently predicted the rest of the European Union would have adopted his country's pragmatism by the year 2000. But even the Netherlands' pragmatism is a step back from actually enacting the permitting legislation. And from other people in Holland I detected a retreat from the freedoms they had allowed themselves in the past.

Coincidentally, in remarks made only five weeks apart, Italy's leading anti-Mafia judge, Liliana Ferraro[13] and French criminologist Professor Xavier Raufer[14] both used practically identical phrases to predict that organised crime would continue to flourish in Europe until its excesses so outraged public opinion that governments would be forced to act – to have the will imposed upon them – irrespective of any immediate anti-popularity consequences.

The cost of waiting until that happens is surely too great to bear.

Conclusion

The European Union *is* gripped by organised crime, each of its member nations squeezed internally by syndicates that are externally partnered by the totally uncontrolled mafias of the East and the West. It is the best – and biggest – business in the Community, conducted by boards of masonically-linked directors and their laundering financiers with tax-free, murder-sanctioning efficiency.

And through petty jealousies, myopic opportunism and a total lack of any genuine pan-European political will on the part of the government of the fifteen, no effective, federal law enforcement agency is being created to oppose it.

Pieter Stoffelen and Professor Jan van Dijk and the far-sighted few who agree there is a now-or-never time limit for concerted action against overwhelming lawlessness are right.

Crime *is* winning. Perhaps permanently.

It would be foolish to expect the absolutely essential cohesion of national wills to arrive overnight. Would that it could.

But neither can it be delayed for the sixty years predicted by Professor Xavier Raufer. I do not totally ascribe to the dire do-or-die belief in a two-year period after which action will be too late. But the threat cannot be overstated: if the EU is to evolve anything like the organisation that is essential for organised crime's containment, then the process must begin *now*, and be pursued with the utmost urgency.

Which is all such a strategem can ever be, one of containment at as low a level as possible. For organised crime to be completely eradicated Europe would have to be turned into a totalitarian police environment, which fortunately can never happen. A philosophy to which I *do* ascribe is that a country without crime *is* a country without freedom.

The need of course is for a delicate balance to be struck between total freedom and total repression. If the growth of organised crime is to be reversed, all law-abiding citizens will have to accept certain curtailments of their civil liberties. The degree of curtailment is the choice of the people – of *all* the people. They have only to scrawl an X on a ballot paper to express that choice. And scrawl it differently the next time, if they make the wrong decision at their first attempt.

Every country in Europe is allegedly democratic, its government utterly dependent upon the ballot box. In the hands – literally – of the raped and the battered and the slashed and the mugged and the burgled and the cheated is the power to curb all those crimes. But always at a price. Are they willing to pay that price in losses of individual freedom?

The fight against the mafias does not need to be heralded by sound-byte pronouncements of toughness and new initiatives and clampdowns. It needs to be a decision made by vote-dependent governments that they will properly accept – which *none* fully do – that they are part of a European federation of countries, and that they must therefore create a federated legal system capable of dealing with a pan-European organised crime problem.

So far only a re-united Germany that has found itself the unwilling host to the indigenous mafias of Europe and their Frankenstein nuclear-smuggling cousins of the East has anything like the necessary political will. Unfortunately – because Germany sees itself as the law and order engine for the whole of Europe – this is more the obstacle than an encouragement to the rest of the EU's member nations.

The legal and emotional hurdles that divide Europe more formidably than any Himalayan range must be surmounted. Europol must be made operational.

The opinion I expressed at the very beginning of this book has been many times confirmed by its end: *no* country forming part of the Community is truly committed to or sufficiently interested in a complete, nationhood-sacrificing union of Europe. And the

United Kingdom is the standard bearer of those dismissive nations to which federalism, which eventually has to be accepted no matter what placebo word is used in its place, is total anathema.

European – and world – crime really is too powerful and well organised for fence-straddling ministers to go on fudging and vacillating: their threadbare words like *tough* and *crackdown* and *battle* and *war* will provide scant protection against the bullets which the Yardies and the Cosa Nostra and the Chechen and the Rodriguez Orejuela Cartel scatter from their automatic weapons. Those bullets maintain crime supremacy, utterly unaffected by sound-byte pontification.

I sincerely believe that the decriminalisation of drugs is the way, eventually, to halt and in time reverse the drug epidemic infecting Europe. Just as I believe that the pursuit and seizure of their billions is the most effective way – perhaps the *only* way – to fight not just the drug producers and traffickers, but every other type of criminal as well. And that this seizure could be achieved by proper and effective use of computer technology.

The decriminalisation of illegal drugs needs political courage. The pursuit of illegal money needs federally compatible seizure laws and federally compatible data legislation, and a federated European police body to enforce those laws.

Drugs *will* be decriminalised. And however great the resulting social upheaval may be, it will be better than the existing status quo. For the first time in any British government policy document, the *Tackling Drugs Together* Green Paper of October 1994 allowed in an appendix that 'the debate can be conducted in good faith by responsible people who can respect each others' views'. This was hailed by some commentators as a step in the right direction. It was scarcely more than a tiptoe. Talk, yes. Legislate, no. In presenting that consultative examination to the British House of Commons, Tony Newton declared: 'We will not legalise or decriminalise any currently banned drugs.' Conflicting though the two statements appeared to be, in announcing *Tackling Drugs Together* Newton honestly admitted – another first – that all traditional policies of crackdown and punishment had failed. 'This is a new emphasis in our approach. Enforcement in itself is not enough to fight drugs.'

Newton's three year, multi-million programme introduced sensible changes of direction. British schoolteachers are to be taught properly how to give anti-drug lessons, within the State school curriculum. One hundred local action teams will coordinate local drug policies, throughout the country. And the almost inevitable advertising campaign was for once designed to inform and educate, not simply to shock.

In early months or even years of the drugs legalisation process, abuse and misery may well get worse before it finally gets better. And democratic governments will be electorally pilloried and will be tempted to revolve in dizzying U-turns. Some will fall for the temptation. But one day drug abuse will be reduced to medically manageable and socially acceptable proportions – just as the abuse of tobacco has been reduced in the early 1990s.

Meanwhile, the Dolgopruadnanskaya and Chechen and Ramenki and Ostankino mafias of Russia will route through twenty new international airports in a virtually unpoliced country the cocaine and heroin produced by their Latin American and Asian mafia partners.

Along with another multi-million dollar commodity, nuclear material.

The Armageddon potential of fissile material laid out for sale as if on a market stall – and it truly is that easy to obtain in the corruptly-policed, mafia-dominated former Soviet empire – stands the horrifying risk of coming true, not only because of the lack of any control in a virtually unpoliced country, but also because no accurate official records exist of what is available anyway.

All the crimes I have illustrated in this book need a pan-European FBI to combat them, but too many one-time Soviet nuclear scientists and technicians have already been lured to the Middle East – and elsewhere – by cheque-waving terrorist governments, and the nuclear leakage from the East demands such an enforcement agency most of all.

Saddam Hussein's generals did not hesitate to murder Iranian women and children (as well as Kurds within his own country) with poison gas in their war against Tehran. Nor would the Fundamentalist zealots of Tehran have hesitated to reciprocate, had they had such weaponry.

Both now have in their employ Soviet nuclear scientists, whose orders for already existing nuclear technology are being amply filled from poorly-recorded, poorly-guarded Russian stockpiles.

And not just Middle East orders.

Within a week – in August 1994 – of German investigators naming Islamabad as the destination for significant quantities of enriched Russian plutonium, former Pakistan premier Nawaz Sharif confirmed his country's possession of nuclear weaponry. Which wasn't all he said. Pakistan was, according to Sharif, prepared to use its atom bombs against its hated neighbour, India. Which also has an atomic capability. Twice since the 1947 partition of Muslim Pakistan from India the two countries have gone to war over disputed sections of Kashmir. It is predictable – although not inevitable – they will again.

The United Kingdom's Home Secretary, Michael Howard, was – for once – right when, at a ministerial meeting on organised crime in Berlin in September 1994, he described nuclear smuggling as the most alarming feature of the new European order. 'We must turn our fine words into fine action' were Howard's own fine words. Since when no fine actions have occurred.

Within the United Kingdom Michael Howard's performance as Home Secretary is lamentable. He should – and will – be replaced. And his departure should signal the amendment of the misconceived, regressive clauses in the Criminal Justice and Public Order Act that are causing so much concern among the judiciary as well as among the general public.

Of course violent criminals should go to prison: and for terms long enough to protect the public. But there is *no* empirical evidence to support Howard's constant assertion that prison works. It doesn't. Prisons are universities of crime, a judgement reached in 1989 by the Conservative Party itself, after it had come to power on a law and order mandate that remained unfulfilled for the following fifteen years – during which time, in fact, the crime rate in Britain grew faster than in any other developed country in the world. And this finding is supported by well-assessed and well-conducted research, some coming from the department of which Howard is head but to whose permanent civil servants he scarcely listens.

In November 1994, the Chief Inspector of Prisons, Judge Stephen Tumim – ignored when he warned of the dangerous conditions in a jail from which IRA terrorists later escaped – pleaded in his annual report for a limit on the British prison population. He warned, too, of the availability of illegal drugs in jails, echoing an earlier Home Office survey for the previous year which had disclosed that drugs were common currency in practically every jail in the country: there were 14,700 internal prison drug prosecutions. Michael Howard ignored every one of these warnings.

In England I did not encounter a single enforcement official or officer who believed that Michael Howard and the British government were sincerely dedicated to maintaining the size and strength of the police force in England and Wales. Statisics support that scepticism: the first four years of this decade were marked by manpower-reducing economies and a move towards the privatisation of many police functions. Unsurprisingly, in October 1994, at the Police Superintendents' Association conference, it emerged that serious crime had become so pervasive in the United Kingdom that in both London and Manchester there had been established special witnesses' protection units to safeguard – from murder or violent intimidation – people needed to give evidence at criminal trials. In two-and-a-half years 127 people in a total of 70 trials had gone into the protection programme. Some had to be given entirely new identities, homes and jobs outside the United Kingdom. Despite such protection – which the Home Office was urged to extend to other forces and areas throughout the United Kingdom – trials continued to be abandoned as a result of intimidation.

On a pan-European scale many important reforms to police machinery and practices could be introduced before Europol gets any operational remit, or before the police forces of the fifteen achieve anything resembling harmonisation.

The opportunity exists with the 1996 review and revision of the Maastricht Treaty, upon which European governments and the Brussels Commission started work in 1994. The most essential overhaul possible was to the constantly-defrauded, money-gorging Goliath of the Common Agricultural Policy. There was also the chance democratically to open up to the sort of public scrutiny that should – but doesn't – exist in some of the closed-door bodies, chiefly the Council of Ministers. And to continue giving greater powers to the European Parliament. Whether any serious reforms will be achieved, however, is very doubtful, obscured and hampered as the negotiators inevitably are by their opposing national views and opposing national electoral pressures.

The main stumbling block to any changes, in London's opinion, is that the underlying thrust of every proposal brings the European Union closer to a federated grouping, which London finds politically unacceptable as a general principle, and all the more abhorrent since Britain will probably be close to a general election when the 1996 decisions have to be taken. There was, in London's view, a further abomination in the recommendation from a Maastricht-updating structural commission that the European Parliament should be given the same powers as those of the national representatives on the Council of Minister. The effect would be to make the Council the Senate of a two-tier Congress. Another suggestion is for all the treaties in the EU to be consolidated into a single constitution, unthinkable again to a government so dismissive of British judges' demands for a people-guardings Bill of Rights.

From my meetings with financial watchdogs like John Tomlinson and Terry Wynn – and others who were re-elected in the 1994 European elections – I know the battle to correct CAP is going to be fiercely and savagely fought, to try to stop the drain of billions a year by fraudsters and organised crime. In Italy, particularly, that battle will not just be political. The traditional mafias of Cosa Nostra and Camorra and 'Ndrangheta are deeply involved in the agricultural cheating and will do everything they can to ensure CAP remains unreformed.

For the first time the European Parliament has as a member the world expert on masonically-shrouded mafias: Leoluca Orlando was elected to the Strasbourg assembly in the 1994 elections. Orlando intends using the European platform constantly to expose and warn of the pernicious, society-within-a-society spread of organised crime throughout not just the EU but Eastern Europe. I am aware, too, of a 1994 re-elected British Euro-MP who intends to attack and expose the masonic and mafia influence in Strasbourg, Luxembourg and Brussels.

Abuses of different kinds will emerge again and again in Europe: for one, thefts of organs for transplant from waifs and mentally retarded children; for another racially-motivated xenophobia. Virtually on the eve of Austria's entering the Community, avowed anti-immigrant politician Jorg Haider's Freedom Party (FPO) achieved a general election vote there that saw the country's two ruling parties lose their two-thirds parliamentary majority. In local elections in Belgium, the anti-immigrant *Vlaams Blok* and *Front National* gained council seats, and in France Jean Marie Le Pen hailed these racist successes with the ominously familiar cry, 'Nationalists of all countries, unite. Today more than ever!' In Italy there was open speculation that Gianfranco Fini, leader of the reformed party founded originally by Benito Mussolini would emerge the leader of the next democratically-elected government of the Second Republic.

Although – apart from Austria and to a far lesser extent Italy –the political shift to the right has not been substantially reflected in the results from Europe's mid–decade elections, it does suggest that the people of the crime-ridden EU are looking for governments traditionally strong on law and order.

Before that tip toe becomes a stampede not to totalitarianism but to flawed, cover-all-and-everything legislation like Britain's 1994 Criminal Justice and Public Order Act, the message should be heard and finally reacted to.

Unless it is the depressing message with which I began this book remains valid at its end.

Crime pays.

Notes

The Wages of Sin

1 Personal interview. Strasbourg. 29.6.93.
2 Detective Inspector Graham Saltmarsh, money laundering expert at Britain's National Criminal Intelligence Service. Paris. 15–16.6.94.
3 Personal interview. Strasbourg. 2.7.93.
4 Personal interview. Palermo. 22.10.93.
5 *Independent* newspaper. London. 24.11.94 and 25.11.94.
6 The Criminal Justice and Public Order Act. 1994.
7 Personal interview. Strasbourg. 2.7.93.
8 Personal interview. Dublin. 15.9.93.

CHAPTER TWO

By Way of the Orient

1 Personal interview with John Hamill. London. 16.11.93
2 Unattributable interview. London. 14.7.93.
3 Unattributable interview. Rome. 25.10.93.
4 Personal interview. Palermo. 22.10.93.
5 Personal interview. Palermo. 22.10.93
6 Unattributable interview. Strasbourg. 28.6.93.

7 Unattributable interview with a source who provided widespread insight into Mafia history and its workings. Rome. 27.10.93.
8 Personal interview. Palermo. 22.10.93.
9 Unattributable interview with Euro-MP. Brussels. 9.11.93.

CHAPTER THREE

Weapons of War

1 Unattributable briefing. Paris. 13.12.93.
2 Ibid.
3 United States House of Representatives' Republican Task Force Committee on Terrorism and Unconventional Warfare. 30.11.92.
4 Iranian Organisation of Atomic Energy. British *Sunday Times*. 26.1.92.
5 *US News and World Report*. 28.3.92.
6 House of Representatives' Task Force Committee on Terrorism and Unconventional Warfare. 30.11.92. and unattributable briefing. Paris. 13.12.93.
7 Max Peter Ratzel, Deputy Head of the Organised Crime Bureau of the Bundeskriminalamt, Federal Republic of Germany. International crime conference. Bramshill, England. May 1993.
8 Ministry of Interior. Bonn. 1.12.93.
9 Wiesbaden. 6.12.93.
10 Unattributable briefing. Paris. 13.12.93.
11 Ibid.
12 Yossef Bodansky and Vaughn S. Forrest. US House of Representatives' Committee on Terrorism and Unconventional Warfare.
13 Unattributable briefing. Paris. 14.12.93.
14 Unattributable scientific monitoring source.
15 House of Representatives' Task Force Committee on Terrorism and Unconventional Warfare. Washington. 30.11.92.
16 Ibid.
17 Ibid.
18 Wiesbaden. 6.12.93. Rome. 24.10.93.
19 London. 4.9.93.

CHAPTER FOUR

Guns Will Make Us Powerful

1 Hermann Goering. Nazi radio broadcast. Summer, 1936.

2 Intelligence briefing. London. 10.2.94.

3 Ibid.

4 London. 10.8.93.

5 Confidential paper to international organised crime conference. Bramshill. Hampshire. 26.5.93.

6 London. 19.2.94.

7 Intelligence briefing. London. 10.2.94.

8 Dublin. 4.12.94.

9 Stephen Rea. Dublin. 16.9.93

10 *The Threat and Impact by Organised/Enterprise Crime upon United Kingdom Interests*. National Criminal Intelligence Service.

11 *Death of a Nation. The Timor Conspiracy*. John Pilger and David Munro. Central Television. 22.2.94.

12 *The International Arms Trade – an Ethical Reflection*. Vatican Justice and Peace Committee. The Vatican. 22.6.94.

CHAPTER FIVE

There's No Business Like Snow Business

1 Christopher Luckett, Pompidou Group. Strasbourg. 2.7.93.

2 Ibid.

3 Pompidou Group assessment. Strasbourg. 2.7.93.

4 Dr Zeigniew Thielle, head of the Polish Drug Treatment Programme.

5 Ibid.

6 Pompidou Group assessment. Strasbourg. 2.7.93.

7 John Benyon, Lynne Turnbull, Andrew Willis, Rachel Woodward and Adrian Beck. *Police Co-operation in Europe*. Centre for the Study of Public Order. Leicester. 1993.

8 National Programme on Drug Abuse Control. *Measures for Drug Abuse Control*. Ministry for Youth, Family Affairs, Women and Health. Bonn. 1993.

9 Luciano Violante, chairman of the Italian Parliamentary Enquiry into the Mafia. Rome. 1993.

10 Italian drugs intelligence briefing. Rome. 25.10.93.

11 General G. Chebotarev, Moscow Ministry of Interior. International police conference. Hampshire. 24.5.93.

12 Drug intelligence briefing. London. 8.1.94.

13 US drug intelligence estimate.

14 Drug intelligence briefing. London. 8.1.94.

15 Ibid

16 The Trevi Group. (Named after the famous fountain in Rome, close to where the formation meeting was held in 1975). A forum composed of Justice and Interior Ministers at its head, with input from crime and judiciary experts. Expanded from its original remit to combat terrorism to include drug trafficking. Widely – and in my opinion justifiably – criticised for lack of accountability. Under the terms of the ratified Maastricht Treaty, Trevi was superseded by the Police Co-operative Council.

17 Dublin. 15.9.93.

18 Ibid.

19 Drugs intelligence briefing. London. 9.2.94.

20 Ibid.

21 Drug Dependancy interview. London. 3.3.94.

22 National Criminal Intelligence Unit briefing. London. 21.4.94.

23 Briefing. London. 21.3.94.

24 National Criminal Intelligence Unit briefing. 21.4.94

25 Ibid.

26 Ibid.

CHAPTER SIX

A Yard Of Their Own To Call Home

1 *The Threat of Jamaican Criminals in the UK: An Outline Assessment of the Threat and Impact by Organised/Enterprise Crime upon the United Kingdom Interests.*

2 National Criminal Intelligence Service. London. 25.2.94.

3 Foreign drugs intelligence briefing. London. 10.8.93.

4 International organised crime conference hosted by the National Criminal Intelligence Service. Bramshill. 25.5.93.

5 National Criminal Intelligence Service. London. 8.1.94.

6 International criminal conference. Bramshill. 25.5.93.

7 National Criminal Intelligence Service. London. 8.1.94.

8 Ibid.

9 Ibid.

10 *The Fix. The Inside Story of the World Drug Trade.* Brian Freemantle. 1985.

11 Foreign intelligence narcotics briefing. London. 10.8.93.

12 National Criminal Intelligence Service. London.

CHAPTER SEVEN

Money Makes the World Go Around

1 Operation Green Ice. Anecdote recounted by Judge Liliana Ferraro. Rome. 28.10.94.
2 P. F. Vallance. C2 Division of the UK Home Office, at the Council of European Money Laundering Conference. Strasbourg. 29.9.92.
3 Personal interview. Paris. 7.9.93.
4 London. December, 1993.
5 Ibid.
6 General Gennardy Chebotarev, Russian Interior Ministry. Conference on Organised Crime. Hampshire. 26.5.93.
7 Palermo, Sicily. 22.10.93.
8 Personal interview. London. 14.7.93.
9 General Gennardy Chebotarev. Hampshire. 26.5.93.
10 Ibid.
11 London. December, 1993.
12 Palermo. 22.10.93.
13 Gerald Mobius. Bundeskriminalamt representative at the Council of Europe Money Laundering conference. Strasbourg. 30.9.92.
14 *Outline Assessment of the Threat and Impact of Organised/Enterprise Crime upon the United Kingdom Interests.* Second briefing. February, 1994.

CHAPTER EIGHT

Rien Ne Va Plus

1 Unattributable interview. Monte Carlo. 17.5.93. And with Professor Xavier Raufer. Paris. 7.9.93.
2 *France-Soir.* 5.1.94.
3 Personal interview. Paris. 7.9.93.
4 Paris Match. 3.8.93.
5 Unattributable interview. Monte Carlo. 18.5.93.
6 Paris. 6.9.93.
7 Rome. 25.10.93.
8 Unattributable interview. Paris. 6.9.93.
9 Ibid.
10 *Paris Match.* 3.8.93.
11 Rome. 26.10.93.

CHAPTER NINE

The French Affair

1 London. 21.1.94.
2 Police briefing. Hyères. 3.3.94.
3 Unattributable interview. London. 14.4.94.
4 Ibid.
5 Police briefing. Hyères. 3.3.94.
6 Unattributable Interview. Toulon. 4.3.94.
7 Ibid.
8 Police briefing. Hyères. 3.3.94.
9 Ibid.
10 Unattributable interview. Paris. 6.3.94.

CHAPTER TEN

There's Something in the Air

1 Briefing. Hans Nilsson. Strasbourg. 30.6.93. Deborah Fisch Nigri, Harrow. 11.1.94.
2 Unattributable briefing from German specialist. XVth International Conference of Data Protection and Privacy Commissioners. Manchester. 27–30.9.93.
3 Interview with Deborah Fisch Nigri. 11.1.94.
4 Guidlines for the Security of Information System. OECD. Paris. 1992.
5 *The Hackers Crackdown. Law and Disorder on the Electronic Frontier.* Bruce Sterling. Viking. London. 1992.
6 British Computer Misuse Act. 1990.
7 Unattributable briefing. XVth International Conference of Data Protection and Privacy Commissioners. Manchester. 27–30 September 1993.
8 *Dealing with Computer Misuse.* Prepared by Coopers and Lybrand Deloitte in association with Cameron and Markby Hewitt. October, 1992.
9 Unattributable briefing. Strasbourg. 29.6.93. London. 15.1.94.
10 Personal interview. Harrow. 11.1.94.
11 *International Herald Tribune.* 11.1.94.
12 Council of Europe Convention for the Protection of Individuals with Regard to Automatic Processing of Personal Data, 1981. Council of Europe Recommendation (R(87)15) on the Use of Data in the Police Sector, 1987. EC Data Protection Directive, 1992. Guidelines for the Security of Information Systems, OECD. Paris. 1992.
British laws: Computer Misuse Act, 1990. Data Protection Act, 1984.

Acts with applications to computer crime; Police and Criminal Justice Act, 1994. Theft Act, 1968 and 1978. Forgery and Counterfeiting Act, 1981. Criminal Damage Act, 1971. Copyright, Designs and Patents Act, 1988.

13 Bonn. 1.12.93.
14 Unattributable briefing. Institut de Criminologie de Paris conference on global Mafia financial power. 15–16.6.94.
15 Unattributable briefing. Manchester. 27–30.9.93.
16 Intelligence briefing. Institut de Criminologie de Paris conference on global Mafia financial power. 15–16.6.94.
17 British Criminal Justice Act, 1994.
18 British Home Office briefing. 7.7.94.
19 Deborah Fisch Nigri. Harrow. 11.1.94.
20 Interview. Strasbourg. 4.11.92.
21 Interview. Strasbourg. 4.11.92.
22 Deborah Fisch Nigri. Harrow. 11.1.94.
23 Interview. Strasbourg. 30.6.93.
24 Chaos Computer Club statement. Hamburg. 15.9.87.

CHAPTER ELEVEN

Snuffed Out

1 London. 15.7.93.
2 Amsterdam. 9–10.12.93.
3 Detective Superintendent Michael Hames. London. 15.7.93.
4 Report (MJU–16 (88) 3) by the Norwegian delegation at the 16th Conference of European Ministers of Justice. Lisbon. 21–22.6.88 on Sexual Exploitation, Pornography and Prostitution of, and Trafficking in, Children and Young Women.
5 Strasbourg. 4.1.92.
6 Unattributable interview. Institut de Criminologie conference on the Global Mafias' Financial Power. Paris. 16.6.94.

CHAPTER TWELVE

Love for Sale

1 Amsterdam. 9.12.93.

2 Amsterdam. 9.12.93 and 10.12.93.
3 Bonn. 2.12.93.
4 Wiesbaden. 6.12.93.
5 Professor Dr Jan van Dijk. The Hague. 8.12.93.
6 European Council of Police Unions conference. Strasbourg. 3–6.11.92.
7 Ibid.
8 By telephone. Paris. 5.7.94. Letter from Versailles. 7.7.94.
9 Apeldoorn. 10.12.93.
10 The Hague. 8.12.93.
11 Mark Fuller. *The Times Magazine*. 28.8.93.
12 NCIS briefing. December, 1993.
13 *Independent* newspaper. London. 6.4.94.
14 European Council of Police Unions conference. Strasbourg. 3–6.11.92.
15 Guidance briefing. Wiesbaden. 6.12.93.
16 *Daily Mail*. London.
17 Video Violence and Young Offenders. Home Affairs Committee. 13.7.93.
18 Superintendent Michael Hames. Scotland Yard Obscene Publications Squad. London. 15.2.93.
19 Paedophile Unit Briefing. National Criminal Intelligence Service. London. 10.2.94.
20 Unattributable Home Office briefing. London. 14.7.94.

CHAPTER THIRTEEN

The Body Snatchers

1 Unattributable interview. Institut de Criminologie Conference on Global Mafia Financial Power. Paris. 16.6.94.
2 Ibid.
3 *Report of the European Parliamentary Committee on the Environment, Public Health and Consumer Protection on prohibiting trade in transplant organs*. 25.2.93. Debate in the European Parliament 13.9.93.
4 *Transplant Organs – a self-sufficiency in blood* (A3–0074/93): Resolution on prohibiting trade in transplant organs. 4.10.93.
5 Paris. 4.7.94.
6 Strasbourg. 13.9.93.
7 *Everyman*. 21.10.93.
8 Leiden, Netherlands. 9.10.93.
9 Telephone interview. 5.7.94.

10 *Le Quotidien du Médecin.* 24.5.93. *Libération.* 20.4.93. *France Presse* 27.3.93.
11 *Observer* newspaper, London. 26.9.93.
12 Ibid.
13 Telephone interview. 4.7.94.
14 *Le Monde Diplomatique.* March, 1992.

CHAPTER FOURTEEN

*Give Me Your Tired, Your Poor,
Your Huddled Masses . . .*

1 Extract from The New Colossus, by Emma Lazarus, inscribed on the pedestal supporting The Statue of Liberty, the first sight that greets immigrants arriving at New York. Presented to America by France to celebrate the centenary of American independence from British rule on 4 July 1776.
2 Committee of Enquiry on Racism and Xenophobia. European Parliament (rapporteur Mr Glyn Ford). Luxembourg. 1991.
3 Asylum and Immigrant Appeals Act. 1992.
4 European Parliament Committee of Enquiry on Racism and Xenophobia. Luxembourg. 1991.
5 Evrigenis Report, 1985. Committee of Enquiry on Racism and Xenophobia. 1991.
6 Unattributable briefing. Strasbourg. 11.11.92.
7 Briefing at National Criminal Intelligence Service. London. 9.2.94. Unattributable briefing. Triad specialist. Institut de Criminologie de Paris conference. Paris. 16.6.94.
8 Ibid.
9 Ibid.
10 Alan Friedman. *International Herald Tribune.* reprinted 20.3.94. *Independent* on Sunday. London.
11 Ibid.
12 Ibid.
13 Ibid.
14 Personal interview. Bonn. 2.12.93.
15 European Parliament Committee of Enquiry on Racism and Xenophobia. 1991.
16 Ibid.
17 Ibid.
18 Ibid.

19 Ibid.

20 Article 1(1) states: 'The dignity of man shall be inviolable. To respect and protect it shall be the duty of all State authority.' Article 3(3) states: 'No one may be prejudiced or favoured because of his sex, his parentage, his race, his language, his homeland and origin, his faith or his religion or political opinions.'

21 European Parliamentary Committee of Enquiry on Racism and Xenophobia. Luxembourg. 1991.

22 Ibid.

23 Personal interview. Paris. 7.9.93.

24 *Independent on Sunday*. London. 17.4.94.

25 European Parliamentary Committee of Enquiry into Racism and Xenophobia. Luxembourg. 1991.

26 Ibid.

27 *Observer*. 11.9.94.

28 European Parliamentary Committee of Enquiry into Racism and Xenophobia. Luxembourg. 1991.

29 Ibid.

30 Ibid.

31 Kenneth Clarke. *The World at One*. BBC Radio. 27.11.92.

32 European Parliamentary Committee of Enquiry into Racism and Xenophobia. Luxembourg. 1991.

33 Ibid.

CHAPTER SIXTEEN

The Golden Goose

1 The truism that Northern Ireland was a province in which there was far too much religion and insufficient Christianity was first coined by Alfred Draper, a friend and former fellow *Daily Express* reporter whom I much admired.

2 Unattributable intelligence briefing. Belfast. 3.5.92.

3 Boris Yeltsin. *The View from the Kremlin*. HarperCollins. May. 1994.

4 Sir Hugh Annesley, Chief Constable, at the publication in Belfast of the RUC's annual report. 4.7.94.

5 Unattributable briefing. London. 1.9.94.

6 Ibid.

7 Ibid.

CHAPTER SEVENTEEN

Inshallah

1 'If God Wills' or 'God Willing.' The most common form of Muslim wish after any expression of hope, wish or intention.

2 Home Office briefing. 8.4.94. Intelligence briefing. Brussels. 9.11.93.

3 Home Office briefing. 8.4.94.

4 Unattributable briefing. Paris. 14.6.94.

5 Ibid.

6 Unattributable briefing. London. 1.9.94.

7 Background briefing. Washington. 6.6.88.

8 Unattributable briefing. London. 1.9.94.

9 Background briefing. Lyon. 25.5.93.

10 Background briefing. Washington. 7.6.88.

11 Ibid.

12 Unattributable briefing. London. 1.9.94.

13 Unattributable briefing on intelligence analysis. London. 1.9.94.

14 Ibid.

15 Unattributable intelligence briefing. Paris. 14.6.94.

16 Unattributable briefing. London. 2.9.94.

17 Ibid.

18 Ibid.

19 Ibid.

20 Ibid.

21 Ibid.

22 Briefing at National Criminal Intelligence Service. London. 8.2.94.

23 *Elephteros Typos*. Athens. 25.4.94.

24 Unattibutable intelligence briefing. London. 2.9.94.

25 Institut de Criminologie de Paris conference. Paris. 15–16.6.94. Intelligence briefing.

26 Those of the United Kingdom, Germany and Turkey.

27 Institut de Criminologie de Paris conference. Paris 15–16.6.94. Intelligence briefing.

28 'Even if you indirectly support terrorist activity, this will turn bad on you. Certain circles in Greece support the PKK, especially when it comes to bombing Turkish tourist resorts' Turkish Foreign Ministry spokesman Ferhat Ataman. Ankara. 4.7.94

29 Home Office briefing. London. 2.9.94.

30 Counter-intelligence briefing. Paris. 14.6.94.

31 Ibid.

32 Ibid.

33 London. 8.10.93.
34 Unattributable telephone briefing. Madrid. 7.9.94.
35 Unattributable intelligence briefing. Paris. 7.9.93.
36 Counter-intelligence briefing. Paris. 14.6.94.
37 Ibid.
38 Ibid.

CHAPTER EIGHTEEN

Art for Art's Sake

1 Unattributable interview. Winchester. 5.8.93.
2 Ibid.
3 Ibid.
4 Ibid.
5 Unattributable dinner party briefing. Winchester. 9.10.93.
6 Interview with Brigadier James Emson, CBE, managing director, International Art Loss Register. London. 23.8.93.
7 17.8.93.
8 Personal interview. London. 2.9.93.
9 Unattributable briefing. London. 5.9.93.
10 Personal interview. London. 23.8.93.
11 Telephone interview. Zagreb. 25.8.93.
12 *Catalogue for Peace and War.* Ministry of Culture and Education. Republic of Croatia. Zagreb. August, 1992. *The War in Croatia. Archeological Sites.* Ministry of Culture and Education, Republic of Croatia. Zagreb. April, 1992. *Museums and Galleries of Croatia.* Ministry of Culture and Education. Republic of Croatia. Zagreb, January 1993. *Informatica Museologica.* Muzejski Dokumentacioni Centar. Zagreb, 1993.
13 *Museums and Galleries of Croatia* (see above).
14 Robert Fisk. *Independent on Sunday.* London. 19.6.94.
15 Ibid.
16 Ibid.
17 Vienna Convention on the Succession of States with Respect to International Agreements. 23.8.78. Vienna Convention on the Succession of States with Respect to Property, Public Records and Debts. 8.4.83. Judgement of the International Arbitration Commission. 4.7.92. that the Socialist Federal Republic of Yugoslavia no longer existed and that 'FR Yugoslavia (Serb and Montenegro) is a new state which cannot be

considered as the only successors to the SFRY.' Matching conclusions of
the UN Security Council, Resolution 777 (1992).

18 Personal interview. London. 23.8.93.

19 Strasbourg. 5.11.92.

20 London. 23.9.93.

21 European Council of Police Unions conference. Strasbourg. 3–6.11.92.

22 Ibid. Unattributable briefing.

23 Institut de Criminologie conference on Global Mafia Financial Power.
    Paris. 16.6.94.

24 European Council of Police Unions conference. Strasbourg. 5.11.92.

25 *International Herald Tribune*. 30.12.92.

26 Unattributable background briefing. London. 23.8.93.

27 Ibid.

28 The International Art and Antiques Loss Register 1993/1994 annual
    review.

29 International Foundation for Art Research monthly report. *Trace
    Magazine. The Antiques Trade Gazette. La Gazette de l'Hotel Drouot.
    Wektkunst. Annuaie International.*

30 Michael Nash. Feudal Hangover. *New Law Journal* 23.4.93.

31 Bishop of Worcester case. Determined 22 December 1594, generally
    referred to in British law as 'case of the market overt'.

32 Sale of Goods Act, 1979. Section 22 (1). 'Where goods are sold in market
    overt, according to the usage of the market, the buyer obtains a good title
    to the goods, provided he buys them in good faith and without notice of
    any defect or want of title on the part of the seller.' Market overt includes
    'any open, public and legally constituted market' including fairs. It has
    been legally held that this definition includes markets authorised by statute
    and custom.

33 Personal interview. Colin Reeve. London. 2.9.93

34 Unattributable dinner party gathering. Winchester. 9.10.93.

35 Unattributable briefing. London. 11.10.93

36 Interview with John Suter, of Davies and Co. Winchester. 16.2.94.

37 Unattributable briefing. London. 11.10.93.

38 Unattributable interviews. London. 11.10.92. Winchester. 9.10.93.

39 Unattributable briefing. Institut de Criminologie de Paris conference on
    Global Mafia Financial Power. 15–16.6.94.

40 *Portrait of Madame Baudot, nee Blanche Sennegon. Boy Wearing a Cap.
    The Orchard. Semur-Sunset. The Soiree.*

41 Unattributable briefing. Institut de Criminologie de Paris mafia
    conference. 15–16.6.94.

42 Ibid.

43 Ibid.
44 Ibid.

CHAPTER NINETEEN

Back to the Future

1 Rome. 4.4.94. London. 28.4.94.
2 Unattributable briefing. Rome. 24.10.93.
3 Rome. 26.10.93.

CHAPTER TWENTY

The Man They Called Uncle

1 RAI. 31.3.93.
2 Rome. 26.10.93.
3 Unattributable intelligence briefing. Rome. 27.10.93.
4 Conference on global Mafia finance control. Paris. 15.6.94.
5 Unattributable intelligence briefing. Rome. 27.10.93.
6 Ibid.
7 Ibid.
8 Unattributable briefing from La Rete staff member. Rome. 4.4.94.
9 Intelligence briefing. Rome. 27.10.93.
10 Palermo. 22.10.93.

CHAPTER TWENTY-ONE

Il Big Bang

1 Filed evidence. Prosecutors' office. Milan.
2 Ibid.
3 Ibid.
4 Ibid.
5 Ibid.
6 Ibid.
7 Court Records. Milan.
8 Deposition of Giuseppe Garofano. Milan Prosecutor.
9 Filed evidence. Prosecutors' Office. Milan.
10 RAI. 9.1.93.

CHAPTER TWENTY-TWO

The Hydra Factor

1 Operation Husky. 10.7.43.
2 Rome. 25.10.93.
3 Unattributable guidance briefing. Palermo. 20.10.93.
4 Palermo. 20.10.93.
5 *Men of Honour. The Truth about the Mafia.* Warner Books. 1993.
6 Unattributable intelligence briefing. Palermo. 21.10.93.
7 Leoluca Orlando, Palermo. 22.10.93. Nando Dalla Chiesa, Rome. 28.10.93.
8 Public Prosecutor's files. Naples.
9 Ibid.
10 Rome. 20.10.93.
11 Unattributable intelligence briefing. Palermo. 10.10.93. Rome. 19.10.93.

CHAPTER TWENTY-THREE

I Have a Right to be Blind Sometimes

1 Admiral Lord Nelson, at the Battle of Copenhagen. 2 April 1801 'I have only one eye – I have a right to be blind sometimes. I really do not see the signals!'
2 Unattributable interview. London. 6.5.94.
3 Ibid.
4 Ibid.
5 Interview with European Parliamentary spokesman. Unattributable. London 8.1.94.
6 Public Prosecutors' files. Milan.
7 Ibid.
8 Unattributable interview with Parliamentary official. London. 8.11.94.
9 Public Prosecutors' files. Milan.
10 Liège. 14.1.94.
11 Ibid.
12 Ibid.
13 Unattributable interview. London. 5.7.93.
14 Ibid.

CHAPTER TWENTY-FOUR

For Tobacco Road, Read Easy Street

1 Unattributable interview. London. 5.6.93 and 6.7.93. John Tomlinson, Labour MEP for Birmingham and Terry Wynn, Labour MEP for Merseyside East. Brussels. 11.11.93
2 Special Court of Auditors' Report No 8/93. *Observations pursuant to the second subparagraph of Article 188c (4) of the EC Treaty. The Common Organisation of the Market in Raw Tobacco*. Luxembourg 3.2.94.
3 Unattributable briefing. London. 6.7.93. Brussels. 10.11.93.
4 Ibid.
5 Special Court of Auditors' report. 3.2.94.
6 Ibid.
7 Unattributable briefing. Brussels. 9.11.93.
8 Brussels. 10.11.93.
9 Unattributable briefing. Brussels. 9.11.93.
10 Ibid.
11 Unattributable briefing. London. 6.7.93.
12 Special Court of Auditors' report. 3.2.94.
13 Ibid.
14 Brussels. 10.11.93.
15 Special Court of Auditors' report. 3.2.94.
16 Ibid.
17 Unattributable guidance. Commission briefing. 10.11.94.

CHAPTER TWENTY-FIVE

The Frankenstein Scarecrow

1 John Tomlinson. Brussels. 11.11.93.
2 Delayed draft report. Court of Auditors. 10.11.91.
3 *Daily Telegraph*. 12.4.93.
4 John Tomlinson. Brussels. 11.11.93.
5 Brussels. 10.11.93.
6 Brian Scott, chief executive of the Processed Vegetable Growers' Association. 26.10.92.
7 Brussels. 11.11.93.

CHAPTER TWENTY-SIX

When Two Plus Two Makes Five

1 Personal interview. London. 16.11.93.
2 Ibid.
3 Personal interview. Brussels. 11.11.93.
4 Letter from Leslie Huckfield. 31.8.93.
5 Unattributable interview. London. 6.7.93.
6 Background briefing. Brussels. 12.11.93.

CHAPTER TWENTY-SEVEN

The Rule of Law

1 Personal interview. Paris. 7.9.93.
2 John Alderton. Former Chief Constable of Devon and Cornwall and
   one-time Research Fellow with the Centre for Police Studies at Exeter
   University.
3 London. 30.11. to 1.12.92.
4 Personal interview. Lyon. 25.5.93.
5 Unattributable DEA briefing. Washington. 21.1.94.
6 *International Herald Tribune*. Paris. 19.5.93.
7 Bonn. 2.12.93.
8 The Hague. 8.12.94.
9 Unattributable interview. The Hague. 9.12.93.
10 Personal interview. Exeter. 5.10.93.
11 Unattributable interview. London. 3.5.94.
12 *Police Co-operation in Europe: an investigation.* Centre for the Study of
   Public Order. University of Leicester. 1993.
13 Unattributable interviews. Strasbourg. November, 1993. Paris 9.6.94.
14 Which the police force of Kent and a team of linguists from Cambridge
   University tried to alleviate by compiling *Policespeak*, Cambridge, 1993.
   Policespeak is a lexicon of more than 5,000 French-English words in
   common police usage, created to ease understanding between French and
   English police with the opening of the Channel Tunnel.

CHAPTER TWENTY-EIGHT

The Dirge of the Dreadnought

1 The Criminal Justice Act, 1987.

2 Ibid.

3 The Companies Act, 1985, the Financial Services Act, 1986, the Insolvency Act, 1986, the Banking Act, 1987 and the Criminal Justice Act, 1987.

4 The Richard Dimbleby Lecture *The Judiciary in the Nineties*. BBC 1 10.11.92.

5 Ibid.

6 Unattributable Home Office guidance. 21.6.94.

7 Personally ascribed feature entitled *Punishment Must Fit the Crime*. *Mail on Sunday*. 18.9.94.

8 Ibid.

9 *Independent* newspaper. London. 15.2.94.

10 Wold, Humberside, Blakenhurst, Redditch, Worcestershire, Doncaster.

11 *Independent* newspaper. London. 30.8.94.

12 *Independent* newspaper. London. 15.2.94.

13 Home Office guidance. 21.6.94.

14 *Independent* newspaper. London. 16.10.94.

15 National Association for the Care and Resettlement of Offenders annual report, published 8.11.93.

16 *Crime. Punishment and Rehabilitation*. London. 12.10.93.

17 *Independent* newspaper. London. 16.10.93.

18 Ibid.

19 Ibid.

20 Home Office guidance. 21.6.94.

21 Michael Howard speech at Wokingham, Berkshire, 15.10.93.

22 *World at One*. BBC Radio 4. 17.10.93.

23 Prison Service Conference. Blackpool. 3.11.93.

24 Committee on the Penalty for Homicide, by former Lord Chief Justice Lord Lane. comissioned by the Prison Reform Trust. 7.12.93.

25 John Major. Speech to the Social Market Foundation. 9.9.94

26 Mark Hook, then 17, was sent in 1993 on a 'character building' African safari and an Egyptian cultural tour from the Bryn Melyn detention centre, North Wales, prior to a court appearance on a number of charges. Within three days of his return, he was arrested on suspicion of drunk-driving and possession of drugs.

27 *Independent* newspaper. London. 19.1.94.

28 Personal interview. Surbiton, Surrey. 17.11.93.

29 *Counting the Cost*. 4.9.94. Compiled by Crime Concern.

30 *Prevention Strategy for Young People in Trouble*, compiled by consultants Cooper and Lybrand, commissioned by the Prince's Trust and ITV Television.

31 *Criminal Statistics England and Wales 1993*. Her Majesty's Stationery Office.
32 NCIS Briefing. 21.3.94.
33 Personal interview. Surbiton. Surrey. 17.11.93.
34 The Guildford Four (Carole Richardson, Patrick Armstrong, Paul Hill and Gerard Conlon): convictions for the murder of seven people in the bombing of pubs at Guildford and Woolwich. Birmingham Six (Hugh Callaghan, Richard McIlkinney, Patrick Hill, William Powell, Gerard Hunter and John Walker.) Convicted of the murder of 21 people in two Birmingham pubs. Maguire Seven (Anna Maguire, Patrick Maguire, Vincent Maguire (son) Patrick Maguire (son), William Smyth, Patrick Conlon and Patrick O'Neill). Convicted of possessing explosive substances. Thirteen other people, all convicted of murder, were freed because their original convictions were unsafe.
35 Personal interview. London. 8.10.93.
36 Personal interview. Surbiton, Surrey. 17.11.93.

CHAPTER TWENTY-NINE

A Question of Identity

1 The Convention of the Council of Europe (Convention No 108) of January 1981, for the Protection of Individuals with Respect to Automatic Processing of Personal Data.
2 Italy, United Kingdom, Ireland, Belgium and Germany.
3 Unattributable briefing, Strasbourg. November, 1992. June, 1994 Andrew Puddephat, General Secretary, Liberty UK. 31.8.93 and XVth International conference of Data Protection and Privacy Commissioners. Manchester. 27–30.9.93.
4 Unattributable Home Office briefing. 21.6.94.
5 Ibid.
6 Dr Stephan Gull. Dr Keith Percival-Barker. Cavendish Laboratory, Cambridge.
7 The NeuroMetric System. Florida.
8 *Independent*, London. 15.8.94.
9 Ibid.

CHAPTER THIRTY

Thinking the Unthinkable

1 *The Fix. The Inside Story of the World Drug Trade.* Brian Freemantle. Michael Joseph. 1985.
2 *Drug Usage and Drug Prevention. The View and Habits of the General Public.* Home Office.
3 Paris 6.9.93.
4 Paris. 7.9.93.
5 Amsterdam. 7.12.93.
6 The Hague. 8.12.93.
7 *Crime, Punishment and Rehabilitation.* London. 12.10.93.
8 *Europhile.* BBC 4. 27.11.93
9 UN Single Convention of Narcotic Drugs, 1961. UN Convention on Psychotropic Substances, 1971. UN Convention Against Illicit Traffic in Narcotic Drugs and Psychotropic Substances, 1998.
10 Strasbourg. 2.7.93.
11 Surbiton, Surrey, 17.11.93.
12 *The Fix. The Inside Story of the World Drug Trade.*
13 Judge Liliana Ferraro. Rome. 28.10.93
14 Professor Xavier Raufer. Paris. 7.9.93.

Sources

Council of Europe

Convention for the Protection of Human Rights and Fundamental Freedoms. Rome. 1950.

Explanatory Report on the European Convention on the International Validity of Criminal Judgments. Strasbourg. 1970.

Explanatory Report on the European Convention on the Repatriation of Minors. Strasbourg. 1971.

European Convention on the Suppression of Terrorism. Strasbourg. 1977.

Explanatory Report on the European Convention on the Suppression of Terrorism. Strasbourg. 1979.

Convention for the Protection of Individuals with regard to Automatic Processing of Personal Data. Strasbourg. 1981.

Protection of Personal Data used for Scientific Research and Statistics. Strasbourg. 1984.

Parliamentary Assembly Report on International Crime. Strasbourg. 1986.

Protection of Personal Data used for Social Security Purposes. Strasbourg. 1986.

Protection of Personal Data used for the Purposes of Direct Marketing. Strasbourg. 1986.

Parliamentary Assembly report on the Traffic in Children and other forms of Child Exploitation. Strasbourg. 1988.

Regulating the Use of Personal Data in the Police Sector. Strasbourg. 1988.

Sexual Exploitation, Pornography and Prostitution of, and Trafficking in, Children and Young Women. Strasbourg. 1988.

New Technologies: a Challenge to Privacy Protection. Strasbourg. 1989.

Human Artificial Procreation. Strasbourg. 1989.

Protection of Personal Data used for Employment Purposes. Strasbourg. 1989.

Computer Related Crime. Strasbourg. 1990

Data Protection and the Media. Strasbourg. 1991.

The Introduction and Use of Personal Identification Numbers: the Data Protection Issue. Strasbourg. 1991.

Data Protection, Human Rights and Democratic Values. Strasbourg. 1992.

Convention of Laudering, Search, Seizure and Confiscation of the Proceeds of Crime, Strasbourg. 1992. Also papers submitted by the representatives of the Czech Republic, France, Germany, Greece, Hungary, Ireland, the Netherlands, Poland, Switzerland, Sweden, Slovenia, the United Kingdom, the United States of America, the Financial Action Task Force of the Organisation of Economic Co-operation and Development, the annual report for 1991–92 of that Task Force and extracts of the United Nations Convention Against Illicit Traffic in Narcotic Drugs and Psychotropic Substances.

The Use of Analysis of Deoxyribonucleic Acid (DNA) within the Framework of the Criminal Justice System. Strasbourg. 1992.

Parliamentary Assembly Report on Police Co-operation and Protection of Personal Data in the Police Sector. Strasbourg. 1992.

European Commission

The Community of Twelve: Key Figures. Brussels. 1991.

Working Together – The Institutions of the European Community. Brussels. 1991.

Information and Communication Technologies in Europe. Brussels. 1991.

The Single Market in Action. Brussels. 1992.

European Union. Luxembourg. 1992.

From Single Market to European Union. Brussels. 1992.

Annual Report of the Commission on the Fight Against Fraud. Brussels. 1993.

Court of Auditors

Special Report No 2/92 into the audit of export refunds paid to selected major traders in the milk products section. Luxembourg. 1992.

Summary of the Court of Auditors' annual report, Luxembourg, 1991.

Court of Auditors' annual report, Luxembourg, 1991.

Court of Auditors' external auditing of Community Finances, Luxembourg. 1992.

Court of Auditors' complementary report on Community Expenditure since 1988 on the European Agricultural Guidance and Guarantee Fund. Luxembourg. 1992.

Court of Auditors' annual report. Luxembourg. 1992.

European Parliament

Committee of Enquiry into the Rise of Fascism and Racism in Europe. (The Evrigenis Report). Strasbourg. 1985.

Committee of Enquiry into the Drugs Problem in the Member States of the Community. Strasbourg. 1986.

Committee of Enquiry on Racism and Xenophobia, Luxembourg, 1991.

Committee of Budgetary Control on Notification by member States of Fraud and Irregularities against the EC Budget. Brussels. 1993.

Committee of Budgetary Control report on the Relations between Bodies Responsible for Control of the Community Budget. Brussels. 1993.

Committee of Budgetary Control summary of the public hearing on the Protection of EC Taxpayers' money. Brussels. 1993.

Report of the Committee on the Environmental, Public Health and Consumer Protection on Prohibiting Trade in Transplant Organs. Strasbourg. 1993.

Europe in Figures. Statistical Office of the European Community (Eurostat). Brussels. 1992.

House of Lords Select Committee on the European Community. 1992: Border Control of People (with evidence). London. 1989.

Foreign Office. The European Community: Facts and Fairytales London. 1993.

Royal Commission on Criminal Justice report. London. 1993. Amnesty International;

Republic of Ireland. Allegations of Ill-treatment in Police Custody. London. 1990.

United Kingdom. Allegations of Ill-treatment in Northern Ireland. London. 1991.

United Kingdom. Human Rights Concerns. London. 1991.

United Kingdom: The Right to Silence. London. 1993.

United Kingdom. Northern Ireland: Fair trial concerns in Casement Park trials. London. 1993.

United Kingdom (Northern Ireland). Alleged coerced confessions during ill-treatment at Castlereagh Holding Centre of Eight Youths from Ballymurphy, Northern Ireland. London. 1993.

Italy. Increase in Alleged Ill-treatment by Prison Guards. London. 1993.

Spain. Torture and Ill-Treatment: Summary of Amnesty International Concerns. London. 1993.

General Council of the Bar (Britain). The Bar Council's Response to the Royal Commission on Criminal Justice. London. 1993.

United States House of Representatives Task Force on Terrorism and Unconventional Warfare. Nuclear Trafficking in Europe. Washington DC. 1992.

National Criminal Intelligence Service. Assessment of the Threat and Impact by Organised/Enterprise Crime upon United Kingdom Interests. London. 1992.

National Criminal Intelligence Service. Annual Report 1992/1993. London.

Bibliography

Arlacchi, Pino. (Translated by Martin Ryle). *Mafia Business: The Mafia Ethic and the Spirit of Capitalism*. Oxford University Press. Oxford. 1988.

Benyon, John. (with Lynne Turnbull, Andrew Willis, Rachel Woodward and Adrian Beck). *Police Co-operation in Europe: an Investigation*. Centre for the Study of Public Order, University of Leicester. 1993.

Cornwell, Rupert. *God's Banker. An Account of the Life and Death of Roberto Calvi*. Victor Gollancz. London. 1983.

Cottrell, Richard. *The Sacred Cow. The Folly of Europe's Food Mountains*. Grafton Books. London. 1987.

Falcone, Judge Giovanni (with Marcelle Padovani). *Men of Honour. The Truth about the Mafia*. Warner. London. 1993.

Holden, Neville. *The Single European Act and Maastricht*. Thornhill Press. London. 1992.

Johnson, MA, BEd, Edward. (with Mark Garner, MA, PhD; Steve Hick, BA; David Matthews, MA, PhD; in association with Doreen Bailey, Angele Cadge, Catherine Eve, Francois Gabard, Joy McQueen and Anita Ogier. Also Kent County Constabulary officers Chief Inspector R. Cruttenden, Inspector J. Gledhill, Sergeant K. Grant, Constables J. Blackman and J. Gent, assisted by Inspecteurs Divisionnaires Joel Rose and Andre Torres. *PoliceSpeak. Police Communications and Language and the Channel Tunnel*. PoliceSpeak Publications. Cambridge. 1993.

Morgan, W.P. *Triad Societies in Hong Kong*. Government Press, Hong Kong. 1982.

Orwell, George. *Nineteen Eighty-Four*. Penguin. 1954.

Sampson, Anthony. *The Essential Anatomy of Britain. Democracy in Crisis*. Hodder and Stoughton. 1992.

Spencer, Michael. *1992 and All That: Civil Liberties in the Balance*. The Civil Liberties Trust. 1990.

Spencer, Sarah. *Called to Account: The case for police accountability in England and Wales*. National Council for Civil Liberties. London. 1985.

Spicer, Michael. *A Treaty too Far: A New Policy for Europe*. Fourth Estate. London. 1992.

Sterling, Bruce. *The Hacker Crackdown*. Viking. 1993.

Toner, Michael and Christopher White. *Bluff Your Way in the European Community*. Ravette Books. Horsham. 1992.

Tugendhat, Christopher. *Making Sense of Europe*. Penguin. London. 1986.

Tutt, Nigel. *Europe on the Fiddle: The Common Market Scandal*. Christopher Helm. London. 1989.

Index

Page-numbers in **bold** type denote main treatments.
NB: Certain Arabic names are not inverted; e.g. 'Abu Nidal', not 'Nidal, Abu'